Transferences

PSYCHOANALYTIC HORIZONS

Psychoanalysis is unique in being at once a theory and a therapy, a method of critical thinking and a form of clinical practice. Now in its second century, this fusion of science and humanism derived from Freud has outlived all predictions of its demise. **Psychoanalytic Horizons** evokes the idea of a convergence between realms as well as the outer limits of a vision. Books in the series test disciplinary boundaries and will appeal to scholars and therapists who are passionate not only about the theory of literature, culture, media, and philosophy but also, above all, about the real life of ideas in the world.

Series Editors
Esther Rashkin, Mari Ruti, and Peter L. Rudnytsky

Advisory Board
Salman Akhtar, Doris Brothers, Aleksandar Dimitrijevic, Lewis Kirshner, Humphrey Morris, Hilary Neroni, Dany Nobus, Lois Oppenheim, Donna Orange, Peter Redman, Laura Salisbury, Alenka Zupančič

Volumes in the Series
Mourning Freud, Madelon Sprengnether
Does the Internet Have an Unconscious? Slavoj Žižek and Digital Culture, Clint Burnham
In the Event of Laughter: Psychoanalysis, Literature and Comedy, Alfie Bown
On Dangerous Ground: Freud's Visual Cultures of the Unconscious, Diane O'Donoghue
For Want of Ambiguity: Order and Chaos in Art, Psychoanalysis, and Neuroscience, Ludovica Lumer and Lois Oppenheim
Life Itself Is an Art: The Life and Work of Erich Fromm, Rainer Funk
Born After: Reckoning with the German Past, Angelika Bammer
Critical Theory Between Klein and Lacan: A Dialogue, Amy Allen and Mari Ruti
Transferences: The Aesthetics and Poetics of the Therapeutic Relationship, Maren Scheurer
At the Risk of Thinking: An Intellectual Biography of Julia Kristeva (forthcoming), Alice Jardine
The Analyst's Desire: Ethics in Theory and Clinical Practice (forthcoming), Mitchell Wilson

Transferences

The Aesthetics and Poetics of the Therapeutic Relationship

Maren Scheurer

BLOOMSBURY ACADEMIC
NEW YORK • LONDON • OXFORD • NEW DELHI • SYDNEY

BLOOMSBURY ACADEMIC
Bloomsbury Publishing Inc
1385 Broadway, New York, NY 10018, USA
50 Bedford Square, London, WC1B 3DP, UK
29 Earlsfort Terrace, Dublin 2, Ireland

BLOOMSBURY, BLOOMSBURY ACADEMIC and the Diana logo are trademarks of
Bloomsbury Publishing Plc

First published in the United States of America 2019
Paperback edition published 2021

Copyright © Maren Scheurer, 2019

For legal purposes the Acknowledgments on p. vi constitute an extension
of this copyright page.

Cover design by Daniel Benneworth-Gray
Cover image © Fighting Forms, 1914, Franz Marc (1880–1916).
Bavarian State Painting Collections, Munich, Germany.

All rights reserved. No part of this publication may be reproduced or transmitted in any form or by any means, electronic or mechanical, including photocopying, recording, or any information storage or retrieval system, without prior permission in writing from the publishers.

Bloomsbury Publishing Inc does not have any control over, or responsibility for, any third-party websites referred to or in this book. All internet addresses given in this book were correct at the time of going to press. The author and publisher regret any inconvenience caused if addresses have changed or sites have ceased to exist, but can accept no responsibility for any such changes.

Library of Congress Cataloging-in-Publication Data
Names: Scheurer, Maren, author.
Title: Transferences: the aesthetics and poetics of the therapeutic
relationship/Maren Scheurer.
Other titles: Aesthetics and poetics of the therapeutic relationship
Description: New York: Bloomsbury Academic /
Bloomsbury Publishing Inc, 2019. | Series: Psychoanalytic horizons |
Includes bibliographical references and index.
Identifiers: LCCN 2019011540| ISBN 9781501352447 (hardback: alk. paper) |
ISBN 9781501352454 (eBook) | ISBN 9781501352461 (epdf)
Subjects: LCSH: Psychoanalysis and literature. | Psychoanalysis and the arts. |
Aesthetics–Psychological aspects. | Psychotherapy in literature. |
Poetics–Psychological aspects. | Storytelling–Psychological aspects. |
Literature, Modern–History and criticism.
Classification: LCC PN56.P92 S34 2019 | DDC 700.1/05–dc23
LC record available at https://lccn.loc.gov/2019011540

ISBN: HB: 978-1-5013-5244-7
PB: 978-1-5013-8144-7
ePDF: 978-1-5013-5246-1
eBook: 978-1-5013-5245-4

Series: Psychoanalytic Horizons
D.30

Typeset by Deanta Global Publishing Services, Chennai, India

To find out more about our authors and books visit www.bloomsbury.com
and sign up for our newsletters.

Contents

Acknowledgments — vi

Part One Introduction

1 Psychoanalysis and the Arts — 3
2 The Therapeutic Relationship — 21

Part Two Discourses in Dialogue: The Aesthetics and Poetics of Therapeutic Relationships

3 The Art of the Therapeutic Relationship: Psychoanalytic Aesthetics — 53
4 Art as (Therapeutic) Relationship: Relational Models of Creativity, Reading, and Interpretation — 95

Part Three Reading Relationships: Therapy in Literature, Theater, and Television

5 "I'm Telling Everything": Psychoanalytic Gameplay in Philip Roth's *Portnoy's Complaint* — 141
6 "A Gap, a Hole, a Darkness": Epistemic Desire in J. M. Coetzee's *Life & Times of Michael K* — 167
7 "To Keep the Sultan Amused": Scheherazadian Narration in Margaret Atwood's *Alias Grace* — 192
8 "Act It Out, If You Like": Anti- and Stage-Psychiatry in Peter Shaffer's *Equus* — 217
9 "Locked in a Room, Listening": Talk-Show Therapy and Co-Construction in *In Treatment* — 241

Part Four Conclusion

Notes — 285
Works Cited — 293
Index — 324

Acknowledgments

I am deeply indebted to Edgar Pankow, Julika Griem, Justus Fetscher, Frank Schulze-Engler, and Achim Geisenhanslüke, without whose guidance, encouragement, and support this book would not have been possible. My warmest thanks go to all the colleagues and friends who have helped shape this book. For the countless hours they have invested in reading my work, for their critical interventions and invaluable suggestions for improvement, and for the inspiration I could always draw from our conversations, I thank Iva Apostolova, Adrian Chapman, Annika Eisenberg, Vincent Fröhlich, Guido Furci, Erik Grayson, Andrea Gremels, Samuel Kessler, Ruth Knepel, Agnes Jäger, Aimee Pozorski, Anne Rüggemeier, Caroline Sauter, Iris Schäfer, Oliver Völker, Julia Wilch, and Jan Wilm. Last but not least: To all my friends and family, I am deeply grateful for their love and support throughout this project.

Part One

Introduction

1

Psychoanalysis and the Arts

Practical poetry

Not as a scientist, not as an apt technician, not even as a healer, perhaps as a magician or a prostitute, "in the 'intimacy with strangers' business"—certainly, however, as a poet: this is how psychoanalyst Dr. Jamal Khan understands himself in Hanif Kureishi's 2008 novel *Something to Tell You* (413). He tells us: "For Freud, as for any other poet, words, the patient's spoken words and those of the analyst, were magic; they brought about change" (99). Describing the founder of psychoanalysis as a poet is not, however, as radical or surprising as it may appear at first. After all, Freud himself had recognized in his earliest writings that his case studies read like "short stories" (*Novellen*) ("Studies" 160), and in 1930, he was awarded the Goethe Prize of the City of Frankfurt: "The honor dedicated to you is meant as much for the scholar as for the writer and the fighter," Alfons Paquet writes to Freud in the name of the committee (qtd. in Freud, "Goethe-Preis" 546, my translation). It is also well known that Freud was fascinated with literature and saw himself called to deliver "audacious interpretations" of the works of poets (545, my translation).

In Kureishi's novel, Jamal understands the psychoanalytic profession from the viewpoint of his teacher Tahir Hussein, a fictional disciple of Donald Winnicott. Jamal's view goes further than appreciating the artistic achievements of a few outstanding psychoanalysts or legitimizing the practice of applied psychoanalysis with interpretations of artists and their work. In this understanding, psychoanalysis[1] is not just a discipline that produces literary vignettes or sometimes poaches on the hunting grounds of literary, art, and media scholars. Instead, it is a practice that is itself based on an aesthetic process:

> My profession is not, and should not be considered, a straight science. It was impossible for Freud to say that he cured people by poetry. Yet observe the important figures and see how like poets they are, with their speculative jumps and metaphors: Jung, Ferenczi, Klein, Balint, Lacan,

each singing their own developmental story, particular passion and aesthetic. Their differing views don't cancel each other out but exist side by side, like the works of Titian and Rembrandt. (*Something* 97)

If, as both psychoanalysts and writers seem to think, psychoanalysis were an artistic discipline that cures by poetry and allows every analyst her own aesthetics, it would mean that the most important link between psychoanalysis and other arts could be found not in its theories—not in the Oedipus complex, in dream interpretation, or in the structural model of the mind—but in its therapeutic process. Not without reason, British psychotherapist Adam Phillips describes psychoanalysis as "a kind of practical poetry" (*On Flirtation* xi) with its own poetic methods. But what would the resulting aesthetics and poetics of psychoanalysis look like? And what do they have to do with the fascination psychoanalytic work apparently holds for a writer like Hanif Kureishi?

The art of the therapeutic relationship

Most psychoanalysts today identify the therapeutic relationship as the foundation of the therapeutic process.[2] Pedro Laín Entralgo defines this relationship as "a quasi-dyadic and helpful cooperation, whose purpose is that the patient should achieve the psychosomatic situation we call health" (152). Entralgo describes an asymmetric configuration, in which a therapist is placed in the service of a patient.[3] With the term "therapy" being derived from the Greek θεραπεύω, "to serve, to care," all therapeutic work can be understood as a service to the patient (Petersen 15), as a practice that is oriented toward an Other—toward a relationship—from the outset. Through such a relationship, "a bond in the space between [two or more individuals] which is more than the sum of the parts" (Clarkson 148), something new is developed, which, in the case of a psychoanalytic encounter, is shaped by the particular conditions of the treatment situation and goes far beyond a mere professional service. The bond between analysand and analyst encompasses their real relationship in the therapeutic setting as well as all imaginary aspects of their encounter. These imaginary aspects, which are essential for the psychoanalytic understanding of the therapeutic relationship, were called "transference" (*Übertragung*) by Freud. They were soon recognized as a crucial factor in psychoanalytic work and led to a concentration on the relationship between patient and therapist.

In his papers on technique, Freud describes the configuration of a therapeutic setting in the service of establishing and regulating transference and countertransference and facilitating a sustainable analytic stance. However, the discovery of transference challenged several elements of the conventional definition of the therapeutic relationship: the orientation toward the norm of health and the purpose of healing as well as the possibility of an objective, professional encounter. Along these lines of inquiry, a relational variant of psychoanalytic theory has developed via Melanie Klein's object relations theory and prominent analysts like Donald Winnicott and Wilfred Bion, who were influenced by her. They focus on the individual, quasi-poetic features of the therapeutic relationship—and thus it is no coincidence that Kureishi places his fictional psychoanalyst Tahir in close psychoanalytic kinship with Winnicott. At the same time that 1950s American Ego Psychology sought to adhere to the standards of an objective science (Mertens 21), Klein's disciple Paula Heimann turned countertransference—and thus the inevitable subjectivity of the analyst—into the central instrument of analytic technique. Winnicott emphasized the emotionally supportive function of the therapist and the creative aspects of the analytic process, while Bion developed a theory of unconscious communication. If today most psychoanalytic schools accept the interaction between therapist and patient as the essential aspect of psychoanalytic theory and technique, it is only because they have adopted these approaches. In Chapter 2, I will trace this development from Freud through his immediate disciples to object relations theory and contemporary theories of therapeutic interaction. Unfolding the intricate and conflicted history of psychoanalytic knowledge about its relational foundations is the best way to delineate a model of the therapeutic relationship that takes full account of the complexity of the debates surrounding this constituent element of psychoanalysis. By introducing the terms and theories that are the premises of the theoretical and fictional works that will be discussed later in this study, this overview of the therapeutic relationship will provide a conceptual background and help us understand why psychoanalysts might turn to art and why artists might turn to psychoanalysis in order to discuss the relationships in which they participate.

Narrative has been identified as a second important factor in the therapeutic process. Storytelling seems to happen everywhere in therapy, whether general practitioners take a history, psychoanalysts explore the submerged infancy of the patient, or patients report everyday events. The results are seldom polished or completed stories, but, for therapeutic purposes, Roy Schafer defines a narrative simply and pragmatically as "whatever qualifies as a version of a happening or an event or scene of any kind" (*Retelling* xiv). Ever since the 1980s, when the "narrativist turn" took hold in the therapeutic professions (Charon et al. 601; Rousseau 175), narrative has become an even stronger focus of physicians and psychotherapists. Clinically oriented proponents of "Narrative Medicine" and the "Medical Humanities" seek to sensitize doctors in training to the importance of the therapeutic relationship and storytelling with select examples from literature and art. From the humanities, they hope to gain "insight into the human condition, pain and suffering, selfhood, personhood, depression, mental illness, and our ethical responsibility to each other," an understanding of the "interactions of the individual experience of illness" as well as a reinforcement of skills like observation, analytic comprehension, empathy, and self-reflection; but they do not necessarily seek to provide a contribution to the humanities in turn (Rousseau 175). In their understanding, narrative is a component of all experience, as Rita Charon and Maura Spiegel, co-founders of the "Narrative Medicine" movement, explain:

> In one inflection, narrative is the medium we exist in; the air we breathe; it is how the mind makes sense of things, interprets stimuli. In this formulation, we must become conscious of the ways in which we are claimed by and make claims according to narratives. . . . In a darker variation, narrative is a mechanism for interpolating us into the workings of domination, and oppression. Narrative is on the side of power and control; our stories are already plotted. In yet another account of narrative, however, stories are not limiting or controlling; they enable exploration and release; they are expressions and acts of movement, possibility, redefinition, intervention, and intersubjectivity. (vii)

Narration thus gains an immense importance and seems to contain endless potential for healing that must be revealed and deployed in or out of therapy. The Medical Humanities promise not only that it is possible to tell or write oneself out of illness but also that physicians can be dissuaded from the inhumane objectivization of their patients and briefed to empathize with them through literary methods (Rousseau 171). Thus, they have contributed to highlighting the significance of linguistic forms of experience in various therapeutic fields. Sometimes, however, they create the impression that all we have to do to revolutionize the world of medicine is learn to tell the "right" story. That the "darker variations" of storytelling mentioned by Charon and Spiegel are often excluded from consideration and that the disturbances and blockages created by language are seldom discussed may be due to the resistance the Medical Humanities fight against in their increasingly technologized and particularized medical environment. Their controversial project to reform medicine does not allow much room for self-doubt, but even if we grant the practical necessity of the resulting glorification of narrative practices, an uncritical take on narrative in therapy does not contribute to a differentiated aesthetic perspective on the link between narration and the therapeutic relationship.

The therapeutic significance of storytelling is not a new discovery; even the "first" psychoanalytic patient Anna O. famously described her treatment as a "talking cure" (Breuer 229). Psychoanalysis has always been understood as a fundamentally narrative practice, which is often but not always linked to an epistemic endeavor: the search for hidden knowledge in the past. "The principal business of psychoanalysis is to interpret and reinterpret in life-historical perspective the verbal and other utterances of the analysand," states Schafer (*Language* 6). Peter Brooks goes even further when he designates psychoanalysis not just as a narrative practice but also as a theory of narrative: "Psychoanalysis is necessarily narrative, and indeed, in its theoretical formulations, necessarily a 'narratology': a study of how narrative works" (*Body* 231). Now psychoanalysis is interested in a very particular potential of narrative. "Mostly, I believed in the efficacy of conversation," Jamal muses in Kureishi's novel; "all Freud demanded of his patients was wilder words" (32). Freud did indeed establish demands and rules geared toward the defamiliarization of narrative work: rules for untethered and wild talk, attentive listening, and effective interpretation, which will also be introduced in the following Chapter 2. By highlighting the formal and methodical specificity of the psychoanalytic narrative, I argue that the therapeutic aesthetic may actually shed light on narrative features that stand in the way of straightforward projects of therapeutic self-improvement—in contrast to the Medical Humanities, which often subsume and enlist narration in all its forms for curative visions of "healthy" identity formation. Moreover, as we will see, the way psychoanalysts frame their practices in their writings also highlights the fact that the narrative of psychoanalysis as a "narratology" fails to capture important—though not necessarily narrative—aesthetic elements of the therapeutic experience.

Thus, a cross section through the discourse on the therapeutic relationship and its narrative work actually sheds light on the fact that psychoanalysis contains a specific aesthetic experience that is not adequately described by pointing to the therapeutic potential of storytelling. In other words, psychoanalysis is not just an epistemic project or an exclusively narrative practice, geared toward discovering or creating knowledge about people, but an aesthetic project that involves the intricate experience of a relationship. In order to describe this experience, the basic, intertwined constituents of which are narrative and transference, psychoanalysts since Freud have drawn on art and exploited concepts from literature, film, theater, or music to find words for what happens in the therapeutic relationship. It seems as if they can only gain a mediated access to the way characters, space, and time take effect in analysis, how showing and telling interlock, how a particular, disguised kind of poetic dialogue enters every therapeutic utterance, and how analysis is conducted in serial patterns. Paradoxically, through recourse to such comparisons, metaphors, and analogies, it becomes clear that psychoanalysts attempt to describe the therapeutic relationship as an aesthetic experience in its own right. In Chapter 3, this feature of psychoanalytic discourse will be traced and discussed from its beginnings in Freud to select examples in the present. Analyzing the language psychoanalysts use to describe their practices, I will extract central aesthetic elements that they consider to be the formal principles of their work. It turns out that literary and film studies are not alone in having drawn inspirations from other disciplines like psychoanalysis. Contemporary psychoanalysis has, in turn, adapted terms from literary scholarship or semiotics to conceptualize its therapeutic work.

The potential of the psychoanalytic process for aesthetic theory, however, is not exhausted with these descriptions of the therapeutic exercise as an artistic practice. In a strategic reversal, psychoanalysis offers hypotheses for aesthetic processes beyond its own disciplinary borders. Thus, we find rhetorical comparisons in which the therapeutic relationship is illustrated with metaphors and a vocabulary drawn from aesthetics as well as analogies in which artistic practices are compared to therapy and explained in psychoanalytic terms. "The anxious quest for reassuring analogies," which Phillips identifies as an integral part of the history of psychoanalysis in search of a proper self-understanding ("Poetry" 1), is a quest that is apparently also a part of the history of the humanities and literary scholarship. Dominic Angeloch assumes that the foundation of the analogy between psychoanalysis and literature lies in a shared subject area, as both are concerned with interaction (*Beziehung* 187). From the relationship that an artist develops with her work to the multiple relations readers, viewers, and critics establish with works of art and artists, a whole range of constellations can be identified that psychoanalysts and psychoanalytic critics read in analogy to the therapeutic relationship. Indeed, the psychoanalyst has often been described as the prototype of the reader and critic, despite the conceptual difficulties implied in this double role. "Sitting with my first analysands, trying to bear the anxiety of hearing someone unknown, whose dreams and ramblings I could not comprehend, I felt, at times, as though I were trying to decode *The Waste Land* at a first reading," psychoanalyst Jamal admits (265). In Chapter 4, I will study similar analogical models, which will provide us with a whole array of competing and contradictory theories of art and methods for interpretation, but also, more importantly, with an opportunity to study the theoretical problems and strategic motivations psychoanalysts and critics try to solve with their analogies.

Taken together, these perspectives on the therapeutic relationship furnish psychoanalysts with important ideas for an aesthetics of the psychoanalytic process. And by critically reading the various forms of description and comparison psychoanalysts employ, we gain further insight into the way we think about therapy, relationships, and reflective practices in general. Psychoanalysts use aesthetic analogies to highlight the artistic components of their work beyond or inherent in their therapeutic and epistemic methods. According to Phillips, the reason for the psychoanalysts' unrelenting interest in poetry is their need to reassure themselves about the powers of language and seize the psychological knowledge to which poets have access: "Poets and psychoanalysts have a shared aim (or object of desire), but different means for attaining it" ("Poetry" 4). However, when art and psychoanalysis choose each other as an object for "reassuring" analogies, the reason is not necessarily the results they produce. In contrast to Phillips's assessment, the unbroken interest in the procedures of the other discipline testifies to specific methodical intersections. By implication, art and psychoanalysis meet not only in the things they talk about but also in the *way* they talk about them, and thus refer to each other in theoretical and artistic representations of themselves and each other.

The second part of this study will thus be dedicated to exploring a variety of strategies and imagery employed in the self-descriptive discourse of psychoanalysts and critics. By placing these chapters before the following readings of literary, theatrical, and televisual texts,[4] I intend to accomplish two goals. First of all, the chapters shed light on metaphorical constellations, structural frameworks, and theoretical problems that the artistic texts will draw from psychoanalysis—and thus they provide me with a heuristic foundation for my readings. Secondly, but no less importantly, I believe that the interdisciplinary exchange between psychoanalysis, the arts, and scholarship in the humanities can only be properly studied by taking into full account the voices of psychoanalysts—and the way they turn to the arts in their similes, metaphors, and analogies.

However, this thinking in analogies—which includes "analogy derivatives" such as the metaphor, the comparison, and the model (Wilcox and Ewbank 2)—harbors a number of problems. As soon as they share a single feature, two sets of facts can be linked in an analogy, but this does not exclude the possibility that the compared sets differ in other characteristics (Coenen 31). Based on similarity rather than identity, analogies do not provide logically valid conclusions (168). In addition, metaphors and analogies do not necessarily describe existing similarities. They may also create connections by establishing relationships between disparate objects or ideas. Despite this, an analogy is often constructed in order to point out correspondences and deduce conclusions from the comparison (Sacksteder 235), which, with specific interests in mind, are supposed to create knowledge about the target. A certain, however limited, similar behavior of the source and the target is usually assumed (Coenen 169), but it is precisely the absence of such a stable base that opens analogies for "invention and discovery" (Sacksteder 251), allowing them to explore possible correlations and differences between source and target as long as they do not pretend to establish absolute truths. The analogies and metaphors I study are experiments, often called upon for the purpose of consolidating the disciplines of psychoanalysis and the humanities.

In my readings of these analogies, I am, however, conducting an experiment with a different purpose. My aim is not the extrapolation of the "correct" version of the analogy but a study of how the *employment* of analogies creates a variety of interdisciplinary exchanges. Therefore, I am not so much concerned with the question whether a particular analogy describes artistic or therapeutic relationships adequately as I am grasping the nexus of descriptions, ideas, and problems that is created through the use of such analogies. My analysis will highlight how these comparisons between the psychoanalytic and the artistic process point to commonalities of a certain significance but not to a consistent theory of art or psychoanalysis. After all, thinking in analogies does not provide reliable answers and works best where it is not taken as dogma but as a form of play.

After having started, in the second part of this study, with an analysis of the language and the models psychoanalysts and scholars of literature, theater, and television have developed in their writings, in the third part, I will further examine the dialogue psychoanalysis and the arts entertain with each other by turning to artistic representations of therapy.[5] Psychoanalytic criticism has often taken such representations as an excuse to resort to its traditional methods, the psychoanalytic interpretation of the author, the reader, and the characters of the text, telling us, as Brooks has noted, "precious little about the structure and the rhetoric of literary texts" (*Psychoanalysis* 20) and mistaking its critical thrust as "inherently explanatory" (22). Shoshana Felman pointed out as early as 1977 that the relation of "psychoanalysis and literature" has often been seen as hierarchical, "a relation in which literature is submitted to the authority, to the prestige of psychoanalysis. While literature is considered as a body of *language—to be interpreted*—psychoanalysis is considered as a body of *knowledge*, whose competence is called upon *to interpret*" ("To Open" 5). In the following chapters, the arts and psychoanalysis will be understood as equal forms of thought, and neither is considered a key to the other's interpretation. The goal of such a comparative, multilateral reading of psychoanalytic and fictional texts is the discovery of literary constructs and adaptations of psychoanalytic concepts, of ways of playing with common questions and of developing a poetics shaped by the methods and insights of both disciplines. As Sam Durrant has suggested, I will respect the fictional and psychoanalytic texts "as different yet analogous modes of cultural thought," but I will not just read them "next to" each other (21). This would not do justice to their relationship, which is not characterized by parallel coexistence but by mutual exchange and controversy. Felman demands "a real *dialogue* between literature and psychoanalysis, as between two different bodies of language and between two different modes of knowledge" (6). She wants to replace "*application*" by "implication": "to explore, bring to light and articulate the various (indirect) ways in which the two domains do indeed *implicate each other*, each one finding itself enlightened, informed, but also affected, displaced, by the other" (8-9). In doing so, she assumes that it is necessary to bring the "real" dialogue to light because it is based on an indirect exchange. With many post-Freudian artistic texts, however, this is not the case. Hanif Kureishi's novel *Something to Tell You*, which I use here as one example among many, shows the relationship between art and psychoanalysis can no longer be described as unidirectional. And, what is more, Kureishi knows the discipline he deals with so well that he can provide his own theory of the therapeutic process derived from a direct intertextual relationship with psychoanalytic knowledge.[6] The literary, theatrical, and televisual texts I am interested in are similarly informed about psychoanalytic theory and practice, and they continue the interdisciplinary exchange by infusing artistic form with a psychoanalytic aesthetic and confronting the metaphors and analogies discussed in psychoanalytic and aesthetic theory with their own positions.

Aside from further methodological problems and misconceptions—how would one properly psychoanalyze an author who is multiply abstracted from his published work or a literary character, who is, after all, nothing more than "a tissue of words" (Holland, "Shakespearean Tragedy" 219)?— these traditional variants of psychoanalytic criticism are not adequate to get at the principles at stake here. Authors who talk freely about their experience with therapy or their embeddedness in therapeutic cultures and texts that knowingly engage with psychoanalytic concepts, depicting patients in therapy that openly discuss their mental conditions, cannot be tackled by diagnosing writers and characters—such an approach would simply reduplicate the overt psychoanalytic structure of texts that play with the very concepts psychoanalytic criticism would use to analyze them. The "unconscious" cannot be *un*covered if it already covers the surface of the text. A writer like J. M. Coetzee, who rarely speaks about his work, states that "the traces of my dealings with Freud lie all over my writings" (Coetzee and

Attwell 245), thus implicitly reminding us that if we seek knowledge about his relationship with Freud, the answer will be found in his work, not in his biography or his mind.[7] A related problem arises with the analysis of readers: the texts ask readers and spectators to enter playful interactions, inviting them to recognize aesthetic innovations and analogies with psychoanalysis rather than influencing them on an unconscious level. Reading methods inspired by psychoanalytic practice, such as countertransference analysis, thus also fail to take into account this level of the text's engagement with therapy. In fact, the fictional texts probe the very premises of these reading practices, such as the reader's emotional involvement in the reading process, which makes them unsuitable to engage with the texts' primary interests.

In his lectures *Psychoanalysis and Storytelling*, Brooks has claimed: "The best—and perhaps the only—model for the *use* of the psychoanalytic model in literary study is the model of metaphor" (43). In other words, he suggests using the terms and concepts of psychoanalysis as metaphors, with which to explore analogical relationships between literature and psychoanalysis that shed light on their "human stakes" (35). I have already emphasized that I wish to examine rather than simply reproduce Brooks's method, but what is crucial here is that the works that I will discuss—the novels, the play, and the television series—also employ the therapeutic relationship as model, metaphor, and analogy. When they speak about therapeutic relationships, they simultaneously speak about themselves and the narrative relationships constituting and constituted by them. Through this analogy with psychoanalysis, they achieve a poetological reflexivity that opens a plethora of new starting points for inquiry. The inclusion of therapeutic relationships allows these texts, in Felman's terms, to consider not only "what psychoanalytical theory has to say about the literary text, but also . . . what literature has to say about psychoanalysis" ("Turning" 102), and, I might add, what literature has to say about literature *via* psychoanalysis. These works engage formally and theoretically with therapeutic relationships in order to reach their own understanding of art, or, in other words, to develop a theory of art through a confrontational dialogue with psychoanalysis.

The issue is thus not how psychoanalysis can be employed to render a text or its context intelligible or whether a text delivers an authentic representation of therapy. Instead, the crucial question is how the texts employ psychoanalysis to test their aesthetic potential and develop models for creative work and interpretation. Again, my aim is not to develop another analogy but to show what analogies do for psychoanalysts, artists, readers, and critics alike. In psychoanalysis, the therapeutic relationship is understood as a sort of laboratory for relationships (Zwiebel, "Ist" 152), in which relational behavior and narrative approaches can be safely studied and experimented with. Thus, it is not surprising that literature, theater, and television use the same experimental design to explore their own aesthetic and poetic stakes. What we need are strategies to analyze the texts in these acts of self-reflection.

The therapeutic relationship in the arts

As much as art has challenged psychoanalysis, Freud's theories have attracted and irritated artists from the outset, with both disciplines fighting for self-assertion and the demarcation of their terrain (Anz 23). "Psychoanalysis already plays into the poetry of our entire cultural sphere, it has rubbed off on it and will possibly influence it to an increasing degree in the future," Thomas Mann writes in 1926 (23, my translation). Nevertheless, in early artistic depictions of psychoanalysis, the psychoanalytic process itself remains in the dark. In the "analytic" chapter of Mann's *Der Zauberberg* (*The Magic Mountain*, 1924), psychoanalytic theories are discussed, but the actual *Seelenzergliederung*—literally the dismemberment of the soul—takes place behind closed doors (19). And in what may be the first novel that turns psychoanalysis into the starting point of a narrative, Italo Svevo's *La coscienza di Zeno* (*Zeno's Conscience*, 1923), Dottor S. encourages the written reminiscences of Zeno Cosini as "a good prelude to psychoanalysis" (8, my translation), but this prelude is not yet the product of actual psychoanalytic sessions. Freud himself refused his cooperation in Georg Wilhelm Pabst's attempt to shoot an instructional film about psychoanalysis, *Geheimnisse einer Seele* (*Secrets of a Soul*, 1926), because he was convinced of the impossibility of respectably representing the abstractions of psychoanalysis in the cinema (Freud and Abraham 357). And even twenty years later, Alfred Hitchcock's feature film *Spellbound* (1945) and Jo Sinclair's novel *Wasteland* (1946) are dedicated to therapeutic encounters, but in their didactic and romanticizing thrust they do not actually engage with the aesthetic challenges of the psychoanalytic process.[8]

For a long time, novelists and directors were mostly interested in the romantic entanglements of doctor and patient and the frightening or ridiculous effects of overpowering, demonic, or incapable therapists (Schneider 56). Not until the 1960s do artistic engagements with the psychoanalytic process go beyond the exploitation of its repertoire of characters and materials or its employment as a plot device to unveil secrets in suspenseful stories. At this point, however, psychoanalysis and alternative forms of psychotherapeutic treatment as well as a substantial critique of their practices have finally penetrated Western culture (Porter, *Madness* 212).

Ingrid Hotz-Davies and Anton Kirchhofer show that, from the late 1960s onward, psychoanalysis goes through a phase of general cultural availability that promotes a creative use of its theories: "It thereby becomes available as an ironically inflected mode of self-perception and self-fashioning" (30). Particularly in Anglo-American cultures, where psychoanalysis prospered after the Second World War,[9] its increasingly differentiated theories doubtless belonged to the intertextual and contextual reservoir of writers and readers.

Thus, representations of therapy might be read as an expression of the development of a therapeutic culture. The therapeutic disciplines have, as Nikolas Rose argues, radically changed the way we perceive ourselves as psychological beings:

> The beliefs, norms and techniques which have come into existence under the sign of psy over the last century about intelligence, personality, emotions, wishes, group relations, psychiatric distress and so forth ... have profoundly shaped the kinds of persons we are able to be—the ways we think of ourselves, the ways we act upon ourselves, the kinds of persons we are presumed to be in our consuming, producing, loving, praying, sickening and dying. (226)[10]

Eva Illouz also sees therapeutic discourse as "a formidably powerful and quintessentially modern way to institutionalize the self" (9). According to her, it has recodified the work space and family life and has provided a new language for them, turning the private into an object of public performance. The emphasis on the inner world through self-observation and control has paradoxically led to a standardization and rationalization of our emotional worlds (149–50; 171; 238–39). Although, without a doubt, some representations of therapy mirror and comment on these developments, they are of minor importance in this study. The therapeutic discourse discussed by these critics is based, as Illouz explains at one point, on popularized versions of psychoanalytic theories and therapeutic methods, such as self-help books or business consulting, which have turned psychoanalytic assumptions into commodities for mass consumption (157) and which are often diametrically opposed to actual psychoanalytic practices.[11] Studies like Rose's or Illouz's also assume that the therapeutic narrative, "the therapeutic mode of self-understanding" (Illouz 106), holds a "basic self-schema" for "organizing stories about the self and, more specifically autobiographical discourse" (178). Instead of looking at therapy as a process, they criticize its potential results—models and metaphors for the self.[12] In doing so, they fail to engage with the processual aesthetics of the therapeutic narrative, and even less with the perspective this might provide for other aesthetic processes.

This aesthetic perspective is also neglected in studies that look at the fictional representation of psychoanalysis in literature, film, or television. Most of the time, these texts are tested for how accurately they depict the therapeutic process. In numerous studies on psychoanalysis in the movies, critics remark that film is not capable of capturing the intricacies of the therapeutic encounter (Gabbard and Gabbard xvi; Sabbadini 4). To explain this observation, they often refer to the unrepresentability of psychoanalysis, its resistance against "interesting visual representation," the slowness of its processes, its complex relationship to time and narrative, and its concentration on speaking and listening (P. Gordon 144). If an affinity between psychotherapy and narrative media is established, it is usually based on content, "storytelling that is grounded in emotional experience, personal discovery" (Young 54), and the suspenseful encounter of two people in an intimate space that remains hidden from others. The actual relationship—apparently devoid of excitement, with its slow, detailed, repetitive progress—seems to put up a resistance against realistic representation and thus has to be stocked up with sensational elements. This is where many critical evaluations get stuck. They explain distortions with "common fantasies and fears of what psychotherapy is really about" (P. Gordon 143) or ask "what we learn from the movies about our professional selves and the nature of the therapeutic endeavor" (Brandell 2). Understandably, psychoanalysts are afraid that misrepresentations of their profession could influence their acceptance and public credibility: "Even sophisticated viewers . . . may find their understanding is affected in the absence of any other picture of therapy" (Young 58). What is not taken into consideration in these debates is the potential artistic appeal of the complex aesthetic structures of psychoanalysis.

When Thomas Anz explains that psychoanalytic knowledge can be adapted in literature via characterization, themes and motifs, or plot constellations, his analysis hardly engages with the particular aesthetics of psychoanalysis (26). Hotz-Davies's and Kirchhofer's overview of artistic strategies of "utiliz[ing]" psychoanalysis lists only a single formal feature: plot structures "fashioned along the lines of psychoanalytic 'cures'" (26). Even the few monographs dedicated to the representation of therapy in literary texts, such as Jeffrey Berman's *The Talking Cure: Literary Representations of Psychoanalysis* (1985) and Lilian Furst's *Just Talk: Narratives of Psychotherapy* (1999), deal almost exclusively with psychoanalytic content. Furst concentrates on the literary representation of psychotherapy from the patient's perspective, asking, "what narratives of psychotherapy reveal about the healing process over and beyond what is taught in the textbooks of technical case management" (xv). Furst also engages with plot construction and discusses the function of the therapeutic dialogue, but she does not develop these criteria systematically out of the therapeutic process. In addition, her concentration on one figure of the therapeutic dyad is a problematic simplification if the psychoanalytic process as such is to be studied. Siri Hustvedt argues with good reason: "A truly human portrait of a working therapist ... must also address the problem of the between, the charged space that is neither analyst nor analysand, but a mutual creation" ("Analyst" 229). The representation of psychoanalysis cannot be tackled from one perspective—analyst or analysand—but must always include both sides or, better even, look at the relationship as the space between. This is, after all, also the pivotal point of psychoanalytic techniques and aesthetics, from which the literary texts borrow formal and theoretical ideas. Although Berman claims to study transference relationships in his book, he has hardly any room, after his justified critique of stereotypical representations of psychoanalysts and a historic account of the "ways in which the popular conception of psychotherapy has changed" (*Talking Cure* 25), to discuss the aesthetic ramifications of the encounter. No study of the literary and filmic representation of therapy has so far combined an analysis of psychoanalytic discourse, its aesthetics, and its understanding of art with readings of adaptations of therapeutic encounters in different media. And none has studied the therapeutic relationship not just as a motif but also, as I will, as an aesthetic formal principle and as a figure that allows the texts to reflect their own poetics.

Admittedly, in her book *The Literary Use of the Psychoanalytic Process*, Meredith Skura turns her attention toward the therapeutic process. She argues for the use of psychoanalysis in literary scholarship not as a theoretical structure but as a procedure, a method for interpretation (5). Demonstrating that theories like dream interpretation cannot explain literature, she develops a new literary theory out of the psychoanalytic process. She believes

> that it was something like psychoanalysis, not the naked unconscious, which the poets discovered. The complex ways in which literary texts elaborate and call attention to the play of consciousness have no parallel in simpler phenomena like fantasies and dreams.... But they do have a parallel in the way that these phenomena are handled in analysis—in the moments of integration and insight about them which characterize the psychoanalytic process. (11–12)

However, with her virtual identification of literary and psychoanalytic processes Skura does not respect art and therapy as independent disciplines in Felman's sense. Accordingly, I am not interested in continuing this line of argument. Instead, I aim to explore the significance of such analogical scenarios in art and psychoanalysis—why anyone would entertain the *idea* that art or literary scholarship is like psychoanalysis or the *idea* that psychoanalysis is like art.

Philip Roth's *Portnoy's Complaint* (1969) is the first novel that systematically employs a therapeutic relationship as a structural framework for the entire book, thus demonstrating its fascination with the aesthetic potential of a psychoanalytic session. With this concentration on the analytic monologue of the patient-protagonist Alexander Portnoy, Roth manages to find a new, playful form for the novel and, at the same time, involve the reader as a co-analyst in self-reflexive narrative action. *Portnoy's Complaint* adapts psychoanalytic theories about relational and narrative behavior, finds inspiration in psychoanalytic aesthetics, and creates a performative expression of the analogy between art and the therapeutic relationship. The novel thus inspires a range of questions that will also be the guidelines of my other readings in this study: How does the therapeutic relationship develop in the text and what are the relational structures the text is particularly interested in? How is the form of the text related to these features of the relationship? How does the text use the interplay of therapeutic relationship and artistic expression to reflect upon itself, develop theoretical models, and confront the reader with this self-reflexive process?

My readings of the intricate relational dynamics depicted in texts like *Portnoy's Complaint* are aimed at making visible the textual constructs employed to reflect upon psychological, ethical, and political concerns and at preparing for the following closer analysis of the text's formal and theoretical devices. The oral situation of the imagined therapeutic dialogue is transformed—into literary variants or stylized dramatic and televisual renditions of the encounter. The "text" of psychoanalysis, its fundamental relational structure encapsulated in a dense network of verbal, paraverbal, and nonverbal communication, offers a rich foundation for artistic transformation. For whatever juxtapositions and entanglements are produced between oral and literal, mimetic and diegetic forms of expression in psychoanalysis, depictions of therapy in different media will always find entry points in common modes of discourse and representation. In a second step I explore how the texts react on a formal level to the creative challenge of representing therapeutic relationships with their unique patterns of the psychoanalytic aesthetic. Since every text emulates different aspects of the therapeutic relationship, every chapter offers an opportunity to look at a different way in which psychoanalysis and art may interact on a formal level with the specific features of the medium. In a final step, I will explore how the texts exploit the self-reflexive character of the therapeutic relationship to engage in their own exploration of therapeutic and narrative relationships. The texts involve readers and spectators in a performative dynamic that acts out central theoretical concerns. Felman describes a similar *"reading-effect"* in her study on Henry James's *The Turn of the Screw* ("Turning" 102). According to her, the story creates a trap for its readers: They are supposed to first adopt and then recognize a problematic attitude of overinterpretation illustrated by the characters (190). To grasp such reading effects, like Felman I will draw connections between the ideas played out at the character level and the structure of the text and will verify these effects with actual readers' reactions, reconstructed through exemplary critical readings and reviews (196). I am interested in how the fictional texts tackle the theoretical questions prevalent in critical discourse, such as the relationship between authorship and patienthood, figurations of the text's resistance, and the reader's oscillation between the analyst's emotional involvement and her critical activity. When art and psychoanalysis meet, narratability, readability, and interpretability are all at stake, and both disciplines, in a critical dispute with each other, have to negotiate possibilities, limitations, and liminal cases of their respective communicative practices. In the employment of the relational analogy, the theoretical strands of this study are thus reconnected. Its examination allows us to question relational modes, extend narrative theories, elucidate aesthetic problems, and discuss discursive and performative enactments of narrative interaction and interpretive conflict. And, what is more, through a close analysis of how the fictional texts enact rather than just discuss theoretical problems, we may also gain further insight into the specific nature of the engagement with theory in literature, theater, and television.

Not every representation of therapy is equally suitable for the exploration of these questions. Peter Brooks believes that framed narratives are particularly suited to study narratological relationships and the narrative situation itself because the frame represents the "'real life,' that outer margin that makes the life within narratable" (*Reading* 235). Texts that use a psychoanalytic frame, in which the therapeutic relationship envelops the narrative process, epitomize this potential. The "real life" of the frame is here just another figure of reflection, precisely not "real life" but, analogous to its employment in the text, an artificial relationship initiated to tell stories about "real life." In other words, the therapeutic relationship is a unique self-reflexive structure that can be employed in texts to think about the very process of self-reflection. To explore further the questions prompted by *Portnoy's Complaint*, the most suitable texts do not only use the therapeutic relationship sporadically to characterize their protagonists, as do, for example, Kureishi's *Something to Tell You*, Siri Hustvedt's *The Sorrows of an American* (2008), or the Showtime series *Huff* (2004–06). Representations in which therapeutic situations appear only at brief, albeit pivotal, moments in the fabric of the plot, as in the films of Woody Allen,[13] or in which therapy is used as a mere plot device to make storytelling possible, as in Alice Munro's "Dimensions" (2009) or Lewis Nkosi's *Mating Birds* (1983), also do not contribute to an exploration of this reflexive figure. To elucidate it in all its facets, the therapeutic relationship must be given a central structural function, be made a subject of discussion, and introduce a process of self-reflection via analogies.

To study this thematic, formal, and theoretical engagement with psychoanalytic concepts, a close reading of specific texts is imperative. The representations of therapy that will be dealt with in this study cover a large part of the second half of the twentieth century and the beginning of the twenty-first century, and they span the United States, South Africa, Canada, and Great Britain.[14] They trace the history of psychoanalysis from the height of its success in the 1950s and 1960s through the anti-psychiatric movement in the 1970s and its eventual erosion in the following decades up to its fictional renaissance in contemporary television. However, even within this span I can provide neither a historical nor a global overview of the artistic engagement with the therapeutic relationship. This would call for a more extensive "distant reading" (Moretti 48–49), which would not be in accord with the minute aesthetic questions of this study. With my case studies, I will instead provide exemplary in-depth explorations of the possibilities the structure of the therapeutic relationship may hold for formal and theoretical concerns in a variety of media. I have made a selection in which the basic elements of a therapeutic aesthetics—play, enactment, narrative, dialogue, analysis, seriality—find expression in corresponding medial and artistic environments: literature, theater, and television.[15]

After Philip Roth's paradigmatic *Portnoy's Complaint*, which allows me to introduce a playful, aesthetic engagement with psychoanalysis (Chapter 5), I will turn to J. M. Coetzee's *Life & Times of Michael K* (1983). This gives me the opportunity to study a diametrically opposed literary approach to the therapeutic relationship: in his novel, set during a fictional civil war in South Africa, Coetzee has the doctor—a medical officer—narrate the story of a therapeutic encounter, and he is less interested in therapy's ludic than in its epistemological potential (Chapter 6). The epistemic desire Coetzee's Medical Officer experiences in *Life & Times of Michael K* is also something that Dr. Simon Jordan struggles with in Margaret Atwood's historical novel *Alias Grace* (1996). By embedding her investigation of a murder case from nineteenth-century Canada in the fragmented and serialized narrative of a therapeutic relationship, Atwood is concerned with the intersections between storytelling and gendered power dynamics and the instability of history and identity (Chapter 7). With Peter Shaffer's *Equus* (1973), I turn to the theater and anti-psychiatry. The play shows how the entanglement of diegetic and mimetic representational forms determines the dramaturgy of treatment, which circles around the possibilities of therapeutic and artistic creativity and destructiveness (Chapter 8). I conclude my study with the HBO series *In Treatment* (2008–10), an example that concentrates most radically on the therapeutic space, thus putting the sustainability of the analogy between therapy and television—or art in general—to a final test (Chapter 9).

Art and (psycho)analysis

When the therapeutic relationship is integrated into the structure of literary, theatrical, or televisual texts, it clearly serves as a figure of reflection, in which the functions of storytelling in therapy and in fictional representations are read as analogous. Thus, it creates more than just a frame to treat the suspenseful relationship of therapist and patient; it is also a challenge for formal composition and metafictional self-reflection.

So why do psychoanalysis and the arts turn to each other through the therapeutic relationship? If they establish a dialogue, it is certainly not always mutual, equitable, open, or even favorable. What is at stake is not, as normative visions of interdisciplinary exchange often suppose, the establishment of a "mutual" or "true" dialogue, but interactions that come in various disguises and with specific goals and consequences. The artistic texts mentioned above show that psychoanalysis is really used, as Adam Phillips believes, as a touchstone for the achievements of art and that, in their engagement, they explore their relationship as both complementary and antagonistic practices ("Poetry" 2). But the aesthetic dimension of the therapeutic relationship challenges not just the arts but psychoanalysis itself. Art and psychoanalysis seek each other out as venues for the negotiation of the fundamental theoretical questions they are occupied with. In this study, I will examine how these apparently interdependent fields use each other in various forms of interaction and critical intervention. By comparing the aesthetics and poetics of the therapeutic relationship as they are explored both in therapeutic and critical discourse and in literary, theatrical, and televisual texts, I posit that this relationship is an important nexus for mutual and contending self-reflections. The engagement with the aesthetics of the therapeutic relationship produces new forms and meanings in both directions and opens possibilities for interdisciplinary dialogues—dialogues that seek not so much to find the therapeutic in the aesthetic or prepare for an analysis of art but to explore the aesthetic in the therapeutic and to practice the art of analysis.

2

The Therapeutic Relationship

Introduction: Lessons from Dora

When she took up treatment with Sigmund Freud in October 1900, eighteen-year-old "Dora" had long suffered from an unbearable family secret. She had been molested by the family friend Herr K. and suspected that this was the result of a tacit agreement between K. and her father, who was having an affair with Frau K. and profited from K.'s silence in exchange for his daughter's attentions (Freud, "Fragment" 25). The case became important for Freud not just because it helped refine his thinking about family relations but also because Dora's behavior challenged his theories about psychoanalytic technique and the therapeutic relationship.

Most of Freud's case history is concerned with exploring the history of Dora's hysteria through her personal biography and her dreams. Freud casts himself as a benign interrogator who seeks to make Dora see the hidden motivations behind her behavior, but, apparently, Dora is a less-than-compliant patient. "Dora had listened to me without any of her usual contradictions" ("Fragment" 108–09) is one of many indirect hints that she resists Freud's interpretations. Their relationship is antagonistic, even if Freud notes a sign of affection in Dora's sudden wish for a kiss:

> The addendum to the dream could scarcely mean anything else than the longing for a kiss, which, with a smoker, would necessarily smell of smoke.... Taking into consideration, finally, the indications which seemed to point to there having been a transference on to me—since I am a smoker too—I came to the conclusion that the idea had probably occurred to her one day during a session that she would like to have a kiss from me. (74)

Freud assumes that Dora has made a transference from her father and Herr K.—both smokers like Freud—to himself, but he does not follow up on this connection, and shortly after she terminates the analysis. Freud concludes that she has repeated material from her immediate past and reads the termination as "an unmistakable act of vengeance" (109), not just on himself but on K. as well:

> In this way the transference took me unawares, and, because of the unknown quantity in me which reminded Dora of Herr K., she took her revenge on me as she wanted to take her revenge on him, and deserted me as she believed herself to have been deceived and deserted by him. Thus she *acted out* an essential part of her recollections and phantasies instead of reproducing it in the treatment. (119)

The passage is crucial, as it reflects Freud's recognition that patients may not always be able to tell the analyst about their troubles. Instead, they *reenact* crucial experiences in the transference. As Freud realized, the relationship in which this reenactment takes place needs special attention. Dora's therapy failed, not because Freud might have misinterpreted her but because he did not work on their relationship and underestimated the significance of Dora's transference.

What is even more important than Freud's admission of a failure to recognize the transference in time is his blatant ignorance of his own behavior and his palpable "countertransference" (Berman, *Talking Cure* 11; Mentzos 124). Although Freud described Dora as a "girl of intelligent and engaging looks," "in the first bloom of youth" ("Fragment" 23), most of his remarks testify to a subliminal hostility. Freud is not prepared to accept her repugnance against Herr K. and takes her words as a challenge to detect unconscious motives for her behavior (Gay 248, 250). In a language that testifies to that detective desire, Freud speaks of a "coincidence" of symptoms (in German, he identifies a *verräterische Übereinstimmung*—a telltale or, literally, treacherous concurrence) ("Fragment" 39), of proof, of a "confession" (76), and of his own perplexity: "Her behaviour must have seemed as incomprehensible to the man . . . as to us" (46). Freud turns into a sleuth-like interpreting persecutor, from whom Dora backs away. When she returns a few years later and asks for further therapy, Freud believes that her request is not made in earnest and claims to forgive her for one thing only: "for having deprived me of the satisfaction of affording her a far more radical cure for her troubles" (122). Peter Gay reproaches Freud's lack of empathy and his refusal to recognize Dora's need for reliable orientation "in a cruelly self-serving adult world" (249). At the same time, he notes Freud's own mortification and the painful recognition that "he was far from invulnerable to her efforts at seduction and to her irritating hostility. . . . Freud could be assailed by emotions that at times clouded his perceptions as a therapist" (254). For many therapists after Freud, the Dora case is a compelling reminder that both sides of the therapeutic relationship are involved in a mutually influential emotional process.

The difficulties Freud reports in this case, whether open or hidden, reflect the powerful dynamics of the therapeutic relationship, which forced Freud further to refine his methods—to turn away from an arrogating and dominant interpretive technique and to deepen his understanding of the relational forces at work in psychoanalysis. In what follows, I will discuss the core themes of Freud's technical papers—the setting, the transference, the analyst's stance and his countertransference—delineate their further development in psychoanalytic history, and point out avenues for further investigation. As an introduction to the psychoanalytic therapeutic relationship and as a close reading of Freud's and his disciples' historical discourses, I present these concepts not as static entities but as heuristics in constant flux and debate, exposing the tensions and ambiguities inherent in the therapeutic relationship—tensions and ambiguities that turn it into a salient figure for psychoanalytic self-reflection, aesthetic reconfiguration, and artistic exploration.

The setting

The therapeutic relationship is often described as a special relationship—"one of the most formal and at the same time one of the most intimate of human relationships," as Thomas Ogden says ("Comments" 230). Indeed, therapeutic intimacy is only available under the condition of the formality created by the therapeutic setting. In his papers on technique, Freud designs an ideal environment for the treatment, which includes iconic elements like the couch and free association along with other rules for communication and spatiotemporal arrangement (Habermas, "Freuds Ratschläge" 207, 211). Even so, Freud emphasized that his guidelines were nonbinding words of advice (*Ratschläge*) at best: the occurrences in therapy are too varied to lay down a single modus operandi ("Beginning" 123). His advice does not provide rules of the game, as it were, but gaming strategies that can be discussed and modified (Habermas, "Freuds Ratschläge" 215). And much like rules or strategies in a game, the therapeutic setting determines the kind of game that can be played within its framework.

The fundamental rule or *Grundregel* of psychoanalysis is the most important communicative gaming strategy. It asks the patient to say anything that comes to mind, not to select or shape the material that comes up, and to hold nothing back, no matter how painful or shameful (Freud, "Beginning" 134–35). The fundamental rule is related to the technique of free association, but, strictly speaking, neither these associations nor anything else the patient says is entirely free. Freud assumes that unconscious processes direct the flow of thoughts, which is what gives the patient's speech its shape and the analyst an opportunity to tap into the patient's unconscious ("Autobiographical" 40–41). The analyst is also given a rule to follow: Just as the patient is supposed to tell everything, the analyst is supposed to listen to everything with "evenly-suspended attention" ("Recommendations" 111). With this term, Freud describes a form of attention that opens itself calmly to all of the patient's utterances: "He should simply listen, and not bother about whether he is keeping anything in mind" (112). A specific agenda or screening for specific content, for scientific purposes, for example, should be avoided at all costs:

> For as soon as anyone deliberately concentrates his attention to a certain degree, he begins to select from the material before him..., and in making this selection he will be following his expectations or inclinations. This, however, is precisely what must not be done. In making the selection, if he follows his expectations he is in danger of never finding anything but what he already knows; and if he follows his inclinations he will certainly falsify what he may perceive. (112)

The fundamental rule and evenly suspended attention are both designed to prevent analyst and patient from selecting prematurely the material they work with; they are guidelines to get at as much untampered material as possible. Wilfred Bion goes as far as allowing both partners, psychoanalyst and patient, to "dream" during the treatment: in a state of "reverie," they are supposed to open themselves to random thoughts, daydreams, fantasies, ruminations, and bodily sensations (Habermas, "Freuds Ratschläge" 218; Ogden, *Conversations* 99).

The therapeutic relationship is thus constituted through language (Laplanche and Pontalis 174), or, more specifically, it conventionalizes unconventional communication. Dieter Flader and Wolf Grodzicki have proposed that the fundamental rule establishes an asymmetrical communicative structure that is purposefully opposed to conventional communicative patterns (560–61). Psychoanalysis suspends the sequential rules for speech acts. The patient has to say everything and answer to any question, while the analyst does not and, in fact, must not (565). The reticence of the analyst denies the patient the much-needed interpersonal confirmation that is common practice in everyday speech. As a result, the patient is no longer able to use available interpretive patterns to make sense of the situation or to rest assured that his words are understood and appreciated (574–77);

he becomes insecure and often attempts to retell his story with even more detail and attention to intelligibility. The fundamental rule is thus designed to disrupt the calming effects of storytelling and is intentionally painful and burdensome in order to transform the story (Boothe, *Patient* 13).

The external features of the therapeutic setting serve a similar function of constituting a specific climate for storytelling. The analyst's consulting room is supposed to provide a protective frame that ensures safety and secrecy (Boothe, "Erzählen" 56) but also disrupts conventional patterns of communication. The classic setting requires the patient to lie on a couch while the analyst takes a seat at its head, invisible to the patient. Freud justifies this arrangement with his discomfort at being incessantly stared at by a patient, but it is also supposed to allow the patient to turn to her unconscious and surrender herself to her fantasies, while the analyst attends to his own unconscious impulses and to listening (Freud, "Beginning" 134). Being outside of the other's mimic and gestural sphere of influence goes hand in hand with an asymmetrical visual arrangement, which strengthens the authority of the analyst and fosters infantile fantasies in the patient (König 89–90; Habermas, "Freuds Ratschläge" 209). That is why the paradigmatic couch has become an object of contention and is now often replaced by two chairs facing one another. This debate, however, only goes to show that the seating arrangement, as much as the furnishing of the analyst's office and his use of the available space, is an important feature of the setting (Bateman and Holmes 155). Like the rules for communication, the spatial arrangement structures the relationship and determines the stories that can be told within it. The same significance applies to the temporal framework of psychoanalysis. It usually includes high-frequency sessions (as often as six times a week in the early days of psychoanalysis) and the fifty-minute hour that Freud established. The extreme length of psychoanalytic treatments has been criticized because it supposedly allows patients to wallow in their problems instead of solving them and because such lengthy therapy, which often takes many years, remains inaccessible to underprivileged patients. However, the high frequency and the long duration are a condition for the development and exploration of complex relationships. Like the spatial arrangement, the temporal arrangement is geared toward facilitating and modifying the terms of the relational encounter.

Hence, all these psychoanalytic guidelines are tied to ethical and therapeutic goals. The elements of the setting are geared toward facilitating access to the unconscious and overcoming or preventing resistance. The patient is isolated from all avoidable environmental influences so that his problems will have a chance to come to the surface (Habermas, "Freuds Ratschläge" 207, 210). Nevertheless, stability and safety are not the only implications of Freud's measures; they might also create an atmosphere of domination, violence, and rigidity (Berns 336). The setting provides a basic framework for the relational dynamics of the therapeutic relationship, and if the patient has difficulties with one aspect of the setting, it usually signals a dysfunction in the relationship created within the setting (Habermas, "Freuds Ratschläge" 220). While thus taking on relational implications of their own, the communicative, spatial, and temporal parameters of the setting are a foundation for the creation of meaning, the shape of the stories, and the relationship in which they are told—but their individual significance may also be read as an emanation of the relationship they create.

Virtuality: Transference as weapon and as instrument

Freud's advice regarding the organization of the psychoanalytic encounter is an important component of his strategy to gain control of the unwieldy phenomenon of transference, which derailed Dora's treatment. Transference soon became such a central concept in psychoanalysis that Freud declared it to be an indispensable element in his new "science" with immense methodical and theoretical implications ("History" 16; "Autobiographical" 42). In consequence, transference is one of the most extensively and controversially discussed concepts of psychoanalytic theory (Laplanche and Pontalis 550). Most psychoanalysts, however, would agree that transference describes a process in which (mostly unconscious) experiences, feelings, expectations, wishes, and fantasies that originate in the (infantile) past or in fantasy are transposed onto a relationship in the real present. Dora treated Freud, so he assumes, not as her doctor but as if he had been her father or the unpleasant Herr K. Behind such transference reactions lies a complex, multilayered, and ambivalent phenomenon, which Freud, not without reason, emphatically termed "the most difficult as well as the most important part of the technique of analysis" ("Autobiographical" 43). After all, transference always introduces a proliferation of semantic levels, juxtaposing past and present and inner and outer realities, turning resistance into an instrument and falsehoods into truths.

In a first brief reference to the phenomenon in *Studies on Hysteria*, Freud sees transference only as a "false connection" (*falsche Verknüpfung*) (303): an unconscious and seemingly inexplicable transposition of embarrassing notions and wishes onto the doctor. A more comprehensive definition of transference, which takes it beyond the initial suspicion of being merely an unintentional fallacy, arises only after the failed relationship with Dora. Freud relates the transference to the impulses and fantasies that are being analyzed and argues that the previous relationship, in which they were first experienced, is replaced by the relationship with the doctor ("Fragment" 116). The result of this re- or displacement is often so different from what one might expect in the actual therapeutic relationship—the activated emotions seem so incomprehensible, excessive, or unrealistic—that Freud is forced to explain the occurrence of this transference with the intrusion of unconscious experiences derived from the past. Freud assumes that, through an interplay of constitution and experience, every human being develops idiosyncratic modes of experiencing and acting in relationships. In earliest childhood, these modes solidify into "stereotype plate[s]" of relational experience, which are then repeated in other relationships throughout life (Freud, "Dynamics" 100). This also explains the ambivalence of the transference, which often varies from passionate love to extreme hatred, as it feeds on the conflicting feelings the patient experienced in past relationships (Freud, "Autobiographical" 42). For Freud, transference is thus first and foremost a temporal transposition, which reactivates past conflicts between drive and defense, wishes and fears (Mitchell, *Influence* 104). With her object relations theory, Melanie Klein has supplemented this understanding of transference. In her opinion, familiar objects and the real and imaginary relationships that have been established with them are internalized and serve as patterns for externalization via transference (König 31, 53). This view understands transference not as a transposition in time but as a transposition in space, in which inner conflicts are displaced to the outer world (Mitchell, *Influence* 105–06). Hence, transference is not limited to the shape of the original relationships. As external impressions are absorbed into psychic reality and modified retroactively, and as internalized object relationships are not static copies of the past but creative transformations of earlier object relationships (König 52), object representations and fantasies are revised and roles actively reassigned in the course of transference. Whether through the past or through fantasy, repetition, or revision, transference seems to transpose the "unreal" into the present relationship.

However, transference is also linked to the real relationship between psychoanalyst and patient. It is both prefigured by specific dispositions in the individual and activated by triggers in her counterpart (König 24, 36). Similarities with an internalized object, for instance, may induce specific transference reactions, as Sándor Ferenczi reports: "Even ridiculously small similarities: the hair color, some facial features, the way he holds the cigarette, the pen in his hand, the similarity in the sound of one's given name with an important person's: even such remote analogies suffice to establish the transference" ("Introjektion" 15, my translation). Thus, the connections established by transference are not completely "false," but take the other person's real features into account. All external aspects of treatment may constitute such influencing factors: the setting and personal features of the participants; their behavior; their outward appearance; their gender and sexuality; their age; and their educational, cultural, ethnic, and social background (Kernberg, "Influence" 873, 880; Bateman and Holmes 208). Differences based on discursive power and social rank are of particular importance since they act directly upon the frame of the therapeutic encounter and thus contribute to the formation of asymmetrical relationships. The reality of the relationship thus shapes the transference as much as unconscious fantasy. Transference emerges as a complex "as-if" mode of experience: it reanimates and distorts past and fantasized relational constellations in a present in which they are inappropriate *and* eerily fitting.

As an unconscious mechanism designed to process relational material, transference does not operate only in psychoanalysis. In his "Autobiographical Study," Freud describes transference as "a universal phenomenon of the human mind," which transpires in every analysis, every medical treatment, and, more generally, every relationship (42). The ubiquity of transference has been confirmed by empirical psychologists and neurologists (Pincus et al. 623; Andersen and Berk 81).[1] According to their studies, transference is a basic psychological function that helps us organize experience, integrate perceptions within previously established schemata, and change these schemata through new experience (Bettighofer 39–40). This, in turn, allows us to have recourse to vast patterns of experience and action in every interpersonal encounter, albeit at the risk of judging a new relationship wrongly or prematurely (42). Transference is, as it were, a lens for reading relationships with quite varying accuracy. Seen through this lens, every relationship can be understood as a partially imaginary construct, engaged in a paradoxical search for the familiar and the unexpected (König 13). Based on this potential to access the familiar past and change its impact on the present, the therapist must take transference seriously as "the strongest weapon of the resistance" and deftly turn it into "the best instrument" of psychoanalysis (Freud, "Autobiographical" 43).

At the beginning of the treatment, Freud's patients behave toward him with interest and appreciation, which makes their work together pleasant and productive (Freud, "Introductory Lectures" 440). This beneficial transference, which Freud calls "unobjectionable" ("Dynamics" 105), serves as the foundation of the working relationship between the physician and the patient. Freud's first goal of the treatment is thus to "attach" the patient to the therapist and the treatment ("Beginning" 139) because a strong therapeutic relationship instills confidence and respect toward the authority of the analyst in the patient and sustains her motivation for treatment. To a modern understanding of doctor-patient equality, this institutionalization of deference may sound like an "act of submission" (Mitchell, *Influence* 38), but in Freud's terms, the treatment is based on a mutual "working contract":

> The analytic physician and the patient's weakened ego, basing themselves on the real external world, have to band themselves together into a party against the enemies, the instinctual demands of the id and the conscientious demands of the super-ego. We form a pact with each other. The sick ego promises us the most complete candour . . . ; we assure the patient of the strictest discretion and place at his service our experience in interpreting material that has been influenced by the unconscious. (Freud, "Outline" 173)

The collaboration of the patient, her candid communication and self-observation, the confidentiality of the analyst, his experience, and his commitment to the needs of the patient make up a rational, purposeful alliance between two partners that enables them to work together—a "working alliance" (Greenson 153) as the foundation for psychoanalytic exploration, which soon encounters forces beyond rationality and mutual understanding.

For a while, the mild, positive transference of the first sessions constitutes "the most powerful motive [*Triebfeder*] in [the treatment's] advance" (Freud, "Introductory Lectures" 443). However, as soon as the first difficulties arise and sensitive conflictual material is touched upon, this initial progress evaporates along with the favorable attitude toward therapy (Freud, "Outline" 176). Patients start to feel strong resentment against the doctor or, on the contrary, fall unexpectedly and inexplicably in love with her—irrespective of its content, transference is thus invariably turned into a source of resistance (Freud, "Dynamics" 105): "The patient brings out of the armoury of the past the weapons with which he defends himself against the progress of the treatment—weapons which we must wrest from him one by one" (Freud, "Remembering" 151). Transference, which first served the progress of therapy, is now turned into the patient's weapon, which endangers the treatment and the doctor. After all, it confronts the therapist with her own emotionality—her vulnerability to attack and her susceptibility to falling in love with a passionate patient. The therapist must not respond to the patient's desire for love because she is ethically obliged not to take advantage of an infatuation induced by the treatment; an outright refusal or deception, however, might destroy the patient's trust. Freud's paradigmatic solution for this dilemma reflects his sober treatment philosophy. The analyst has to endure the transference-based tension in order to facilitate interpretation:

> He must keep firm hold of the transference-love, but treat it as something unreal, as a situation which has to be gone through in the treatment and traced back to its unconscious origins and which must assist in bringing all that is most deeply hidden in the patient's erotic life into her consciousness and therefore under her control. ("Observations" 166)

In Freud's opinion, the transference can only be vanquished by proving to the patient that his feelings are a repetition of previous experiences and not actually meant for the analyst ("Introductory Lectures" 443–44). Freud thus transfers the patient's experience into a virtual, self-reflexive realm, in which emotions are analyzed rather than acted upon.

Instead of telling the analyst about their memories, however, patients often repeat the past by acting it out, thus building up considerable resistance against conscious remembering. "Acting out" (or "enactment") is defined as a destructive act on a prereflective level, in which the patient revolts against analytic work, through drug abuse, violence, or, as in Dora's case, premature termination (Bateman and Holmes 194–95; Thomä and Kächele 318). Because of the dangers that lurk behind acting out, Freud prefers "remembering in the old manner" ("Remembering" 153). Again, he clearly privileges the verbal and thus more reflective access to the past, but he also realizes that for most patients this level is initially unattainable. Transference, he argues, felicitously ranges halfway between remembering and acting out; it allows the patient to repeat old patterns in the safe space provided by psychoanalysis. Transference thus becomes the ideal medium to gain access to the patient's inner world. It concentrates all psychoanalytic work within the therapeutic relationship, creating an "intermediate region" between illness and life, a sort of stage on which the illness, its symptoms, and all related relational constellations can be unfurled and "reenacted" in front of the analyst's eyes. This is why Freud describes transference as a "playground" (*Tummelplatz*) on which previous events can be freely repeated (Freud, "Remembering" 154). By thus "staging" the history and the inner life of the patient, transference makes them available for analysis (Freud, "Outline" 176). In Freud's writings, transference emerges as a multifaceted phenomenon that fosters the creative reenactment of old conflict material. I will discuss the theatrical metaphors that buffer these descriptions of transference in the following chapter, but even at this stage we can discern a tension between mimetic and diegetic modes of analytic representation that will characterize psychoanalytic discourse and its aesthetic potential from Freud onward.

To manage the transference, the patient needs plenty of time fully to explore her experiences and resistances and ultimately surmount them (Freud, "Remembering" 155). Ordinarily, interpretation and isolated insight do not suffice to resolve a conflict—due to the "adhesiveness" of the libido, the psyche is too inertial to allow for quick change (Freud, "Introductory Lectures" 455). Therefore, Freud emphasizes the necessity of working through—the eradication of resistance and the complete penetration of the analyzed material through repeated intervention and interpretation (Greenson 196–97). In neurological terms, long-term change in neural networks can only be effected through long-term conditioning (Gedo 352), which explains both the length and the repetitiveness of psychoanalytic therapy. The idealistic aim of "complete analysis"—eradicating all repressions and memory gaps—is theoretically impossible. The unconscious, Freud holds, can never be completely purged ("Analysis Terminable" 220). At least on a virtual level, the treatment is, as Freud claimed, interminable, and transference never entirely resolved. Similarly, transference remains an interminably unresolved factor in psychoanalytic treatment and theory, and, as we can now intuit, in psychoanalytic aesthetics. Transference is a force that thrusts the analyst into a relational connection with the patient's fantasy and her past, with strong emotions like love and hatred, and the patient's performance of them—it creates an as-if mode of experience that has inspired numerous analysts to establish a link with artistic experience.

Neutrality: Transference and the analytic stance

In addition to providing insight into the unconscious, transference also holds the possibility of learning through repetition and alternative conflict solving (Freud, "Outline" 175 and "Introductory Lectures" 451). Thus, analysts after Freud have often considered playing along with the roles they are offered in transference to allow patients to make different experiences with new objects (Racker 81; Bettighofer 98, 107). This active engagement in therapeutic action, however, does not sit well with the neutral stance that Freud demanded from the analyst. He explains: "*Analytic treatment should be carried through, as far as is possible, under privation—in a state of abstinence*" ("Lines" 187). Thus, the physician is neither allowed to satisfy his needs at the patient's cost nor supposed to give the patient an opportunity to gain satisfaction from their relationship. This is not only a safeguard against sexual abuse and misguided therapeutic ambition, but it also ensures that the patient is denied her desire for approval, affection, consolation, and premature reassurance (Habermas, "Freuds Ratschläge" 216). Whereas the first part of Freud's rule is the ethical baseline of any treatment, the second part may sound cruel—but noncompliance with the patient's wishes is actually a way to serve her needs. If the patient uses therapy as a substitute for true satisfaction, she loses her motivation for treatment and runs the risk of becoming dependent on the analyst for the satisfaction of her needs (Freud, "Lines" 163–64). Freud believes that unsatisfied desire will push for curative clarification and thus facilitate the psychoanalytic process (Bateman and Holmes 190; Habermas, "Freuds Ratschläge" 216–17). Crucially, the rule of abstinence is not a rule against emotions but a rule involving their intentional dissatisfaction and suspension for further exploration.

Freud also counsels the analyst not to be guided by his ambitions, opinions, biases, or precursory theoretical premises. Freud never uses the word "neutrality," which was later to become the catchphrase for this guideline (Laplanche and Pontalis 331–32). He does, however, warn against the temptation to use one's own personality as a curative device. There is always a risk that the patient's interest in the physician's character will dominate the therapy and that the resulting intimacy complicates the resolution of the transference (Freud, "Recommendations" 118). Only if the analyst does not contribute anything to the therapeutic equation, so the argument goes, can he collect impressions of the patient's behavior independent of his own influence (Russell 39; König 63). And finally, Freud also cautions his colleagues against role-playing and attempts at educating the patient. Psychoanalysts are not supposed to form the patient in their own image but help him "to liberate and fulfil his own nature" ("Lines" 165). All is geared toward providing a clear space for the patient's story.

In order to underscore the importance of a neutral stance, Freud draws on a number of further similes, which have lastingly shaped the image of the analyst. Among other things, Freud likens the analyst to a telephone receiver: "[The analyst] must turn his own unconscious like a receptive organ towards the transmitting unconscious of the patient. He must adjust himself to the patient as a telephone receiver is adjusted to the transmitting microphone" ("Recommendations" 115–16). Although this telephone simile implies the passivity of the analyst, it also emphasizes that Freud's rule is geared toward creating specific conditions "for a particular sort of receptivity and 'play' of the mind" to become attuned to the patient's experience (Ogden, *Reverie* 132). For Freud, the analyst is supposed to be all medium—all receiver. In a similar manner, he argues that the physician should be "opaque" for the analysand and, like a "mirror," reflect nothing but what is shown to him ("Recommendations" 118). This stance is supposed to ensure that the therapy is completely devoted to the patient's needs and that her utterances will not be distorted by the analyst. It also suggests that the analyst relies on mirroring communication and silence instead of intervening empathetically or expressing herself spontaneously. In a manner that is far from unproblematic, it paints the analyst as cold and unfeeling, which also finds resonance in Freud's more elaborate recommendation that analysts be as unaffected as a surgeon during an operation. Freud advises his colleagues

> to model themselves during psycho-analytic treatment on the surgeon, who puts aside all his feelings, even his human sympathy [*Mitleid*], and concentrates his mental forces on the single aim of performing the operation as skilfully as possible. . . . The justification for requiring this emotional coldness in the analyst is that it creates the most advantageous conditions for both parties: for the doctor a desirable protection of his own emotional life and for the patient the largest amount of help that we can give him to-day. ("Recommendations" 115)

Conspicuously, Freud anticipates the possibility of being accused of cold unfeelingness and justifies this stance with therapeutic considerations; at the same time, he points to the danger that the emotional life of the analyst might be encroached upon. As yet unaware that media always have an influence on the story they facilitate, Freud strives to provide as neutral a medium as possible. However, this repeated insistence on neutrality, in addition to the numerous war metaphors Freud uses to describe the "battlefield" of transference and his patient's "armoury" of resistance ("Introductory Lectures" 456 and "Remembering" 151), indicates that powerful emotions are at work beneath the surface of the supposedly smooth, neutral mirror. Freud's metaphors are potent reminders that the question of the analyst's stance is not solved by a simple call for neutrality, and we will see that the analyst's "mediality"—his inevitable influence, as facilitating medium, on the therapeutic process—remains one of the central questions of analytic self-understanding, interdisciplinary debate, and artistic cross-inspiration.

Mastery: Countertransference as interference and as instrument

Eventually, Freud's call for neutrality runs up against the ubiquity of transference. The analyst is inevitably caught up in his own transference in addition to not being able to extricate himself from the patient's transference. This is what has become known as the analyst's countertransference (*Gegenübertragung*). In Dora's treatment, Freud did not succeed in reflecting on his own countertransference, which, as his case study still shows, is comprised of a mixture of sexual attraction, hostile rejection, and paternal authority (Glenn, "Freud" 524). When Freud introduces the term "countertransference" much later, he does so only with reservations: "We have become aware of the 'counter-transference,' which arises in [the physician] as a result of the patient's influence on his unconscious feelings, and we are almost inclined to insist that he shall recognize this countertransference in himself and overcome [*bewältigen*] it" ("Future Prospects" 145). This assessment is soon followed by an appeal to all analysts to analyze themselves continually in order to work through their own conflicts and, finally, by the establishment of training analyses (Freud, "Recommendations" 116; "Question" 219). Beyond these recommendations, Freud's public countertransference policy rests on his insistence on neutrality and on his reluctance to speak about the phenomenon at all. Clearly, emphasizing the impressionability, weakness, and imperilment of the physician in the psychoanalytic treatment might have hurt Freud's chances at establishing his new method as a serious treatment option and as a scientific endeavor (Nerenz 504). Accordingly, countertransference, much like transference before, was first considered a danger to the stipulated equanimity, so that evasion or extermination seemed like the only recourse.

Meanwhile, Freud's private statements provide a much more nuanced understanding of countertransference. In a letter of March 20, 1913, Freud writes to Ludwig Binswanger:

> What one dispenses to the patient should never be immediate affect but always consciously assigned, and then more or less depending on need. Potentially very much, but never from one's own unconscious. This is what I would take for the formula. Therefore, one must recognize and overcome one's countertransference every time, only then is one free oneself. To give someone too little because one loves them too much is an injustice toward the patient and a technical mistake. All of this is not easy, and maybe one needs to be older for it, too. (126, my translation)

Thus, Freud does not actually require the analyst to be without emotions. In his opinion, one must simply keep these emotions away from the patient and dedicate oneself to her needs. Freud's words clearly indicate, however, that both experience and technical sensitivity are required to achieve this level of restraint. In one of his last works, "Analysis Terminable and Interminable," Freud returns to the psychoanalyst's own fear of unconscious turmoil (248–49). Emphatically, he advises analysts to be brave and face the dangers of emotional work. Even as Freud acknowledges the necessary involvement of emotion, however, his main concern remains the analyst's mastery of the countertransference rather than its employment as an instrument of analysis. Overall, Freud's concept of countertransference remained underdeveloped, and the problem of delineating and handling the phenomenon was delegated to his successors.

Ferenczi considers this problem in his paper on psychoanalytic technique. He admonishes analysts "to *dose* their sympathy well . . . , since being dominated by affects or even passions creates unfavorable ground for the reception and proper processing of analytic data" (Ferenczi, "Zur psychoanalytischen Technik" 50, my translation). According to him, one can only overcome the countertransference by observing the patient and simultaneously controlling one's own position. He warns explicitly against attempts at avoiding this precarious balancing act. If the analyst fails to control his countertransference and tries to manipulate the patient emotionally, he misses out on the unconscious influence he exerts and produces wishful projections—the patient might see him as a "patron or as her 'knight in shining armor'" (52, my translation), which would inhibit the analysis. If, on the contrary, the analyst tries to disconnect from his feelings, he makes it impossible for the patient to establish a viable relationship and fails to understand her "battles of the soul" (50, my translation). Ferenczi's metaphors already show a much more involved therapist at work. He acknowledges that allowing the countertransference to work harbors the danger of losing control in the face of intense emotions, but defending against it may also establish resistance and inhibit the analyst's access to the patient's world (Racker 75, 162; Pick 157, 165; Bettighofer 63). And what is more, resistance against countertransference conceals the potential it shares with transference to be transformed into a powerful instrument.

In an influential 1949 lecture, Paula Heimann pointed out the utility of countertransference feelings, thus initiating a decisive turn in psychoanalytic practice. According to her, mastering the countertransference cannot be accomplished via emotional restraint; instead, the analyst needs to process his emotional responses as a "key to the patient's unconscious" (Heimann 78). Heimann reinterprets the mirror metaphor by committing the analyst "to *sustain* the feelings which are stirred in him, as opposed to discharging them (as does the patient), in order to *subordinate* them to the analytic task in which he functions as the patient's mirror reflection" (74). In this way, countertransference is turned into an emotional transmission device, which reflects all forms of communication between analyst and analysand (Kernberg, "Notes" 38–40). Heimann's paper was a decisive step toward the recognition that the therapeutic relationship can be read from both sides.

Further investigation into the unconscious communication between analyst and analysand has followed the reinterpretation of Melanie Klein's "projective identification," which was originally conceived as a mechanism of defense in which the subject imaginatively inserts parts of herself into an object to harm, possess, or control it (Laplanche and Pontalis 226). But whereas Klein limited her concept to the subject's internal life, projective identification is now mostly seen as an interactional phenomenon. Therein, the patient not only projects a part of herself onto the analyst but also induces him to identify with the projected material and react accordingly (Bateman and Holmes 111). This experience, as Ogden summarizes in the words of Wilfred Bion, "is like having a thought that is not one's own" (*Projective Identification* 26). He explains the underlying psychological mechanics in the following way: "In association with this unconscious projective fantasy there is an interpersonal interaction by means of which the recipient is pressured to think, feel, and behave in a manner congruent with the ejected feelings and the self- and object-representations embodied in the projective fantasy" (34). Drawing on James Grotstein's "body rhetoric," William Meissner hypothesizes that subliminal signals, which are transmitted via facial expressions, gestures, posture, intonation, and autonomic bodily reactions like blushing and sweat production, are the medium of this interpersonal pressure (103, 121). On this basis, projective identification may be understood as a primal, everyday form of communication, which is commonly used in relationships from the mother-child dyad onward, and which allows the analyst to partake directly in the analysand's relational experience. Therefore, speech and action are now considered equally valid means to communicate within and about the shared relationship in a "dialogue of action" (Bohleber et al. 1221, my translation). Countertransference and many related phenomena are no longer seen as dangers to the neutral analytic stance but as valuable, interpersonal carriers of information and tools of transformation. As a device that disrupts the separation between the members of the communicative dyad, countertransference is exploited in therapy and, as we will later see, in literary theory and many fictional renditions of the therapeutic relationship.

Elasticity: Countertransference and the analytic stance

With this recognition of the complicated interplay between transference and countertransference, Freud's insistence on a neutral analyst could hardly be upheld; indeed, contemporary psychoanalysts tend to question the very possibility of a neutral stance. Owen Renik claims: "It is *impossible* for an analyst to be in that position *even for an instant*: . . . our technique, listening included, is *inescapably* subjective" (560). Complete anonymity and abstinence cannot be maintained in any close contact between two human beings; indeed, the concentrated attempt to remain neutral is nowadays interpreted as a strong trigger for transference on the patient's side (Mitchell, *Influence* 178, 180; Bettighofer 130–33), and, on the analyst's side, as a defense against anxiety. Samuel Gerson compares Freud to "the ancient Ulysses" who protected himself from the Sirens' seduction by "lash[ing] himself to the mast" ("Neutrality" 629). Neutrality, as seen from this angle, actually protects the analyst—from his own emotional turmoil and his resentment against what he sees as his (female) patients' seductive behavior. In the course of this critical backlash, Freud's metaphors provide a perfect target, as the mirror and the surgeon seem to epitomize the coldness of the analyst and the objectification and deactivation of the patient (Ivey 64).

Orthodox psychoanalysts had indeed understood Freud's recommendations as rigid laws and cultivated an analytic stance of anonymous and sterile authority (Greenson 174). Upon closer inspection, however, Freud's metaphors do not really reflect his own practice—his patients report him to have been a warm and involved therapist, and Johannes Cremerius portrays Freud's technique as open, vivid, and artistic (*Handwerk* 349). In this light, Racker has suggested a reinterpretation of Freud's central mirror metaphor, arguing that it is less about sterility than about focusing all attention on the patient and helping her see herself anew (41). In addition, guiding images like the surgeon may reflect a desire to protect analyst and patient—a much-needed caution, given that Freud's first disciples often engaged in detrimental love affairs with their patients (Bräutigam 181). Clearly, neutrality and involvement as well as abstinence and care are not opposite binaries in the therapeutic setting, which is why psychoanalysts have searched for new conceptualizations of the analyst's stance to counterbalance and supplement Freud's influential images.

Objections to Freud's neutrality had already been voiced by Jung and Ferenczi. "A certain impact on the doctor is unavoidable as well as a certain disturbance or impairment of his nervous health. After all, he actually 'takes over' the suffering of the patient and shares it with him," Jung argues ("Psychologie" 183, my translation). He believes that the unconscious conflict of the patient is also activated in the therapist (187): He is no longer a "judge and advisor" with superior knowledge, not just an interrogator, but also a respondent and a witness, or literally "a co-experiencer" (*ein Miterlebender*) ("Grundsätzliches" 7, my translation). In this rendition of the therapeutic relationship, the analyst is no longer just a neutral canvas but an integral and actively involved part of the process.

Similarly disassociating himself from Freud, Ferenczi also tried to conceptualize and operationalize the analyst's involvement. He compares the analyst to an "obstetrician," who must remain a passive observer during a natural process, but, at the critical moment, must also be able to intervene with his forceps (Ferenczi, "Zur psychoanalytischen Technik" 45, my translation). In addition, he emphasizes the importance of responding to the developmental processes in therapy with elasticity: "Like an elastic band, one must bend with the tendencies of the patient, but without giving up pulling in the direction of one's own opinions" (Ferenczi, "Elastizität" 390, my translation). The resulting, proper analytic stance involves "continuous oscillation" between empathy, self-observation, and judgment (391, my translation). In a similar manner, other psychoanalytic authors seek to abolish all pretensions to a specific stance. Bion reminds his colleagues that "the fact that any session is a new session and therefore an unknown situation" must not be obscured "by an already over-plentiful fund of pre- and misconception" (*Learning* 39). And Stephen Mitchell wants to remain open for all "modes of participation" and thus not even strive for "a state of nonintention" (*Influence* 193–94). Obviously, these calls for elasticity and nonintention also have metaphoric implications—again, the analyst is turned into a medium, only this time it is a medium that is ready to be formed and changed by whatever the analysand brings to the relationship.

Other conceptualizations of the analytic stance see the analyst as providing a supportive medium—elastic, but also warm and protective. Michael Balint believes that the therapist

> should be willing to carry the patient, not actively but like water carries the swimmer or the earth carries the walker, that is, to be there for the patient, to be used without too much resistance against being used. . . . Over and above all this, he must be there, must always be there, and must be indestructible—as are water and earth. (*Basic Fault* 167)

In a similar vein, Donald Winnicott describes psychoanalysis not as an interpretive exercise but as "the provision of a congenial milieu, a 'holding environment' analogous to maternal care" (Phillips, *Winnicott* 12). Thus, the analyst is primarily called upon to "hold" the patient and his conflicts instead of anxiously searching for a cure (Winnicott, *Therapeutic Consultations* 2). In this way, he creates a medium for growth, which Winnicott, much like Balint, associates with a holding element. Adam Phillips identifies an "implicit analogy" in Winnicott's writings "with simpler forms of organic life" and "the belated provision of the right soil for the plant" (*Winnicott* 88). Water and earth: in Winnicott's and Balint's terms, the analyst is turned from an unresponsive mirror to a rich, interactive, and supportive—quasi-parental—medium. Clearly, they seek to find more acceptable and humane models for the therapeutic relationship as a response to the criticism lashed against Freud's early metaphors; at the same time, however, these hold their own problematic potential. After all, Jung and Ferenczi, the early advocates of the analyst's involvement, were the disciples about whose affairs with patients Freud was most worried. Nevertheless, and in concert, these reconceptualizations have added considerably to a shift in psychoanalytic thinking, which turns away from one-sided interpretation to mutual interaction.

Several new approaches to psychoanalytic treatment are therefore united by their concern with interpersonal elements in metapsychology and treatment philosophy rather than with intrapsychic experience. A differentiation between transference and countertransference reaction seems no longer pertinent to them. Instead, both mechanisms are seen as the result of a mutual process, a shared creative construct in a new relational context, in which both analyst and analysand are subjectively involved (Bohleber, "Editorial" 815; Kunzke 599). In order to describe these forms of interaction and utilize them in treatment, psychoanalysts have developed several theoretical models for the relational interplay of transference and countertransference. In what follows, I will focus on three models with particular relevance to an inquiry focused on narratology and aesthetics: Stephen Mitchell's "relational matrix," Thomas Ogden's "analytic third," and Antonino Ferro's "bi-personal field." Along with the elastic and supportive reconfigurations of the psychoanalytic stance, interactive models such as these have considerably altered the way psychoanalysts think about their own endeavor, which, as we will see in later chapters, have also provided new entry points for aesthetic theory and artistic critique, capitalizing on the implications of involvement and support—love and desire.

The relational matrix

Stephen Mitchell's turn toward interpersonal, relational processes finds its roots in a radically different theory of what constitutes the psychological structure of the individual. For Mitchell, human beings are not governed by their internal drives, as orthodox Freudianism assumes, but

> shaped by and inevitably embedded within a matrix of relationships with other people, struggling both to maintain our ties to others and to differentiate ourselves from them. In this vision the basic unit of study is not the individual as a separate entity whose desires clash with an external reality, but an interactional field within which the individual arises and struggles to make contact and to articulate himself.... The person is comprehensible only within this tapestry of relationships, past and present. (*Relational Concepts* 3)

Recent findings in infant psychology confirm Mitchell's belief that, from the outset, the individual is grounded in relational structures. According to the theory of "mirroring," a child can only develop as a thinking and feeling subject through the reflection of her emotions and reactions by an early caregiver: the child learns to see herself in the eyes of the mother. By reflecting the child's utterances or feelings through her own words or gestures, this intersubjective human mirror allows the child to become aware of herself (Altmeyer and Thomä 19). In this exchange, she develops a sense for the borders between conscious and unconscious, fantasy and reality, you and I, as well as a reflexive regard for her own self (Ogden, *Matrix* 209 and *Subjects* 60). The capacity for mutual recognition evolves at the same time. The child finds in her mother a separate psyche outside of her own control, who can share, confirm, and reflect her feelings, but who can also deviate from them. In the give-and-take of encouragement and dissent, detachment and attachment, the child learns to differentiate herself from others and recognize them as independent subjects (Benjamin, "Outline" 38–39). Hence, the individual is created and forever embedded in relationships.

With such a radical relational orientation, Mitchell seems to give up on a fundamental perspective of early psychoanalysis—the focus on the unconscious internal life of the individual (Bernstein 278). However, he is not interested in dismissing intrapsychic experience. He seeks to integrate both perspectives, arguing that human beings clearly depend on their physiology and their psychological constitution but interpret these physical and intrapsychic processes within relational patterns (*Relational Concepts* 4). He coins the term "relational matrix" to describe the interplay of intrapsychic experiences with interpersonal interaction and development: "*The most useful way to view psychological reality is as operating within a relational matrix which encompasses both intrapsychic and interpersonal realms*" (9). Thus, the model does not suppress the intrapsychic dimension but extends, as Lynne Layton argues, our understanding of the structure of the psyche to include "the unconscious rules of relating that every dyad creates" (308). In other words, relationships shape a substantial part of the psyche and remain readable in future behavior.

In the clinical practice of Mitchell's "Relational School," the therapeutic relationship is conceived as an exchange between two equal and complete psychological entities (Renik 553), who bring their own relational matrices to the encounter. The analyst's personality, with all its experiences, emotions, passions, beliefs, and sociocultural background, becomes an integral element of the treatment (Kunzke 603). Whereas orthodox approaches have taken pains to restrain the analyst's involvement, Mitchell pleads in favor of interaction: "The analyst becomes the various figures in the analysand's relational matrix . . . ; the analyst and the analysand gradually rewrite the narrative, transforming those characters in a direction which will allow greater intimacy and more possibilities for varied experience and relatedness. One never stands completely outside the transference-countertransference configurations" (*Relational Concepts* 296–97). To make room for these enactments, spontaneous reaction, and self-reflexive receptivity, Mitchell calls for methodological open-mindedness; according to him, it is less important what happens than how what happens is being discussed with the patient (*Influence* x; Kunzke 604, 608). For him, it is also essential to introduce the analyst's passionate emotions into the therapeutic exchange. All participants in the analytic encounter are invited to indulge in their emotions; but whereas the analysand may cultivate "a kind of analytically constructive irresponsibility," the analyst is still obliged to protect the relationship (Mitchell, *Relationality* 131). This self-discipline and the ability to experience intense emotions do not exclude each other in Mitchell's model. On the contrary, only a combination of the two allows the patient to access his deepest emotions: "What makes it possible to love and hate with abandon is involvement with an other who has feelings in return, . . . but who is working to employ the feelings on both sides of the relationship in the service of analytic work" (133). Mitchell is still in line with Freud when he calls on the analyst to keep the boundaries of therapy in check, but the emphasis is rather more on the reality of the emotions than on their control. Instead of comparing the analyst with a surgeon or a mirror, Renik accordingly perceives a kinship with a skier or a surfer, "someone who allows himself or herself to be acted upon by powerful forces, knowing that they are to be managed and harnessed, rather than completely controlled" (565). The Relational School clearly tends toward immersion rather than distanced observation.

Mitchell's emphasis on the asymmetry of therapy and the analyst's responsibility for the patient's safety (*Relationality* 130; Kunzke 605) must be read in light of the backlash against the Relational School. Cordelia Schmidt-Hellerau, for instance, criticizes relational psychoanalysts for being busier with themselves, their own pleasure and subjectivity (as reflected in the surfer metaphor) than with the patient (664–66). Sharing this critical stance, Werner Bohleber is afraid that the Relational School is no longer capable of conceiving of the other as radically Other because the analyst concentrates exclusively on what is shared within the dyad and not on what separates the participating individuals ("Intersubjektivismus" 207). These concerns actually point to central tenets of the Relational persuasion: the theory does not allow for a notion of radical Otherness because every individual is always connected with and constituted through others, and it is exactly this connection—be it erotic, antagonistic, or otherwise relationally charged—that offers the analyst insight into the "Other."

In one particular case history, Mitchell describes his analytic relationship with Gloria, who felt deeply torn between various imaginary lovers and her actual partner: "Our analytic relationship was characterized by a romantic tension and subtle erotic flirtation on both our parts. I did not self-consciously choose to be flirtatious, but I also did not self-consciously restrain ways of being with her that might be construed as potentially flirtatious" (*Relationality* 137). Mitchell clearly allows passion to grow within a potential space: "It seemed to live in a world made possible by our acknowledging its presence, . . . but not . . . examining it too closely" (138). For a long time, Gloria seems to benefit from this relationship, but after several years, she develops an obsession with actually having a love affair with her therapist. At that point, Mitchell tells her clearly that there are boundaries he will not transgress, which "ushered in a difficult, painful, but also very important period in our work. . . . The gains she made became consolidated, and her relationships with other men deepened" (138). What is striking about Mitchell's report is not just his willingness to take the analytic relationship far into the realm of "cultivated and questioned love" (138), guided by his responsibility for the patient's safety. Mitchell also never speaks about the interpretations he might have given Gloria; instead, the entire case history focuses on the description of their relationship. It is as if not just the story but also its interpretation rests within the relational work itself.

The analytic third

A different variant of mutual influence and joint construction is described by Thomas Ogden's model of the "analytic third,"[2] which he defines as an independent intersubjective phenomenon arising out of the interaction of therapist and patient (Gerson, "Relational Unconscious" 79). For Ogden, the therapist and the patient are not only separate beings in a therapeutic encounter; they also create a specific "intersubjectivity" that "coexists in dynamic tension with the analyst and the analysand as separate individuals with their own thoughts, feelings, sensations, corporal reality, psychological identity, and so on" (*Subjects* 63). Through the interplay of the couple's unconscious communication via transference and countertransference, a third subject is created, which represents all that analyst and analysand share, create together, and thus have no individual control over. The third cannot exist without these separate individuals, but they, in turn, depend on it for their interaction *as* analyst and analysand (Ogden, *Subjects* 64, 93). Both individuals are anchored in and influenced by the shared third, which changes their experience and their behavior: "No thought, feeling, or sensation can be considered the same as it was or will be outside of the context of the specific (and continually shifting) intersubjectivity" (73–74). Sometimes, Ogden's descriptions of the analytic third make it sound like a common stock of relational material, "an experiential base, a pool of unconscious experience to which analyst and analysand both contribute and from which they individually draw" (*Conversations* 19–20). And yet, in other contexts, the analytic third emerges as an independently acting subject capable of dialogue: "The analytic situation . . . is comprised of three subjects in unconscious conversation with one another" (Ogden, "This Art" 863). Ogden could be charged with conceptual uncertainty, but the fluctuating metaphors actually reflect the polymorphism of the phenomenon he tries to capture—a co-created entity with a life of its own.

Since Ogden believes that each partner perceives the third exclusively from her own point of view, the shared creation is never experienced identically. He emphasizes that the patient's experience is still to be privileged in an asymmetrical therapeutic encounter (*Subjects* 93–94). Nevertheless, the psychoanalytic process creates such an intimate connection that both participants and their experiences are irrevocably altered. Upon entering analytic space, the patient "loses" her mind, her thoughts, dreams, feelings, and sensations, her experiences and her history, which alter their shape and meaning within the relationship (Ogden, *Subjects* 6, *Reverie* 141 and "This Art" 858). This all-encompassing, pervasive connection with another being results in a transformative experience, and therapist and patient may "'retrieve' their separate minds" at the end of the analysis, "but the minds 'retrieved' are not the minds of the individuals who had entered into the analytic experience" (Ogden, *Reverie* 9–10). These processes occur in all relationships. The interaction itself unconsciously changes the behavior and the experience of the participating individuals. As a consequence, Ogden assumes that the Other and her experiences are only accessible to the extent in which she acts in and upon a shared relationship. Thus, Ogden's third is not mere mystification, as Helmut Thomä and Horst Kächele worry, and he does not actually fail to consider the difference between the patient's thoughts and his own, as they suspect (95). His very point is that it is not possible to locate the precise origin of a thought within a relationship; analyzing the third provides the only possible access to the patient. Ogden is not concerned with distinguishing each participant's contribution but with accurately appreciating "the interplay of individual subjectivity and intersubjectivity" (*Subjects* 64). From the perspective of the analytic third, there are no wholly individual actors in a relationship and their thoughts must be interpreted as co-creations.

The assumption that all sensations the analyst experiences are connected to the analytic third and thus with the analysand allows Ogden to revise his interpretive technique and pay attention to "mundane, unobtrusive, quotidian thoughts, feelings, sensations, fantasies, daydreams, ruminations" (*Reverie* 98) and use them to reflect on the relationship. In this way, he employs his own unconscious to become receptive to "the 'drift' . . . of the unconscious of the analysand" (109–10). However, Ogden does not communicate these thoughts directly but waits until he can translate them into an interpretation or a metaphor that can be used by the analysand. In his case study "The Purloined Letter," Ogden relates how a random envelope suddenly becomes meaningful in a session with his patient Mr. L.: "The envelope . . . came to life at that point as a psychological event, a carrier of psychological meanings . . . . I understand the event as a reflection of the fact that a new subject (the analytic third) was being generated by (between) Mr. L. and myself" (*Subjects* 74–75). At this moment, Ogden, who had believed that he was being entrusted with a secret in this letter, realizes that it has been part of a bulk mailing. After further scrutiny of the envelope, however, he finds that the address was written with an antiquated typewriter, a refreshing antithesis to the anonymity of the dispatch itself. While describing these ruminations, Ogden appears distracted from his patient and self-absorbed, but he eventually connects his thoughts with the therapeutic relationship, which revolves around a similar search for "something human and personal" (70). By no means does he tell his patient about his preoccupation with the envelope; instead, he translates his insight by speaking out of his experience of the analytic third: "I told the patient that I thought that our time together must feel to him like a joyless obligatory exercise, something like a factory job where one punches in and out with a time card" (71). For Ogden, every event and every object may become meaningful and thus a part of the relationship, communicable through metaphors and stories. The "analytic third" is not only a theory about relationships but a reading strategy to understand the communicative products of the relationship.

The bi-personal field

The model of the bi-personal field also rests on the assumption of a four-way matrix between the conscious and unconscious systems of patient and analyst, which structures every analysis in a unique way (Bateman and Holmes 117). However, while the "field" is designed to describe similar phenomena as the analytic third or the relational matrix, its spatial imagery introduces further conceptual possibilities into a theory of psychoanalytic interaction. This is apparent in the writings of Antonino Ferro, currently one of the most productive representatives of field theory, as well as in the earlier work of Madeleine and Willy Baranger, on which Ferro's concept is based.

Metaphorically, the idea of the bi-personal field is derived from physics. The image describes how particles invisible to the eye generate a force field across space—only in this case, the field, much like the analytic third, is produced in the interplay of transference, countertransference, and projective identification (Baranger and Baranger 808; Kittler 181; Ferro, *Bi-Personal Field* 16). At the same time, the metaphor evokes the earlier Freudian associations with the battlefield and the playing field. When the Barangers touch upon these metaphors, however, they are interested in the structure of the exchange between analyst and analysand. For them, analysis is not archaeological work but playful interaction, like a game of chess: "The 'chessboard' between them is a shared structure and each of them is acting by virtue of it. . . . This chessboard could very well symbolize what we have termed the bi-personal field while the game would be the structure of the treatment as a whole" (Baranger and Baranger 811). Like the chessboard, which prescribes a spatial configuration, rules, and moves, the field is generated by internal and external structures. Spatial and temporal coordinates as well as the communicative contract of the setting determine its quality. Any change in these microstructures, such as a change in the position of the couch, effectuates a change in the entire field and thus in the analytic relationship (Baranger and Baranger 797; Stern, "Field Theory I" 492). Freud's thoughts on the setting, including his reference to the game of chess, are thus integrated into a theory of the therapeutic relationship.

Due to the continuous exchange between both partners in the dyad, the field theory also assumes that no event in this relationship can be assigned to a single agent (Baranger and Baranger 796). However, the field is "bi-personal" only with regard to the two persons actually engaged in the analysis; by way of narratives and fantasies, other persons continuously intrude upon the dyad. Even the analytic partners may perceive each other as embodiments of other, third persons or entities: "In ordinary situations, the bi-personal therapeutic structuring remains as a background, present but not perceived, on which the constantly changing tri- and multi-personal structures are made and unmade" (Baranger and Baranger 798). The Barangers conceive of the field as a relational stage, on which external relationships are reenacted. The analytic relationship can be distinguished from other relationships by its strange capacity to represent them: "It is a couple in which all other imaginable couples are experienced while none of them is put into action" (807). For the

Barangers, the analytic experience is both virtual and ambiguous through its capacity to reflect many other relationships in simultaneity. Through this overload of continuous projections and transferences, all elements in the field assume a polysemous as-if quality: "It is this temporal ambiguity, the mixture of present, past and future, that permits patients not only to become aware of their history but also to modify it retroactively" (800). The analyst's task consists in keeping all of these relational forces in flow and allowing them to intrude upon and be transformed within the analytic field (816). What the Barangers describe as a curative factor, however, the field's ambiguous virtuality, also points to an aesthetic quality of the field, which I will further explore in the following chapter.

Ferro's concept of the bi-personal field builds on the Barangerian model, but he emphasizes the role of the analyst's own fantasies and weaves insights from narratology into his account of the therapeutic process. He pays attention to unconscious dynamics that are not yet palpable in the relationship but can already be apprehended through tensions within the field, such as the influence of the setting or of the fundamental rules of therapy (Ferro, *Bi-Personal Field* 17). In the transitional space of the field, ideas can be grasped even though they are not yet connected, may still be taking shape, or remain "unsaturated" (158). Ferro understands the field as a medium for symbolization, narration, and transformation, in short, as a "matrix of possible stories" (*Psychoanalysis* 13). Starting from the assumption that the unconscious dynamic of the pair becomes apparent in narrative derivatives within the analytic dialogue, he argues that both partners have to learn to symbolize what happens in their subliminal exchange with the help of dreams, drawings, stories, or play (28). Storytelling, in various guises and shapes, becomes Ferro's leitmotif for psychoanalytic work.

However, Ferro's goal is not to reveal hidden meaning but to transform existing meaning from *inside* the field and to enable the analysand to effect such transformations herself (Stern, "Field Theory II" 633, 636). For instance, Ferro proposes that the analyst can only face the transference of a father figure by asking himself from which point of view he might *actually* represent the father and how he must behave to transform this, possibly anxiety-inducing, father imago into another, more benign imago (*In* 63). In order to enable such experiences, Ferro rejects straightforward interpretation in favor of psychological work within the field, which is best represented by joint narrative work. Like Mitchell and Ogden, Ferro also grants that the therapy must remain asymmetrical, privileging the patient's stories and delegating the responsibility for the analytic work to the analyst (*Psychoanalysis* 92–93). Nevertheless, even with this emphasis on the analyst's responsibilities, Ferro's concept turns away from psychoanalysis as authoritative interpretation toward a more equalized model of joint narration—with implications that need further exploration.

Numerous case studies from Ferro's work with children demonstrate his theory in practice. In a vignette dealing with five-year-old Renato, Ferro reports that the hyperactive child "reminds [him] of a bison-calf"; his speech only "seems to goad him, as though my words were bullets" (*Bi-Personal Field* 41). Thinking that "it would take a fence to keep him in," he starts drawing fences on a piece of paper (41). Renato participates in the game by drawing a red funnel designed to break the fences. When he draws something that looks like a teepee, Ferro recognizes in the drawing "A place for Red Cloud," and in response Renato draws "a teepee, an Indian child and a whirlwind" (41). Jointly, Ferro and Renato establish a narrative framework that allows them to symbolize what happens between them without immediately abstracting from it. The relational material is preserved in narrative interaction and can be transformed through new narrative or pictographic events, such as "Red Cloud" or the "Indian child." Like Ogden, Ferro delineates a reading practice in his case study; unlike Ogden, however, Ferro privileges creative practice over interpretation or, rather, presents us different forms of storytelling *as* interpretation within a complex spatiotemporal relational matrix.

Mitchell's, Ogden's, and Ferro's case studies represent a turn in psychoanalysis, in which narration and interpretation are no longer seen as a unidirectional process with a privileged interpreter-analyst but as a joint search for meaning (Zwiebel, "Ist" 164). Contemporary psychoanalytic models seek access to a relational truth, assuming that an individual can only understand herself in an encounter with another (Coetzee and Kurtz 137). In such an undertaking, analyst and patient co-develop their interpretations, whose primary object is no longer the past but the present therapeutic encounter (Bettighofer 119). The interactive models of the therapeutic relationship thus all point toward an interactive theory of storytelling, which has huge theoretical implications both for psychoanalysis and the aesthetic models that draw on it. Interaction and narrative co-construction promise an ethically balanced mode of gaining insight into an Other, and yet, the insight gained in this way may be fraught with an (inter-)subjectivity that destabilizes analytic certainties.

Conclusion

As a very brief introduction to the psychoanalytic understanding of therapeutic relationality, this chapter could only provide a glimpse of the variety of controversial approaches discussed throughout the history of psychoanalysis and it does not pretend to present an all-encompassing or conclusive model of the therapeutic relationship. The main purpose of this chapter was to extract the nodal points of the psychoanalytic model and discuss central concerns of the theory that make it amenable to aesthetic and fictional reconfigurations. Indeed, we have seen that central elements of the therapeutic relationship are fraught with so much emotional and intellectual resistance that they have been continually redefined, even and particularly in aesthetic terms.

A therapeutic relationship is contractually established as an artificial working relationship with explicit therapeutic purpose. The setting, in which it is embedded, takes on its own meaning for the relationship because, with its implementation of formalized intimacy and conventionalized unconventionality, it sets specific limitations and support structures for interpersonal and narrative development through a communicative and spatiotemporal framework. Transference and countertransference, however, provide the most important foundation for the therapeutic relationship. The dyad consisting of therapist and patient is virtually colonized by a potentially infinite number of other relationships, which endow every event within the therapeutic space with multiple, ambiguous meanings. In fact, one could argue that the psychoanalytic therapeutic relationship differs from all other relationships in this very potential to incorporate other relationships and suspend them in virtuality, where they may be examined. Transference turns psychoanalysis into an as-if experience, which suspends reality but still allows for the fully felt emotionality we associate with "real" experience. The surprising number of analogies between artistic and therapeutic experience that spring from this theory of transference will be closely examined in the following two chapters.

The unreality and high emotionality of transference and countertransference have challenged the analyst's conduct, and his stance from a neutral distance to unrestrained engagement has been a continuous subject of debate since Freud. The earliest demands for complete neutrality soon came under attack, both for sterilizing the relationship and for neglecting the important modes of communication in the transference-countertransference dynamic that can only be picked up if the analyst allows herself to be touched and changed in the relationship. In other words, the analyst's "mediality" is at stake as is her capacity to let the relationship reflect and transform the stories the patient brings to analysis. This is manifested and emphasized in the three models of interaction I have introduced here. Mitchell's relational matrix allows us to understand the individual as always embedded in relational contexts. For him, passionate interaction and mutual immersion in psychoanalysis are a way to make relational patterns felt rather than translated into a discursive interpretation. Ogden's analytic third turns our attention to the fact that every thought, every event, every thing that is experienced within a relationship is actually a product of that relationship rather than of a single one of its participants. Thus, it is as much a relational theory as a reading strategy that opposes straight lines of interpretation. Similarly, Ferro's bi-personal field suggests that we must understand the spatiotemporal and emotional contexts of a relationship as part of a process of meaning-making and, in turn, read the relationship as a projection surface for the developing relational drama, not in order to deduce an interpretation but continue the storytelling through narrative interaction. This interdependence between the story and the relationship, the love and the desire awakened in psychoanalysis, and the ethical and epistemological concerns raised by the analyst's stance have not just continued to test therapeutic theory, they are also one of the prime reasons why novels, plays, and other media remain interested in the therapeutic relationship. It is clearly not just a generator of stories about a patient, a therapist, and their encounter, but a complex medium that has been endowed with aesthetic and poetic potential by psychoanalysts and artists since its inception. In the following chapter, I will show how these quasi-artistic dimensions of the therapeutic relationship have turned it into a richly suggestive figure in psychoanalytic and aesthetic theory that continues to be discussed and transformed in literature, theater, and television.

Part Two

Discourses in Dialogue: The Aesthetics and Poetics of Therapeutic Relationships

3

The Art of the Therapeutic Relationship: Psychoanalytic Aesthetics

Introduction: Psychoanalysis as aesthetic experience

The interest of modern psychoanalysis in (joint) narration and interpretation points to a crucial question that has been debated since Freud: Is psychoanalysis a scientific or an artistic practice? "Freud . . . rejected the suggestion that there might be something non-scientific or unscientific, something resembling art, about psychoanalysis" (277), Hans Loewald explains, but he himself does not seem so sure: "Due to significant shifts and changes in modern understanding of what constitutes truth, in our insight into the relations between reality and fantasy or imagination and between objectivity and subjectivity, we begin to recognize that science and art are not as far apart from one another as Freud and his scientific age liked to assume" (278). In his classic paper "Psychoanalysis as an Art and the Fantasy Character of the Psychoanalytic Situation," Loewald promotes a scientific-artistic understanding of psychoanalysis. Admittedly, his concept of art concentrates on technique and refers the analyst's art (τέχνη) to interpretation and investigation (278), but still, he suggests a broader definition of psychoanalytic art that pertains to its relational configuration: "Considered as a process in which patient and analyst are engaged with each other, psychoanalysis may be seen as art in another sense: the psychoanalytic situation and process involves a re-enactment, a dramatization of aspects of the patient's psychic life history, created and staged in conjunction with, and directed by, the analyst" (278–79). In this sense, psychoanalysis provides a framework for stories and reenactments through its analytic techniques, the specific requirements for storytelling and storymaking, and the structure of the therapeutic relationship. In other words, Loewald defines psychoanalysis as a distinct mode of experience and genre of art.

Psychoanalysts tend to emphasize the exceptionality of the formal constraints they encounter in their practice: "What is done, spoken of, thought and valued on the couch is so different from what happens in the rest of the patient's life, that the space between them yawns in ways that can be expected to cause alarm," Susan van Zyl claims (90). Thomas Ogden also stresses the specificity of the relational experience in psychoanalysis: "The invention of a new form of human relatedness may be Freud's most remarkable contribution to humankind. Being alive in the context of the analytic relationship is different from the experience of being alive in any other form of human relatedness" ("This Art" 866). This belief in the exceptionality of their practice forces psychoanalysts to pay more attention to the form of their interactions. Ogden urges his colleagues to focus less on the meaning of an event than on the emotional and linguistic relationship between analyst and patient, in which the event is discussed: "Our use of language must be equal to the task of capturing and conveying in words a sense of 'what's going on here'—in the intrapsychic and intersubjective life of the analysis, the 'music of what happens' in the analytic relationship" (*Conversations* 80). It is striking but not accidental that Ogden uses metaphors borrowed from aesthetics to describe the analyst's task. A comparison between art and psychoanalysis is, in fact, a regular feature of psychoanalytic discourse. Sebastian Leikert, for instance, speaks of psychoanalysis as an "artwork without a work," arguing that it aims to create new subjective and intersubjective realities by deploying all kinds of aesthetic mechanisms (984, my translation). For Loewald, the psychoanalytic session also has similarities with the structure of a work of art: "In the mutual interaction of the good analytic hour, patient and analyst . . . become both artist and medium for each other" (297). The "work" of psychoanalysis is a work in progress, mutually developed within the therapeutic relationship. Psychoanalysts have thus referred to their work as a form of creative, procedural "art," which must be "reinvent[ed] . . . for each patient" (Ogden, "This Art" 862) and calls for "a greatly heightened sensitivity" (Ogden, *Conversations* 75)—or, one might be tempted to add, an aesthetic attunement—to do justice to the experiential uniqueness of every therapeutic relationship.

These various ways of describing psychoanalysis as an art or as an aesthetic practice are summarized in Reimut Reiche's position that psychoanalysis, apart from its knowledge about artists or art, has more genuine access to aesthetic experience and artistic form—through its very own form of *psychoanalytic* experience (315). Indeed, aesthetic experience is not tied to the encounter with artworks but may be an aspect of all kinds of experiences; Joachim Küpper and Christoph Menke describe it as a specific way of dealing with objects, situations, or people, or as a specific way of orienting oneself in the world (11). It is created, as Martin Seel argues, by perceiving something in its (aesthetic) appearance and paying attention to its "momentary sensual givenness" (17, my translation). Aesthetic perception is thus no more but no less than a particular form of attention to the sensual qualities of an experience, and, in the strands of psychoanalytic discourse I will examine here, it has thus been wrested from the traditional field of beauty in art and nature and applied to psychoanalytic experience.

However popular this application may be, Ogden has warned his colleagues against simplistic comparisons between therapeutic and literary experience: "A critical divide separates the two pursuits: psychoanalysis is a therapeutic activity, while reading and writing poetry are aesthetic ones. To try to draw one-to-one correspondences between the two represents, I believe, a form of reductionism that obscures and distorts the essence of these two quite different human events" (Ogden, *Conversations* 113). Ogden opposes the equation between psychoanalysis and poetry because the "analytic aesthetic" is defined by the therapeutic function of their encounter ("Some Thoughts" 10). For him, the therapist's duty to treat the patient separates his endeavor from art, which is classically defined as an experience that should be appraised with disinterested pleasure. Ogden is well aware that analogies are never complete, but that does not stop him from being one of the most prolific creators of aesthetic metaphors for psychoanalysis. Like all metaphoric thinking, the pervasive use of art as an analogue to therapy is supposed to draw out and make plausible particular insights and concerns about psychoanalysis. The aim of this chapter is not, in an extension of the psychoanalysts' metaphors, to describe psychoanalysis as an art, but to examine the significance of these metaphors.

Through a close reading of these psychoanalytic writings, I intend to trace a line of argument from Freud to contemporary psychoanalysts, which hinges on a comparison with the arts and attempts to describe the specific aesthetic experience of the therapeutic encounter. In this discourse, the therapeutic relationship emerges as a "text" with "characters," as a realm where space and time become fictionally overdetermined, as a "theatrical" form of play and as a space for storytelling, producing narratives that are both poetic and dialogical and follow the mythological prototypes of Oedipus and Scheherazade. With the philosophical extension of aesthetic experience outlined earlier, it may very well be possible to conceive of psychoanalysis as possessing its very own aesthetics in which the therapeutic and the aesthetic are actually intertwined. The chapter, however, goes further in arguing that these strategies for aestheticizing the psychoanalytic practice are an attempt to deal with the discipline's fundamental ambivalence about its own "scientific" status and point to a not (yet) completed theory of the importance of aesthetic experience in the therapeutic process.

Transference texts

The "raw material" of analytic work consists in a variety of utterances the patient introduces into the relationship (Freud, "Constructions" 258), but these utterances do not necessarily have to be verbal. Freud extends his understanding of language to include every kind of expression of psychological activity ("Claims" 176), under which he subsumes stories, ideas, memories, parapraxes, associations, sign language, symptoms, writing, the language of dreams, and the actions of transference and resistance. The unconscious, Freud maintains, speaks "more than one dialect" (177). One of the characteristics of the psychoanalytic exchange is that everything that happens or is being said in analysis is treated as a "potentially meaningful" form of communication (Ogden, *This Art* 113). That is why psychoanalysis is interested in all modes of expression that emerge in the therapeutic relationship.

Vittorio Gallese summarizes all these verbal and nonverbal utterances of the patient as a "text," which is to be deciphered and interpreted (532). This "text" of the patient is reflected and supplemented by the interplay of transference and countertransference. In this sense, James Gorney understands the analytic "text" as the sum of the entire analytic discourse, which is created "through an act of reciprocal co-authorship" between analyst and analysand (540). Thus, when analysts speak of "text," they create a metaphor for the complex network of conscious and unconscious communications in the therapeutic encounter, and in doing so, they do not necessarily follow an understanding of the text as a piece of writing. Instead, the psychoanalytic concept of therapeutic "text" could be described, with Roland Barthes, as a "methodological field" that cannot be pinned down to a stable physical manifestation because it substantiates itself in a process—it is, again, a work in progress (*un travail, une production*) ("De l'oeuvre" 73).

In this sense, textuality is also an important metaphor for Freud's thoughts about transference. With regard to the fact that under its influence the material of psychoanalysis is shaped and produced, Freud has described transference as a "species" that generates "new editions," "new impressions or reprints," and more "ingeniously constructed . . . revised editions" ("Fragment" 116). Transference is "textual," as Peter Brooks explains, because it represents the past "in symbolic form, in signs, as something that is 'really' absent but textually present" and can only be fully established through mutual interpretive work (*Psychoanalysis* 53–54). This text has a content (the transferred patterns of previous relationships) and a specific form in which it manifests itself in psychoanalysis. Through transference, a (sub)text is introduced into the analytic work, which forms part of the analytic text and which can itself be a creative adaptation of previous (relational) texts that are no longer or have never been available for conscious representation (Crapanzano 405). As such a text, transference furnishes the therapeutic dyad with models and patterns for reading and interpretation, but it may also be read and edited itself. In consequence, the goal of the therapeutic process is to decipher this text or to add on to, revise, or rewrite it. The text metaphor thus emerges as a broadly applicable analogy to conceptualize different aspects of the transference with further metaphors of reading and writing. The theoretical and practical shift from the primacy of interpretation toward working within the transference and creating new experiences demonstrates that access to the relational material does not depend on interpretation; instead, it is primarily rooted in the (aesthetic) experience of its textual manifestation.

Strikingly, these metaphors tend to obliterate the difference between spoken and written "text," and they ignore the fact that the therapeutic relationship is based on oral rather than written communication. This may be more than simply an acknowledgment of the fact that definitions like Barthes's no longer rely on the text's written constitution. Describing the therapeutic situation or, more precisely, the transference as text allows psychoanalysts to home in on specific characteristics of the therapeutic encounter, such as its revisionary work, the co-authorship of a newly created story, and the tensions between absence and presence in analytic storytelling and listening. In short, it provides a model for the multiple connections that are established in the psychoanalytic dialogue along the axes of artistic experience.

Characters

The "text" of the psychoanalytic encounter is populated by two kinds of characters: the people who are actually present in the therapeutic dyad and the imaginative characters that are drawn into the therapeutic process through stories and enactments. Both kinds of characters are caught up in asymmetrical constructions. The relationship between analyst and analysand is forever unbalanced because however much the therapist may participate in the process, she is supposed to focus all her attention on the patient. His psyche is ultimately the one to be cured, and his story ultimately the one to be explored.

This asymmetry is further dynamized by the transference. In her memoir *The Last Asylum*, Barbara Taylor writes:

> All psychoanalysts are, to a greater or lesser degree, fictive beings, creatures of their patients' needs and imaginations. This was certainly true of [my analyst], who at different times in my analysis was a god, a devil, a shaman, a snake-oil salesman. I never really met the man himself, apart from his analytic persona, nor will you in these pages. (xvii)

The figure of the analyst contains fictive elements through a number of persistently overlapping mechanisms. Taylor's term "analytic persona" suggests that the therapist enters into the process with the self-constructed mask of a psychoanalyst—including all the behavioral norms and attitudes that suit this role. At the same time, the analyst is charged with even more contradictory meaning through the transference of the patient. On the one hand, he is being equipped with the features of characters and personal experiences drawn from the inner life of the patient, and on the other hand, he is being associated with the cultural stereotypes of the healing professions. Taylor lists gods, devils, shamans, and charlatans, but other figures should also be included in that list: detectives, judges, saviors, and saints; crazy scientists, lovers, and persecutors; conquerors, playmates, prostitutes, sages, gurus, magicians, and poets. Of course, patients are not exempt from this fictionalization. Although analysts are asked to curb their countertransferential tendencies, patients are treated according to familiar patterns and may emerge as disciples, victims, criminals, and lunatics, but they can also be elevated to saviors, "wise fools," or artists. Such descriptions convey a quasi-mythic dimension to the therapeutic endeavor and add layers of meaning beyond the immediate encounter.

This overdetermination of analytic characters has been intensified in the Barangers' and Ferro's conceptualization of the bi-personal field. The dyadic construction of most therapeutic relationships excludes other people from the immediate therapeutic situation. However, Madeleine and Willy Baranger point out that the therapeutic process is not truly limited to analyst and analysand; within the established space of therapy, a plethora of other characters come alive in narrative representations (798). These figures may be humans or meaningful animals, objects, or even abstractions (Ferro, *Psychoanalysis* 95). Antonino Ferro emphasizes that these "characters" are readable in three different ways and links these analytic modes of interpretation to parallel developments in literary studies. The first, Freudian psychoanalytic conceptualization of narrated characters understands them as representations of real characters in the patient's history—a notion that

Ferro relates to the very first narratological studies, in which a character is understood as a psychological person with feelings of his or her own. In the second conceptualization roughly associated with formalism or structuralism, literary studies focus on the general rules of storytelling: characters in the text are seen in terms of their function in the narrative (Ferro, *Psychoanalysis* 87). This stance is matched in Kleinian psychoanalysis by a tendency to interpret characters as a reflection of internal objects and bodily fantasies. The third position is represented by "the more recent theories of character construction by way of the intersection of text and reader" (29). Thus, it is the functional equivalent of Ferro's own conceptualization of characters, which assumes that all "persons" and other figures that emerge in the analytic dialogue are "holograms" of the function of the analytic pair (*Bi-Personal Field* 2). They are jointly constructed figures who also reflect joint concerns and are to be read in that way. Ferro introduces these comparisons with literary theory not only for clarification but also for intensification. The psychoanalytic character is even more complex (and, so the implication goes, interesting) than the literary character. Behind the asymmetrical constellations highlighted by psychoanalysts and patients—the patient at center stage, the therapist in the backseat while both explore jointly created characters that are fictionalized holograms of history, fantasy, and the relationship—thus rests a sense of aesthetic ambiguity that points to a proliferation of meaning in the therapeutic encounter.

The psychoanalytic space-time continuum

Brooks describes transference as "a special 'artificial' space for the reworking of the past in symbolic form" (*Psychoanalysis* 53), designating it as a locus of symbolic action and as a special realm of experience. Reiche also locates the intersection between psychoanalysis and art in their common potential to create "intermediary" or "imaginary spaces," in which signs and meanings can be transformed (308). It seems that the creation of "space" is particularly important for the aesthetics of psychoanalysis.

Spatial metaphors elucidating the therapeutic experience can be found as early as Freud. He describes transference, as we have already seen, as a "battlefield" ("Introductory Lectures" 456) and as a "playground" ("Remembering" 154). Through James Strachey's influential English translation, the second metaphor has become especially potent. As Siri Hustvedt intimates, along with the German original *Tummelplatz*, which describes a meeting place that is not limited to children, the image calls to mind "children romping at play," "hurry and commotion among adults," and a "hotbed of action" ("Freud's Playground" 197). Indeed, both the battlefield and the playground metaphor emphasize that psychoanalysis involves the joint activity and interaction of two parties playing in dead earnest. This interactivity caught between fantasy and reality is further specified in two psychoanalytic concepts that were designed to illustrate the space created by transference: potential space and the analytic field.

According to Winnicott, "potential space" is a realm between fantasy and reality, "an intermediate area of *experiencing*, to which inner reality and external life both contribute" (*Playing* 3). It is "not *inside* by any use of the word," "nor . . . *outside*, that is to say, . . . not a part of the repudiated world, the not-me, . . . which is outside magical control" (41). Children experience a jointly created potential space through play with their mothers, but they also learn to create it themselves through transitional objects—curious possessions that children use to cope with the mother's absence and to test out the differences between I and Not-Me, reality and imagination. Later, the capacity to create this potential space also plays a role in play and cultural experience. It is the kind of mental space that, according to Ogden, makes creativity possible in the first place (*Matrix* 213). For him, analytic space is one version of this jointly created potential space, a space "in which personal meanings can be created and played with" (238). The notion of potential space thus endows analytic space with the "potential" for interactive creativity, but it does not yet consider the actual dimensions of therapeutic space and time.

The concept of the bi-personal field is likewise based on the creation of a joint space for experience and fantasy, but it also considers the spatiotemporal coordinates of this realm. While the field is generated by two participating individuals, it is also substantially influenced by the analytic setting. The Barangers' reminder that "any modification of the experienced spatial field naturally means a global modification of the analytic relationship" pertains to the dependence of the field's configuration on spatial, temporal, and communicative conditions (797). For instance, it is of central importance that therapy takes place in one specific room. Its dimensions, the use of the couch and its properties, the distance between analyst and analysand, the interior design of the therapist's office—everything may influence the relationship. In turn, these real coordinates may be overwritten by imaginative spaces and extend beyond their own dimensions. The Barangers attribute this experience to the imaginative juxtaposition of two different spheres: "The space of the analytic situation is similar to the space in dreams, where the geometric scandal of ubiquity becomes the rule" (801). Thus, when analysts speak about "space," we need to think of it as a kind of "experienced space," which cannot be measured geometrically but creates an experience of orientation, position, attunement, and security within certain behavioral codes (Dennerlein 55, my translation). Analytic space, as a potential space and as a bi-personal field, is thought of as an "experienced" space-time-continuum, which is created by the ambivalent as-if mode of transference. It is located in a between-space, in which the boundaries between self and other, subject and object, fantasy and reality, symbol and symbolized, here and there, and then and now are dissolved.

The experience of time in psychoanalysis is similarly described as a juxtaposition of several time frames. The Barangers speak of "temporal ambiguity":

> The time of the analysis is simultaneously a present, a past and a future. It is a present as a new situation, a relationship with a person who adopts an attitude essentially different from that of the objects of the patient's history, but is at the same time past, since it is managed in a way which permits the patient the free repetition of all the conflicting situations of his or her history. (800)

In addition to this simultaneity of temporal levels, Ogden also holds that psychoanalytic time is characterized by transformation, as the past cannot be reexperienced as such and is always recreated in the present (*Matrix* 243). Against this background, time appears distorted, as the significance of events replaces the chronological sequence in the organization of experience:

> At one moment childhood is telescoped into the present. . . . At another, time becomes elongated—the trivial becomes extended and preoccupying—while that which is portentous and apparently pregnant with meaning is treated with a speed and casualness that does not seem to fit with all that lingering over a slip of the tongue or over an almost imperceptible change in the tone of a voice. Yet this temporally anomalous experience within each session is framed by the fixity of the fifty-minute hour. (Zyl 95)

Susan van Zyl sketches a protean experience of time that is still held within a rigid frame—the psychoanalytic setting. In other words, she defines therapy as a regulated medium, in which a particular aesthetic experience takes place, an experience that the Barangers have characterized as ambiguous in both space and time: "It is never just one situation but superimposed or mixed situations, different but never clearly delimited" (799). This juxtaposition of past and present, real and fantastic spaces is produced by the transference. In its amalgamation of ambivalent relationships, levels of reality, and mundane experience with fantasy material, transference gains a creative potential that cannot be read unidirectionally or unequivocally and that may create "mixed situations" that are more akin to aesthetic or fictional experience than scientific evaluation.

By definition, transference involves the impulse to transfer earlier experiences onto new ones and thus forge a "false" connection between past and present. The therapeutic relationship as a whole is, as Brooks points out, "metaphoric, in that it is based on the analyst's role as surrogate for past figures of authority. . . . And of course, the word *transference* itself is merely the Latinate version of *metaphor*" (*Psychoanalysis* 42). The properties of transference produce the characteristic metaphoricity of experience in psychoanalysis, in which events that are antecedent or external come alive in internal incidents. However, if transference is read as a metaphor, then it also acquires its instabilities. Transference would then no longer be a mere equation between two similar relationships but a unique interaction between two semantic levels, which produces these similarities in the first place and, in the process, creates new insights (Black 293). Such a reading of transference ties in with conceptualizations of the analytic space as a field where factual and psychic realities overlap. Although past, factual reality is the basis for transference, its specific shape is determined by the psychic reality of the therapeutic relationship and the adaptations it has undergone in the patient's mind. Through the act of transference, the act of μεταφορεῖν, the outer layers of reality are perforated, for the relationship is then seen as something different from what it actually is. The tang of fictionality that is attributed to psychoanalytic experience is thus drawn from the productive relationship between external and internal reality. And yet, what psychoanalysts describe is not quite fictional, but a hybrid of factuality and fictionality.[1]

Freud claims that transference feelings are not "real" although they are experienced as such, and he lists a number of reasons: the obvious influence of resistance on transference, its traceable origin in earlier relationships, and its lack of foundation in reality. And yet, Freud concedes that transference love is indeed very similar to "real" love: "We have no right to dispute that the state of being in love which makes its appearance in the course of analytic treatment has the character of a 'genuine' love" ("Observations" 168). Whatever the relation between transference and factual reality, the emotional experience it creates is real. "Emotions are not fictive either in dreams or in transference," Hustvedt explains ("Freud's Playground" 200). Thus, transference is not simply fictional; it is, according to Jeremy Holmes, "both a fact and a fiction" ("Language" 214–15) and is experienced as both real and unreal at the same time (Ogden, *Matrix* 239). Freud deals with the tension between transference and true feeling by holding them in suspension—not just a "willing suspension of disbelief" but rather a suspension of all critical judgment, which enables the analyst to test reality and fiction against each other.

What defines the specific aesthetic experience of psychoanalysis is the virtuality with which Freud decides to treat the semi-fictional constructions of transference. Leo Bersani remarks: "It is conversation suspended in virtuality. Perhaps the therapeutic secret of psychoanalysis lies in its willingness to entertain the possibility of behavior or thought as only possibility" (28). At the same time, Ferro insists, this virtual level is undercut by the emotional reality of what is discussed:

> In the consulting room "we are constantly having sex and nothing but sex"—in the sense, of course, that we relate to each other, and that this relationship *is sex*, even if it follows from the necessary rules of abstinence that we have "chaste" sex. However, it is certainly not chaste with regard to the emotions activated and experienced, and to the fantasizing, also in sexual terms, of the continuous matings *between minds*. (*Psychoanalysis* 48)

In other words, Ferro contends that the virtuality described by Bersani is, again, only semi-virtual: Psychoanalysis suspends action and fact, but their substitutes, language and fiction, are no less potent, no less fraught with intense and "real" emotion and meaning. Based on this sense of virtual experience in therapy, it is no longer surprising that psychoanalysts align their own practice with the virtual experiences we encounter in art.

Constructions

Quite often, however, psychoanalysts suspect they are dealing not just with "mixed situations" but with pure invention. From Freud onward, they have worried about the truthfulness of their patients' stories and their access to the "real" past. In his later case studies, Freud is no longer convinced that it is possible to reconstruct past events without a significant loss. He compares the patient's lifelong work on his own stories with the way in which a nation "constructs legends" by constantly reworking previous experiences in the light of new insights (Freud, "Obsessional Neurosis" 206). These "tales [*Dichtungen*] of the individual's prehistoric past" are developed and given sense through retroactive adaptation (207); the event itself escapes the analyst's grasp. As much as this recourse to *Dichtungen*—"poetry" as a metaphor for the patient's stories—suggests a departure from scientific investigation, Freud remains ambivalent about opening his practice to quasi-literary pursuits.

Freud specified these thoughts in his essay "Constructions in Analysis." Comparing psychoanalysis with the work of an archaeologist, Freud argues that the analyst probes meticulously reconstructed evidence before he ventures into an interpretation of the past:

> His work of construction . . . resembles to a great extent an archaeologist's excavation of some dwelling-place that has been destroyed and buried or of some ancient edifice. The two processes are in fact identical, except that the analyst works under better conditions and has more material at his command to assist him, since what he is dealing with is not something destroyed but something that is still alive. . . . But just as the archaeologist builds up the walls of the building from the foundations that have remained standing, determines the number and position of the columns from depressions in the floor and reconstructs the mural decorations and paintings from the remains found in the débris, so does the analyst proceed when he draws his inferences from the fragments of memories, from the associations and from the behaviour of the subject of the analysis. Both of them have an undisputed right to reconstruct by means of supplementing and combining the surviving remains. ("Constructions" 259)

Freud recognizes that the material the analyst works with is fragile, fragmentary, overdetermined, and ambiguous (Grubrich-Simitis 18) and that the analyst must often construct what has been forgotten and cannot be recovered. However, the archaeological metaphor suggests that Freud needs to dispel the danger of fictionality. Archaeology is based on hard work and evidence, not on poetical invention. Similarly, Freud claims that psychoanalysis is an evidence-based science that can eventually link all its assumptions to living proof: "All of the essentials are preserved; even things that seem completely forgotten are present somehow and somewhere, and have merely been buried" ("Constructions" 260). And even when Freud admits that the psychological object is more complicated than the archaeological object and decides to suspend the question of the truthfulness of memory, he does so based on experiential evidence: whichever (re-)constructed narrative proves therapeutically effective—whether derived from biography, fantasy, or a mixture of both—is a valid narrative ("Infantile Neurosis" 60). Evidently, Freud acknowledges the fictional and retroactive aspects of his constructions, and his approach to interpretation is far from reductive or naïvely positivistic (Haubl and Mertens, *Archäologe* 32). His metaphor, however, clearly signals his preference for a scientific and historical understanding of psychological truth.

This archaeological understanding of psychoanalysis provides legitimacy, but it also proved difficult to maintain. Donald Spence questions the psychoanalyst's ability to elicit historical facts and posits that interpretations are effective and persuasive "not because of their evidential value but because of their rhetorical appeal; conviction emerges because the fit is good, not because we have necessarily made contact with the past" (32). In other words, an interpretation is convincing when it leads to a coherent version of narrative truth.[2] According to Spence, effective interpretations stand out mainly because they make a good story, furnish the patient with new perspectives, and thus fill distressing gaps within the patient's account of the past: "The psychological benefits of such an account may produce the belief that it *must* have happened that way; thus it becomes true" (168). Psychoanalytic interpretations are to be understood as pragmatic, performative utterances that effect a change in the patient by creating an aesthetic experience (37). By thus describing psychoanalysis as a hermeneutic and aesthetic discipline, Spence replaces the scientific metaphor ("archaeology") with metaphors drawn from the arts.

In identifying these implicit metaphors, Rolf Haubl and Wolfgang Mertens suppose that Spence regards analysts no longer as scientists but as "poets and inventors," whose explanations are not found but created (*Archäologe* 72, my translation). For them, however, the literary metaphor becomes problematic. One's individual biography, they argue, remains operant in life even if it remains inaccessible; one cannot shed one's history through a narrative (*wegerzählen*) or rewrite one's experiences like a "screenwriter." For them, psychoanalysis is productive and capable of grasping the full complexity of human behavior only because it hovers undecidedly between science and art and negotiates between historical and narrative truth, explanation and understanding, and exterior and interior experience (100–01, 110, my translation). Most analysts today would similarly hold on to a tension between real history and the individually constructed and partially fictional narratives based on that history, narratives that are better understood as versions of a life and a preliminary and processual form of truth. Ogden, for instance, prefers to work on "what is true to the patient's emotional experience" (*This Art* 21). This emotional truth is not created by interpretation, but it is inevitably changed by its verbalization: "What is true is a discovery as opposed to a creation, and yet, in making that discovery, we alter what we find and, in that sense, create something new" (Ogden, "What's True" 597). In this understanding, the metaphors of archaeology ("discovery") and poetry ("creation") are no longer an alternative; they become fused and remain in paradoxical tension with each other. The practice of psychoanalysis is thus hailed as both, a science *and* an art, or as their productive synthesis.

Poetry

The association between psychoanalysis and poetry is often based on the particular attention that is paid to language in both practices. Meg Williams asserts that "dream-imagery together with musical resonances" and nonverbal signals like the analysand's posture demand the therapist's attention in psychoanalysis (219). This stress on musical, lyrical, and embodied communication points to two characteristics often assigned to analytic language—performativity and poeticality.

The idea that illocutionary and perlocutionary acts play an important role in the therapeutic encounter has become more and more common in analytic circles (Pflichthofer 35). It coincides with Freud's insistence that the word has its own power: "After all it is a powerful instrument; it is the means by which we convey our feelings to one another, our method of influencing other people. Words can do unspeakable good and cause terrible wounds" ("Question" 187–88). Clearly, Freud emphasizes that language has agency beyond its referential function, and hence psychoanalysts consider interpretation to be a speech act that may change the patient's behavior (Bettighofer 115). In addition, the interpersonal dynamics between patient and therapist—transference, resistance, acting out—invade language and are shaped by language in turn. Through the transference, which influences the strategies of persuasion, narrative design, and embellishment, the psychoanalytic exchange thus acquires a "rhetorical" component, "because it is defined not only by what is being said but also by the way in which the speaker takes account of and tries to move or otherwise affect his audience" (Skura 175). When the patient speaks to her analyst as if he were her father, her speech acts point to wishes, demands, and fantasies the patient associates with her father. Thus, overdetermination takes hold of language, which opens up beyond its referential meaning, making the emotive and conative elements of speech, its personal and relational implications, highly visible and allowing therapist and patient to work on them. However, the performative and rhetorical aspects that psychoanalysts identify in their practice do not explain why they would also align it with poetry.

The patient's particular language use has gained new importance in contemporary narrative psychologies, which examine the linguistic and narrative structures of patients' stories to diagnose underlying disorders (Wepfer 115). A great variety of analytic tools is employed to investigate semantic and dramaturgic structures, narrative form, and style. This narrative analysis is supposed to elicit information about the patient, based on the assumption that the structure of the patient's psyche will influence the structure of her narratives. Her self-constructions, the intensity and quality of her emotions, and her ability to mentalize have all been found to influence grammatical structures, her choice of words, and her use of imagery (Habermas, Meier, and Mukhtar 755–57; Habermas, "Who" 500–01). More specifically, particular pathologies have been linked with particular narrative styles. Wilma Bucci and Norbert Freedman, for example, have shown that depressed patients retreat from communication (349–50), and Lisa Capps and Elinor Ochs have detected consistent gestures of helplessness in the grammatical structures of an agoraphobic woman (66). These researchers are wary of generalizing their results—the multiple ways in which their difficulties are experienced and the individual narrative possibilities are too complex to define *the* language of a particular pathology—but their emphasis is less on providing specific diagnostic tools than on turning the analyst's attention to grammatical and stylistic subtleties. Otherwise, Capps and Ochs claim, "therapists miss meaningful aspects of the way a sufferer represents and maintains his or her predicament" (178). And yet Brigitte Boothe, Agnes van Wyl, and Res Wepfer also point out that the particular style of the patient, the way in which her narrative "sings," and the "poetry of narration" cannot be captured by these analytic tools (203, my translation). In other words, although they suspect poetry to be inherent in the analytic encounter, its origin is assumed to lie beyond the patient's measurable mental structures.

Graham Frankland attributes the poetical quality of analytic discourse to the fundamental rule, which liberates the patient's speech while aiming a specific form of attention at her speech patterns:

> The patient, then, is asked to improvise and produce something closely related to poetry. The results of this suspension of inhibitions do indeed display certain poetic qualities. The associations are subtle, evocative, and unpredictable, relying on connotation rather than denotation. It would even be accurate to say that they fulfil a more "modern" criterion of literary language—the priority of the signifier over the signified. (124)

By disabling conventional models of structuring a conversation, the fundamental rule opens psychoanalytic discourse to experimental modes of speaking and listening, focusing on the effects created in the patient's specific linguistic choices. Ogden, for instance, tells analysts to ask themselves, "What is it like to be with this patient?" just as they would ask, "What is it like to read this poem?" ("Some Thoughts" 4). Along with many other analysts, Ogden thus privileges the poetic function of language in psychoanalysis. Drawing on Roman Jakobson, Heinz Müller-Pozzi argues that the aesthetic form of the message becomes more important in psychoanalysis than its referential function, and it is the transference with its unconscious work on language that makes this attention to *how* the patient speaks to the analyst necessary (49–59). This, however, suggests that psychoanalysis does not just deal with poetry but also practices poetry, which becomes especially obvious in recent psychoanalytic writings about the therapeutic uses of metaphor.

Whereas Susan Sontag believed that "the most truthful way of regarding illness . . . is one most purified of, most resistant to, metaphoric thinking" (*Illness* 3), analysts like Ogden describe their work as a work on metaphors (*Conversations* 29). But what Sontag demanded was the casting off of culturally conditioned, idealizing or demonizing metaphors, which is exactly what the psychoanalytic metaphoric work aims for through the creation of new meaningful contexts. Psychoanalysts seek to get rid of dead metaphors and the wooden language of psychoanalytic theory to enliven the therapeutic dialogue (Holmes, "Language" 218; Ogden, "Some Thoughts" 12). Ogden believes that the metaphor enables the analytic dyad to transform the unspeakable into a communicable unit: "We find that we cannot say a feeling, but we may be able to say what an emotional experience feels like" ("This Art" 866). The metaphor's openness to meaning and its imaginative components allow the patient to allude to what he cannot grasp with literal speech. Thus, the metaphor is not only an etymological relative of transference, but it also generates a similar transitional space for meaning (Buchholz 569), which reflects the psychoanalytic process as a whole—the mediation of imaginative ambiguity. When psychoanalysts describe their practice as a lesson in poetry, then, it is primarily to open up new spaces for meaning and acknowledge that there are aspects of experience that cannot easily be captured in prosaic, non-literary discourse.

Theater

Another way of trying to describe these new spaces for meaning is the recurrent comparison between analytic and theatrical space. Structural and metaphorical conjunctions between therapy and theater led many forms of therapy, such as psychodrama, playback theater, gestalt therapy, or drama therapy, to employ scenic play as a way of making the patient's reality accessible (Arndt 380). However, therapeutic methods that have not been explicitly modeled on theater are also frequently compared with it. Simon Grolnick describes the playing in theater and therapy as "structural, and . . . to some extent functional relatives" (255). In a similar theatrical metaphor, Brigitte Boothe argues that transference turns the patient into the equivalent of playwright, director, dramatic adviser, and character ("Begegnung" 270). She also identifies a comprehensive stage model ("Bühnenmodell") (*Patient* 23), which is used throughout psychoanalytic discourse to explain the specific relational experience created in therapy. The pervasiveness of the theatrical metaphor is surprising, given that the analogy is far from perfect. After all, talk is still the dominant mode of communication in all nontheatrical versions of the talking cure; and therapy aims at healing and demands utter privacy, whereas theater is a public performance designed for entertainment (Nuetzel 298). Nevertheless, the theatrical metaphor persists just as much as the metaphor of poetry, while highlighting and privileging different aspects of the psychoanalytic endeavor.

The comparison between theater and psychoanalysis can be traced back to Freud and rests on terminological as well as conceptual intersections. Tobias Döring points out that Freud borrowed central ideas, such as catharsis, from classical drama (170). Given that Freud eventually gave up the cathartic method, however, transference is most commonly identified as the central theatrical element in psychoanalysis. Freud believes that an important function of transference is its theatricality: "that in it the patient produces before us [*vorführt*, i.e. 'performs'] with plastic clarity an important part of his life-story" ("Outline" 175–76). Likewise, he describes transference as a compulsion for play-acting that forces the patient "to stage a revival of an old piece" ("Question" 227). Since the patient's problems can only be dealt with if they are present—"it is impossible to destroy anyone *in absentia* or *in effigie*" (Freud, "Dynamics" 108)—the story must be reproduced on the psychoanalytic stage before it can be tackled by analysis. And although this staging contains just such a representation "in effigy," the juxtaposition of reality and fantasy in transference creates just enough psychological presence to work through the conflicts of the patient (Brooks, *Reading* 235). This Freudian connection between transference and theater continues to dominate psychoanalytic descriptions of the process. Even brief definitions, such as Eric Nuetzel's, bring up the kinship between transference and theater: "Transference is casting another in a role," he insists (303), and Tony Bennett also describes transference as "a theatrical situation": "the analyst gets drawn in as a performer in the symptomatic drama" (211). Illustrating transference through theatrical metaphors helps to explain and normalize a phenomenon that would otherwise be closed off from the experience of laypeople; in addition, it highlights the performativity that is indeed inherent in the concept. Still, Freud was not captivated by a blind enthusiasm for the theater. His work "on the stage" of transference was a technique born out of necessity, which is always the second-best option when compared to remembering and verbalizing an experience. Freud explicitly rejects the taking up of roles for himself: "I have always avoided acting a part, and have contented myself with practicing the humbler arts of psychology" ("Fragment" 109). For Freud, the theatricality of transference should always be mediated through and referred back to a linguistic description. The theatrical metaphor is thus imbued with ambivalence from the start, as it is supposed to mediate between verbal and nonverbal experience and proper and improper analytic technique.

Other elements of psychoanalytic experience, however, are also likely to evince theatrical descriptions. Winnicott's "potential space" is often used to analogize therapy and theater, based on the assumption that the theatrical stage is a variety of transitional space: "Dramatic activity brings about this very situation by creating an intermediate world between fantasy and real life— the stage" (Bennett 211). The discussion of the problem of space in theater studies is indeed similar to Winnicott's concept of intermediate spaces. Max Hermann describes the theater as a spatial art in which the space of the theater is never identical with the real space of the stage. Instead, it is an "artificial space" created by the experiential transformation of actual space into another space (502, my translation). The fictionality of drama is superimposed on the actual presence of actors in the theatrical and scenic space, and another in-between experience is created by the interactive relationship between the audience and the stage (Balme 135, 151). In other words, theater functions as a relationally constructed as-if space. The Barangers use this similarity to compare the patient to an "actor playing the part of Hamlet," who "acts and feels as if he were Hamlet, but . . . is not, and . . . does not lose consciousness of his own person" (799). Thus, they draw on the virtuality of theatrical space to characterize the virtuality of analytic space.

Marvin Carlson's conceptualization of theatrical space as a "permanently or temporarily created ludic space, a ground for the encounter of spectator and performer" (6), points us to another aspect of the theatrical analogy. In a similar manner, Winnicott conceives of psychoanalysis as a ludic encounter with two participants: "*Psychotherapy has to do with two people playing together*" (*Playing* 51). As a child analyst, Winnicott employs play strategically, but he also conceives of psychoanalysis more generally as a highly specialized form of playing in order to enter into a dialogue with others and with oneself (56). Grolnick describes psychotherapy as an analogue of Winnicott's squiggle game, in which therapist and patient take turns to add on to each other's doodling: "There is trial and error, creative method, a reciprocal shifting between the patient and therapist, co-players, trying out images, metaphors, meanings that fit together, that make sense, that seem plausible to both parties" (255). This play is exciting and precarious because it balances on the thin line between "the interplay of personal psychic reality and the experience of control of actual objects. This is the precariousness of magic itself, magic that arises in intimacy" (Winnicott, *Playing* 64). By thinking of psychoanalysis as play, Winnicott imbues it with an inherent creativity, which must, however, rest on a safe relationship, cooperation, and openness for new meanings (Phillips, *Winnicott* 144). Beginning with Freud, who had compared his guidelines to a set of rules for a game, the psychoanalytic setting has frequently been seen as the foundation for such a playful stance. In these descriptions, psychoanalysis emerges as a safe space for play. This aspect of the theatrical metaphor thus frees the psychoanalytic practice from associations of coercion and mental correction and reframes it as a ludic interaction of players.

Hans Loewald synthesizes the performative aspects of transference and play and relates them back to the theater in order to characterize specific aspects of this interaction. He understands transference as a form of Aristotelian mimesis: "imitation of an action in the form of action" (279). In contrast to a dramatist, however, the patient is not completely conscious of his creation of a "dramatic play," and in order to establish the transference neurosis, one must work on this "make-believe aspect of the psychoanalytic situation" (279). With the help of the analyst, the patient is supposed to become ever more cognizant of his role as an actor and author. Thus, the analyst takes over an important part in the staging of the patient's play: "Patient and analyst in a sense are co-authors of the play: the material and the action of the transference neurosis gain structure and organization by the organizing work of the analyst" (280). The analyst thus becomes director, author, and co-actor, while the patient casts him in a variety of roles, which the analyst may choose to play along with or reflect back (281). The play the patient extracts from his history is not just adapted according to the circumstances of the setting and the interaction but retroactively rewritten; a new reality is created through a performative process (Pflichthofer 30). This interactive, poetic aspect of the theatrical metaphor also points to the fact that it is closely connected to the central importance of storytelling in psychoanalysis.

Loewald notes that it is difficult to separate the performative aspects of the treatment from its narrative components in the theatrical "enactment" of therapy:

> Narrative, historical account, may be regarded as imitation of action too, as a reproduction of action . . . . As I mentioned earlier, the dividing line between the two forms of remembering or repetition is not always sharply drawn: the patient who describes an experience with a great deal

of affect is more identified with that experience, is less objective about it; the past invades the present. Such narration is closer to re-enactment. The repetition of action in the form of narrative may be compared to a novel. (292)

Since language is itself a form of action, Loewald is unable to distinguish storytelling from dramatic action; all narratives, as "language action," are tied to the dramatization in transference (293). However, since all actions are continually interpreted through narratives, enactment is also drawn into the force field of narrative and reflection (296). "Showing" and "telling," mimesis and diegesis shape the treatment in close interaction. Transference is often the only possible form of representing the past; but, at the same time, every story is embedded in a transference context and thus part of a nonverbal enactment and a form of action, a fantasy, and a barometer of current emotions (Schafer, "Action" 68, 79; Ferro, "Some Implications" 600). When Loewald has recourse to the metaphor of theater on the one hand and to the metaphor of the novel on the other to explain different forms of analytic communication, he hits upon the generic interrelation of theater and storytelling. The theater depends on diegetic devices as much as storytelling depends on mimetic ones. Therefore, psychoanalysis might be described as caught up in the entanglement of mimetic and diegetic narrativity.[3] The theatrical metaphor is constantly infiltrated by the leitmotif of storytelling. For while theater always remains a metaphor in psychoanalytic therapy, patient and therapist really do tell stories all the time—or do they?

Storytelling

Many psychoanalysts assume that storytelling is the most important medium of getting access to the patient's experience. Ferro claims that every impression in psychoanalysis may find expression in a "narrative derivative": depending on the narrator's situation and her preferences, this may be "a childhood memory; an account of 'external' life; a report of a film; a diaristic genre; an intimate-type genre; or an infinite number of other possible modes" (*Psychoanalysis* 27–28). As Ferro's recourse to everyday forms of aesthetic experience indicates, material, form, and purpose of the psychoanalytic narrative are by no means accidental, and they are continually reflected upon. Thus, psychoanalysis is understood not just as a narrative but as a metanarrative practice. Narratives are the material, narration the technique of therapy—and yet, as one probes the specific "narratology" of psychoanalysis, "storytelling" also emerges as a problematic aesthetic standard against which therapeutic communication is measured.

According to the fundamental rule, the patient is supposed to tell everything that comes to his mind and not give heed to any doubts about the suitability or decency of his stories. Freud suggests using the following words to introduce the patient to this rule:

> What you tell me must differ in one respect from an ordinary conversation. Ordinarily you rightly try to keep a connecting thread running through your remarks and you exclude any intrusive ideas that may occur to you and any side-issues, so as not to wander too far from the point. But in this case you must proceed differently. You will notice that as you relate things various thoughts will occur to you which you would like to put aside on the ground of certain criticisms and objections. You will be tempted to say to yourself that this or that is irrelevant here, or is quite unimportant, or nonsensical, so that there is no need to say it. You must never give in to these criticisms, but must say it in spite of them—indeed, you must say it precisely *because* you feel an aversion to doing so. Later on you will find out and learn to understand the reason for this injunction, which is really the only one you have to follow. So say whatever goes through your mind. Act as though, for instance, you were a traveler sitting next to the window of a railway carriage and describing to someone inside the carriage the changing views which you see outside. ("Beginning" 134–35)

This rule opens the analytic narrative to topics that could never be uttered in conversation with friends, family members, or acquaintances. Formally and thematically, Freud asks for material that would normally be deemed too private, too shameful, too irrelevant, or too offensive to be expressed. Utterances determined by the fundamental rule thus deliberately break with conventions and can be both more spectacular and scandalous and more banal than customary contributions to a conversation. Dieter Flader and Wolf Grodzicki have shown that the fundamental rule disrupts the familiar patterns of communication to enable the patient to develop a new self-understanding through what they call "becoming strange" (*Fremd-Werden*) (575, my translation). Thus, they describe a kind of "defamiliarization," which aligns the fundamental rule with art. "The technique of art is to make objects 'unfamiliar,'" Viktor Shklovsky writes in his influential essay "Art as Technique" (4). Although Freud's descriptions suggest that the patient's speech is formless and unsystematic, the term "fundamental *rule*" indicates that the resulting narratives are not "free" but follow a precise formal and structural organization (Schafer, "Action" 69). This organization renders the story quasi-artistic, and it has made analysts turn their attention to the formal arrangement of the patient's associations: "We also have to take into account the rhythm, the force, the 'music' with which the words are pronounced. ... We listen to form as well as to content" (Bronstein 479). An attention to form is clearly associated with aesthetic experience, yet when analysts start to describe the particular artistic features of their patients' narratives, things get more difficult.

Stories in psychoanalysis never have a single narrator. Frederick Wyatt argues that psychoanalysis must be understood as a shared narrative process: "Stories ... are somehow jointly produced ... between patient and therapist through a subtle and elusive interaction of the two" (195). This interaction is based on the influence of transference on the shape of the story: some stories can only be shared with certain people; some narrative styles are considered inappropriate for a particular counterpart; and the feelings harbored toward a narratee inevitably soak into the stories told in his presence. Telling stories in dialogue changes the way they are told: "We construct what we know of ourselves by identifying with the other and 'listening' through his ears to the story we are telling" (Stern, "Partners" 707). Through transference and countertransference, analyst and analysand develop what Ogden calls an "intersubjective dream space," in which specific narratives are generated and shaped by the therapeutic relationship (*Reverie* 108).

Beyond this inevitable and unconscious conjunction of storytelling, the analyst is actively working on changing the stories of the patient through questions, clarifications, contextualizations, suggestions, and additions. As a co-narrator, the therapist participates in the retelling of the past: "A life is re-authored as it is co-authored" (Schafer, *Retelling* xv). Rather than simply accepting the "improved" stories of the analyst, psychoanalytic storytelling is thus a complicated process involving the shared production of text. Schafer understands these narratives as "stories in process," which are continually constructed, reconstructed, and imagined by both analytic partners ("Listening" 278). Old relational patterns are replaced by new narrative patterns or a new "communicative palette" (Capps and Ochs 179), co-developing new constructions of the self and the world (175). Ferro calls this process "*co-narrative transformation*" (*Psychoanalysis* 1) and emphasizes that the stories created in this way also reflect the relationship itself. Therefore, he concentrates not so much on historical or intrapsychic dimensions of the story, but on its meaning for the present relationship; every utterance relates in some way to the events of the session. "From this point of view the analytic couple speaks *only and always* about itself and about its mutual functioning," Ferro emphasizes (*Bi-Personal Field* 161). The developing narrative is therefore "the offspring of the minds of both" (*Psychoanalysis* 2), a specific creation that cannot be repeated because it reflects what both partners need in a given moment (*Bi-Personal Field* 118). The relationship and the story of the relationship are thus described as interdependent and in constant flux, influencing the possible topics and the shape of relational and narrative work.

As narrative co-constructions, psychoanalytic narratives do not separate strictly between narrator and addressee. In asymmetrical interaction, both patient and analyst continually work on the stories they tell each other. In narratological terms, these narrators are split once again: the distinction between narrating and narrated I is created by Freud's demand for a pact, in which the patient's Ego promises the analyst to join him in analyzing the aspects of the psyche over which she has lost control ("Outline" 173). Thus, they create a narrative form in which an autodiegetic narrator tells her story subjectively and introspectively, strongly emphasizing her position as a narrator because it is constantly called into question. As psychoanalysts acknowledge the influence of the unconscious, they almost always characterize the narrator in psychoanalysis as an "unreliable narrator" (Schafer, "Narration" 39). Although the fundamental rule is geared toward promoting open and truthful speech, unreliability is a necessary result of processes that are considered fundamental to the analytic exchange—transference, countertransference, and resistance. Unreliable narration is to be taken as ubiquitous, but the analyst is not supposed to be "lulled by the dramatic rendition of life" (Schafer, "Narration" 39). Apparently, unreliability, for all its inevitability, adds an unwanted note of uncontrollability to the treatment that renders the resulting narration suspicious.

Another feature psychoanalysts frequently and somewhat disappointedly associate with analytic storytelling is a lack of linearity. In *Fragment of an Analysis*, Freud deplores that complications such as resistance or overdetermination prevent the patient from developing a "fine poetic conflict" (59). Freud believes that one possible goal of the treatment is to arrive at a comprehensible and complete case history; but on the way, one encounters a number of difficulties:

> This first account may be compared to an unnavigable river whose stream is at one moment choked by masses of rock and at another divided and lost among shallows and sandbanks.... [The patients] can, indeed, give the physician plenty of coherent information about this or that period of their lives; but it is sure to be followed by another period as to which their communications run dry, leaving gaps unfilled, and

riddles unanswered; and then again will come yet another period which will remain totally obscure and unilluminated by even a single piece of serviceable information. The connections—even the ostensible ones—are for the most part incoherent, and the sequence of different events is uncertain. (16)

With this description of the "shallows" of the story, of gaps, dark passages, and fissures, Freud privileges form over content and shows us how the analytic story is never unified but develops as a dynamic entity through ruptures and repetitions over a long period of time (Freud, "Beginning" 136). Chronological structures are regularly broken, analepses, prolepses, and ellipses, excessive compression and acceleration of time, iterations, repetitions, and summaries are more characteristic of the narrative work in analysis than clear and linear stories. Thus, Brooks submits that the resistant shape of the narrative in analysis—its "plot"—may not yield a direct link to the original "story": "It works intermittently, interruptedly, in a dialogic manner" (*Psychoanalysis* 56). It is for this very reason that Freud believes that analytic narratives defy an audience: "To a spectator, therefore—though in fact there must be none—an analytic treatment would seem completely obscure" ("Autobiographical" 41). In any case, it does not really sound as if psychoanalysis has compelling stories to offer.

Measured by conventional standards, the formal arrangement of analytic stories might indeed be considered unsatisfactory. Adam Phillips notes: "In psychoanalysis life-stories fragment in the telling; in order to be read, interpreted, they have to be unreadable. The patient has to refuse himself the conventional satisfactions of narrative. Abrogating his need for beginnings, middles and ends, he often has to become a very bad story-teller and make a nonsense of his life" (*On Flirtation* 68). In this reading, nonsense and bad storytelling are the formal features of the therapeutic narrative. There is apparently no real poetry and no good story in psychoanalysis. Anita Eckstaedt believes that patients are unable "really" to tell stories (*wirklich zu erzählen*) because they can only tell them in stumbles and fragments, and the analyst is thus not absorbed in "dreamily suspenseful stories" (*traumhaft spannenden Geschichten*) (27–28, my translation). Eckstaedt and Freud obviously struggle with the aesthetic imagery and the metaphoricity of the "story" in psychoanalytic discourse. Whatever patients and therapists produce in therapy, their so-called stories seem less successful as artistic and communicative artifacts than suspenseful and chiseled literary narratives. And yet, Eckstaedt's objection only serves to show that at least in part, "story" is a metaphor in psychoanalytic discourse denoting a particular "literariness" that Eckstaedt finds lacking, although her reference to stumbles and fragments actually emphasizes the *specific* aesthetic qualities of psychoanalytic narratives. And her objection cannot stop the production of the metaphor. On the contrary, for Jan Marta, the apparently "bad" storytelling is exactly what aligns psychoanalysis with literature: "There are no redundancies in psychotherapy (or in literature); each reiteration, repetition, or identification contributes new meaning" (153). Good or bad—psychoanalysts are not willing to give up the quasi-literary qualities of their practice. Although the comparison introduces contradictions into their descriptions of analytic work, the powers of language associated with literature allow psychoanalysis to reflect and appease their own "scepticism about language" (Phillips, "Poetry" 34).

Coming to terms with the instabilities of language is important because psychoanalysis ultimately sees itself as a form of narrative plot work. The narrative the patient brings to analysis

> lacks the dynamic necessary to creating sequence and design that integrate and explain. The fuller plot constructed by the analytic work must be more dynamic, thus more useful as a shaping and connective force.... Truth, then, arises from a dialogue among a number of *fabula* and a number of *sjužet*, stories and their possible organizations, as also between two narrators, analysand and analyst. (Brooks, *Reading* 283–84)

In this way, the dissolution of all temporal and logical structures is usually opposed by a process in which the narrative is returned to linear, compressed, and causal storylines. Psychoanalysis appears as joint story work, and dialogue enters the narrative to activate the work of therapy.

Dialogue

During a vacation in the mountain range High Tauern in the 1890s, Freud was asked for help by a young woman named "Katharina." The unusual setting forced him to proceed without hypnosis, which, at that time, was still his go-to technique. The surrogate Freud resorted to, which would become the foundation of psychoanalysis, is described by him as a "simple talk" (*Gespräch*) ("Studies" 127). The dialogic nature of psychoanalysis, which is also reflected in its understanding of the therapeutic relationship, its narratology, the construction of analytic space, and its theory of language, is seen by many analysts and critics as its central feature. Peter Atterton, for example, claims: "A large part of the therapeutic value of psychoanalysis ... is due to its dialogical character" (555). Like storytelling, however, "dialogue" is both what actually happens in psychoanalysis—two people talking with each other—and an aesthetic signifier used to characterize and evaluate the specific nature of the psychoanalytic encounter.

Nevertheless, whether there is even such a thing as a dialogue in analysis has been disputed. The asymmetrical orientation of the therapeutic discourse, the privileging of the patient's psyche and speech, seems to be opposed to the mutual exchange that is usually associated with the term "dialogue." Due to the patient's tendency to project, Eckstaedt claims that the psychoanalytic dialogue is not a real, genuine dialogue (35). This estimation is reminiscent of Martin Buber's three forms of dialogue, which he defines as follows:

> [There is] the real [dialogue] . . . , where every one of the participants really means the other one in his or her existence and essence [*Dasein und Sosein*] and turns to them with the intention of instituting a vivid reciprocity [*lebendige Gegenseitigkeit*] between him and them; the technical one, which is merely given by the necessity of factual communication; and the dialogically disguised monologue, in which two or more people gathered in a room talk with themselves through miraculously convoluted detours and still think themselves abstracted from the pain of being dependent on each other. (166, my translation)

In psychoanalysis, "real" dialogue seems impossible. The speaker, who is always caught up in the transference, never addresses his counterpart exclusively as that person only (although, from an analytic point of view, this does not exclude "vivid reciprocity"). In a psychoanalytic conversation, the dialogue partner intentionally refuses to make herself available in her essential existence. To a certain extent, the analytic dialogue could be understood as a "technical" dialogue, but it is hardly factual and businesslike. One is most inclined to label the analytic dialogue as a "dialogically disguised monologue," as the fundamental rule represents an invitation to speak with oneself in the presence of another. Is psychoanalysis not a dialogue then but a disguised monologue?

The term "dialogue" is charged with ethical values in the work of Buber and many other critics, which manifests itself in the insistence on a "real" or "true" dialogue. In this regard, the therapeutic dialogue is usually found lacking. Hans-Georg Gadamer, for instance, claims that there is no true (*wahrhaft*) communication in the therapeutic dialogue (389). According to Lewis Aron, Buber also did not recognize any mutuality in the analytic dialogue: "He viewed each of these relationships as instrumental, in that one person acts upon the other to accomplish a specific goal. Mutuality requires authenticity and genuineness, an absence of pretense. Since the therapist is trying to achieve specific goals, and since the therapist assumes a greater responsibility than the patient does, full mutuality cannot be achieved" (156–57). Nevertheless, there have been attempts to establish Buberian forms of therapy (M. Friedman), and the term "dialogue" features prominently in programmatic titles of the Relational School and related psychoanalytic persuasions.[4] However, instead of understanding dialogue principally as a phenomenon of "good"—benevolent and equal—interpersonality, the psychoanalytic dialogue might also be conceptualized in aesthetic terms, without moral judgment. With Mikhail Bakhtin, psychoanalyst Beatriz Priel interprets the dialogical elements in psychoanalysis as negotiations between differing positions that do not necessarily have to be symmetrical or interpersonally aligned:

> Bakhtin defines a dialogical relation (between different internal voices or between self and other) as an asymmetric dualism and not as an abstract dialectical binary opposition between concepts. . . . In Bakhtin's dialogical conception, different and opposed voices coexist in a process that does not lead necessarily to integration or progression; contradictory voices . . . coexist side by side in a process in which both progression and regression are possible directions. ("Bakhtin" 489–90)

With this concept, authenticity and mutuality are no longer the only determinants of the "conversation," and it becomes possible to explore the recurrent descriptions of the psychoanalytic encounter as a "dialogue" in terms of their intersections with Bakhtin's notion of dialogicity.

Freud's description of therapy as a conversation lacks such normative stipulations; indeed, it sounds positively laconic: "The analyst . . . gets [the patient] to talk, listens to him, talks to him in his turn and gets him to listen" ("Question" 187). At the same time, however, Freud admits that the conversation develops under "unusual conditions" (188). By putting a qualitative and quantitative emphasis on the speech of the patient, the dialogue is rendered asymmetrical. Even the forms of speech are distributed unevenly. Storytelling, reporting, and describing are the responsibility of the analysand, whereas the analyst is supposed to question, interpret, and confirm the developing story. In addition, Freud describes the dialogue as an intimate space that is kept private from others. As we will see, it is this asymmetry and exclusiveness that allows the psychoanalytic situation to realize "dialogic" experiences such as the interpersonal encounter with another, the intrapersonal conversation with oneself, and the proliferation of meaning through interior and exterior dialogues.

Transference stands in the way of a mutual and "authentic" exchange in psychoanalysis, but it also determines the specific quality of its dialogic nature. By privileging the transference—the generator of fictionality, inauthenticity, and asymmetry—psychoanalysts build the foundation of their conversation out of its potential hindrances. The rhetorical term "dialogue" is used to characterize unique elements of the psychoanalytic experience; but strikingly, the patterns that are ultimately highlighted in the dialogic nature of psychoanalysis turn on hindrances against conventional notions of dialogue, which emphasize the balanced presence of two interlocutors. Although this might at first appear paradoxical, the notion of the psychoanalytic dialogue is therefore linked to the imagery of writing. André Green posits:

> Writing is, according to Freud, communication with the absent, the reverse of speech, which is rooted in presence. In psychoanalysis, the contrived conditions of the analytical situation seek to create a kind of present absence or absent presence. The analysand does not see the analyst; at times he may feel a loneliness bordering on despair because of the analyst's non-visibility. . . . But he also knows that there is someone else . . . ready to assume any role the analysand attributes to him. (282)

Despite the therapeutic encounter's groundedness in the spoken word, writing figures as an adequate metaphor for the paradoxical absence-presence created by the analytic situation. While the written text renders the absent quasi-present, the psychoanalytic setting establishes the quasi-absence of the present analyst.

Indeed, free association and the couch create conditions that undermine the dialogue but constitute it at the same time. In this light, the rhetorical quality of transference can be described with much more precision. Bakhtin understands language as inherently permeated by dialogic relationships: "These relationships lie in the realm of discourse, for discourse is by its very nature dialogic" (*Problems* 183). Every word has been shaped by historical and social contexts and carries them with it: "When a member of a speaking collective comes upon a word, it is not as a neutral word of language, not as a word free from the aspirations and evaluations of others, uninhabited by others' voices. No, he receives the word from another's voice and filled with that other voice" (202). The word, which always speaks of its history, is thus itself a medium for transference, but its dialogic nature can be intensified by specific literary means. For Bakhtin the hidden polemic, the polemic confession, the sideward glance at someone else's word, the rejoinder, and the hidden dialogue are all versions of active dialogic devices (199). These categories help illuminate how psychoanalysts have described their specific version of therapeutic dialogue. In Bakhtin's terms, the analysand "sharply senses [his] own listener, reader, critic, and reflects in [himself] their anticipated objections, evaluations, points of view" (196). The hidden dialogue, in particular, resembles Green's conceptualization of the psychoanalytic situation as a state of present absence or absent presence:

> Imagine a dialogue of two persons in which the statements of the second speaker are omitted.... The second speaker is present invisibly, his words are not there, but deep traces left by these words have a determining influence on all the present and visible words of the first speaker. We sense that this is a conversation, although only one person is speaking, and it is a conversation of the most intense kind, for each present, uttered word responds and reacts with its every fiber to the invisible speaker, points to something outside itself, beyond its own limits, to the unspoken words of another person. (Bakhtin, *Problems* 197)

Read with Bakhtin, the hidden dialogue of psychoanalysis retains its alignment toward another, no matter how absent she may be. The dialogicity analysts identify in the therapeutic encounter rests on the fundamentally interpersonal orientation of the patient's speech.

However, the analyst is not the only dialogue partner who emerges in analysis. Transference also allows a dialogue with internal objects. Essential elements of the internal relational world are displaced to the outside world and become available for analysis, enabling analyst and analysand to enter a dialogue with themselves: "The ... psychoanalytic technique ... [is] designed to enhance the capacity of each participant to achieve a state of mind in which he might gain access to the continuous unconscious conversation with himself" (Ogden, *Conversations* 5). What he finds there is also conceptualized as a set of multiple or dialogic self-constructions. Peter Raggatt, for example, assumes that "the life story is really more like a *conversation of narrators*" (16). In consequence, "identity can be read in narrative as a polyphony of texts or stories" (17). With this recourse to Bakhtin's polyphonic novel, dialogue becomes a metaphor for the self. What had previously been defined by its "identity," its single-voicedness, is here portrayed as a multitude of voices, which not only reflects the psychoanalytic insight into the unconscious multiplicity of the internal world but also provides a foundation for a dialogic reconceptualization of therapeutic technique. For Ogden, the patient's encounter of a multitude of "I"s is an essential analytic experience (*Reverie* 131), and Priel adds that the reverie of the analyst—his internal dialogue—provides access to the internal dialogue of the patient, turning the psychoanalytic setting into "a multivocal dialogue, an actual polyphony" ("Bakhtin" 500). The "outcome" of such a Bakhtinian polyphonic analysis is envisioned "in terms of the degree to which analysand (and analyst) come to be able to carry on richer, more interesting, livelier conversations with themselves . . . , and consequently with each other" (Ogden, *Conversations* 14). In Ogden's and Priel's juxtaposition of internal and external dialogues, psychoanalysis becomes an open playing field between a multitude of voices, all encapsulated in the patient's experience of the therapeutic encounter. Thus, one might understand the therapeutic dialogue—in a Bakhtinian reversal of Buber's term—as a "dialogue disguised as monologue."

Apparently, many psychoanalysts turn to Bakhtin's dialogicity and polyphony to establish a form of dialogue that escapes the norms of coherence, authenticity, and mutuality. In doing so, they tend to celebrate new ideals revolving around cooperation and multiplicity. Bakhtin's terms, however, actually valorize controversy, which represents an often-neglected challenge to many psychoanalysts' self-understanding. Bakhtin argues that empathy and agreement, which are often favored as ethical guidelines in psychoanalytic discourse, foreclose the advantages of open and controversial dialogues: "What would I have to gain . . . if another were to fuse with me? He would see and know only what I already see and know, he would repeat in himself the inescapable closed circle of my own life; let him rather remain outside of me" (*Creation* 53–54). A dialogue that leads to mutual consent is far from desirable for Bakhtin—and thus a Bakhtinian turn in psychoanalysis would have to acknowledge that the analyst and the unconscious remain countervoices that cannot be assimilated. Dialogicity does not protect psychoanalysis from the charge of inauthenticity and inequality. Despite its limitations, however, the metaphor of dialogue also delineates a model of communication that refuses to disqualify asymmetry and fictionality as noncommunicative modes and recognizes that controversy and silence are not the failure but the foundation of their interaction.

Analysis

In order to delineate two types of therapeutic interaction, Brigitte Boothe and Bernhard Grimmer have turned to two mythological figures—Oedipus and Scheherazade. The "Oedipus model" turns on the discovery of repressed material as the foundation of psychological transformation:

> In surmounting resistances and anxieties, someone is intensely interested in the revelation of hidden, repressed, repelled connections and prepared to face their own biographic development even in its most painful and threatening aspects, do the work of mourning, and admit a process of transformation. (51, my translation)

In contrast, the "Scheherazade model" rests on narrative seduction, in which a gradual transformative effect may be achieved through continual storytelling:

> Her engagement in the game of relationships was . . . the taking over of the assigned function of satisfaction, and in this function, she offered underhandedly the alluring bounty of narration and thus opened an additional gratification to the patient, which steered his desire into a new direction: entertaining distraction that does not dissipate but is retained in memory and seduces him into secondary processing as much as into enjoyable reflection. (54, my translation)

Boothe and Grimmer's models offer two different, gendered perspectives on the therapeutic relationship, in which the male, Oedipal model remains the norm, and the female, Scheherazadian model is reserved for difficult cases, in which the ideal of psychoanalytic technique cannot be achieved and patients must be coaxed into a therapeutic relationship. Aside from these questionable technical implications, however, these two models also encapsulate two different ways of understanding the narrative structure of the therapeutic process, its search patterns, and their specific aesthetic implications. In probing these models further, I intend to show how Oedipus and Scheherazade are not accidental figures in Boothe and Grimmer's work but pervasive technical and aesthetic figures throughout psychoanalytic discourse.

Oedipus is the central myth of psychoanalysis around which Freud builds a dense cluster of theories on psychosexual development and psychopathology. However, he is attracted not just by the content of the myth—the nucleus of Freud's ideas about family rivalries—but also by the particular way in which Sophocles treats his material in *Oedipus Rex*: "The work of the Athenian dramatist exhibits the way in which the long-past deed of Oedipus is gradually brought to light by an investigation ingeniously protracted and fanned into life by ever fresh relays of evidence. To this extent it has a certain resemblance to the progress of a psychoanalysis" ("Introductory Lectures" 330). Oedipus fascinates Freud not because he marries his mother but because he tries to find out the truth about his past. With his interest in the detective process in the play, the psychoanalyst identifies both with the protagonist searching for enlightenment and with the dramatist who determines the structure of the play—the confrontation with secret longings and the art of "Oedipal unravelling" (Döring 172). As Oedipus's attempts to illuminate the past seem to prefigure his own analytic endeavors, Freud's interest in the play ultimately derives from its analytic structure.

Freud's remarks can be compared with the influential comment Friedrich Schiller sent Johann Wolfgang Goethe in a letter dated October 2, 1797: "Oedipus is just a tragic analysis, as it were. Everything is already there, and it is just unraveled. That may happen in the simplest action and within a very small moment in time, no matter how complicated and dependent on circumstances the events may have been" (331, my translation). In Sophocles' tragedy, Oedipus does indeed promise to rescue the city of Thebes from the plague by solving the murder of his predecessor Laius: "Then I'll uncover all of it again" (11). Schiller's deliberations introduced the "analytic drama" as a dramatic subgenre, which Matthias Strä ßner defines as a play in which events of the past that were unexplained or consciously kept secret are eventually explained or revealed (38). Sophocles' play is usually considered the prototype of this genre because, as Peter Szondi argues, it shows how analysis is turned into action: "Oedipus, seeing and still blind, constitutes the empty midpoint, as it were, of a world that knows about his fate, whose messengers conquer his interior world step by step to fill it with their terrible truth. This truth, however, does not belong to the past, not the past but the present is being revealed" (23–24, my translation). The investigative element is the reason why the myth of Oedipus is so often used to attribute a common structural basis to psycho*analysis* and the analytic drama (Brooks, *Reading* 270; Gooblar 68; Timm 129).[5] Manfred Beyer even designates the analytic drama as the "formal equivalent" of psychoanalysis (154). But what would it mean to describe the psychoanalytic process as an "analytic drama," as it were?

The term "psychoanalysis" harbors several components of meaning that point us toward a critical appreciation of the aesthetic structures Freud identified with it. He claimed to have borrowed the term from chemistry:

> Why "analysis"—which means breaking up or separating out, and suggests an analogy with the work carried out by chemists on substances which they find in nature and bring into their laboratories? Because in an important respect there really is an analogy between the two. . . . We teach [the patient] to understand the way in which these highly complicated mental formations are compounded; we trace the symptoms back to the instinctual impulses which motivate them; we point out to the patient these instinctual motives, which are present in his symptoms and of which he has hitherto been unaware,—just as a chemist isolates the fundamental substance, the chemical "element," out of the salt in which it had been combined with other elements and in which it was unrecognizable. ("Lines" 159–60)

To "analyze" means, first and foremost, to decompose psychic activity into its elementary components. Jacques Derrida, however, tells us that in "analysis" the motif of decomposition ("lysis") is connected to an archaeological motif ("ana"):

> There is, *on the one hand*, what could be called the *archeological or anagogical* motif, which is marked in the movement of *ana* (recurrent return toward the principal, the most originary, the simplest, the elementary, or the detail that cannot be broken down); and, *on the other hand*, a motif . . . marked in the *lysis* (breaking down, untying, unknotting, deliverance, solution, dissolution or absolution, and, by the same token, final completion). (19–20)

Thus, the activity of "analyzing" is composed of an interplay of dissolution and discovery, which is what links psychoanalysis with archaeology and detection rather than with chemistry.

That the direction of "analysis" suggests a movement into historical depth—both backward and downward—is obvious in all of Freud's descriptions of the activity of the analyst. Rolf Haubl and Wolfgang Mertens argue that this "depth" psychology is linked to a spatial conception of the psyche. It is supposed to have deep and dark depths related to repressed aspects of the biographic past. This depth is deemed more precious than the deceivingly simple surface, and recovering this precious material implies that one must search for biographic traumas that have consequences for the present (*Archäologe* 23). The analyst has been described, as we have already seen, as the archaeologist of the self, and the retroactive orientation of the psychoanalytic plot is one of its most essential features. Just as Oedipus traces the plague over Thebes to its roots in the city's and his own history, psychoanalysis proceeds retrospectively, from a symptom to its assumed origins (Gooblar 68). In this mythical node, the analyst as archaeologist intersects with the analyst as detective. Both rest on the assumption that the recovery of remnants from the past will elucidate the present. In early case histories such as *Studies on Hysteria* or *Fragment of an Analysis*, Freud works like a detective, "pressing his patients for the symptomatic clues, reaching back to uncover a moment of trauma, a scene of crime that makes sense of all subsequent events" (Brooks, *Reading* 270). He was fascinated by the detective story and its implications for understanding and perception. Peter Hühn's description of the classic detective as "predominantly defined by his cold detachment from all human concerns, the clarity of his analytic intellect, and his interest in the truth-finding process for its sake" (460), and the process of detection as "reconstructing a hidden or lost story" (451), clearly resonate with Freud's image of the neutral analyst searching for psychological truth. It is not surprising, then, that the metaphor of the analyst as detective is one of the most pervasive in psychoanalytic discourse and that most laypeople conceive of psychoanalysis as a detective story (Haubl and Mertens, *Detektiv* 14). The metaphor, however, is also criticized among psychoanalysts. Haubl and Mertens worry that it stigmatizes patients as potential criminals (*Detektiv* 15), and Buchholz disapproves of the implication that there is a single truth that can and must be unveiled (561). Indeed, upon further investigation, the detective metaphor becomes increasingly complicated and problematic.

Psychoanalysis requires not only going back in time but also reaching the unspeakable, the unimaginable, and the imperceptible. This exploration goes beyond the excavation of sunken history to the descent into psychodynamic and emotional depths. Accordingly, Alfred Lorenzer claims that both psychoanalyst and detective have to extend their understanding beyond the conventional and the comprehensible and concentrate on "the most outré" (4, my translation). At this point, the archaeological and investigative tendencies interface with dissection and dissolution. Such a depth of intrusion becomes possible only through taking apart what is given, and putting it back together becomes either impossible or must be supplemented by the imagination. Thus, the work of analysis is both more destructive and less straightforward than the metaphors seem to imply at first. Psychoanalytic work does not proceed with the linearity of the crime story and its teleological path toward an explanation. Brooks emphasizes that the detective model ultimately eluded Freud because his patients' narratives were governed by ambiguity and instability: "The result is not the neat Holmesian solution but rather a proliferation of narratives with no ultimate points of fixity" (*Reading* 278). This lack of rectilinearity separates the psychoanalytic process from cathartic or confessional models of psychotherapeutic care and their promise for a solution through one single (self-)revelation with immediate curative effect. Analysis is not linear but shaped by "contradictory, ambiguous, or episodic aspects" (Loewenstein 51). Therefore, Era Loewenstein assumes that the analyst is actually confronted with a "ready-made" explanation in the beginning, "a mythical construction of [the patient's] past," which must then be dissected: "The psychoanalytic dialogue is set into motion once the analyst begins to question the analysand's epical construction; once the analyst probes and ultimately punches holes in the analysand's coherent story, allowing the traces of other stories to surface. Progressing dialectically each analytic phase ends not with a final formulation but with a question, with a riddle" (56). A moment of clarification, so typical of analytic drama (D. Weber 22), fails to materialize. The purpose of analysis is a joint, asymptotic confrontation with the unknown that cannot lead to finite constructions (Loewenstein 58). We might come to the conclusion that the metaphor of detection and the myth of Oedipus ultimately fail to reflect the psychoanalytic aesthetics—but only if we do not read Oedipus's original analytic work carefully enough.

Ultimately, Oedipus's trajectory is neither straightforward nor does he proceed on his own. As detached as they may often be depicted to be, most literary detectives need to become involved and interact with others to solve a case (Lorenzer 9), and so does Oedipus. He proceeds not through narcissistic self-exploration but through the confrontation with witnesses and critical interrogators. In their explanation of the Oedipus model, Boothe and Grimmer explicitly point out the relationality of the concept. Self-perception, self-exploration, and self-revelation become possible only through the encouragement of and the identification with the analyst; transference influences communication; and, most importantly, the process of revealing oneself to another establishes a relationship (51–52). Oedipal detection is not possible in isolation and it is not linear. Shoshana Felman shows how the orientation of Sophocles' play toward interpretation ultimately leads to blurring the roles of the analyst and the object of analysis:

> It is doubtless no coincidence, therefore, that the myth of Oedipus—the psychoanalytical myth *par excellence*—should happen to recount . . . the very *drama of interpretation*. The tragedy of Oedipus is, after all, the story no less of the analyst than of the analysand: it is specifically, in fact, the story of the deconstruction, of the subversion of the polarity itself which distinguishes and which opposes these two functions. ("Turning" 197–98)

In *Oedipus Rex* and in psychoanalysis, the work of detection ultimately falls back on the investigator—the detective becomes the perpetrator, the patient his own analyst, and vice versa. Whatever truth Oedipus finds at the end of the play, it is not the one he sought; his detection has led him astray to find meaning where he did not expect it—and looking closely, that truth is encapsulated not only in his past deeds but also in his present relationships.

At this point, the analytic structure's dependence on relational others refers us back to Ferro's three types of analytic characters. His critique of the Freudian model is, in fact, a critique of an analytic plot that searches for a straightforward explanation of the present in the past. The Kleinian model provides an alternative analytic structure, which might be described as allegorical—personal experiences always have an additional symbolic meaning. Stephen Mitchell associates this model less with "a paleontologist" than with "a war correspondent" (*Influence* 107), who glosses what he sees with insightful commentary on the origin of the conflicts he witnesses. Both, the Freudian detective model and the Kleinian allegorical model, go beyond the phenomena of the present therapeutic relationship and seek explanations elsewhere, which adds further layers of meaning but also threatens to obscure the meaning that is already available and, by focusing on the complexity of past or fantasized depths, neglects the complexity of the surface. In contrast, Ferro's own model points to a third possibility, which focuses analytic work on the present therapeutic encounter. Ferro associates this model with Todorov's suspense novel, in which suspense is created by a story in the present that is more substantial than a collection of facts by "a Poirot-like analyst" (*Bi-Personal Field* 163). Therefore, I read Ferro's contribution not necessarily as the only possible trajectory for psychoanalysis (and neither does he) but as an alternative for conceptualizing the aesthetics of the therapeutic encounter. In Ferro's analytic plot, the here and now would be in the foreground, and movement toward the past or a hidden depth is unnecessary because all meaning is embodied and readable in the present. Analysis would then be a surface action that explores visible relational dynamics. It would look into horizontal instead of vertical planes of meaning and would thus develop its own density of significance. Such alternative vectors for analysis can, at least in part, be found in the serial structure of therapy.

Seriality

Whereas Oedipus often serves as an emblem for the internal structure of psychoanalysis, its external session structure has found its most potent symbol in another mythological figure—Scheherazade. And yet, it is not just the serial stringing together of the figural one thousand and one sessions and the potential infinity of her storytelling that has turned her into an emblem of psychoanalysis. In *One Thousand and One Nights*, Scheherazade employs the nocturnal telling of stories, which are skillfully interrupted with cliffhangers at the end of the night, to prevent her husband, the sultan, from murdering more women, including herself. In other words, she tells therapeutic stories in a serial format, in which every nightly unit corresponds with a session (Fröhlich, *Cliffhanger* 158). Thus, Scheherazade may, on the one hand, appear as a therapist who treats the sultan, and narration emerges as a long-term curative and educative process (Mielke 111). On the other hand, Scheherazade is herself at risk and tells stories for *her* life—and psychoanalysts do indeed tend to describe their clients in this way: "each patient would be her own Scheherazade, telling the stories that keep her alive" (Flores 1237).

Like the Oedipus myth, then, Scheherazade's story reflects the entanglement of patient and analyst in a serial relational progression toward transformation.

Even without Scheherazade, the connection between psychoanalysis and serial storytelling has been invoked again and again. Bernard Strauß emphasizes the seriality of psychotherapy (154), and Jane Feuer asserts that television and therapy share a serialized structure. A 2013 conference at the Psychoanalytic Seminar in Zurich was dedicated to the "paradigm" of seriality: "Psychoanalysis, too, is not just a serial practice—one hour following the other—but also the effect of a serial logic. Insight is gained through the connection of significant points" (Psychoanalytisches Seminar Zürich, my translation). How are these connections between Scheherazade, seriality, and psychotherapy established?

Christine Blätter defines the series as a particular kind of pattern (*Ordnungsmuster*) that organizes and combines separate elements ("Einleitung" 12). Episodes and overall serial structure are thus in constant productive tension, in which the episode only makes sense within the series, whereas the series cannot exist without the episodes. The story of the patient evolves in the course of separate sessions and, with the help of the therapist, eventually becomes whole. The intermittent rhythm of the sessions is counterbalanced with the typically serial continuity of story, participants, and setting (Weber and Junklewitz 15–16). Most narrative series are also embedded in a program or publication structure, which dictates a date and a period for consumption (Allen 109). Therapy has a similar structure, in which the schedule of the therapist determines the patient's schedule. "The idea of scheduling by the hour is not the only thing television and psychotherapy have in common," Jane Feuer argues. "Both are, so to speak, serialized. They unfold over time with gaps in between each session." Appointments are made at set intervals to hold regular sessions with a prescribed length. Changes in the overall program influence the single session (as with tardiness or cancellations); missed sessions must be paid as if the treatment had taken place without the patient; and coming early allows the patient a glimpse at the rest of the program (the previous patient). The analogy with seriality thus helps explain several specifics of the analytic experience that arise out of its session structure.

The particular structure of serial narratives combines fragmentation with a promise of continuation. Dawn interrupts Scheherazade's stories abruptly, and she always stops talking immediately: "But morning overtook Shahrazad, and she lapsed into silence, leaving King Shahrayar burning with curiosity to hear the rest of the story" (Haddawy 18). Scheherazade clearly employs cliffhangers to keep the sultan from losing interest. It may be surprising to find that Freud also identified the cliffhanger as an integral part of his psychoanalytic technique, but he does, and quite explicitly so:

> Interruptions which are imperatively prescribed by incidental circumstances in the treatment, such as the lateness of the hour, often occur at the most inconvenient points, just as one may be approaching a decision or just as a new topic emerges. Every newspaper reader suffers from the same drawback in reading the daily instalment of his serial story, when, immediately after the heroine's decisive speech or after the shot has rung out, he comes upon the words: "To be continued." In our own case the topic that has been raised but not dealt with, the symptom that has become temporarily intensified and has not yet been explained, persists in the patient's mind and may perhaps be more troublesome to him than it has otherwise been. ("Studies" 297–98)

Strictly bound to the fifty-minute hour, sessions are often interrupted in the middle of a narrative flow or in the middle of a precarious topic. In this way, suspense is created, which establishes an imaginative connection between the aborted and the future session in the very moment of interruption. The serially ruptured structure of psychoanalysis and the aesthetic effects created by it—the same that bother the reader of a serialized novel—are, for Freud, an integral part of its therapeutic function.

Therapy is thus subject to the same ambivalence that Blättler finds in the series—the tension between the whole and its parts, continuity and discontinuity, difference and repetition (510–12). For Umberto Eco, the series is defined precisely by its paradoxical tendency to present ever new stories within a fixed "narrative scheme" (196). Thanks to the setting and its rules, psychoanalysis possesses such stable narrative patterns. This gives the treatment its specific form but also liberates and protects the narration. Barbara Taylor, for instance, reports: "Over the years I came to lean on this formalism like a rock. I could scream, threaten, arrive drunk and abusive—nothing made any difference" (61). Moreover, the analyst's steady participation in the patient's world is a precondition for its analysis. For Bruno Bettelheim, it is the length of the serial process that links therapy to the Scheherazade myth:

> No single story can accomplish it, for our psychological problems are much too complex and difficult of solution.... It takes nearly three years of continued telling of fairy tales to free the king of his deep depression, to achieve his cure. It requires his attentive listening to fairy tales for a thousand nights to reintegrate his completely disintegrated personality. (*Uses* 87–88)

Similarly, Boothe and Grimmer's Scheherazade model is mainly based on the establishment of a long-term relationship to treat severe disturbances in a safe environment (52). Scheherazade's therapeutic device is seduction (55); she uses suspense to attach her listener and targets his readiness for identification and empathy to educate him (Boothe, "Editorial" 101). In this model, narration cannot have a separate existence from a complex relational dynamic, in which love, seduction, and fear are constant companions of the therapeutic couple. Scheherazade is here turned into an emblem of the psychoanalyst, who needs to keep the patient from leaving therapy in order to save her own position as a therapist. Erika Kittler thus notes that the analyst must become a storyteller like "Scheherazade" to secure her analytic survival (183). Scheherazade's technique can be regarded as a model in which storytelling enables joint working through by way of the long-term attachment of the audience. It posits narration as a relationship.

Most series depend on such relationships as well; they are not simply episodic but hybrid types that combine episodic content with a long-term serial construction. The resulting "narrative complexity" comes with its own difficulties: the demands of episodic and serial storytelling are not resolved but remain in tension with each other and have to be attended to with complex narrative patterns (Mittell 32–34). Therapeutic sessions must achieve a similarly precarious balance. The therapeutic setting provides cyclical stability, whereas the narrative that is embedded within this frame is supposed to progress. Smaller narratives of memories and events that are told as episodes in a single session are integrated into a general narrative whose unifying and forward-pushing function is the development of the patient. The deepening of her understanding through the repetition of similar narratives is opposed with a demand for therapeutic change and the continuation of the story in new directions. Repetition, Brooks argues, always contains a tension between reproduction and change (*Reading* 100). Sometimes it is precisely this variation within the same that fascinates the audience, not only because it creates suspense but also because they take delight in innovative methods of varying old and familiar patterns (Eco 200). We have also seen this "operational aesthetic" (Mittell 35) at work in psychoanalysis, which creates meaning from variations in repetition, pays particular attention to narrative form, and uses it as a major device for development and the transformation of familiar routines and patterns of thinking. The attractiveness of seriality as a metaphor for psychoanalytic work consists in its mediating position between the experiences of stasis and evolution. As such, it can be seen as a principle of everyday action, perception, and organization (Faulstich 51). Serial structures create order and assurance, but also promote development, a dynamic that is closely related to the psychoanalytic concept of "working through." The serial continuation enables psychoanalysis, as Laplanche and Pontalis argue, to enrich a singular insight with additional meaning over a long period of time, thus using repetition but changing it through interpretation (124). Repetition and difference—in suspenseful interaction—are the operational principles of psychoanalysis and seriality.

Another feature of the psychoanalytic experience is its embeddedness in daily life. Through their regularity and high frequency, the sessions become a part of the patient's and the analyst's life just like a series becomes a part of the audience's life. With its open-ended structure that runs parallel to everyday life, the series is directed toward the present and the future of the audience and seems to accompany their day-to-day business in a way that closed structures cannot achieve (Fiske 145). Precisely because psychoanalysis and serials are connected to everyday life in structure and content, experiences from both inside and outside the analytic/serial frame become increasingly juxtaposed as they progress. Seriality might thus be described as a formal equivalent of transference, with similar consequences for narrative interaction. The openness of serial structures toward the future creates the possibility of a "feedback loop" between production and reception, allowing authors to change the progress of the text with respect to the audience's desires (Kelleter 100)—a feature that ties in with the interactivity of psychoanalytic serial storytelling. The incompletion of the serial model thus harbors the promise of therapeutic action and relational interaction.

The openness of serial narratives implies a seductive but problematic endlessness. Serials are designed to be continued without end and they certainly flirt with their potential infinity. They might end at a certain point, but not because every possible story has been told; the series always "assures us that there will be no end to the return of our stories, no end to the multiplication of our conflicted story engagements," reproducing "a sense of infinite futurity" (Kelleter 104). The quandary of psychoanalysis has been similarly described. The process is potentially interminable but must at a certain point be terminated for practical reasons, as Freud finds in "Analysis Terminable and Interminable" (219). Brooks explains: "The dynamics of resistance and the transference can always generate new beginnings in relation to any conceivable end" (*Reading* 281). And although the treatment must invariably come to an end, termination is often painful and remains unsatisfactory in many ways. To continue telling the story symbolizes the continuation of development and, more importantly, life itself. The serial's resistance against the end may be read as an attempt to fight against physical, psychic, and social extinction (Mielke 5–6). Hence, the seriality of psychoanalysis and storytelling allows for a multifaceted exploration of relational experience, while also—and Scheherazade knew this quite well—establishing and securing these very relationships.

Oedipus and Scheherazade—as emblems of psychoanalytic structures—both point to a relational foundation of the aesthetics of psychoanalysis. In psychoanalytic writings, Oedipus has received more attention than his female counterpart Scheherazade, perhaps because she is also—and troublingly so—associated with a gendered opposition between linear and cyclical storytelling, problem-solving and continued-talking, insight and seduction. But as much as Freud would have liked to position the psychoanalyst as an insightful Oedipus, the limitations of that model are clearly apparent in the corresponding tendency to deconstruct Oedipus and supplement him with the less "analytically" minded narrative aesthetics of Scheherazade.

Conclusion

Does psychoanalytic experience involve a specific aesthetic experience? Is it indeed "practical poetry," as Adam Phillips has suggested (*On Flirtation* xi)? Clearly, psychoanalysts and critics have repeatedly made use of comparisons with artistic media and genres in order to characterize psychoanalytic practice. Surprisingly, the "aesthetic turn" of psychoanalysis is not even a recent development. Beginning with Freud, psychoanalysts have developed a therapeutic aesthetic based on the "artificial" transference experience within the analytic encounter. Ambiguous characters step into a virtual, ambivalent space-time continuum, whose as-if quality facilitates reenactments through playing and storytelling. Space, communication, and language are self-referential, asymmetrical, and dialogically arranged, always related to the Other and pervaded by contradictions. The structures of therapeutic explorations evoke a coordinate system of psychological and historical depth (through analysis) and processual length (through seriality), which promises a high density and penetration of individual and relational experience. It is with these building blocks—elements of a psychoanalytic aesthetic—that an artistic representation of psychoanalysis has to grapple with if it intends to engage with this specific aesthetic experience. These descriptions may be questioned, they may even be contradictory when combined, but the pervasiveness of the recourse to the arts suggests that psychoanalytic experience does indeed possess an undeniable aesthetic potency.

If we take a further step back, however, this insistence on comparisons with the arts may strike us as curious. When therapy is likened to theater, literature, even music; to all major literary forms, prose, drama, and poetry; to dialogic and serial structures; and finally even to specific subgenres like crime fiction, we get a sense not only of the multifacetedness of psychoanalytic experience but also of the persistent need to find a description for what goes on in therapy. Apparently, psychoanalysis has no genuine access to its particular aesthetic, no psychoanalytic language available to describe a feature of the therapeutic relationship that remains elusive unless captured in metaphors. The comparison with the arts adds a particular allure and magic to the therapeutic endeavor—a much-needed potion against allegations of analytic rigidity and inhumanity—and yet it also introduces a precarious element into psychoanalysis. Indeed, however much the comparison may seem to "ennoble" psychoanalysis, it also threatens its aspiration to the status of a respected science. Even if one does not believe, with Felman, that literature is "*the unconscious of psychoanalysis*" ("Open" 10), the constant return of the comparison hints at the repressed aspects of psychoanalytic experience that have not yet been properly addressed. As we will see in the next chapter, however, the discursive interdependence between psychoanalysis and the arts points to a mutual relationship based on shared, but not fully "analyzed," intuitions about their relational aesthetics.

4

Art as (Therapeutic) Relationship: Relational Models of Creativity, Reading, and Interpretation

Introduction: Art as relational experience?

For psychoanalytic practice and research, the therapeutic relationship provides an experimental arrangement—a self-reflexive, imaginative space to play out conflicted relationships in the transference—which has been used to explore and understand the foundations of relational structures. This experimental potential can be extended to experiences outside the boundaries of the therapeutic relationship. Recalling the ambivalent position of psychoanalysis between science and art discussed in the previous chapter, Adam Phillips notes that the "uncertain status of psychoanalysis is the point and not the problem. Indeed, psychoanalysis has become one useful site for contesting the relative merits of the arts and the sciences; both what they might be good for, and what we should do with our belief in them" ("Poetry" 2). In this chapter, I will look at the ways in which the therapeutic relationship has been employed as such an *aesthetic* "laboratory" to think about the merits and meanings of relational experiences in art.

Peter Brooks, for instance, points to the heuristic potential in psychoanalytic models: "We sense that there ought to be, that there must be, some correspondence between literary and psychic process, that aesthetic structure and form, including literary tropes, must somehow coincide with the psychic structures and operations they both evoke and appeal to" (*Psychoanalysis* 25). By speaking of "correspondences" or using psychoanalytic concepts as models for literary phenomena, Brooks creates an analogy between psychoanalysis and literature: "the relationship I want to establish between psychoanalysis and literature is itself a transactive and transferential one, based on a 'transaction between contexts'" (42–43); his readings employ psychoanalysis as a metaphoric model that "can function as a tool for both comprehension and discovery" (43). Even though Brooks assumes that literature is a product of the psyche (resulting in inevitable interferences between psychological and aesthetic processes), the metaphoric relationship he proposes suggests that he is not interested in actual, proven correlations between therapy and art. Instead, he uses psychoanalysis as a figure of thought to create insights about the dynamics of literary texts (107). This indicates that we are actually homing in on a two-way relationship between psychoanalysis and art. Just as metaphors have been borrowed from aesthetics to describe psychoanalysis, psychoanalysis may apparently be used to forge analogies and explain art.

In psychoanalytic literary criticism, the dream analogy is a widespread figure of thought linking psychoanalysis and literature. By equivalating the dream work with artistic production, the manifest dream content with the shape of the artwork, and dream interpretation with reading, the analogy yields numerous models for aesthetic processes and products, but it has one problem: the privacy and incommunicability of the dream experience actually forecloses simplistic identifications between literature and dream and fails to capture the interactional complexity of art (Schönau and Pfeiffer 79–81). To replace the dream model, the therapeutic relationship has thus often been turned to as a more promising candidate for an analogical model of aesthetic experience. Any number of possible relationships within the complex web of artistic production and reception are eligible for such a parallel reading of therapy and art. The artist has relationships with other artists, with his work and its features, as well as with a (potential) audience; readers and viewers establish numerous real and imaginative meeting points with authors, texts, and characters while reading and interpreting. The most common version of the analogy compares the author or the text to a patient and the reader and critic to the therapist, but any other combination is possible and has indeed been construed at one time or another. Numerous related problems are at stake in the analogy—the potential therapeutic effects of art but even more so the applicability of psychoanalytic assumptions and methods to our dealings with literature, film, or theater; the importance of transference and the utility of the psychoanalytic approach for a study of the production, reception, and interpretation of works of art.

The tendency to read therapeutic and artistic narrative relationships in analogy with each other, which I will from now on call "relational analogy" for short, has for the most part been developed in the interaction between literature and psychoanalysis and has been transferred to other arts and forms of therapy from there. It is most prevalent from the 1970s through to the 1990s, especially in Germany, where it intersects productively with reader-response criticism, but it has also found a home in the Anglo-American poststructuralist psychoanalytic discourse and continues to influence critical thinking up until today. The analogy is sometimes recognized as such or expanded into an explanatory model, but mostly it just flashes up briefly in a casual comparison or in an implicit concept hidden behind the application of psychoanalytic techniques and terms. I will not attempt to give a comprehensive overview of all possible forms of the analogy, which would only lead to a confusing web of terminological and conceptual contradictions. In what follows, I will first discuss how psychoanalysts and literary scholars construct and employ analogies between literature and therapy to create models of literary production, reception, and interpretation, before exploring the analogy in theater and television studies. In comparing different ways in which the analogy is employed and highlighting contradictions and problems of such analogical thinking, my close reading of theoretical texts is aimed not at confirming the analogy but at discovering how and why it is used. Studying the analogies in this way highlights that art and therapy turn toward each other to address questions that are the troubling foundations of both disciplines. In fact, these relational analogies are often employed where the status of a theoretical concept is at stake—the role of the author/analyst/patient, the nature of the text/patient, and the subjectivity of readers, critics, and (psycho)analysts.

Creative neurotics and analytic artists

The first concern and perhaps the first instance of the relational analogy is the exploration of the creativity of the artist and the relational experiences that dominate the creative act. Before I turn to these actual relationships, however, it is important to note that creativity and art are paradoxically linked to the separate roles of patient *and* psychoanalyst in psychoanalytic discourse. The artist as a potential patient in psychoanalysis is perhaps the most well known and most widely contested version of this link. "To account for poetry in psychoanalytic terms has traditionally meant to analyse poetry as a symptom of a particular poet," notes Shoshana Felman (*Jacques Lacan* 27). In other words, psychoanalytic theories of creativity are based on an analogy between artistic and neurotic production that runs both ways. On the one hand, the aesthetic qualities of neurotic productions are regularly noted by early psychoanalysts. Josef Breuer, for instance, attributes a character of "free poetic creation" (*freier poetischer Schöpfung*) to Anna O.'s narratives (228). Likewise, Sigmund Freud observes: "Hysterics are undoubtedly imaginative artists [*Dichter*], even if they express their phantasies mimetically in the main and without considering their intelligibility to other people" ("Preface" 261). These utterances suggest that Breuer and Freud see a relationship between art and neurosis that reflects their fascination with the "poetry" of hysteria and serves to justify their interest in listening closely to these previously neglected products of the human psyche. One foundation for the analogy between the therapeutic and the creative process can be found here, in the association of the patient with the artist.

On the other hand, another source of the discursive link between artist and neurotic can be found in Freud's theory of sublimation, which turns the analogy around and explains the production of art with a deft avoidance of illness. In this process, libidinal energy is redirected to a more sophisticated goal: "Here we have one of the origins of artistic activity; and, according to the completeness or incompleteness of the sublimation, a characterological analysis of a highly gifted individual, and in particular of one with an artistic disposition, may reveal a mixture, in every proportion, of efficiency, perversion and neurosis" ("Three Essays" 238). However, Freud is far from pathologizing the artist. He suspects that the psychodynamic secret of the artist lies in her ability to *avoid* neurosis, even though she may be predisposed to it. In contrast to the neurotic, the artist is capable of adapting her daydreams in a way that makes them palatable for others. Furthermore, the artist possesses "the mysterious power" of temporarily overcoming her repressions and using artistic materials to express her fantasies ("Introductory Lectures" 376). Although Freud clearly detects an analogical relationship between artist and neurotic, he refuses to resolve the mystery of art by assimilating it to his psychoanalytic terms. Thus, he also opposes Alfred Adler's theory that all artists fight against (organic) deficits: "Not all artists are handicapped with bad eyesight, nor were all orators originally stammerers" ("Narcissism" 99).

Nevertheless, psychoanalytic theories of creativity have mostly been deficit theories. A conflict, a lack, or a loss is usually seen as the foundation for artistic activity. As Freud had declared in "Creative Writers and Day-Dreaming": "We may lay it down that a happy person never phantasies, only an unsatisfied one" (146). In connection with this dictum, various theories of creative motivation have been developed. Frequently, artistic activity is deemed to be an attempt to cope with trauma, or to find a productive and active interaction with a painful experience, an obsession, or an emotional conflict. Whereas Adlerians usually see the narcissistic compensation of personal deficits as the point of origin, Kleinians assume that art is grounded in the desire for reparation. The artist may seek recovery through an identification with the completed work and use the admiration of others to stabilize her self; or she may placate her destructive fantasies and the resulting sense of guilt through the act of creation and achieve an imaginary restoration of lost objects (Schönau and Pfeiffer 12–13; Müller-Braunschweig 835). Basically, then, the analogy describes art as a form of autotherapy for the sick artist. These theories of creativity are the basis of numerous psychoanalytic biographies, which take the form of medical histories and interpret artistic creation and its products as symptoms of a disorder or as a character neurosis. Marie Bonaparte, for example, has famously interpreted Edgar Allan Poe's art as a "defense against madness" (Felman, *Jacques Lacan* 38), and Ernest Jones, following Freud, has linked Hamlet's Oedipus complex to "a similar [conflict] in Shakspere [*sic*] himself" (102). In this "psychopathographic" approach, the author is read in analogy to a patient who must be diagnosed (Frier 223). For readers, this method satisfies their curiosity about the author's life, in which they suspect the meaning and the reality of a work of art to reside (Foucault, *Ordre* 30). The psychoanalytic method promises to pin down the elusive author, and predictably, this theory of creativity also manifests itself in the disquiet many artists feel at the thought of psychotherapy. If their disorders were the foundation of their creativity, they would have to fear losing their creativity, along with their illness, in therapy (Schönau and Pfeiffer 3). Rainer Maria Rilke, to name only one example, was sure: "If one were to exorcise my devils, my angels would also suffer a small, (let's say) a very small shock" (322, my translation). The problem is obvious. The link between sickness and creativity is reductive in that it fails to account for other modes of creative motivation as well as for the genuinely literary qualities of the product. Why, if creative work is no more than an attempt at therapy, does it result in art in some cases and neurosis in others?

Therefore, a number of psychoanalytic critics no longer seek to explain creativity with a disorder, and it is no longer deemed acceptable to put the author on the couch (Pietzcker, *Psychoanalytische Studien* 44). Felman, for instance, resists the idea that a clinical condition is a sufficient foundation for a creative product (*Jacques Lacan* 38). Donald Winnicott also sees creativity as a universal aspect of healthy living (*Playing* 91), and thus not just as a neurotic, substitute satisfaction but as an autonomous psychological function (Clemenz 459–60). His theory of artistic creativity revolves around inherent artistic motivations as an expression of health. Nevertheless, creativity and psychoanalysis remain connected. As discussed in the previous chapter, for Winnicott, playing is the core of the analytic experience, which ultimately links art and therapy in their common potential for restoring and expanding creative powers. In any case, the link between therapy and creativity obviously remains a concern in psychoanalytic discourse, even if the notion of the neurotic artist is rejected. For if art is more complex than a pathological symptom but linked to the universal creative potential in human life, then perhaps it can serve as a model for psychoanalysis.

Freud does indeed expect more from the artist than successfully averting a debilitating mental condition. He sees the writer as a sort of ally, who supports the analyst in his endeavors: "Creative writers are valuable allies

[*Bundesgenossen*] and their evidence is to be prized highly, for they are apt to know a whole host of things between heaven and earth of which our philosophy has not yet let us dream" ("Delusions" 8). It is surely not a coincidence that Freud tries to bond with poets over their superior knowledge in a sentence that is itself an unacknowledged but obvious quotation from *Hamlet*. Adam Phillips notes that psychoanalysts have often turned to literature as a "source of 'profound insight'" ("Poetry" 5), and this is also what makes J. M. Coetzee and Arabella Kurtz link psychoanalyst and writer—their common interest in human experience, development, and their linguistic medium (vii–viii). These connections through language and their concern with the human psyche do suggest a close kinship between the two practices, but Freud complicates the issue. He identifies an essential difference between analyst and poet in their methods:

> Our procedure consists in the conscious observation of abnormal mental processes in other people so as to be able to elicit and announce their laws. The author no doubt proceeds differently. He directs his attention to the unconscious in his own mind, he listens to its possible developments and lends them artistic expression instead of suppressing them by conscious criticism. Thus he experiences from himself what we learn from others. ("Delusions" 92)

The artistic production of a poet, as Freud sees it, may certainly be aligned with the activity of a psychoanalyst; but in contrast to the therapist, the writer exercises it through subliminal self-analysis and shuns away from interaction until the work of art is published. Freud may see the poet as a playing child, who "creates a world of phantasy which he takes very seriously" ("Writers" 144), but in the moment of creation he seems to play with no one else. Freud is still intent on keeping up the boundaries between the two disciplines: the artist is an ally, but he cannot replace the analyst, whose work lacks the genius of art but retains the sober methods of science.

Contemporary approaches of narrative therapy are no longer so eager to keep psychoanalysis and art apart. The concept of therapy as imaginative co-authorship relies on analogies to art and thus no longer sees the patient as the only creative agent. In turning the relational analogy around, they imagine the analyst as an artist or at least as a (co-)narrator. Accordingly, Lilian Furst notes: "The physician not only hears stories but, like the writer, also tells them" ("Pairing" 139). Thus, from the arguments of psychoanalysts and literary critics, we can extract two different analogies for the author—taking on the guises of patient *and* analyst. With contemporary psychoanalytic theories, we can also see a tendency toward depathologizing the poet—which is not surprising, given that, as Felman notes, the now common association of the analyst with the artist would automatically infect the analyst with the artist's "folly" (*Jacques Lacan* 489). In this way, all the fascination of the analogy is retained without the association with illness—only to create new implications. The poet/analyst is no longer imagined as an autonomous figure but as an actor in mutual play.

Creation as relational act

The notion that neither the writer nor the patient nor even the analyst is an isolated storyteller paves the way for a more comprehensive analogy between the therapeutic relationship and creativity. Freud's conceptualization of the creative act as a narcissistic act is rejected and literary creation described as a relational process. Michael Miller, for instance, explains: "Although it is done in private, writing is inherently a social activity" (450). Aside from the potential presence of actual other people during the creation or presentation of a text, the process is supposed to be accompanied by meaningful, imaginary relational constructions. Clemenz even assumes that the artist has an affair (*Liebesverhältnis*) with art itself (455). Elements of a work of art, such as its characters, are also amenable to love or transference relationships. Siri Hustvedt, for example, describes the analyst-protagonist in her novel *The Sorrows of an American* as "my imaginary brother-analyst-self" ("Playing" 39). Psychoanalytically, characters are usually interpreted as mirrors of earlier relational experiences that contain a number of transference fantasies and allow the artist to uphold a relationship with her objects (Gesing 46). This is confirmed by Hustvedt: "Writing novels is . . . a form of open listening to those imagined others, one that draws on memories, transmuted by fantasies and fears" ("Analyst" 233). In her description of the imagined other as a counterpart who can challenge the author, the artistic act remains imaginatively embedded within a relational matrix.

The idea that the work of art is also an object with which the author can establish a passionate relationship is at least as old as the myth of Pygmalion.[1] In numerous variants of the relational analogy, this relationship with the work of art is turned into a therapeutic relationship. Hans Müller-Braunschweig, for instance, illustrates how the artist begins to see his work as a partner in an emotionally fraught and reciprocal relationship. Since the object has been created by the artist, it is experienced as controllable and not as frightening (835). Such an object may fulfill numerous psychological tasks and, as Carl Pietzcker explains, has a calming and comforting effect ("Literarische Form" 77). Now, the artist may see herself in her work. But as soon as she observes it from the outside, the temporal difference between production and reception alone alienates her from her work. This creates a mirror effect, in which the artist may find herself anew or see herself in a different light (I. Jung 196). The writer relates to her work as to an object that triggers transference, reflects emotions, and offers a safe space to face her suppressed desires, fears, and troublesome memories. It is probably not a coincidence that all these descriptions of the artistic object cast the work in the role of the analyst, mirroring, comforting, and challenging the artist to reflect herself. They rest on an implicit analogy between text and therapist, which allows them to turn writing into a therapeutic endeavor—a question I will explore in more detail later in this chapter.

Many relational analogies, however, do not focus on the work and its components but argue that the potential audience is the most important counterpart in the relational constellation of creative work. Even if real audience members also play a role, psychoanalytic art theory is primarily interested in the imaginary addressees the writer creates during the production of a text. Thus, it is pitted against theoretical positions that describe the work of art as a solipsistic creation. Walter Benjamin, for example, postulates that art does not cater to an audience: "no poem is dedicated to the reader, no painting to the spectator, no symphony to the audience" ("Aufgabe" 9, my translation). Hardly any representative of psychoanalytic criticism, however, will be satisfied with such an exanimated image of the creative process. For Brooks, writing is not much different from oral storytelling. The writer turns toward an imaginary listener, even if he has no immediate access to or influence on her reactions (*Psychoanalysis* 76). The potential presence of a listener acts as a trigger for the transference: "That is, the presence of a narratee-interpreter provokes a situation of transmission and transference" (89). According to this hypothesis, the experiences, desires, and anxieties of the author influence the shape of the text to which the audience may later react. Stanley Coen is convinced that an author transfers unresolved issues from his childhood onto his audience (*Between* 29), thus describing the relationship between an author and his audience as a typical transference situation. The analogy with the therapeutic relationship is even more explicit in Stanley Olinick's and Laura Tracy's insistence that "every story teller tells his stories to an imagined reader who is his transference imago. The evident validity of this proposition in the psychoanalytic process is paralleled in the literary process" (330). In these theories, writing always involves a transference toward an imaginary object—be it the text as a whole, text elements, or potential readers—and this foundational transferential structure suggests an analogy with the therapeutic relationship, in which transference is not an accidental phenomenon but an instrument for deeper understanding.

Transference also introduces a paradoxical absent presence into the process as none of the imaginary (therapeutic) partners the writer conjures up is actually there at the moment of writing. André Green argues that this is precisely what links writing and psychoanalysis: "In writing, no one is present. To be more precise, the potential and anonymous reader is absent by definition. . . . Writing fashions this dimension of absence while it re-presents, while (in a certain sense) it renders present" (282). Similarly, the analyst is an absent-present partner for the patient, who will render present the absent characters from his past. If there is a relationship inherent in the act of creation, it consists in its potential to erect characters, works of art, and readers as imaginary Others for creative interaction, and the analogy with psychoanalysis presents itself because it is likewise concerned with the enactment of imaginary relationships. Concerning the act of creation, the relational analogy is thus supposed to draw out and give a name to important relational components within aesthetic experience. On the one hand, it serves to emphasize and theorize the previously disregarded relationality of much (but not all) creative work; on the other hand, it deals with the imaginary relationships we establish as readers and critics with absent authors through our fascination with their mysterious abilities. This, however, points us to another set of analogies that tries to describe the relationships readers entertain with their various counterparts.

Relationships in reading

Perhaps even more frequently than authors, readers are seen as involved in relationships with the texts they read, the characters they encounter, and the authors they imagine. The transference-countertransference dynamic provides critics with a model to explain these relationships and place them in an analogy with the therapeutic relationship. I will here begin by tracing the assumptions about relational experiences in reading before I explore the presumed transferential structures underlying these relationships. These various ways of conceptualizing reading highlight a need for narratives about the reader's experience that engage with its relational, interactional, and affective components.

How much the narratives of reading that we have at our disposal are at odds with each other can easily be demonstrated with one of the simplest relationships recreational readers engage in on a regular basis—the affective relationship with a literary character. From a critical point of view, this experience is merely an illusion. Literary characters do not possess the ability to act autonomously, maintain relationships of their own, or develop a personality to which the reader might relate. In philosophy and narratology, literary characters are seldom regarded as more than "a set of statements" (Eaton 30). And yet, there is a difference between scholarly reflection and "naïve" reading. Even if a reader or interpreter is, strictly speaking, not allowed to treat a character as if she were an analysand on the couch, literary figures are almost automatically attributed complex psyches by their readers (Pietzcker, *Psychoanalytische Studien* 47). The relationship with a character may be so intense that readers turn them into imaginary companions or identify with them—the euphoric cult surrounding Goethe's *Werther* in the eighteenth century being an extreme but socially widespread example of such literary transference relationships (Hamburger 57). Literary characters obviously affect us or "satisf[y] a need for us" (Holland, *Dynamics* 277–78), but there is a gap between how we evaluate their ontological status and how we encounter them in reading.

A similar paradox has taken hold of our appreciation of the reader's relationship to the author. As Brooks has noted, this "classical locus of psychoanalytic interest" is both "the most discredited" and "the most difficult to extirpate," for however often "the disappearance of the author" has been announced, "authorial mutants ceaselessly reappear" (21). Numerous psychoanalytic critics do indeed assume that the reading experience is underpinned by the unconscious communication between author and reader as mediated by the text (Pietzcker, "Überblick" 25) and that reader response is determined by the relational bid (*Beziehungsangebot*) the author has introduced into the text (Matejek 70). In many camps of literary theory, these premises are regarded as highly problematic. Roland Barthes, for example, criticizes the equation between an author's person and her work in his famous essay "The Death of the Author": "The *explanation* of the work is always sought on the side of the one who has produced it, as if . . . it was always finally the voice of a single and the same person, the *author*, who delivers his 'confession'" ("Mort" 64, my translation). Barthes wants to liberate text and reader from this dependence on the revelations of an individual. Michel Foucault also regards the author as a mere function that we project as a psychological entity ("Auteur" 801). In the eyes of most psychoanalytic literary critics, however, there can be no question that the author is very much alive. Benjamin and Thomas Ogden describe the problems a psychoanalytic literary reader ("PLR") will encounter with this poststructuralist critique because of his own disciplinary background:

> [The PLR] firmly believes . . . that a writer cannot create in his writing what he is incapable of experiencing in his own life—an author, he contends, cannot write effectively *about* emotional experiences, he must

write *from* them: they must be alive in the author. The point we are trying to make here about the place of psychoanalysis in literary studies is that the PLR treats voice as a reflection of human psychology. (13)

What we see here is a clash between different interests and questions. The psychoanalyst will look at literature not as an autonomous linguistic construct that chiefly follows literary rules but as a product of an individual mind. Hence, he will also regard reading as a "relationship between the writer's conscious and unconscious psychology and the psychology the reader hears and feels in the writer's use of language" (57). The result is a completely different—psychological—conception of the basic structures of literature. Given the fact that even in psychoanalysis the reconstruction of the past has been renounced in favor of a mutual construction of meaning, it remains doubtful whether psychoanalytic literary criticism will be able to continue reading works of art as a direct consequence of the psychology of the real, historical author (Pietzcker, *Psychoanalytische Studien* 34). Even so, as the psychological element has been widely eliminated from literary theory, the continued resonance of the relational analogy suggests that it comes back to haunt the debate because the problem of authorship has not been solved by its excision from critical discourse.

Many analogies, however, do not even go back to the real author. Several theorists believe that readers establish a relationship with implicit authors as a part of the overall relationship with the structure of the text. Just as the author may imagine his readers in their absence, the reader may react to the author in his absence. "We as readers, except as an academic exercise, do not experience the text as entirely divorced from a person who wrote it," Miller maintains (454). This is true especially when the author has become inaccessible as a real person. Since there is usually no communication between author and reader aside from the text itself, this author figure is both real and imaginary, determined by experiential facts as much as by fantasies: "We construct an author . . . according to our wishes, needs, defenses, assumptions, biases, and everything else we bring to the reading experience" (Coen, "Introduction" 12-13). Thus, from a psychoanalytic perspective, the implicit author is, at least in part, a product of the unconscious and productively irrational impulses of the reader.

Since the implicit author is just one of the structures that make up a text, many scholars who discuss reader response as a relationship focus on the confrontation between text and reader. Aaron Esman suggests "that the reader's relationship is with the text, rather than with the author. . . . The reader's relationship with the text, like that of analyst and patient, requires an abolition of distance, a willed regression, and it can be disrupted or distorted as with transference-countertransference reactions" (24). In this way, the relationship between text and reader is not just equated with the therapeutic relationship; it is also loaded with affective emphasis as well as psychological and relational implications. In many analogies, the encounter with a work of art is conceptualized as a nexus of processes of merger and delimitation, overtures to and refusals of relationships, and reflections on the self and the other. This suggests that the relationship that is being theorized is an interaction between two equally involved parties—the work does not only depend on the reader, the reader also depends on the work. Referring to Winnicott's dictum that there is no infant without a mother ("Theory" 586), Norman Holland claims: "There is no such thing as an audience as an entity-in-itself, for whenever one finds an audience one finds a literary work creating it, and without a literary work there would be no audience" (*Dynamics* 79). When scholars establish the relational analogy as a transference relation between reader and text, they apparently seek to highlight the exchange itself as well as its mutuality as central components of literary response.

A wide range of relationships—between authors, characters, texts, and readers—is thus turned into a central category of literary analysis. This might at first suggest a theoretical conflict with (post)structuralist models of literary art, but when we look closely at Barthes's and Foucault's arguments they do not deny that readers establish these psychological connections—they simply suggest that we should look at authors and texts in different terms. In the relational analogies, however, authors, characters, and texts seem to be returning to life. This is not just so because, as Holland has suggested, psychoanalytic assumptions remain viable only if there are actual (however fictional) minds to which they can be applied ("Shakespearean Tragedy" 217); on the contrary, it seems that psychoanalytic theory is employed to *add* psychological force. The language of these comparisons suggests that there is something we have not fully accounted for and appreciated in our theories about reading, namely, the tendency of texts to be perceived as interactional partners in the reading relationship. Although the analogy almost always leads to impasses in the interdisciplinary conglomerate of theoretical concepts and questions, it points to something that, apparently, we cannot yet relinquish: a relational element in the phenomenological *experience* of reading.

The mechanics and metaphors of literary transference

Given the multiplicity of possible pathways for readers to establish relationships with texts, critics have come up with a wide variety of analogies between reading and the therapeutic relationship. Widely accepted is the link between patient and author/text, who are read by an analyst/reader. In this vein, Norbert Matejek declares that the author guides the reader just as the patient guides the therapist through a story (39). But once again, the asymmetric yet interactional structure of the therapeutic relationship makes this habitual equation problematic. Frier assumes that the reader is actually in a "double situation," in a developmental process like a patient and responding to the text with emotions very much like an analyst who responds to a patient (222, my translation). The analogy patient ≙ text / therapist ≙ reader can thus easily be reversed. The analyst can identify with the patient and be analyzed by her, while the reader might step into the author's imaginary position and accept his transference from that position (Pietzcker, *Lesend* 25). All imaginable relationships are thus in constant flux, which is reflected in the multiplicity of possible analogies. And although critics often extrapolate a basic analogy in which the narrative situation between narrator and listener corresponds to the therapeutic situation between analysand and analyst, they still encounter a number of problems. The positions of the written narrative exchange—(implicit) author, text, (implicit) reader, narrator, addressee— do not correspond neatly to the roles narrator and listener obtain in oral storytelling situations like the "talking cure." Moreover, every theorist seems to have his or her own idea about where analysand and analyst are to be enlisted in the repertoire of narrative roles. Out of this confusion arises a need to clarify the mechanics of the reader-text relationship, and many psychoanalytic critics are preoccupied with explaining exactly how the reader and the text interact in a transference-countertransference dynamic.

An important foundation of the analogy is thus the assumption that reading rests on transferential structures: "The reader's attempt to adapt the work to his or her own identity theme . . . is a manifestation of the transference phenomenon" (Alcorn and Bracher 346). The transference of the reader certainly helps to explain the variability of the reading experience. Just like the patient, so the argument goes, the reader brings her own relational patterns to her encounter with literature, and she will not only respond to the text based on these patterns but also try and adapt her interpretation of the text to her own assumptions. The value of the transference model is obvious. It provides an explanation for the differences in each reader's response to the same text. However, when psychoanalytic critics talk about transference in reading, they might also talk about the transference of the text. Pietzcker, for example, argues that the text enacts its own transference and the reader experiences the text "as something that turns towards him" (*Lesend* 20, my translation). That would turn the reader's response to the text into a closer analogue of countertransference, holding the same explanatory potential as the transference model. Such theories of the transference of the text are often based on the assumption that textual strategies serve as triggers for the reader (Frier 224), analogous to the triggers supposed to involve the psychoanalyst in the transference. Thus, they accept that the relationship between readers and texts is an interaction influenced by the strategies found in the text (Iser 29), but ascribing its own transference to the text goes beyond traditional reader-response models in that it endows both the text and the reading relationship with intersubjectivity and numerous psychological implications (Reiche 309).

Most text-transference models argue that the text's transference is created by the fact that "texts presume a variety of relationships" (Skura 183)—they cast readers in a variety of roles and employ seductive strategies to hold them there (Neukom 165). And what is transference but the presumption of a relationship or an attempt at seduction? The reader's "countertransference" would then be a reaction to the proposals of the text, shaped by her acceptance of or her struggle against the roles the text imposes on her (Raguse 111; Matejek 39). One of the most important carriers of such textual role offers is the implicit author, whose influence can be felt through the text's seductive, aggressive, or anxiety-inducing mechanisms as they manifest in its language, genre, or medium (Pietzcker, *Lesend* 19). The narrator's stylistic register is also supposed to establish a communicative relationship with the reader, who may be made to feel instructed, taken seriously, or confused; or who may be made to feel inferior to the omniscient narrator (Gesing, "Annäherungen" 46). The analogy is thus based on the effect of language on the reader and not on the (absent) "mind" of the text engaged in transference. In the tradition of reader-response theory, it delineates the text's strategies for meaning-making and involving the reader in interaction (Iser 36).

Accordingly, Matejek identifies the implicit reader as another role offer anchored in the structure of the text (18). Through the possibilities that the text provides for the establishment of a relationship, the reader is attached cognitively and affectively to the text and encouraged to behave in a certain way. Iser describes this phenomenon expressly as a process of transference (*Übertragungsvorgang*) (67). Even if it is unlikely that he had the psychoanalytic concept in mind, the idea is similar. Based on her past experiences, the reader will react with an individually tailored response to the role offered to her by the text. Iser's concept of the "gap" (*Leerstelle*) works in a similar way, only in this case, the text does not predetermine a role but offers a space for the reader to bring in her own material. Iser's gaps are open hinges (*Scharniere*), which indicate that a particular position in the system can be filled with the imaginations of the reader (284). They involve the reader in the specific response-inviting structure (*Appellstruktur*) of the text but, through their indeterminacy, leave her the freedom to fill them with her own material, dependent on the structures of her own mind (Langenmayr 34). Psychological conclusions are almost inevitable once the individual reader's response is granted as much importance. Even Iser's model identifies a therapeutic component in the presupposed text-reader relationship. He argues that the text provides a space for transferences, which is constantly filled with projections. If the reader does nothing but project her own material, Iser sees no real interaction; but if the text resists this attempt at appropriation, it may function as a corrective device for the reader's mind-set (263). It is this capacity of literary texts for the transformation of readers that fascinates psychoanalysts and critics alike, even as it fills them with suspicion.

With the plethora of transferential structures provided by the text, it remains controversial how independently the reader responds to these attempts at conditioning. On the one hand, the model acknowledges that different readers may react in all kinds of different, playful ways to an opportunity for transference (Pietzcker, *Lesend* 22–24). Holland makes a similar point when he emphasizes the free and constructive engagement of the reader with the text: "[Reading] makes something new, something human, something personal" (*5 Readers* 122). And yet, on the other hand, it can be argued that the reader is not at all independent; one must expect a limited number of countertransference patterns because texts give readers only a few roles to choose from (Matejek 49), so that reading emerges as an individual and emotionally variable adaptation of invariable textual features (Heigl-Evers and Salfeld 29–31). In this debate, the status of the text and its autonomy is at stake, and with it the agency of the reader. Paradoxically, the transferential model seems to strengthen both positions. The acknowledgment of the transference of the reader supports the notion of the radical subjectivity of reading, whereas the quest for textual structures of transference serves to ascribe a strong and independent agency to the text.

Elizabeth Freund ascertains that the reader-response movement has always wondered who dominates the reading relationship: the text or the reader. While privileging the reader seems to override the autonomy of the text and compromise the separation between an object and its interpretation, in practice this separation is always reinstated to make interpretation, which depends on an interpretable object, possible (152, 156). Tellingly, Freund also falls back on a psychoanalytic analogy to resolve the asymmetrical power dynamics between reader and text. According to her, a consideration of the transference might help transcend the problem of the object's status:

> A transferential model would allow us to take as the object of analysis not the text or the reader alone, but reading itself. . . . If the encounter of analyst and analysand is seen to correspond to the encounter of

reader and text, a double and properly dialectical perspective on reading emerges; the reader reads the text, but the text also reads the reader. (129)

Freund goes back to interactional models of psychoanalysis to solve the problem delineated above. As long as transference and countertransference overlap, it becomes impossible to say whose communicative impulses dominate the production of meaning. Like Thomas Ogden or Antonino Ferro, Freund is no longer interested in separating the participants of the relationship but in studying the relationship itself, as the independent, third creation it is.

By introducing more recent theories about the relationship between analyst and analysand to the analogy, Freund and other critics add a new perspective to the contested dynamic between reader and text. The therapeutic relationship as a complex interactional process on the basis of a fluctuating transference-countertransference matrix is captured in a relational analogy when, for example, Mahler-Bungers elevates the reader to the "co-author" or "co-translator" of the text (517, my translation) or when Langenmayr recognizes her as a possible "co-player" in interaction (117, my translation). Ogden's analytic third is also capable of lending a description to the intersubjective dynamics of the reading relationship, which is most apparent in the words he addresses to his own readers:

> You, the reader, must allow me to occupy you, your thoughts, your mind, since I have no voice with which to speak other than yours. If you are to read this book, you must allow yourself to think my thoughts while I must allow myself to become your thoughts and in that moment neither of us will be able to lay claim to the thought as our own exclusive creation. (*Subjects* 1)

Ogden thus delineates a complex process that resembles the therapeutic relationship in both its antagonistic and its transformative qualities:

> You, the reader, will oppose me, deny me, perhaps humor me, but never entirely give way to me. This book will not be "understood" by you; you will not simply receive it, incorporate it, digest it, or the like. To the degree that you will have anything at all to do with it, you will transform it. (2–3)

In this way, an (analytic) third is created between reader and author: "The creation of a third subject (that exists in tension with the writer and the reader as separate subjects) is the essence of the experience of reading, and ... is also the core of the psychoanalytic experience" (2). This point of view allows Ogden to regard the interaction between author/text and reader as a third that is created by both dyadic poles, created anew in every encounter, reflecting not just the presence of the relationship but also the past of both participants. These constant fluctuations in the construction of the analogies show how much they are shaped by constantly developing theories about literary and psychoanalytic communication and may thus become effective mediators between the two disciplines. In an attempt to understand the complex process of literary reception, critics develop theories about reading that capture its relational components; but, as the multitude of constructed reading relationships show, the analogy is never quite sufficient to clarify what happens between reader and text—which explains the need for ever new analogies, based on the ever-evolving models of the therapeutic relationship.

A somewhat different approach is followed through by Peter Brooks. As I indicated at the beginning of this chapter, his writing is fully aware of the metaphorical nature of the analogy. It is therefore less concerned with clarifying the specific pathways transference and countertransference might take than with the implications of the transference model for the process of reading. When Brooks describes the relationship between text and reader as a transferential relationship, he attributes this link less to the narrative structures of the text than to the nature of storytelling itself. According to him, every story is a form of transference because it transmits the past (a story) to the present (narration) (*Reading* 97). The inevitability of transference is also highlighted by Felman: "The love-relation, i.e., the acting out of the unconscious through a relation of performative interpretation, seems to inhere in, and to govern, the relationship between the addresser of the narrative ('author' or narrator) and its addressee (listener-receiver or reader-interpreter)" ("Turning" 133). Both Felman and Brooks thus home in on the specific relationship created through literary communication, emphasizing its repetitive structure and its heightened emotionality. Brooks bases his model on Barthes's description of narrative as a contract between narrator and listener (*S/Z* 95; Brooks, *Psychoanalysis* 51). However, he does not just take over Barthes's contractual model but expands it with a transference model that puts a different emphasis on the reader-text interaction. Through the admission of transference, Brooks highlights that reading involves the creation of a relationship as an artificial medium, in which meaning is not only transmitted but also created and in which individual anxieties and desires play a huge role in constituting that meaning (*Reading* 234–35). Thus, Brooks conceives of the story as a process of dynamic exchange. This allows him to ask what is at stake in reading in terms of affect and psychosomatic interaction:

> Why [the story] is told, what aims it may manifest and conceal, what it seeks not only to say but to do. There can be a range of reasons for telling a story, from the self-interested to the altruistic. Seduction appears as a predominant motive, be it specifically erotic and oriented toward the capture of the other, or more nearly narcissistic, even exhibitionistic, asking for admiration and attention. Yet perhaps aggression is nearly as common, and, of course, often inextricably linked to the erotic: a forcing of attention, a violation of the listener. The nature of the transference established between speaker and listener can be positive and productive of satisfaction, but it can also involve dependency and abjection, the incapacity to free oneself from the interlocutor. (*Reading* 236)

Just as analyst and analysand explore the hidden dynamics of their relationship, bracing themselves for aggressive and erotic components, Brooks also delineates an imperative for the reader to confront her "inescapable desire for narrative": "The link between teller and listener that produces the story is originally and ultimately an erotic bond, an investment of otherwise inexpressible desires into narrative exchange" (*Psychoanalysis* 100-01). In this way, reader and text are always linked to each other, incapable of breaking away, so that reading and interpretation can only take place in their relationship: "One cannot read, as one cannot cure, from the outside. It is only through assuming the burden and the risks of the transferential situation that one reaches the understanding of otherness" (*Psychoanalysis* 70). Thus, Brooks shifts the attention away from elements of the reading process and their practical consequences to the fundamental question: What does it mean to be affectively and intimately involved in the process of reading? What is asked of the reader and what does she ask herself? Hence, in this analogy, the problem of the hierarchy between reader and text cannot be resolved on universal terms but depends on the distribution of needs and desires in the individually established reading relationship. It is an affective literary theory that employs transference as a signifier for a variety of unconscious factors that enter and influence the reading experience.

At the end of these deliberations on the similarity between psychoanalysis and reading, we should remind ourselves that they also differ in many important ways: analysis is practiced in absolute privacy within a specific relationship geared toward therapy, whereas a text is indirectly but publicly aimed at unknown readers, who may use it as they wish (Schönau and Pfeiffer 53). And yet, as we have seen, many critics develop a comprehensive analogy between analytic and narrative relationships on the basis of their transferential structure. Freud argues that we need such narratives to make the basically inaccessible process of "what readers 'do'" imaginable (87). The relational analogy provides one such narrative to facilitate the imaginative construction of theories about reading. It has often been used to speculate on the mechanics of the relationships involved in reading, when it is more precisely organized as a metaphor that helps us think through the meanings we attribute to texts, readers, and their interaction.

The analyst/critic and the text/patient

From the analyst-as-reader it is only a small step to the analyst-as-critic. Arguing that the proper analytic model of understanding is not diagnosis but therapy, Schönau and Pfeiffer believe that psychoanalytic literary criticism should be modeled on the interaction of psychoanalyst and analysand (95). In this way, the relational analogy links the analyst with the critic and the text with the patient, and almost always implicitly so when psychoanalytic methods are applied to literature. Quite frequently, however, the analogy is explicitly made to prove a certain point and work toward the corroboration of a psychoanalytic or critical agenda. In order to justify her realignment of psychoanalytic literary criticism toward an analogy with the therapeutic process, Skura declares: "The analytic process offers a more complete model for literary texts than the other methods we have examined; all the ways we understand each other are the ways we understand texts, too" (201). For Schafer, the comparison between psychoanalyst and literary critic helps explain his hermeneutic therapeutic technique:

> Thus, the analyst treats the analysand in the same manner that many literary critics treat authors—with interest in what the analysand says about the aims of his or her utterances and choices, but with an overall attitude of autonomous critical command rather than submission or conventional politeness, and with a readiness to view these explanatory comments as just so much more prose to be both heard as such *and* interpreted. (*Retelling* 176)

In the same vein, Nanette Auerhahn employs the analogy to learn something about the poetic qualities of the psychoanalytic process: "It appears that the psychoanalytic narrative resembles a literary text in having the quality of literariness. This would suggest that there might be specific ways in which the analyst's tools would be similar to that of the critic" (429).[2] Coen, in contrast, imagines a reverse flow of inspiration: "I would argue that it is the *method* of the practicing psychoanalyst that can enrich the work of the literary critic" (171). These various positions show clearly that different intentions lie behind the construction of relational analogies. They are assembled to enrich one's own interpretive process by drawing inspiration from the other discipline's methods or to legitimize one's own practices by demonstrating their far-reaching significance.

The analogy has been particularly influential in a branch of psychoanalytic literary criticism called countertransference analysis (*Gegenübertragungsanalyse*). In this technique, the critic reads the strategies of the text as part of a communicative situation. His starting point for every interpretation is his own personal reaction to the text, adopting the way in which psychoanalysts use their own countertransference to gain access to their patients' unconscious. At first glance, such an attention to one's countertransference seems to stand in the way of a clear appreciation of the object of interpretation. If the critic were to follow his reactions to the text blindly, his statements would apply only to himself but not to the text. However, as Murray Schwartz counters, "becoming conscious of transference responses enables the critic to bring repetitions into the area of reflection, and thus to use them to enrich his representations of the work of art" ("Literary Use" 43). So there are good reasons why psychoanalytic critics stand by countertransference analysis. Contemporary psychoanalytic theory no longer allows them to believe that countertransference can be overcome as Freud used to think, and the adoption of this opinion in literary criticism reinforces the theory that it is impossible to have a neutral relationship with the text. Following this model, countertransference analysis is presented as a way toward greater self-awareness and thus acquired objectivity. Speaking to an audience of psychoanalysts, Holland explains a further attraction of the model:

> As I understand it, by tuning in to the way you are feeling as you hear what this patient is saying, you discover what you are hearing. In the same way, the critic who is alert to his own role in the re-creation of a book listens to his feelings as he reads, and that way he arrives at a fresh understanding, a new appreciation, really, of the book. ("Why" 32)

Seen in this way, countertransference harbors the potential to find new meaning in the text precisely because the critic gets involved (Pietzcker, *Lesend* 34). Thus, not only does the text say more than is at first apparent, the relationship between text and critic adds further, unpredictable elements of meaning to the process of understanding.

To safeguard against the accusation of abandoning the text's own message in favor of indulging in the critic's subjectivity, Pietzcker makes a point of embedding countertransference analysis within the hermeneutic tradition (*Lesend* 66), demanding respect for the text's otherness (*Fremdheit*) and ambiguity (54). In one point, however, the technique is clearly different from the hermeneutic approach. Joachim Pfeiffer emphasizes that psychoanalytic approaches further complicate Gadamer's notion of the prejudicial structure of understanding by pointing to its unconscious underpinnings (340). Countertransference analysis thus has a genuine claim to addressing an unruly component in the process of interpretation that previous models of criticism have been ill-equipped to deal with.

In accordance with the underlying analogy, the new critical equipment is derived from the psychoanalytic setting. Angeloch, for instance, believes that the critic should remain abstinent, abstain from unreflecting identifications with the text and its characters, and contemplate the relationship on offer with evenly suspended attention ("Beziehung" 541–42). Evangelia Tsiavou similarly wants the critic to build a relationship with the text. But for her, it is also important that the critic remains open to his own unconscious fantasies and keeps oscillating between reading as countertransference experience and interpretation as an act of self-analysis (121)—in short, she asks the critic to cultivate the analytic stance of elasticity. Just as in psychoanalysis, these techniques are geared toward controlling the inevitable subjectivity brought forward by countertransference analysis. This subjectivity is an inherent feature of psychoanalysis and literary criticism, these theorists argue—but not without betraying a certain discontent and defensiveness with regard to the instability of their results. Schwartz identifies this critical paradox within psychoanalysis, which originated in Freud's self-analysis but at first cultivated a stance of "disinterestedness" that tried to disavow the analyst's inevitable subjectivity ("Where" 53). Similarly, we have seen how the countertransference critics are eager to show that despite their efforts to tap into the subjectivity of the critic, their results are nevertheless contained within a "proper" hermeneutic frame that leads to reliable results. Madelon Sprengnether, however, argues that the turn to psychoanalysis in literary studies might actually help overcome the illusion that one might ever escape the "radical instability of texts": "The dream of total objectivity is a dream of total outsidedness, whereas the message of modern psychoanalysis is one of participation, of complicity, of the simultaneous elusiveness of boundaries and of the self" (93–95). Wilfred Bion, in a reference to John Keats, has similarly emphasized that the psychoanalytic stance requires a "Negative Capability," a capacity for being "in uncertainties, mysteries, doubts, without any irritable reaching after fact and reason" (*Attention* 125). An analysis of the relational analogy thus exposes two disciplines similarly struggling with the subjectivity and instability of their practice—the recognition that interpretation will never be fully contained in scientifically reliable models. Literature and psychoanalysis turn to each other in the hopes of drawing more solid techniques from the other discipline and reassuring themselves about the values of subjectivity.

Another important problem of countertransference analysis is the communicative situation the critic faces with a text. Psychoanalysis is based on the presence of two interacting people and the ongoing production of spoken material by the patient; it is a conversation and not a reading experience. In short, unlike the patient, the text cannot talk back (A. Cooper 51). The solutions that proponents of countertransference analysis in general have come up with will show that the relational analogy between critic and psychoanalyst highlights not only the subjectivity of the encounter but also assumptions about its interactional nature.

The objections brought forward against the application of the psychoanalytic method to literary interpretation are based on theoretical models in which the text is incapable of responding to the reader's questions. James Gorney describes the literary text as "circumscribed, delimited, and incapable of responding directly with new words to interrogation," whereas the analytic conversation is alive, "open-ended [and] immediately reactive in speech" (546). Marius Neukom even declares that the text remains "absolutely silent" (163, my translation). Thus, the asymmetrical communication of analysis, in which the patient is supposed to speak while the analyst remains silent, is actually reversed because the analyst/critic is faced with an unresponsive "entity" (Pietzcker, *Lesend* 36). It seems that the relational analogy would reach an impasse here.

In an effort to solve this difficulty and uphold the analogical relation, theorists enlist subjects outside of the text to create a dialogic situation. Hartmut Raguse asks the critic to act as her own supervisor (113), implicitly splitting her into two voices so as to arrive at a proper dialogue. Similarly, Pietzcker is convinced that, by imaginatively taking over the role of and speaking for the text, the critic can actually establish a dialogic situation (*Lesend* 57). These critics still proceed from a static textual model—a text that is factually out there and immutable. Critics who embrace more radical models, however, do not necessarily see the text as mute and static and are thus capable of driving the analogy even further. Schwartz states: "The text only remains what it is because the critic has not changed" ("Literary Use" 43). If the text as such is only established in the interaction between work and reader, as Stanley Fish believes (144), then it is indeed capable of changing, or even, as Schafer claims, of being "given therapy":

> Following [the] analytic interpretation of the poem . . . , the reader may better experience the poem's structural unity, richness of meaning, and potential impact, within the perspective provided. For this reason, we may legitimately say that the poem has become more alive and integrated, that it has been rendered available to enter into a more developed relationship with the reader, something more on the order of a mature, mutual, and modifiable relation of whole persons. . . . It would be arbitrary to insist that in consequence of interpretation only the reader has changed, for it can be argued that the poem changes with the reader as the reader becomes more expert. It is no longer the same poem. (*Retelling* 184)

Schafer argues that the reader assumes the virtual co-authorship of the text, creating and changing—"therapizing"—it as she reads; but the analogy hinges on the text being created within this interaction rather than having a separate existence. This assumption has the effect of rendering dynamic the text-reader relationship, as it allows for actual interaction and transformation, but at the same time it robs the text of its independent agency.

It is thus not surprising that the relational analogy also pivots on a third model for the text's interactive capacities, which is not just ready to assign the text/patients more agency but turns them into the element that actually drives the analytic process—the literary analyst might become the analysand of the text. In this vein, Felman posits:

> It could be argued that people who choose to analyze literature as a profession do so because they are unwilling or unable to choose between the role of the psychoanalyst (he or she who analyzes) and the role of the patient (that which is being analyzed). Literature enables them not to choose because of the following paradox: 1) the work of literary analysis resembles the work of the psychoanalyst; 2) the status of what is analyzed—the text—is, however, not that of a patient, but rather that of a master. . . . Like the psychoanalyst viewed by the patient, the text is viewed by us as . . . the very place where meaning, and *knowledge* of meaning, reside. ("To Open" 7)

Felman establishes a two-sided analogy, in which the critic stands in for the analysand as well as for the analyst. For her, this does not just explain how we might treat a text but, more importantly, why we turn to literature in the first place. With the relational analogy, the status of the text itself is at stake: is it "dead" material, unsuited to the dialogic process of psychoanalysis, or does it have an agency of its own, capable of challenging the critic? The more the text itself "knows" and "speaks," the more the analogy is capable of being reversed, and the text may become the analyst of the reader. It is therefore often designed to solve methodical and ethical problems, such as how to approach texts that are radically Other without subsuming them under an interpretive paradigm—or, indeed, to make it possible to subsume them. Thus, the analogy between psychoanalysis and interpretation may not only yield pointers for the technique of countertransference analysis but also provide a possibility to reconsider the relationship between text and critic.

Suspicious interpretation and psychoanalytic dialogue

Psychoanalysis has often been charged with disrespecting the Otherness of the patient (or the text), exercising hermeneutic violence, or imposing prefabricated interpretations on their patients (Brooks, *Psychoanalysis* 47, 113). Regarding psychoanalytic interpretations of literature, Pierre Bayard fears the worst kind of imposition is being inflicted on the text: "To interpret is to substitute my word for the word of the other, to produce a meaning that is not that of the other but mine." As an alternative, he suggests respecting the multiplicity of meaning and "how *the text resists interpretation*" (212–14). However, a brief glance at the history of psychoanalytic hermeneutic theory shows that, while these allegations may have a historical basis, they actually go up against a straw target—an obsolete stereotype of psychoanalytic practice.

Originally, the psychoanalytic access to interpretation was modeled after dream interpretation—the psychoanalyst was an investigator who must unearth hidden meaning from a text (Haubl and Mertens, *Archäologe* 29). In his early cases, Freud used a quasi-detective technique based on circumstantial evidence, in which he guessed at the hidden origins of a disorder and confronted the patient with his findings. Accordingly, Paul Ricoeur identified Freud as one of the pioneers of a "hermeneutics of suspicion," or as he actually put it, of "interpretation as an exercise in suspicion" (40, my translation), for it involved acts of transgressive revelation by a superior, distanced exegete (Sedgwick 124). Much of psychoanalytic literary criticism—and literary criticism in general—has since followed that model of "suspicious interpretation" (Felski, *Limits* 3).

However, there is enough evidence to support a case against this conceptualization of psychoanalysis. Freud quickly realized that this detective method was not successful ("Beginning" 140). Patients like Dora reacted strongly against the intrusion into their minds and showed him that interpretation is a relational act that must respect the needs of the patient, the subjectivity of the analyst, and the development of their shared relationship (Ermann 26). With regard to this investment of interpretation in the relational process, Freud's remarks on the interpretive techniques of psychoanalysis turn on tactics and tact (Sandler 106; Felman, "Turning" 109). He recognizes that a patient can only accept an interpretation when he is ready for it, and the analytic task thus consists in enabling the patient to draw his own conclusions ("Outline" 178). Freud also seeks to support these interpretations with a safe relationship, so that the patient's attachment to the doctor prevents him from a premature "flight" from analysis ("'Wild' Psycho-Analysis" 226). This fear of the patient's escape, however, signals that even with precautions such as these, interpretation retains an antagonistic component that must be contained in the strategic framework of the therapeutic relationship.

Interpretations that rashly turn the patient's utterances into conclusive interpretations are therefore under suspicion of creating a threatening atmosphere. Ferro believes that they actually increase the patient's paranoia rather than fostering psychic growth. Apparently commenting on the interpretive climate in his treatment, one of Ferro's young patients remarked: "I saw some scientists on television slicing up an egg to see how it was made inside; what a pity that stopped the chick from hatching" (*Psychoanalysis* 39). Ferro reads this story as a comment on the destructiveness of interpretation. He argues for a psychoanalytic technique that will "allow the 'chick' to hatch" (39) by way of so-called "unsaturated" (33) interpretations that participate in the narrative process instead of concluding it prematurely. Ferro's motives are therapeutic—the patient must be given room to develop her story—but they coincide curiously with aesthetic motives, as he justifies his technical preference with "'taste' and respect for creativity" (*Psychoanalysis* 2).

In Ferro's work, we find a conscious turning away from a hermeneutics of suspicion, which has already been suggested in Winnicott's writings (Phillips, *Winnicott* 11). For Winnicott, the analyst is not an examiner of the unconscious of the patient but a host who facilitates the patient's encounter with it: "Psychoanalysis is not just a matter of interpreting the repressed unconscious [but] . . . the provision of a professional setting for trust, in which such work may take place" ("Cure" 114–15). However, Winnicott not only accentuates trust instead of suspicion but also emphasizes the creativity of the patient and his agency in choosing useful interpretations: "A good interpretation in analysis cannot be given to a patient: it can only be found by him to be so ('meaning,' unlike information, cannot be imposed, but only found through personal recognition)" (Phillips, *Winnicott* 115). The analyst's relation to insight is thus destabilized. From an omniscient exegete she is turned into a mediator in a developmental process, and her interpretive power is challenged and restrained to preserve the creativity of the patient (Phillips, *Winnicott* 144; Ogden, *Conversations* 43). Thus, psychoanalysis has not only moved from a hermeneutics of suspicion to a hermeneutics of trust but also to a poetics, which aims not at interpretation but at creative production.

Returning to the allegations against psychoanalytic interpretation, it is remarkable that psychoanalysis, in its own disciplinary development, has already grappled with them. Respect for the Otherness and resistance of the text/patient and acknowledging overdetermination and the infinity of the interpretive process are part and parcel of how psychoanalysts see their work (Rickard and Schweizer 15), and doubt, self-reflection, respect, and openness have become requirements of the analytic stance (Brooks, *Psychoanalysis* 113; Mahler-Bungers 503). The elucidation of past or submerged layers of meaning is no longer the single goal of analysis; it is replaced by an increasing interest in how meaning is created and experienced in the first place (Ogden, "Some Thoughts" 4–5). The field has thus reacted to a critique that is certainly still relevant, given the seductive allure of suspicious interpretation and the hermeneutic power relations established in psychoanalysis as well as literary reading. And while protesting to the contrary does not necessarily make it so, in their efforts to create tactful and interactive modes of psychoanalytic dialogue, psychoanalysts have developed salient models of nonsuspicious interpretation.

Critics who employ the relational analogy are interested precisely in this psychoanalytic history of struggling with the difficulties of interpretation. To make sure that a text and its Otherness are not assimilated in literary interpretation, Schwartz expressly recommends looking toward psychoanalysis: "The psychoanalytic critic must be his own analyst, questioning the quality and sources of his responses" ("Literary Use" 43). Brooks, in turn, finds inspiration in Freud's remark that constructions can only be accepted if the patient reacts to them with new memories and narratives. Freud argues that an interpretation must be confirmed by the patient's behavior. False interpretations do not change anything, whereas a good interpretation helps move the analysis forward ("Constructions" 262). Similarly, Brooks argues that a good literary interpretation moves the text forward:

> Evidently the only confirmation one can have that the narrative has been correctly constructed and construed lies in the *production of more story*.

As readers, for instance, we know that our hypotheses of construal are strong and valuable when they produce in the text previously unperceived networks of relation and significance, finding confirmation in the extension of the narrative web. (*Psychoanalysis* 56–57)

In other words, Brooks seeks to let the text decide whether the meaning that has been imposed on it is valid, thus trying to avoid the charge of hermeneutic violence. But he goes even further. With psychoanalytic interpretation as a specific target, Susan Sontag had demanded that "in place of a hermeneutics we need an erotics of art" ("Against" 14). What she does not recognize is that, with transference, psychoanalysis already possesses an elaborate theory and practice recognizing the "erotics" of the relationship on which interpretation is built. Brooks's emphasis on the desire of the reader or Felman's on the "love-relation" between narrator and addressee, which have been discussed earlier, point specifically toward Sontag's insight that interpretation is not the only relationship we enter in with texts and that even interpretation itself is embedded within a variety of other, quasi-erotic affective dimensions that cannot be controlled or dominated by the critic or returned to a neutral or balanced analytic exchange.

For Brooks, the psychoanalytic model of interpretation is thus an important cue to give the reader a new position in her relationship with the text. She becomes a partner in dialogue, who struggles with the text for the constitution of meaning: "As in most dialogues, the relation of teller and listener is simultaneously one of collaboration and struggle: collaboration toward the creation of the coherent and explanatory text, yet struggle over its interpretation" (Brooks, *Psychoanalysis* 57). Anxieties over interpretive domination or use of force are alleviated because in this relationship, there is "no clear mastery," "no position of privilege, no assurance, indeed, that the analyst and the analysand won't trade places" (58). This dialogical quality of the psychoanalytic method is frequently linked to philosophical hermeneutics (L. Friedman 229; Kartiganer 17; Clarke 61). Indeed, Hans-Georg Gadamer conceives of the task of hermeneutics as entering a dialogue with the text (*In-das-Gesprächkommen mit dem Text*) (374). The metaphor of the dialogue is thus of a twofold potency. It has served psychoanalysts to emphasize the aesthetic dimensions of their work, but it is equally important in literary discourse to emphasize the communicative dimensions of critical practice. However, while Gadamer's dialogue depends on the recognition of its embeddedness in a literary and historical tradition, psychoanalytic literary critics complicate the dynamics of reading even further by arguing that transference and countertransference exert an unconscious influence on the creation of meaning (Holm-Hadulla 217). Thus, a complicated relational structure is interfaced with the dialogue, which often leads to the conclusion that Gadamer's fusion of horizons (*Horizontverschmelzung*), a dialogic consolidation, is impossible, considering the multiplicity of voices that enter the dialogue. By infusing it with psychoanalytic content, the hermeneutic metaphor of the dialogue is thus reinforced but also made more complicated, as asymmetry, resistance, and transference are imported along with a desire for the mutual construction of meaning.

With the modern, interactional strands of psychoanalysis, the relational analogy leans toward understanding the interpretive relationship not as a relation of dominance but of dialogue, even if this dialogue remains mediated and metaphorical and does not necessarily lead to agreement. It supports the assumption that reader and critic may be co-authors of the text in the same way that psychoanalyst and patient are co-authors of the therapeutic narrative (Coen, *Between* 28). Ogden believes that in literature and in the analytic process, meaning is dependent on the encounter of the participants: "[It] is newly created each time, not only in the medium of words, but just as important, in the medium of someone else's words" (*Conversations* 177). One-sided attempts at decoding the text would go against the psychoanalytic method just as they would obstruct any interaction with the text. The relational analogy is thus used to debate a problem area in a shared pool of interpretive methods, which transports the ethical urgency from the therapeutic relationship to the engagement with texts—the responsibility toward an Other in a mutual process of negotiation.

Fabula sana and anti-narrative

The relational analogy is even more strongly charged with ethical implications when the debate turns toward therapy. Here, we confront two different analogical arrangements. The second, which will be discussed in the following section, argues that literature works like therapy—in the experience of being read. The first, which will be my focus now, argues that storytelling in general, and thus writing literary texts in particular, works like therapy. In psychoanalysis, the promise that storytelling will lead to healing is invested with a great deal of hope. Freud himself pointed out that psychoanalysis relies to a certain extent on "the magic of the word" to relieve the patient from suffering (Freud, "Question" 188). He was notoriously suspicious of the supernatural, so this turn of phrase signals something important. The insistence on the therapeutic qualities of the word and the story is itself a kind of incantation, supposed to ward off criticism against the "talking cure"—particularly today when it is simultaneously under threat from behavioral and pharmaceutical treatment methods. "*Mens sana in fabula sana*," is Brooks's reformulation of that incantation: "Mental health is a coherent life story, neurosis is a faulty narrative" (*Psychoanalysis* 49). If that is true, clearly the path to healing must go through the story.

The idea that storytelling is therapeutic is fed by another analogy, which suggests that the self is a story. Influential narrative psychologist Jerome Bruner believes that the self is constructed through biographic narrative processes: "Telling oneself about oneself is like making up a story about who and what we are, what's happened, and why we're doing what we're doing" (64). Since the notion that we might actually consist of a single story has increasingly come under attack—Schafer argues that instead of possessing a unified self, "there is one person telling stories about single selves, multiple selves, fragments of selves, and selves of different sorts" (*Retelling* 51)— Shelley Day Sclater suggests that we should think of the self not as a finished narrative but as a process "in which aspects of the self are created and transformed in relationships with others and within the matrices of culture" (326). The analogy is thus simply modified to encompass a wider range of narrative self-experience, which is actually more amenable to an analogy with therapy because of its processual character. The general analogical assumption remains in place: if the self is a story, then the self may be cured through revised storytelling.

From the association of the sane psyche with a sane story follows the assumption that patients enter therapy with an "insane" story. Therefore, Roy Schafer believes that the analysand comes to analysis as a "defective self-observer as well as defective life-historian" (*Language* 17). The collection of faulty narratives of which the self is made up can, however, be changed with narrative means (Schafer, "Listening" 277). Characterizing the patient's story or storytelling capabilities as defective implies that there are "good" and "bad" ways of telling stories, which would suggest a certain aesthetic normativity at the basis of psychoanalysis. And indeed, many analysts describe their work as a form of bringing order to emotions and relational matrices. In storytelling, the narrator reshapes her experiences and presents them to an audience, thus establishing a link to the past, satisfying wishes retroactively, warding off anxiety, and integrating ruptures in the story of one's life (Boothe, *Patient* 22, 55; Boothe and Wyl 55). In this way, storytelling is supposed to shape experience and assist with self-understanding, identity formation, social integration, psychic restitution and reorganization (Boothe, *Patient* 21, 53–55; Boothe and Wyl 36). The possibility of sharing emotions with others, creating resonance with another person, and experiencing intimacy through storytelling provides consolation and stabilization (Habermas, Meier, and Mukhtar 752; Luif 219–20). Gabriele Lucius-Hoene also emphasizes that through specific aesthetic means, such as plot constructions, performative features, and stylistic choices, patients develop an active, productive, and creative adaptation of their experiences, which helps them regain control and agency in the face of past trauma (144). The emphasis is thus laid on regulating emotions and coping with experience through narratives that are embedded in a relationship.

The potential of storytelling to impose control on personal experiences is one of the principles that takes the analogy from storytelling in general to literary production. As we have seen earlier, Freud speculated that the artistically gifted person can translate her fantasies into art, thus avoiding illness. By implication, then, artistic production substitutes for therapy. And although many critics argue that the absence of therapeutic intent in most literary production renders the comparison invalid (Schwartz, "Literary Use" 40; Schafer, *Retelling* 183), it is still frequently made. Irene Jung, for instance, admits that most artists are neither conscious of their conflicts nor their relation to creativity and that most art is not made with the intention of self-treatment (Jung 71–73). Nevertheless, she is convinced that literary production and therapeutic intervention may possess significant similarities, based on the common practices of scanning, rearranging, and experimenting with personal experiences within a safe space (67–68). In this way, she argues, writing creates new possibilities for experience, facilitates reflection and insight, and provides release without compromising the writer (192). In explicit analogy to the fundamental rule, Jung argues that literary production liberates the writer from the normalized and stereotypical expressions of everyday communication and allows her to realign personal experiences, provided she uses writing not just as a reservoir for unwanted feelings but recuperates them for conscious reflection (192–93, 197). Far from being a general feature of creative activity, the therapeutic qualities of writing are thus introduced by the writer's self-therapeutic intentions.

In an editorial entitled "Writing and Healing" in the influential Medical Humanities journal *Literature and Medicine*, Charles Anderson argues that "healing narratives ... comprise some of our most compelling literary efforts" (xii). Citing studies that show "improved immune responses; decreases in the number of clinic visits; participants' descriptions of improved health," he claims that writing "creates the conditions in which healing may take place" (x). Crucially, Anderson does not believe that writing equals or guarantees healing; instead, physical and mental improvement seems to be an "ambient effect" of literary production, as it allows writers "to represent, to understand, and to integrate experience" (xi). So, is the therapeutic potential of writing created by the writer's own agency or through the side effects of writing? In any case, the analogy clearly does not identify an essential quality of the creative process—and it tends to reduce the act to its psychological components, excluding linguistic, social, or literary factors that play into the creation of a particular work. But there are also other, inherently psychoanalytic considerations that may serve to problematize the analogy.

The implications of this promise of cure/control through narrative have become the target of much criticism. Coetzee doubts that human beings are ever able to become the autonomous authors of their pasts, and he wonders not only whether it is possible to control the story but also whether it is ethically responsible to rewrite it to one's liking: "Do we trust the human imagination as an invariable force for good?" (Coetzee and Kurtz 15). Narratives are certainly not all-powerful, but they are always charged with ideological and mythological content (Clark 3–4). Who, then, determines what "good" and "bad" stories are? The division between oppressive and curative narratives suggests that therapeutic storytelling, as well as the discourse produced around it, may become a normative practice that celebrates certain kinds of storytelling while banning others. For stories to be essentially therapeutic, they would always have to be a "force for good." It follows that therapeutic storytelling would not just be about the control of the storyteller's past but also about the control of the story. If literature were to be an invariable source for healing and self-understanding, it would have to ensure that destructive stories do not get told or are eventually mended by constructive narration, resulting in a sort of therapeutic censorship.

Galen Strawson goes even further by questioning the assumption of a universal narrative self behind such therapeutic projects: "There are deeply non-Narrative people and there are good ways to live that are deeply non-Narrative" (429). Privileging narrative methods in therapy occludes not only that some people do not construct their identity in narrative terms but also that many people may *not* benefit from storytelling: "The Narrative tendency to look for story or narrative coherence in one's life is, in general, a gross hindrance to self-understanding. . . . It's well known that telling and retelling one's past leads to changes, smoothings, enhancements, shifts away from the facts" (447). What Strawson zooms in here, however, is equally problematic. The potential benefits of storytelling cannot be limited to self-understanding, and the "shifts away from the facts" enabled by narrative may indeed be what is valuable about their way of presenting materials of all kinds.

I propose that the tenets of psychoanalytic practice itself may help demythologize the power of narrative. As Sclater has pointed out, psychoanalysis is geared toward questioning narrative constructs in their ability to approach experience and the self. It rests on the insight that the most complex psychological processes, based on physical, intersubjective, and unconscious experience, are actually beyond the access of speech or narrative (318, 324). There is thus no certainty that the "storied selves" emerging in therapy will be liberating; they might just as well turn into a defense against the intolerable, hidden, or threatening aspects of the psyche that psychoanalysis seeks to uncover (318). By exploring not just what the patient says but also what she does not say, the psychoanalytic process tries to get at this unacceptable material with a strategy that is patently nonnarrative—free association. The modes of speech that psychoanalysis privileges and the repetitive and disruptive modes of working through that it recognizes as an inevitable part of the psychoanalyst's work are not geared toward creating synthesis (Freud, "Lines" 161). The fundamental rule and evenly suspended attention are mechanisms supposed to open the conversation through alienation and the complication of ready-made explanations rather than paving the road for a straightforward process of healing. They create a dynamic that dissects and defamiliarizes narratives, questions authorship, and eliminates smooth conclusions. Thus, the goal of psychoanalysis may not be the construction of a story but the interrogation of existing narratives. Phillips believes that the task of the psychoanalyst is not so much to replace a story with a better one but to learn to cope with fragments and anti-narratives: "A psychoanalysis is as much about the making of gaps as about the making of links" (*On Flirtation* 68). The deconstruction of and hole-poking into existing stories is not to be understood as an entirely anti-narrative practice; in fact, it remains an intricate—albeit destructive—work on narratives, often involves a return to a coherent story, and thus confirms the dominance of the narrative mode in psychoanalysis. This commitment to storytelling is not surprising: as the "talking cure," psychoanalysis is built on the analogy with storytelling and conversation from its very outset. To break with that paradigm would be to break with the foundations of psychoanalysis. Nevertheless, it should be acknowledged that psychoanalysis confirms and resists the narrative paradigm at the same time. Narrative work remains essential, but it is not inherently or exclusively powerful or even beneficial. Its simultaneous emphasis on the magic and the precariousness of narrative should at least complicate how we look at the relational analogy, especially if it demands straightforward therapy from storytelling.

The therapeutic promise of art

Narrative therapy employs writing as a central feature of the therapeutic process (White and Epston 84), but reading has also been enlisted as a therapeutic device. Bibliotherapy assigns patients specific books to read that are supposed to help them evaluate and alleviate their suffering (McCulliss 23).

Literature itself is full of readers who benefit from reading books—but of course it is also full of readers who are misled and damaged by reading. Despite a growing trend to use literature therapeutically, critics have voiced doubts about the therapeutic effects of reading. Coen, for instance, suspects that most readers use texts as reservoirs for unwanted feelings rather than as stimulants for creative mastery or the integration of darker aspects of the self (*Between* 183). Certainly, literature is not designed to treat physiological or psychological disorders, but the vivid discourse surrounding the therapeutic effects of reading nonetheless suggests that readers identify a potential in literature that needs to be examined more closely.

In therapeutic variants of the relational analogy, the reader is no longer the analyst of the text—instead, the text becomes the therapist of the reader. Catharsis is one of the oldest concepts in literary history that addresses a transformation of the audience through a work of art. Aristotle's observation of a "*katharsis* of such emotions" through the sentiments evoked by tragedy, "pity and fear" (37), is known to have inspired the cathartic method of Breuer and Freud. They saw the most important function of the narrative in the discharge of emotion and the resulting purgation of burdensome memories and feelings. Later, Freud turned away from the cathartic method and developed psychoanalysis, which is geared toward creating insight into relationships and the self. The therapeutic qualities of psychoanalysis reside in its intent to tap into repressed and unconscious material through transference, work it through, and change the patient's perspective in a dialogic process. Therefore, the analogy does not come to a halt with the cathartic method but turns toward the possibilities for the regulation of emotions, transference experiences, and the space for simulation that therapy and literature provide.

Based on the related analogical assumption that readers establish transference and countertransference relationships with texts, the therapeutic analogy assumes that events and emotions can be reexperienced and reenacted in literature. Skip Dine Young notes that narrative media such as literature and film have a number of psychological effects. They provide entertainment and escape from one's everyday life, help with the regulation of emotions, the stabilization of social bonds, the compensation of loneliness, and the exchange of information (160–61). Even if most of these options sound like a drug treatment—for example, Young describes the regulation of emotions as "'mood management': using media to achieve an optimal level of arousal"— he still believes that there is a possibility for development: "Sometimes the experience of escape can offer a glimpse of other ways of being" (161). When literature is thus enlisted as progressive therapeutic medium that fosters self-development, this potential is most frequently located in the narrative work it enables readers and viewers to engage in. Leonard Jackson, for instance, assumes that narrative allows us to confront our personal histories, even and especially if they involve traumatic experiences:

> It looks as if the human mind is so constructed that it can come to terms with traumatic experiences by rehearsing imaginary prototypes of them. It may well be that that is what literature is for: to enable us to come to terms with traumatic experience in fantasy, before or after we have to cope with the real thing. (60)

Literature is capable of creating a "space for simulation," a "playing field" for fictive action, where one may transgress one's experiences and routines without any real risk (Wellershoff 22, my translation). Or, as Anne Hoffmann argues, "While of course reading cannot be equated to the interpersonal work of analysis, it can nevertheless be compared, in certain respects, to the ongoing exchange of conscious and unconscious thoughts between analysand and analyst. The activity of reading opens up space for the play of a reader's thoughts and associations" (401). Hoffmann's explicit analogy signals that, in all of these therapeutic conceptualizations of reading, the link between therapeutic relationship and literature is established through their common ability to create potential space.

This space for simulation is supposed to play a role in the discovery and development of new narratives. In Young's terms, fictional narratives furnish the reader with additional experiences she would not otherwise be able to make:

> Stories are laboratories that provide lifelike situations in which audiences can test possible reactions. . . . These narrative simulations symbolically prepare us for future challenges, as well as help us understand situations from the past. Because engaging with stories often has an emotional component and involves identification and empathy, it can increase our capacity to empathize with real-life "characters": other people. (162–63)

The encounter with a text also becomes an incentive for individuation, as Marielle Macé and Marlon Jones point out: "an opportunity to test out ways of being, attitudes, rhythms through which books affect, affirm, or disorient readers along with their gestures and tendencies, their ways of perceiving and paying attention" (224). All these theories argue that by providing alternative experiences, reading offers a potential for change; Young's recourse to another metaphor, laboratory, also suggests an experimental element in these experiences.

With all these modes of transformation, critics usually assume that the reader asserts control over the text and uses it for her own needs. In some therapeutic analogies, however, the texts themselves are the agents of therapeutic change. Marshall Alcorn and Mark Bracher claim that literature confronts the reader with new ideas and takes a stance of abstinent opposition toward her, which turns the text into a functional analogue of the psychoanalyst:

> In psychoanalysis the analyst thwarts the patient's attempt to repeat the script of infantile wishes by passively refusing to participate in the script and also, on other occasions, by actively pointing out to the patient the discrepancy between the real analyst and the patient's projection-ridden image of the analyst. Literature, of course, does not offer the expert, individually tailored response provided by the analyst. But literature often, and the teacher of literature perhaps even more often, functions in a general but very effective way to resist and undo the reader's projections and the corresponding introjects from which they derive. (347)

Alcorn and Bracher thus compare the neutral stance of the analyst and her interventions to a literary text, which works as a resistant corrective of the reader's perspective—a conception of the text that is diametrically opposed to the positions discussed earlier, in which the text provided security and a space to learn and experiment. According to Alcorn and Bracher, however, the text has a therapeutic effect not because it offers easily accessible help but because, like the analyst, it irritates assumptions, resists desire, and sometimes remains silent when answers are desperately needed. This, however, would suggest a loss of control on the part of the reader that most analogies try to avoid, as their goal is to return agency to the patient/reader by making use of literature rather than being subjected to its influence. And who is to say that this influence is benevolent?

With the therapeutic analogy, several problems come to the fore. While therapeutic functions may indeed be a part of literary production and reception, trusting the curative potential of literature harbors the danger of reducing art to such "useful" forms of employment. Doubtless, they come with some hope of legitimizing literature and, therewith, literary scholarship. And yet, while it is not even clear whether texts can bring about curative effects based on abreaction, provocation, or the quasi-pharmacological provision of helpful narratives, scholars have already begun to develop normative models to discern "good," which means "therapeutic," literature from nontherapeutic, "bad" literature. Especially if we grant more agency to the text—as an object that may change the reader without her intention—we would have to differentiate between benevolent and dangerous texts if any positive therapeutic aspiration were to be upheld. Value would then be assigned to texts that promote a specific change, and texts or readers that resisted such therapeutic utilization would forfeit their right to participate in the "value of reading" (Galgut 916). In such arguments, the range of what literature may be and may achieve is limited and short-circuited with the therapeutic disciplines. The result is a clear statement about the otherwise slippery "value" of reading and thus a higher utilitarian valorization of literature, but what is lost is precisely what the relational analogy praises literature for—an encounter with the previously unknown and the potentially disturbing.

The transmedial analogy

Focused on general relational processes in literature, the analogy may easily be extended to other arts and media, especially if they have a narrative structure. Thus, and for other reasons that will be analyzed here, the analogy has found a particularly productive response in theater and television studies. Psychoanalytic methods have been widely used in theater and television criticism—an analogy between therapeutic situation and interpretation is always implicit in such psychoanalytic criticism and so similar to its employment in literary scholarship that it does not warrant further analysis. However, with some modifications it has also been applied to the creation of theatrical and television drama and the reception of theater productions and television series—and it is precisely these modifications that will allow us to complicate our appreciation of the analogy in its transmedial employment.

Although Shakespeare was "put on the couch" as early as Freud's *Interpretation of Dreams* and Ernest Jones's *Hamlet* study, providing a famous prototype for the alignment of dramatist and patient, the relational analogy of authorship is difficult to establish in the theater once its performative components are fully appreciated. Psychoanalyzing the playwright on the basis of his text does not take into account, for instance, that many dramatists develop their plays during rehearsals, thus making it impossible to speak of solitary authorship. The production of television series in teams would similarly require an analogy between author team and patient or analyst. However, if we were to assume that the analogy ends here, we would be wrong, for this is exactly how it surfaces. Irvin Yalom, for example, asks the participants of group therapy to think of themselves as co-producers and actors of a film: "If they do not perform, the screen is blank" (*Theory* 119). In reverse, Jenni Konner, executive producer of the HBO series *Girls*, describes the atmosphere in the writing room in therapeutic terms: "You could tell stories in the room that might have made you uncomfortable telling elsewhere. Some said it felt like group therapy" (qtd. in Tomashoff). The actual collaborative and interactive nature of much theater and television work thus surprisingly enhances the possibility of conceiving of the creative work as a therapeutic constellation, but it takes the analogy from the dyadic construct of psychoanalysis to group therapy.

With regard to the relationship between text and audience, the analogy remains virtually unchanged because the decisive structures of the text that are seen as responsible for the experience of transference, such as the implicit author and audience, narrative agents, and textual gaps, have often, albeit with slight variances, been identified in theater and television (Balme 133; Richardson 682; Burgoyne 4; Dablé 221). Nevertheless, the quality of the relationship between an audience and a work of art changes with the way it is presented, and the analogy helps emphasize these changes. A book is received differently from the production of a theater piece or the broadcast of a serial episode. In theater, the audience has a more immediate role and participates in the experience: "Writers and performers can use theatre and performance to process and share their experiences in a manner that resembles the therapeutic encounter. . . . [W]e see how the spectator not only watches theatre, but is often deliberately cast in the role of therapist/listener" (Walsh 61–62). Fintan Walsh sees numerous possibilities for dramatists, actors, and audience members to create a space for the negotiation of emotional experience (47). Similarly, Patrick Campbell argues: "In making the hidden visible, the latent manifest, in laying bare the interior landscape of the mind and its fears and desires through a range of signifying practices, psychoanalytic processes are endemic to the performing arts" (1). The theatrical experience thus lends itself to the relational analogy, in particular with regard to shared mechanisms such as performativity, enactment, interpersonal encounter, and ephemerality. Theater also introduces a further interesting figure into the repertoire of the analogy and the possible relationships established within aesthetic experience—the actor or performer. Peer Arndt readily establishes a comparison between the actor and the therapist: according to him, the actor does not just move between different roles like the analyst, he also has the quasi-analytic assignment—in the terms of Denis Diderot's "Paradox of the Actor"—to reflect emotions without getting affected by them (382, 386). The audience is thus offered therapy by the "neutral" actor. This is where the analogy coincides with the theatrical metaphor in psychoanalytic discourse, highlighting the transformative potential of theater through a staged encounter.

Just like the theater, television is also discussed as a transitional or potential space that allows the audience to experiment, fantasize, and try out identifications (Dewing 215). Occasionally, commentators even note that television and psychoanalysis both use the couch to stop the viewer/patient from moving (Salje 44). The implicit invitation to relax and regress is supposed to open the viewer to the experience of transference, which is often criticized as a form of manipulation, especially in older commentaries. In Gunter Salje's account, for instance, psychoanalysis and watching television depend on participation and interiorized experience, in which analysand and audience are asked to concentrate on hearing and listening and are forbidden from influencing the material through action, creating a characteristic, pseudo-dialogic structure (Salje 39–40). Although the member of the audience is not allowed to speak or associate herself, she is thus often conceptualized as a "pseudo-patient," regardless of whether she sits on a theater seat or on her living room couch. In Salje, the virtuality of the viewer's patienthood is frowned upon—somehow, television is not able to provide "good-enough" therapy in that it seems to educate viewers to accept "wrong" ideas and adopt "wrong" habits; but freed from such normative evaluations, the virtuality of the therapeutic experience that is being read into the televisual and the theatrical experience seems to suggest they harbor specific aesthetic qualities that are somehow related to the psychoanalytic experience.

Thus, the analogy is most commonly used in theater and television criticism when their therapeutic potential is examined in relation to their medial constraints: "Every fictional medium has advantages and disadvantages in the way it can be used as our equipment of living," Young summarizes the problem at stake in these discussions (163). Theater, in particular, has a long tradition of being identified as a therapeutic medium, which has already been discussed in the previous chapter. The idea rests on the possibility of catharsis and transference, and it enables theatrical therapeutic methods, such as psychodrama and drama therapy. Matthias Warstat traces the link between theater and therapy to a kinship between playing, healing, and learning, which has shaped European theater since its origins (535). Accordingly, Arndt argues that theater has a beneficial effect on the audience, by making its members reflect on the similarities between the play and their own lives (385). In modern and postmodern theater, however, the idea that the audience is supposed to be led to catharsis, consolation, and the containment of aggressive impulses is often openly attacked. Whereas the epic theater after Brecht is still linked to techniques of defamiliarization and enlightenment that are also found in psychoanalytic theory,[3] the anti-individualistic postdramatic theater should foreclose any therapeutic perspectives for the audience. However, Elizabeth Wright argues that there is still a similarity: modern theater, according to her, acts as the analyst of the audience by exposing its linguistic and social illusions (186, 188). It seems that theater cannot shirk its therapeutic implications, even if it becomes anti-psychological. The common emphasis on play, performance, audience involvement, and education in the theatrical tradition suggests that the origin of the persistent comparison lies in theater's ability both to reach a number of people in a public setting—which is paradoxically exactly what separates it from the therapeutic encounter but holds the apparently alluring possibility of "mass therapy"—and to offer fictions that, through their performance, gain a playful semi-reality for the audience members that—so the analogy assumes—engages their minds in such an immediate way that it might change them in the process.

Works of art with a serial structure introduce further possibilities of establishing analogies with the similarly structured therapeutic situation of psychoanalysis. Nevertheless, series have often been accused of furthering regressive tendencies. The repetition of constant narrative patterns might provide the substitute gratifications of recognition and consolation and thus foreclose the cultivation of a critical consciousness: "The series in this sense responds to the infantile need of hearing again always the same story, of being consoled by the 'return of the Identical'" (Eco 196). By creating parallels between everyday life and fictional experience, series may distract from, enrich, accompany, and stabilize one's own life (Giesenfeld 11). From this tendency, critics have often deduced a specific addictiveness of the serial (Fröhlich, "Filling In" 214), so that we might assume that series have a sickening rather than a curative effect. Some scholars, however, have seen this very structure of repetition and continuous support as a vehicle for progress. The return of the same situations creates enough safety to confront the challenges of the serial text, and the repeated juxtaposition of everyday and serial world enables the viewers to identify connections with their own lives (Mikos, *Es* 171, 407). Television series offer a variety of behavioral models for the audience to play with, which are variously modified and relativized by differing perspectives within the serial text (Hickethier, "Fernsehserie" 14, 17). The viewer is free to take these behavioral models as a confirmation of his previous opinions, but he can also let himself be irritated by them into questioning his own values, opinions, and behavioral patterns (Prugger 110). Lothar Mikos believes that the main reason for this progressive dynamic is the tendency of serial narratives to initiate transference experience. A wide variety of characters and perspectives creates numerous options for transference, which trigger the repetition of past and present feelings in the audience ("Übertragungserleben" 30). Paul Smith even compares the way in which television series address social questions with the process of working through, which effects a change in the audience through the regular repetition of the same social themes (73). Thanks to the formal analogy with psychoanalysis, series are thus ascribed a number of curative effects. Nevertheless, everything depends on the agency of the audience, who have to allow themselves to get involved in the process of working through or respond to offers for transference. Whether through literature's narrative, theater's performative, and the serial's repetitive structure, the different media's potential to be used as "equipment of living" is thus first and foremost determined by the audience's engagement. Literature, theater, and television have no inherent therapeutic qualities, but their specific features may be put to a variety of "uses" (Felski, *Uses* 135), including but not limited to therapy.

Although at first it might seem as if literature is most suited to an analogy with the analytic situation, a comparison with theater and television shows that they are equally open to the analogy. While literature is most closely related to psychoanalysis in its linguistic basis, the transmedial expansion of the analogy demonstrates that the nodal point of the analogy is not language or speech but the relational structure art shares with psychoanalysis. The affective confrontation with an entity outside of the self—be it author or authorial team, novelistic, theatrical, or serial text, reader, actor, or spectator—initiates a process in which many scholars recognize a similarity with the psychoanalytic process. Thus, with its reference to unconscious components of artistic and therapeutic relationships, the analogy serves to emphasize the pre- and nonverbal in literature and other arts.

Conclusion

In its multifaceted employment in psychoanalytic and poetological discourse, the analogy artist/text ≙ patient and reader/critic ≙ therapist fans out in all directions, creating unexpected links and paradoxes. The artist, sometimes understood as a patient or as an analyst, has a relationship with her work, its parts, and the imaginary audience. In the creative process, she not only treats herself but also offers treatment for others. The text is mute but speaks incessantly; it is apparently engaged in transference even though it does not have a mind; it analyzes readers and is analyzed in turn. The reader, through his (counter)transference, meets the implicit author, the text, or just himself. Even if he gets involved in a therapeutic encounter, the text not only changes him, but he also changes the text. Finally, the analogy also makes life hard for the critic, who should have just been an analytically minded exegete but is now caught up in the transference-countertransference dynamic like the reader. She may try to become the "ideal" reader through self-analysis, but in the end, she always remains entangled in the text.

The analogy's adaptability to all kinds of object relationships and therapeutic dimensions can be accounted for by the dependence of psychoanalysis and art on elastic role allocations but also by the participants' ability to make use of art and its discourses according to their own needs. In a number of encounters between literature and psychoanalysis, critics demand that psychoanalysts learn about literary history and theory before they apply their assumptions, just as literary critics have been cautioned against employing psychoanalytic concepts without studying the actual practice of psychoanalysis (Hutter 83; Ogden and Ogden 3, 59). This emphasizes that psychoanalysts and literary scholars still see their interdisciplinary exchange as insufficiently dialogic. The variability and the contradictory nature of established links and explanations are also tied to the related premises of literary theory—the importance of the author, the description of texts, and the assumed reader's psychology. As the chapter has shown, the analogy flourishes best in a climate created by psychoanalytic criticism, hermeneutics, and reader-response theory, for their interest in the psychology of author and reader provides more points of contact than structuralist or poststructuralist literary theories. The analogies topple over once critics argue from a position that resists the psychological study of author, reader, or even text. Nevertheless, different versions of the analogy have also been discussed by poststructuralist psychoanalytic critics like Felman and Brooks, emphasizing their metaphorical nature while still turning them into emblems of their literary theories. Thus, the resilience of the analogy cannot be explained away with the deficiencies of interdisciplinary or intradisciplinary debate. On the contrary, and more usefully, the great number of relational analogies point to potential impasses in psychoanalytic and literary theory that have as yet remained underdeveloped or excluded from the discourse. They highlight unresolved aesthetic and poetological questions, which seem to call for the analogy as a way of seeking tentative answers. Are there relationships in art, even if potential partners may be imaginary or absent? What is the origin of creativity—health or illness, narcissism or relationality? What are the elements of text, stage, and screen with which the audience establishes a relationship? Are authors and texts dead and mute or alive and interactive? Is the relationship between text and reader governed by dominance or dialogue? And does—or should—art have a therapeutic effect?

The allure of the analogy can also be explained with a common thread that runs through all the arguments examined here. Apparently, we associate relational experiences with artistic processes but lack a proper vocabulary and methods to deal with them. Psychoanalysis, in contrast, has turned the therapeutic relationship into a focal point of its theoretical and methodical attention. After all, patient and analyst have to deal with asymmetric dyads, radical subjectivity, and paradoxality, and they have to steer a confrontation that is based on linguistic exchange but still remains influenced by subliminal relational forces. This includes an understanding of language that recognizes its "ensouled" and embodied qualities. For the psychoanalyst, even written text is always close to spoken language, "closer to something affective and expressive, tied to the body, tied to unconscious impulses, fantasies and internalized healthy and pathological relationships with one's parents, linked with primitive needs to feel loved and to have one's love accepted and valued" (Ogden and Ogden 59). The appreciation of relational and unconscious processes thus stands out as the original contribution psychoanalysis might bring to a discussion of aesthetic relationships. Psychoanalytic theory highlights elements in art that cannot be controlled because they are tied to individual human beings and relationships. If Winnicott's concepts and their persistent reference to transitional experience (as in "*trans*ference" or "*inter*subjectivity") have been particularly prominent in that discussion, it is so perhaps because he cultivates, as Albert Hutter has put it, a "tolerance for paradox" (74), not just respecting but actively seeking to play with the contradictions between presence and absence, subjectivity and objectivity, individual and relationship.

The analogies achieve such a high degree of complexity because they are employed with different epistemological interests and pragmatic goals. Whereas literary critics or media theorists are primarily interested in psychological models for aesthetic experience or in creating new methods, psychoanalysts use the relational analogy (and the comparison with artistic forms and genres discussed in the previous chapter) as a chance for self-reflection and self-justification. And yet, literary and media critics also employ references to the therapeutic dimension of art as a legitimation for their own practices. Since the "science" of psychoanalysis has been called into question, many critics now look to explanatory models drawn from cognitive psychology or sociology. However, recent publications by Benjamin and Thomas Ogden (2013) or J. M. Coetzee and Arabella Kurtz (2015) show that the alliance with psychoanalysis is not necessarily historical or obsolete and that the relational analogy is very much alive. In fact, the continuing link between psychoanalysis and art (criticism) can be explained with their common concentration on subjective understanding as opposed to models of objective science. This subjectivity creates a precarious instability that may seek stabilization through the alliance with another discipline (Schwartz, "Literary Use" 37; Phillips, "Poetry" 1–2). The aesthetic dimension of the psychoanalytic encounter itself, which is so important for psychoanalysts, is, however, hardly ever recognized in these analogies although the space created by transference is a continual point of reference. This missed connection is what makes many models seem one-dimensional; and, more importantly, it shows that the complex entanglement between metaphoric descriptive languages, strategic employments of analogies, and theoretical models in the interdisciplinary borderlands needs further study.

None of the analogies discussed here says anything about how art and therapy "really" are, especially since they concentrate on imaginary object relationships rather than on other factors like language, historical context, or cultural influence. But even if the relational analogy is often employed as a tool to realign the psychoanalytic process, develop a theory of art or new models for interpretation, its inherent metaphoric structure does not allow definitive conclusions. At its best, it opens another as-if space, in which the relationship between art and psychoanalysis can be explored and described imaginatively. In this way, new narratives emerge—about art as a relationship that recognizes the subtle challenges created by subliminal, emotional communicative processes, the demands of desire and aggression, dialogic interaction, and open-ended and endless co-constructions. None of the models discussed in this chapter, however, asks whether artistic texts employ similar analogies, and seldom do they consider their take on the problems formulated here. In what follows, I will try to remedy this oversight by engaging with explorations of the psychoanalytic aesthetic in literary, theatrical, and televisual texts and probing the relational analogy as it emerges in representations of therapy from Philip Roth to *In Treatment*.

Part Three

Reading Relationships: Therapy in Literature, Theater, and Television

5

"I'm Telling Everything": Psychoanalytic Gameplay in Philip Roth's *Portnoy's Complaint*

Introduction: Playing with therapy

"What it adds up to, honey, is *homo ludens!*" Playing, as the author Philip tells his wife in Philip Roth's *Deception* (1990), is the essence of his creative process (184). The writer, or so his argument goes, likes to play with compromising roles and enjoys a sensual engagement with language: "I'm an écouteur—an audiophiliac. I'm a talk fetishist" (42). A literary fascination with play, with dialogue, and with the relationship between speaking and listening, which, in *Deception*, manifests itself in exchanges between lovers, is also what motivates Roth's work with psychoanalysis.

In his autobiography *The Facts* (1988), Roth does not reveal any details from his own long-standing therapeutic experience, but he hints at its artistic significance: "There was my intense psychoanalysis which, undertaken to stitch back together the confidence shredded to bits in my marriage, itself became a model for reckless narrative disclosure of a kind I hadn't learned from Henry James" (137). Thus, it is probably no accident that Roth's first novel *Letting Go* (1962), which is clearly indebted to James, features a scene in which one of the central female characters visits an analyst.[1] The ensuing episode does indeed make use of the psychoanalytic dialogue to create new insights into Libby Hertz's marital difficulties (Scheurer, "Psychopathology" 18). After *Letting Go*, the importance of psychoanalysis for Roth's work increases. In 1963, a certain Dr. Otto Spielvogel makes his debut in the short story "The Psychoanalytic Special." A few years later, he reappears as Alexander Portnoy's analyst in *Portnoy's Complaint* (1969) and also treats Peter Tarnopol in *My Life as a Man* (1974). Although Roth never completed his projected "Spielvogel cycle," a collection of stories on people in psychoanalysis (Searles 171), the ludic treatment of therapy remains a motif in Roth's *oeuvre*, when literature professor Kepesh is guided by his psychoanalyst after his metamorphosis into a female breast in *The Breast* (1972), when the protagonist of *Sabbath's Theater* (1995) just barely escapes a visit to a therapist with the suggestive name Dr. Eugene Graves—"surname unfortunate but gets the job done" (161), or when Philip Roth himself mimes a psychiatrist in *Patrimony* (1991).

Especially with regard to the period after *Portnoy's Complaint* and *The Breast*, Jeffrey Berman has argued that "Roth's comments about psychoanalysis in his later novels are increasingly hostile" ("Revisiting" 107). He cites examples such as the critique of Freudian overinterpretation voiced in *The Anatomy Lesson* (1983) and *Operation Shylock* (1993) as well as the disastrous therapies depicted in *American Pastoral* (1997) and *The Human Stain* (2000). In addition, Berman concludes that Roth never sees psychoanalysis as "a narrative strategy similar to fiction making" ("Revisiting" 106). It is true that Roth frequently launches attacks against therapy, but they remain humorous and playful in tone (Scheurer, "What" 37). And, what is more, they point toward an interest in the aesthetics of psychoanalysis—its language, its capacity for narrative disclosure, and its theatrics—that do not just make it similar to but transform it into the very foundation of fiction making.

However, none of these texts exploits the narrative premises of psychoanalysis as systematically as *Portnoy's Complaint*. The novel consists almost exclusively of Alexander Portnoy's plaintive monologue before his psychoanalyst Otto Spielvogel, whose expressive name—literally "play-bird"—encapsulates the program of Roth's ludic engagement with therapy. The confrontation with the analyst, his unwitting participation in the drama staged by Portnoy, and the engagement with the narrative possibilities of psychoanalysis are reflected in a narrative design in which readers are drawn into Portnoy's "game" and take on the analyst's position. The novel stages the therapeutic encounter as parody, but despite the farce, despite the witty overstatement and inversion of Freudian concepts, psychoanalysis still serves as a formal source of inspiration, as a liberatory narrative device, and as a foundation for a critical text-reader relationship. Thus, I will argue here that Roth's interest in psychoanalysis is not limited to its exploitation as a motif or to a parodistic criticism of its premises. In *Portnoy's Complaint*, instead, psychoanalysis provides the rules for the entire construction of the novel, starting with the therapeutic relationship between Portnoy and Spielvogel. Although the analyst is silent for almost the entire novel—which has often led to his being dismissed as a mere reservoir for Portnoy's monologue—his presence is of profound importance. In fact, the intricate and thorough exploitation of the therapeutic relationship as a source for the novel's aesthetic and theoretical conception is paradigmatic for the corpus of texts I examine in this study. Thus, before I can explore the psychoanalytic aesthetics of *Portnoy's Complaint* and its interactive design, I will first have to turn my attention to the interpersonal dynamics between analysand and psychoanalyst.

Power games: Alexander Portnoy and Dr. Otto Spielvogel

If it weren't for the blurb and the prefacing lexicon entry "Portnoy's Complaint," first-time readers of the novel might not immediately suspect that they have just started perusing a patient's monologue to his therapist. Not until the unexpected "Doctor" during the final cadence of the first chapter is the reader pulled out of the illusion that this could be a straightforward, unframed narrative about the narrator's childhood (*Portnoy* 16). Since the analyst hardly gets a chance to speak and since the entire novel—except for the epigraph and the "Punch Line"—consists of the patient's words, there is no external perspective that might enable us to determine the parameters of this encounter. As the text progresses, we learn that Alexander Portnoy, a 33-year-old lawyer, has been driven into analysis by an acute case of impotence. All other details, however, remain in the dark, including the interior of Spielvogel's office, his therapeutic persuasion, and the function of Portnoy's speech in the course of his analysis. Spielvogel's invitation at the end of the novel, "Now vee may perhaps to begin" (274), could indicate that the actual analysis has not yet started and that Portnoy's monologue has taken place in his mind (Kirchhofer 105); at the same time, the analyst's words could be an intervention after a long week of individual sessions, each clearly marked by a chapter ending (Bettelheim, "Portnoy" 5). The most plausible solution, however, is to interpret the entire novel as a "preliminary experiment," in which the analyst lets the patient tell his story in order to determine if psychoanalysis is a suitable treatment for him (Freud, "Beginning" 124).[2]

In spite of the paucity of information about the analytic setting, *Portnoy's Complaint* depicts a complex therapeutic relationship, which, in essence, rests on Portnoy's projections. The mixture of hypochondriac surveillance and veneration of medicine that shapes the domestic culture Portnoy grows up in determines how he will respond to his doctor. Physicians are highly esteemed; even the word "doctor" is "one of the words they just love," Portnoy remembers (112). That he hardly ever addresses Spielvogel other than as "Doctor" shows how much, despite his mockery, his own way of thinking is steeped in this culture. It induces Portnoy to attribute authority, superior knowledge, as well as almost magical powers to Spielvogel. From the very beginning, Portnoy thus displays the kind of benign transference toward his doctor that Freud describes, "the same attachment to the doctor, the same overvaluation of his qualities, the same absorption in his interests" ("Introductory Lectures" 442). And yet, at least with Portnoy, deference and adulation do not come without a desire to revolt against authority. Accordingly, Spielvogel's name alludes not only to the satirical use of the psychoanalytic framework in the novel but also to Portnoy's treatment of him: Portnoy plays with and for Spielvogel (Kliman 19) and continually struggles with the allure and the provocation that the analyst's position holds for him. Spielvogel's sustained silence exposes him as the apotheosis of Freud's ideal analyst, who mirrors the utterances of the patient but never reveals anything about himself, thus preventing Portnoy from obtaining the resonance he hopes for.

At first, Spielvogel seems like the perfect addressee for Portnoy's "complaint." Finally, he can dump all his anger, despair, and horror on his analyst and whine to his heart's content: "Doctor, these people are incredible! These people are unbelievable!" (36). Dependent on his physician's attention, he incessantly checks Spielvogel's concentration and understanding: "Doctor, do you understand what I was up against?" (33). By asking questions, Portnoy tries to give Spielvogel a share in his stories and integrate him into his memories and fantasies. These repeated attempts to gain reassurance, however, show that Portnoy is aware of his lack of credibility as he presents fantastical, absurd childhood memories or justifies his actions. For this very reason, he has to keep defending himself, such as with the claim "any guilt on my part is *comical!*" (249), and he needs to make Spielvogel trust him: "Spielvogel, believe me" (215). Portnoy supplements this defensive stance with a confessional mode that is supposed to suggest sincerity: "You want to hear everything, okay, I'm telling everything" (133). With these rhetorical maneuvers of staged honesty and intimacy, Portnoy tries to ease his conscience and to tighten the relationship with Spielvogel. His extravagant confessions also give him the opportunity to impress Spielvogel with his unique psyche, for, "With a life like mine, Doctor, who needs dreams?" (165). In order to convince Spielvogel of his brilliance, Portnoy reports miraculous deeds not only of a sexual but also of a humorous and intellectual nature. Thus, Portnoy's appeals to Spielvogel are designed not only to complain but also, as Berman argues, praise himself: "It is obvious from the manic comic tone of the novel that Portnoy hungers not for redemption, as he mistakenly asserts, but for applause and validation" (*Talking Cure* 244).

However, this does not mean that Portnoy does not suffer or that he does not expect true relief from Spielvogel's help. Repeatedly, he badgers his doctor with questions, asks for advice in family matters and for answers about the conundrum of Jewish identity: "Please, who crippled us like this? Who made us so morbid and hysterical and weak? . . . Is this what has come down to me from the pogroms and persecution?" (37). Apparently, Portnoy sees his Jewishness as a part of his illness and analyzes it as a "complaint" or a kind of neurosis;[3] accordingly, psychoanalysis is the proper place to renegotiate the terms of his Jewish identity. Gene Lichtenstein locates *Portnoy's Complaint* within a specific historical context, in which many Jews, assimilated but still alienated in American society, could no longer find a stable foundation for their identity in their religion: "To be sure, in place of a Jewish heritage and a dead past there were substitutes like those twin cultural heroes, Marx and Freud, who had defined the twentieth century for us" (160). As Freud had already used psychoanalysis to explore the roots of Judaism ("Moses and Monotheism"), Portnoy is free to join the ranks and identify and bond with Freud via his proxy, Spielvogel.[4]

Investing all his hope in the power of language, Portnoy's desire to learn the name of his illness is not a trivial request. All the explanations, instructions, designations, and interpretations that he demands from Spielvogel are supposed to ease his pain. For good reason, he always searches for an "essay . . . I can read on that" (216) and "the sentence, the phrase, the *word* that will liberate me" (185). Portnoy follows a medical school of thought to the letter when he believes that the correct diagnosis will yield a solution to his problem. As Michael Balint has shown, knowing the name of an illness can alleviate a patient's anxiety of the "horrors of the unknown" ("Doctor's Therapeutic Function" 1178). However, since words, according to Freud, can work like a "magical act," do "unspeakable good," and "cause terrible wounds" ("Question" 188), the desire for a diagnosis can be explained much more comprehensively. The analyst, who, by virtue of his profession, has a masterful command of this word-magic, possesses enormous power. Portnoy's interest in overcoming his illness with language is closely linked to his desire to take back the magic of linguistic influence from the analyst. Acknowledging Spielvogel's power, Portnoy supplicates him for the salvation of his manhood. Aside from help and healing, he expects benediction, restoration, and liberation:

> Listen, come to my aid, will you—and quick! (111)
>
> Bless me with manhood! Make me brave! Make me strong! Make me *whole!* (37)
>
> Doctor, my doctor, what do you say, LET'S PUT THE ID BACK IN YID! Liberate this nice Jewish boy's libido, will you please? Raise the prices if you have to—I'll pay anything! (124)

While uttering these cries for help, Portnoy seems ready to trust in Spielvogel as his savior and to follow any command: "Just tell me how, and I'll do it" (112).

However, Portnoy's veneration is not as unambiguous as it appears. The jumbled honorific, "Doctor, Your Honor, whatever your name is" (102), just as much as the German address "Herr Doctor" (48) and the submissive "Your Holiness" (134), are not just deferential gestures but ironic attacks on the analyst's superiority. Portnoy tries to renegotiate his relationship with Spielvogel and position himself as the analyst's equal in rank. His ironic treatment of Spielvogel's elevated status in their relationship is just one of many strategies. Several times, Portnoy insinuates that he knows everything about Spielvogel's professional routine: "But this of course you understand, this of course is your bread and your butter" (120). The presumptuousness with which Portnoy pretends to walk in Spielvogel's shoes signals Portnoy's sympathetic identification with the analyst at all levels of experience—therapeutic practice, psychoanalytic knowledge, and shared ethnic background: "Surely, Doctor, we can figure this thing out, two smart Jewish boys like ourselves" (87). Repeatedly, Portnoy uses the first person plural in this way to speak about the therapeutic dyad, "advertiz[ing] his credentials as an insider" (Brauner, "Masturbation" 80). Thus, he tries to resolve the analytic asymmetry, to identify with his analyst, and to distance himself from the role of the "ignorant" patient.

However, Portnoy is not satisfied with putting himself on an equal footing with Spielvogel—he must bring the analyst down a peg. Mostly, when he addresses Spielvogel directly, his rhetorical goal is to put a humorous emphasis on something or sequester the attention of the analyst. Questions like "But do you buy that? Should I?" (200) serve to involve Spielvogel in the narrative. And yet, it is noteworthy how often Portnoy uses the personal address in sentences with obscene or shocking content, as if he were trying to horrify the analyst and drag him into the nethermost regions of his experience. Similarly, his incessant torrent of words serves to overwhelm Spielvogel and to push him, literally, to the edges of the text: "The patient [is] paying homage to His Majesty Spielvogel while at the same time making plans for his own succession to the throne," Berman observes (*Talking Cure* 245). We can thus understand Portnoy's linguistic effusiveness not just as a favor to his analyst but also as an attack designed to abrogate Spielvogel: "Portnoy's transference relationship to Spielvogel suggests the desire to match his Freudian expertise against the analyst's, to compete with him, secure his approval, and ultimately to replace him as an authority" (244).

And yet, conspicuously, Portnoy cannot utter his aggression against Spielvogel directly; he needs surrogates. His relationship with Spielvogel is mirrored in the description of his girlfriend's relationship with her therapist Dr. Morris "Harpo" Frankel: "The Monkey has thrashed around on Harpo's couch, waiting for him to tell her what she must do" (*Portnoy* 156). But Frankel never delivers the redeeming words; he is, like Spielvogel, a "mute bastard" (249) and so reticent that every bodily signal must be elevated to a communicative gesture in order to gain any understanding at all: "Sometimes he coughs, sometimes he grunts, sometimes he belches, once in a while he farts, whether voluntarily or not who knows, though I hold that a fart has to be interpreted as a negative transference reaction on his part" (157). By way of this displaced—transferred—description, Portnoy manages to transmit his aggression while still bonding with the more powerful analyst via his jargon.

His behavior toward Spielvogel is thus shaped by profound ambivalence, which has its roots—as emphasized by the many parallels between family life and therapeutic relationship—in the experiences Portnoy has shared with his parents. The images Portnoy projects on Spielvogel are fantasy products of his childhood. In young Portnoy's experience, the power of his mother is juxtaposed with his father's "obstructed" helplessness: "Her ubiquity and his constipation . . . these, Doctor, are the earliest impressions I have of my parents" (5). Portnoy diagnoses himself with an Oedipus complex, whose potential for conflict is intensified by the fact that his parents do not fulfill their assigned symbolic roles: "If my father had only been my mother! and my mother my father!" (41). In his memories, his mother emerges as both a castrating and a seductive figure; her dogmas, her anxieties, and her relational scripts will continue to determine his life. As a result, Portnoy interprets all his present conflicts as having been predetermined by his family history. Portnoy's relationship with Spielvogel unfolds against the backdrop of this complex family portrait. Characteristically, Portnoy's transference takes place mainly on a linguistic level, starting with the delivery of his speech. With his "strangled high-pitched adolescent voice" (110–11), Portnoy behaves just like a fifteen-year-old rebellious boy toward his analyst. Repeatedly, he addresses his parents during the analysis directly as "Ma, Ma" (125) or "Poppa" (107), but he also speaks *for* them: "YOU MUST LISTEN TO WHAT WE ARE SAYING AND WITHOUT THE SCOWL, THANK YOU, AND THE BRILLIANT BACK TALK!" (188). In this way, the Portnoy family constellation is transferred to analysis from two different perspectives, child and adult, and Spielvogel, as addressee, is alternately asked to take on the roles of the son and the parents. In this manner, the novel emphasizes Portnoy's transference, prompting us to identify similarities between Portnoy's behavior toward Spielvogel and toward his parents. But as obvious as these intersecting family parallels are to the reader, Portnoy remains blind to them. His textbook Freudian reconstruction of the past prevents him from noticing what happens in the analytic present.

Within Portnoy's monologue, Sigmund Freud gradually emerges as another figure that helps him process his conflicts. In his treatment of psychoanalytic theory and in his relationship with its pioneer, Portnoy gains an additional battlefield to spar with Spielvogel, duplicating his transference. Reading Freud, Portnoy acts as exuberantly, effusively, and corrosively as in talking to Spielvogel: "I have bought a set of the *Collected Papers*, and since my return from Europe, have been putting myself to sleep each night in the solitary confinement of my womanless bed with a volume of Freud in my hand" (185). His reading list includes *Civilization and Its Discontents*, "The Most Prevalent Form of Degradation in Erotic Life," from the *Contributions to a Psychology of Love*, and *Leonardo da Vinci and a Memory of His Childhood*. At once, Portnoy tries to interpret his problems with women with the aid of Freud's theories: "In language plain and simple, are Alexander Portnoy's sensual feelings fixated to his incestuous fantasies?" (186). Expertly splitting his ego and analyzing himself in the third person, Portnoy succeeds in becoming both interpreted object and Freudian analyst. Thus, he effects the desired role-reversal: taking Spielvogel's place and behaving as if he cannot expect a correct diagnosis from Spielvogel (Brauner, "Masturbation" 80), he fulfills the function of the omniscient physician himself. His interpretations reference Freud's work; but since he keeps trailing off into parody with his appropriation of psychoanalytic terminology, the effect is a challenge to psychoanalysis and hence to Portnoy's own analytic endeavor. When he boasts, "I am marked like a road map from head to toe with my repressions" (124), this is not just a testament to his penchant for humorous exaggeration but also a paradoxical inversion of psychoanalytic theory: repressions as inherently unconscious operations cannot be read like a map; they cannot be read at all unless they manifest as symptoms. Here, as in the self-defeating competitiveness of the call, "Let's see somebody beat that, for acting out!" (257–58), Portnoy's interpretive exuberance actually serves to subvert the analysis. Comedic and psychoanalytic maneuvers thus supplement each other, as Sam Girgus argues: "Each challenges the other's assumptions, so the humor subverts the absolute authority of psychoanalysis, while psychoanalysis exposes the potential of a hidden dimension of secret meaning to humor" (121–22). There is a constant tension between two tendencies, "to treat psychoanalysis comically, and to treat comedy psychoanalytically" (Brauner, "Masturbation" 76): humorously, the text turns against psychoanalysis and simultaneously exposes its own comical and critical stance as a resistance against deeper analysis.

This playful yet subversive engagement with psychoanalysis suggests that Portnoy uses Freud to assuage his desires in several ways. At first, his manic interpretations show that he is eager to be dazzled by Freud and to accept him as a new authority (Berman, *Talking Cure* 243–44). Accordingly, Portnoy seeks an alliance with Freud and identifies with the revered primordial psychoanalyst through a deeply felt sympathy with his tenets—"Oh, Freud, do I know!" (103)—and through a connection that he establishes with Freud's analysis of Leonardo da Vinci: "I have read Freud on Leonardo, Doctor, and pardon the hubris, but my fantasies exactly" (121). In this way, Portnoy enters an imaginary dialogue with Freud, which allows him to see himself as a part of the analytic community. However, his reading practice is extremely selective. When he cites the vulture episode in Freud's Leonardo essay, Portnoy only remembers the image of the oppressive mother, whereas he completely ignores Freud's conclusions about da Vinci's latent homosexuality: they would cast further doubt on his already compromised masculinity.

Instead, Freud is used to confirm Portnoy's potency. To expose himself not just as a precedent but as an outlier of psychoanalytic theory is an important strategy to assert his uniqueness: "Doctor, my psyche, it's about as difficult to understand as a grade-school primer! Who needs dreams, I ask you? Who needs *Freud*?" (*Portnoy* 180). In Portnoy, psychoanalytic assumptions manifest themselves so clearly that they become redundant. He is haunted by this idea because of its potential for self-affirmation: Portnoy's insight into his exceptionality accentuates his abilities as an interpreter, putting him on a pedestal with Freud, who also analyzed himself. In addition, it gives Portnoy the satisfaction of possessing an extraordinary psyche that elevates him above the interpretive competence of Spielvogel and Freud, thus condemning them to uselessness.[5] Portnoy's ambivalent engagement with psychoanalysis culminates in his proclivity to masturbate with Freud: "Sometimes Freud in hand, sometimes Alex in hand, frequently both," Portnoy describes his nightly routine (185). And indeed, Portnoy uses psychoanalysis for humorous play, for self-confirmation and self-justification, turning it into a form of intellectual masturbation. Freud, like Spielvogel, has become an "erotic plaything," a "'playbird' to be stroked, serenaded, seduced" (Berman, *Talking Cure* 243). This application of Freud in the service of the self and its satisfaction ultimately subverts his authority: "There is no better image to upset the Freudian apple-cart than that of using Freud's own writing as a phantom penis" (Schehr 225).

Portnoy's wishes and needs determine his exploitation of psychoanalysis, Freud, and his own therapist. At the end of the novel, he has not yet consulted Spielvogel, having only repeated what he knows already. As a silent analyst,

Spielvogel seems to adhere to the Freudian school, to privilege neutrality and abstinence instead of interaction,[6] but in his last sentence, he confronts Portnoy with a new perspective: only now that all has already been said can the real work begin, work that is not exhausted with Portnoy's self-circular movements but that will have to process Spielvogel's intervention.

The fundamental rules of the game: Portnoy's psychoanalytic aesthetics

The silence of the therapist notwithstanding, the psychoanalytic setting penetrates every utterance of Roth's loquacious patient. According to Grebstein, Portnoy displays "the rhetoric of neurosis": "The incredible rapidity and intensity of the language attempt to re-create the reality of hysteria, as the patient relives in his reminiscences those traumas responsible for his present condition" (160). However, the style of the novel does not exclusively depend on Portnoy's neurosis, even if it can be demonstrated that what seems like aesthetic failings, such as "brief, flashy, formulaic [scenes and characters]" (Eiland 261), may actually be read as a consequence of Portnoy's disorder.[7] More importantly, though, Portnoy's attempt at mastering his situation linguistically points to a therapeutic self-experiment: Portnoy "plays with words . . . trying to get them to liberate him from his compulsions, trying to come to some understanding of the meaning of his complaint" (Forrey 69). Thus, the therapeutic relationship and the psychoanalytic situation constitute the starting point from which this particular work with and on language is executed in *Portnoy's Complaint*.

The fundamental rule of free association becomes the foundation for the thematic and stylistic direction of the novel. The format of psychoanalysis not only allows but also demands that the patient tell his own story, with as much freedom, openness, and idiosyncrasy as possible. This liberation through psychoanalytic commandments—"The rule here is that there are no rules," Bernard Avishai summarizes the fundamental rule in the context of *Portnoy's Complaint* (45)—permits Roth to address Portnoy's specific complaints. He recalls:

> What I wanted was the appropriate vessel for the unpalatable stuff that I was ready to dispense. And I found it, I thought, in the *idea* of the psychoanalytic session, wherein pile driving right on through the barriers of good taste and discretion is considered central to the task at hand. In *Portnoy's Complaint* I did not set out to write a book "about" an analysis,

but utilized the permissive conventions of the patient-analyst situation to get at material that had previously been inaccessible to me, and that in another fictional environment would have struck me as pornographic, exhibitionistic, and nothing *but* obscene. (*Reading* 82–83)

In some of his teaching notes, he adds:

> In psychoanal. nothing is too petty, nothing is too grand. The place where you're allowed to say anything. Allows for hatred, aggression, pettiness; *nothing censored.* If that's the bargain, that's the bargain. Coarse realism. Any type of exaggeration is permissible. *It* takes the liberties for you. (qtd. in Avishai 14–15)[8]

In the late 1960s, freedom of personal and literary expression could not yet be taken for granted. Roth once described his role in the battle for liberation with drastic self-mockery:

> I sometimes think of my generation of men as the first wave of determined D-Day invaders, over whose bloody, wounded carcasses the flower children subsequently stepped ashore to advance triumphantly toward that libidinous Paris we had dreamed of liberating as we inched inland on our bellies, firing into the dark. "Daddy," the youngsters ask, "what did you do in the war?" I humbly submit they could do worse than read *Portnoy's Complaint* to find out. (*Reading* 8)

Claudia Roth Pierpont, however, confirms the impression the novel made on its readership:

> *Portnoy's Complaint* was one of the signal subversive acts of a subversive age. The excitement surrounding its publication was so high that even before its appearance, in February 1969, *Life* magazine pronounced it "a major event in American culture." Along with rock concerts and protest marches—with which it seemed to have more in common than with other books—it spoke to the generation-wide rejection of long unquestioned and nonsensical rules, to the repudiation of powerful authorities, and to the larger struggle for personal and political freedom. (53)

To translate this liberatory impulse into literary form, Roth turned to the mold of psychoanalysis.

It is not just the freedom of the psychoanalytic setting, however, that excites Roth. While the patient is free to say anything, he is also *expected* to address certain things, topics that could hardly be mentioned in other situations, such as "intimate, shameful sexual detail" and "hatred and rage" (Roth, *Reading* 82, 131). In addition, in therapeutic reports from the inner regions of the psyche, fantasy and reality are not strictly separated from each other, and thus Portnoy's excursions into the imagined and the grotesque merge seamlessly with the rest of his analysis. His uneven oscillation between reality and fantasy matches perfectly with the transferential mode, the "as-if" of the psychoanalytic setting. Psychoanalysis permits the expression of these emotions and experiences as well as the language and the stylistic registers that go with them: the obscene, the pornographic, the tirade, the excess, and the dream. While these patterns are still considered inappropriate as formal devices or violate socially accepted norms in other contexts, such as everyday conversation, the psychoanalytic situation incorporates them as an important part of communication, seeking to make the unspeakable accessible. This allows Roth to elevate the obscene to the level of a subject fit for literary adaptation (*Reading* 17). It becomes an intentional irritant in the text transmitting important information about Portnoy's psyche and the therapeutic relationship: "This is a man speaking out of an overwhelming obsession: he is obscene because he wants to be saved" (16). Marvin Feldman affirms that the use of obscene language in psychoanalysis can unlock new emotional regions and repressed material (46). In a similar manner, it enables Roth to address character traits in Portnoy that could have never been expressed as vividly if obscenity had remained banned from the text. And without the possibility to use uncensored language, the issues that are attached to it and slowly gain critical recognition in the late 1960s—aggressive masculinity, sexuality and its ties to identity, history, and culture—would also remain excluded from the novel. Now, psychoanalysis allows Roth not just to address these issues but also to circumvent the reader's moralistic resistance: "To judge—or judge prematurely—would not be in the culture of psychoanalysis. No other literary premise gives us what is so coarse about people yet leaves us so unable to distance ourselves from them," Avishai remarks (54). Allowing Portnoy to speak and readers to "listen," this literary premise is what makes their mutual engagement with sexuality and obscenity possible.

As the liberal use of obscene language indicates, the form of the fundamental rule also provides Roth with the opportunity to develop a style inspired by spontaneous colloquial speech. Repetitions, stammering, fragmented sentences, and the purposeful use of Yiddish words underline the oral character of the text, which also has a dramatic quality because Portnoy continuously—"quote unquote" (106)—echoes the speech of others, anticipates Spielvogel's reactions, or dialogizes with himself. However, Roth's aspiration is not to give a faithful transcript of the speech of a real patient in therapy but to create an enthralling mixture of oral and literary style: "I've been attracted to prose that has the turns, vibrations, intonations, and cadences, the spontaneity and ease, of spoken language, at the same time that it is solidly grounded on the page, weighted with the irony, precision, and ambiguity associated with a more traditional literary rhetoric" (Roth, *Reading* 13). As Patricia Meyer Spacks has demonstrated, Portnoy's monologue is a productive "illusion of the extemporaneous," which confronts readers with a literary version of colloquial speech: "The calculated rhythms and ironies, the tonal mixture of nostalgia, affection, amusement, even the punctuation— all suggest the formalities of written rather than oral communication" (630–31). Expressive punctuation and typography, capitalization, italics, and an abundance of exclamation and question marks, which, paradoxically, invest Portnoy's monologue with the emotionality and the exuberance of the spoken word, emphasize this rootedness of Roth's language on the page. The restless graphic impression of the text makes Portnoy's provocation visible on the very surface of language (Gebauer 235). The same could be said of his numerous literary allusions, like "I am the Raskolnikov of jerking off" (*Portnoy* 20). While references to Dostoevsky's *Crime and Punishment* would usually substantiate a text's claim to literariness and self-reflexive intertextuality, Portnoy often juxtaposes such allusions with chatty accounts of sexual practices, destabilizing the relationship between orality and literariness along with the sublimity of the quoted texts.

In a similar manner, psychoanalytic discourse is confirmed and simultaneously destabilized through Portnoy's rant. Freud's language is scattered throughout the entire monologue, both directly, through his terminology, and indirectly, through allusions.[9] Although it is not surprising that an analysand who has dabbled in psychoanalytic theory uses its vocabulary, it is noteworthy that Roth employs the language of psychoanalysis, once again, in a highly stylized manner: "I would guess that it bears about as much resemblance to the drift and tone of what a real psychopathologist hears in his everyday life as a love sonnet does to the iambs and dactyls that lovers whisper into one another's ears in motel rooms and over the phone" (Roth, *Reading* 82). Just as the novel oscillates between oral and literary language, it oscillates between psychoanalytic and literary jargon. Freud and his language provide a continuous ludic subtext to Portnoy's speech. As a result, however, Portnoy does not so much become an object of psychoanalysis as he turns psychoanalysis into his own object for play. Thus, he reinforces his own analytic aspirations only to debunk them, for "he continually vacillates between adopting—and implicitly endorsing—its discourse, and undermining and rejecting it." Overall, this mixture of linguistic levels, "of formal and informal registers, psychoanalytic terminology and demotic exclamation" (Brauner, "Masturbation" 79) gives us an impression of Portnoy's exuberance and his complaints, exemplifying that language and the act of complaining are part of his problem, but it also creates a maelstrom of interpretation, in which Portnoy's various discourses begin to challenge each other.

* * *

Although Portnoy's language appears to be too chiseled and his narrative too well-structured to produce speech akin to free association—the chapter headings alone destroy the illusion that *Portnoy's Complaint* could be the unedited transcript of a psychoanalytic session—the construction of the novel is clearly inspired by this psychoanalytic technique. Roth describes elements of the text as "'blocks of consciousness,' chunks of material of varying shapes and sizes piled atop one another and held together by association rather than chronology" (*Reading* 13). Analogous to the associative structure of the fundamental rule, Portnoy tracks his story not in an orderly fashion but inspired by the vagaries of his imagination. As a consequence, the related events often fit together thematically but not chronologically, they are repeated, expanded, or changed, and Portnoy gets lost in detail or goes too far afield.[10] He struggles through his narrative by means of "amplifications": "The tension generated by these experiences grows as they are described in terms that are increasingly funny and extravagant" (Michel 7). In this way, Portnoy delves into his experiences through storytelling (Grebstein 160), following the progress of his analysis. Therapy is not terminated after a problem has first been discovered; rather, it begins when everything has already been said, when language and thought have been set free by ruminative reflection to take on new meanings and build new connections.

Without regard for chronology, through a myriad of flashbacks and flashforwards, leaps, excursions, digressions, and ellipses, Portnoy nevertheless manages to trace his development from earliest infancy to the episode in Israel that has driven him into therapy. The immediate presence of the session is never spoken of, but it can be sensed at any moment. In its quasi-transferential double structure, the narrative simultaneously reviews the past as it reflects the present. Searching for the origins of his complaint, Portnoy resembles the oft-conjured Oedipus in his attempt to construct an investigative, analytic narrative that sheds light on and solves present conflicts. However, like Oedipus, Portnoy encounters failure in his success: while he manages to lay bare all fragments of his past, he still does not achieve catharsis. The "Punch Line" at the end of the book makes us suspect that Portnoy is too successful as his own psychoanalyst, failing to take into account the interaction with his therapist and his interpretive influence. His self-analysis remains plausible, as David Gooblar has shown, because Roth banks on the widespread cultural knowledge about psychoanalysis in his readership and because Portnoy's conflicts play out visibly on the surface of his experience (70–71). However, if nothing is hidden, then there is nothing to dig out; investigative work and narrative analysis are reduced to absurdity through the overabundance and overavailability of material for analysis. As long as the identification with Oedipus furnishes Portnoy only with another means of resistance, he cannot achieve therapeutic release: instead of a transformative process all that is depicted in the novel is "a stasis, a condition which is barely open to modification" (Kirchhofer 95). Accordingly, the analytic plot is subverted. Reading the novel from the first to the last page, a reader first encounters the conclusive diagnosis and the scientific utilization of Portnoy's case by Spielvogel, then partakes in Portnoy's experience as a patient, and concludes with Spielvogel's suggestion to begin. The correct sequence of psychoanalysis as we might expect it, from a clearly delineated beginning of the treatment through an estimation of the patient's complaints to proper therapy, is completely turned on its head by this "full-scale comical counteranalysis" (Roth, *Facts* 156). Since the reader already knows about Portnoy's condition before first encountering his voice, the tendency to interpret Portnoy independently is undermined and replaced by a strong suggestion to read Portnoy's characterization throughout with the help of Spielvogel's diagnosis. However, this diagnosis appears no less manufactured than Portnoy's attempt to arrange the narrative as a version of the psychoanalytic Oedipal myth of disclosure. Thus, Portnoy's narrative appears as a fiction that is being constructed from all sides rather than, as Portnoy wants it to be read, as a story that has been found and "reconstructed."

* * *

Even if Spielvogel's presence may seem immaterial at first, it becomes essential for the reversal of our perception of Portnoy's constructions. Portnoy's discourse, in fact, cannot function without Spielvogel. As an autodiegetic, autoanalytic narrator with Spielvogel as his constant but silent addressee, Portnoy may take his own medical history and provide several diagnoses. But despite the apparent absence of Spielvogel and the similarity of Portnoy's language to free association, the resulting discourse is still different from an interior monologue or a stream of consciousness—for Portnoy clearly talks to an external addressee. Therefore, Berman compares his speech to "the dramatic monologue" in theater (*Talking Cure* 248). However, it remains doubtful if the text is a monologue at all, even if most critics emphasize Portnoy's self-referentiality: Siri Hustvedt describes the analyst in *Portnoy's Complaint* as "a remote, hidden being, not a *you* for the narrative" ("Analyst" 227–28). Anton Kirchhofer even believes that the constant asides to Spielvogel render him superfluous: "The patient can supplement his presence by simulating the therapeutic (communicative) situation and analysing himself" (107–08). And Lilian Furst recognizes Spielvogel's importance as a "pronounced presence" in the monologue, but only as a contextual device, producing "reminders of the therapeutic context of his verbosity" (*Just* 62). As my analysis of the therapeutic relationship has shown, however, Spielvogel does not just represent the psychoanalytic situation; he also serves as an antagonist to Portnoy's fantasies and as an object of his transference. Thus, Spielvogel is not superfluous at all; instead, his presence transforms the monologue of the patient into a dialogue directed toward a listener. Portnoy's narrative is completely infused with his transference, which causes him to involve Spielvogel or, through him, his parents, into his narrative. The repetition of this mechanism in Portnoy's relationship to Freud emphasizes that transference does not distinguish between real and textual entities. If both Freud and Spielvogel are made present in their absence, Portnoy's speech conforms to what Bakhtin has described as hidden dialogicity, conferencing with the absent presence that André Green has also identified as a feature of the psychoanalyst (282).

Spielvogel, however, is not just a point of contact but actively transforms our interpretation of Portnoy's rant. Debra Shostak believes that Roth relies on a Bakhtinian dialogical method in his writing: "He refuses to imagine such positions in binary terms, which might allow one perspective to gain interpretive privilege over another" (6). Fittingly, Avishai describes Portnoy as "a voice that cannot mock others without first mocking itself" (14). As much as Portnoy struggles for control, his torrent of words seems to develop a life of its own that repeatedly challenges his position. Portnoy knows that his memory is unreliable. Defensive protestations like "I swear to you, this is not bullshit or a screen memory" (97) only testify to Portnoy's own doubts. He realizes that the appraisal of a seemingly innocent situation can change completely in retrospect when "it suddenly occurs to [him]" (83) that his father could have had an affair with a colleague. In consequence, moral assessment and the creation of meaning take place in the aftermath of events. And if that wasn't enough, Portnoy's memory is not even capable of solving the simple question whether a family argument broke out because of his father's hypothetical adultery or because of a pudding theft committed by little Portnoy. Father and son merge imaginatively in his attempt to reconstruct the situation: "But *is* that me—or my father hollering out his defense before the jury?" (87). Memory and imagination are clearly co-dependent in Portnoy's constructions, and suggestions like, "Skip the fight. It's boring" (141), further underline Portnoy's unreliability and his conscious manipulation of events.

So even though Portnoy's voice dominates the novel, his point of view is challenged again and again. Roth was reproached for failing to confront Portnoy with a different perspective, thus purportedly using him as a mouthpiece to steer the reader's opinion (Howe 240). Through openly flaunted manipulations, distorted vision, and memory gaps, however, Portnoy himself undermines his credibility. In addition, the therapeutic situation emphasizes our consciousness of the unreliability of the narrator since his resistance, his fantasy constructions, and his screen memories are pointed out in the narrative. Brauner is correct when he counters that "although . . . other voices are mediated through [Portnoy's], they are audible nonetheless" ("Getting" 52). This includes Spielvogel's perspective, as briefly as it appears, and the voices of other characters, who, though distorted and discounted by Portnoy, still make themselves heard. With the psychoanalytic background in particular, we must proceed from the assumption that the patient never speaks with a single voice but articulates a myriad of contradictory views and opinions.

This is confirmed by Spielvogel's "Punch Line." Although his last statement may emphasize his previous absence, Shostak believes that the sentence destabilizes and thus transforms the entire narrative in retrospect: "Readers oscillate in the last moment between trusting and disbelieving all that has come before" (83–84). Thus, it functions like a psychoanalytic interpretation, by dialogically undercutting the perception of a narrative that readers had thought they had already understood.

Role-play in Spielvogel's Chair: Analysis as creative process

This critical distance to Portnoy is essential because he was often wrongly seen as Roth's, from the author barely distinguishable, alter ego.[11] As "teller of his own story, creator—or re-creator—of his own myth" (Spacks 628) and as producer of the given text, Portnoy can be read as an author figure. However, the connections between psychoanalysis, author, and character are too convoluted to allow for an interpretation of the novel as a simple "confessional" (Roth, *Reading* 100).

In spite of his obvious symptoms, Portnoy's narrative voice is conditioned less by his neurosis than by his patienthood. His "artistic" production—the analytic narrative—does not result from his illness but from its treatment; it is not just a further symptom but rather a consequence of the analytic process. In this context, Roth's statements about his creative process are very instructive:

> If I hadn't been analyzed I wouldn't have written *Portnoy's Complaint* as I wrote it. . . . The experience of psychoanalysis was probably more useful to me as a writer than as a neurotic, although there may be a false distinction there. It's an experience . . . that . . . is tremendously important for [the writer], providing that afterwards he can separate himself enough to examine the experience objectively, imaginatively, in the writing clinic. You have to be able to become your doctor's doctor, even if only to write about patienthood. (*Reading* 128)

Crucially, Roth does not praise psychoanalysis because of its thematic potential or because it helped him work through his own conflicts; instead, he stresses its importance for developing an artistic form and mobilizing the writing process, which demands analytic distance and imagination. *Portnoy's Complaint* is precisely not "a book 'about' an analysis" (*Reading* 83), but a text that is formally "trained" in psychoanalysis, that exploits its material and uses its creative potential in order to dissect a character, generate comedy, and play with roles.

If Portnoy has anything to do with Roth, he is used not for the purposes of confession but for masquerade. Roth claims that the novel is embedded "in parody, burlesque, slapstick, ridicule, insult, invective, lampoon, wisecrack, in nonsense, in levity, in *play*" (*Reading* 28). For him, the creative process is exciting when it allows him to exploit the interplay of autobiography and fiction:

> To act a character. To pass oneself off as what one is not. *To pretend*. The sly and cunning masquerade. Think of the ventriloquist. . . . His art consists of being present and absent; he's most himself by simultaneously being someone else, neither of whom he "is" once the curtain is down. You don't necessarily, as a writer, have to abandon your biography completely to engage in an act of impersonation. It may be more intriguing when you don't. You distort it, caricature it, parody it, you torture and subvert it, you exploit it—all to give the biography that dimension that will excite your verbal life. (*Reading* 123–24)

In psychoanalysis, an autobiographical play with new actors and a changing plot is produced through transference. The simultaneous presence and absence of the analyst, which turns her into a surface for transference projections, shows striking parallels to the way in which Roth wants to make himself available as a masked artist and ventriloquist. The analyst is similarly asked to speak for someone else, the patient and his internal objects, but she is also obliged to question and uncover the patient's masks. Roth suggests that in his creative process the (analytic) role-playing is concentrated in one person, the author, who distorts elements of his own experience, transfers them to an alter ego, and subjects them, right there, to a self-reflexive interrogation that goes beyond self-analysis: playfully, it increases the aesthetic allure of character and linguistic form.[12]

Although Roth is often critical of psychoanalysis in his novels, Berman's claim that Roth does not regard psychoanalysis as a narrative strategy ("Revisiting" 106) is thus inaccurate. On the contrary, inasmuch as Portnoy performs as his own analyst, stages role-plays, and, at the same time, serves as a mask for the author, in a novel that turns the formal guidelines of the fundamental rule into a rule of artistic production, psychoanalysis turns out to be a comprehensive model of Roth's creative process. I agree with Gooblar: "Roth sees in the psychoanalytic process, in its inherent potential for storytelling, a ready-made structure to be exploited for its literary possibilities" (69). And yet, Roth does much more than employ psychoanalytic introspection as a catalyst for the writing process. Many additional factors play into the artistic composition of *Portnoy's Complaint*: the formal rules of psychoanalysis, its asymmetrical dialogicity, and the room it provides to explore thematic and linguistic depths and to play with discourses, roles, and the boundary between fact and fiction. That is why Portnoy never achieves a cathartic conclusion to his narrative. He is too fascinated with his own eloquence and the puzzle presented by the Freudian paradigms to want to terminate the analysis. Similarly, Roth is not concerned with the result of psychoanalysis; he is simply not interested in its therapeutic possibilities and he does not see storytelling as a therapeutic agent. Instead, he is fascinated by therapy as a creative process in its own right.

* * *

For Spielvogel, Portnoy is not just the author of a specific text; he is himself the text that is to be read and interpreted by the analyst. As Portnoy's speech presupposes an addressee, and with Spielvogel not speaking until his "Punch Line," *Portnoy's Complaint* automatically puts the reader into the position of the analyst: "His common recourse to 'you' denotes us, the interlocutors extraneous to the text as well as Spielvogel, the recipient within the text" (Furst, *Just* 63–64). Portnoy's speech is a performance of what Roth himself compares with confession and theater: "Much like the priest discreetly hidden away in the confessional (or the audience beyond the footlights), Spielvogel is silent until the last mortifying detail (or routine) has been extracted from the babbling sinner/showman seeking absolution/applause" (*Reading* 82). The reader listens to the same monologue as Spielvogel, is exposed to the same demands, and is courted and abused with the same rhetorical strategies. The appearance of oral storytelling and the consistent psychoanalytic theme also go a long way in keeping up the illusion of being present at an analytic session. In *Portnoy's Complaint*, the relational analogy between therapeutic and narrative situation is thus put into effect in the process of reading: the patient tells his story while the reader is asked to "listen."

The novel offers the analyst's chair, in which Spielvogel is supposed to reside, to the readers, assigning them a fixed place in the reader-text relationship. Thus, they become the immediate object of Portnoy's transference, which he pours onto the analyst with his rhetorical gestures. Like Spielvogel, readers have to expose themselves to the provocation implied in Portnoy's obscenity, misogyny, and misanthropy, or they may succumb to the seductions of his wit, his intelligence, and his flattery. If they read the novel to its end, Portnoy may have ensnared them, but in the course of reading, they will have suffered through his verbal attacks, his corrosive commentary, and the overabundance of material with which he assails his analyst. And like Spielvogel, they have to come to terms with the fact that they are pushed to the sidelines and overfed with interpretations by a character although, as readers, they should be superior to him and form their own opinions. Thus, apart from the fictional transference of the patient Portnoy, readers are also subjected to the structural transference of the novel. Whereas in an analytic context, transference involves a patient treating an analyst as if he were a person from his past, *Portnoy's Complaint* stages a reversal of this mechanism, in which, for most of the reading experience, the novel treats its readers as if they were analysts. The text plays with its readers, which is drastically brought home to them when Spielvogel's "Punch Line" unexpectedly "kicks" them out of the analyst's chair.

Even earlier, readers are of course free to engage with this role-playing, Portnoy's attacks, and the structural transference of the text—or not. It is, however, evident that *Portnoy's Complaint* almost always elicits strong emotional reactions, and, as Berman notes, "nowhere is the reader's troubled relationship with Portnoy better demonstrated than by the enormous controversy the novel has generated" (*Talking Cure* 249). Avishai claims: "Most people I have asked remember where they were when they read *Portnoy's Complaint*, something like when President Kennedy was shot.... Reading Philip Roth's yellow-clad book felt like the end of innocence" (1).

Avishai thus tries to capture the extraordinary, liberating impact Portnoy's provocation had on his generation. "Readers who were not frightened or shamed by *Portnoy's Complaint* were thrilled by its support for various private overthrowings of their own," Pierpont adds (62). On the other side, critics like Irving Howe passionately despised the novel: "The cruelest thing anyone can do with *Portnoy's Complaint* is to read it twice" (239). This hostile relationship to the book and Portnoy was transferred to Roth, whose public reputation suffered severely from being identified with his character. Pierpont reports: "On television, Jacqueline Susann . . . said on *The Tonight Show* that she would like to meet Philip Roth but wouldn't want to shake his hand" (64). This shows how quickly an emotional reading may bridge the gap between text and author.[13] Apparently, we need to shift our attention from Portnoy's character to his relationship with readers. The reactions Portnoy's behavior and opinions elicit are not just a function of his construction but of the relationship readers establish with and the attitude they are willing to take toward him.

* * *

The analytic stance readers are offered by the text is not necessarily coterminous with an endorsement of Portnoy's opinions; on the contrary, with the tool of psychoanalytic interpretation, it arms readers with a powerful weapon against Portnoy and his author. There is a strong temptation to use the correlation between reader, critic, and psychoanalyst as a justification for interpreting the text psychoanalytically, as Lois Gordon does:

> The critic need have no fear of offering a psychoanalytic interpretation, because the reader (or critic) sits as well in the analyst's chair. Interestingly, this makes explicit certain similarities in the tasks of the analyst of literature and the psychoanalyst. Both must seek the underlying, unifying threads that vitalize and give coherence to the surface narrator, and both must be acutely responsive to the surface and depth at once. (58)

However, the relation between *Portnoy's Complaint* and its interpretation is not exhausted by this imaginary identification of analyst and critic. It does not necessarily follow from Portnoy's cultivation of psychoanalytic interpretations that the novel presents us with a complex that can be interpreted with psychoanalytic means. Steven Lavine explains: "Applying Freud's theory to Roth's novel, we do not psychoanalyze Portnoy ourselves; rather, we discover that Roth has created Portnoy to Freud's prescriptions" (358).

Explanations that supply a psychoanalytic interpretation of Portnoy's disorder thus only duplicate a construction that is laid out in the text. Once again, it becomes apparent that in *Portnoy's Complaint*, psychoanalysis is less a model of critical interpretation than of artistic production.

On these foundations, *Portnoy's Complaint* conceives its own critique of interpretation. Portnoy's orientation toward his analyst is so pervasive that it is impossible to consider any of his utterances without and independent of his relationship to Spielvogel; thus, we must always bear in mind Portnoy's intentions before interpreting an utterance or rejecting it prematurely because of its obscenity or questionable subject matter. As a second step, we have to consider our own relationship to Portnoy and how our interpretations, like Portnoy's, can be part of a dynamic of transference. Psychoanalysis becomes Portnoy's all-encompassing interpretive frame, "a pattern by which to arrange the incidents of his life, to conceptualise his identity and to account for his present situation" (Kirchhofer 107). In addition, he invites therapist and reader to engage in his wild analysis and to follow the traces of his own interpretations. It would be easy for the critic to adopt this pattern and analyze Portnoy with Portnoy. However, this is a trap construed by the text, which, strictly speaking, challenges the very process of psychoanalytic interpretation and ultimately demonstrates to the reader that Portnoy's interpretive activity is the source of his "complaint."

Portnoy's wild reading of Freud prompts Bruno Bettelheim to state summarily: "[Portnoy] has read too much about psychoanalysis and understood nothing" ("Portnoy" 5). Freud was convinced that patients have to learn "that mental activities such as thinking something over or concentrating the attention solve none of the riddles of a neurosis." There are patients, and Portnoy must be counted among them, "who practise the art of sheering off into intellectual discussion during their treatment, who speculate a great deal and often very wisely about their condition and in that way avoid doing anything to overcome it" ("Recommendations" 119). Intellectualization thus works in the service of resistance and may contribute to changing the relationship between analyst and patient. Defying the analytic asymmetry, the patient can imagine himself as a participant in a collaborative research endeavor (König 92–93) rather than undergo proper analysis: "The central paradox of Alexander Portnoy is that his intellectualising . . . only gives him the illusion that he truly understands his condition" (Novak 60). By demonstrating how Freudian interpretation may contribute to a fraying out of meaning rather than to its consolidation, the novel contains a critique of orthodox interpretive methods in psychoanalysis.

This also explains why Portnoy's monologue does not conclude with the desired cathartic solution and liberation from guilt. Portnoy's interpretive fury, his linguistic obsession with mastery, his desire for intellectual distinction, and his neurotic self-observation are part of his complaint; if he tries to resolve them through interpretation, he only goes round in circles. The critic's participation in this interpretive roundabout would only lead to a similar disregard for the novel's critique of Portnoy's interpretations and a resistance against a more intense engagement with Portnoy's provocations. In any case, critics misunderstand the psychoanalytic endeavor if they believe a single, if ever so obvious, interpretation could solve the patient's conflicts. Peter Balbert is a victim of this misunderstanding when he concludes: "Spielvogel no doubt knows there is nothing more to say. It has all been said and understood perfectly by Alex" (74). Portnoy's belief that he has understood everything perfectly, however, may be his biggest misconception. Spielvogel's final intervention emphasizes that the psychoanalytic process has not even begun yet, and, as Shostak argues, "seems to discount Portnoy's insights and accusations" (83). If there is to be a new beginning, Spielvogel's remark suggests, it will have to take into account his transformative perspective as well as pay attention to the transferential form Portnoy has chosen for his analytic discourse.

Although Portnoy uses psychoanalytic concepts in his self-analysis, he also criticizes the reductive attempts at interpretation he ascribes to Freudians:

> More farce, my friend! Too much to swallow, I'm afraid! Oedipus Rex is a famous tragedy, schmuck, not another joke! You're a sadist, you're a quack and a lousy comedian! I mean this is going too far for a laugh, Doctor Spielvogel, Doctor Freud, Doctor Kronkite! How about a little homage, you bastards, to The Dignity of Man! (266)

This outburst is not only an attack on the reductionism of psychoanalysis, erupting once Portnoy no longer perceives the Oedipus complex as liberating (Brauner, "Masturbation" 81 and "Getting" 46). Portnoy also opposes psychoanalysis with literature, with the meaningfulness of a tragedy that cannot be reduced to a simple pattern. Thus, it is only logical that Portnoy perceives the psychoanalytic attack on the complexity of literature as an attack on himself: it underlines Portnoy's constitution as a literary construct that is withdrawn from the psychoanalytic grasp for understanding.

The novel clearly illustrates the results of such an interpretive hold from its very beginning. As the article "The Puzzled Penis," which is cited in the epigraph, demonstrates, Spielvogel has already established himself as a psychoanalytic author:

> **Portnoy's Complaint** . . . *n.* [after Alexander Portnoy (1933-)] A disorder in which strongly-felt ethical and altruistic impulses are

perpetually warring with extreme sexual longings, often of a perverse nature. Spielvogel says: "Acts of exhibitionism, voyeurism, fetishism, auto-eroticism and oral coitus are plentiful; as a consequence of the patient's 'morality,' however, neither fantasy nor act issues in genuine sexual gratification, but rather in overriding feelings of shame and the dread of retribution, particularly in the form of castration." (Spielvogel, O. "The Puzzled Penis," *Internationale Zeitschrift für Psychoanalyse*, Vol. XXIV p. 909.) It is believed by Spielvogel that many of the symptoms can be traced to the bonds obtaining in the mother-child relationship.

Through its position and length, the epigraph exemplifies problematic tendencies that have often been criticized in psychoanalysis. As a summary of Portnoy's complaints, the entry seems one-sided, hardly empathetic, and reductive; not in the slightest does it succeed in imparting an impression of Portnoy, his energy, his suffering, and the depth of his conflicts. As an interpretation and a diagnosis, it always lags behind the experience the reader shares with Portnoy in reading the novel. Prefacing the main body of the text and preempting everything Portnoy will later convey, the entry also stages how the deductive analyst might reach a diagnosis/interpretation before entering a relationship with and listening to the narratives of the analysand. The result is a critique of a reductive interpretive approach (Frank 69), which is epitomized in Spielvogel and his reduction of Portnoy to a diagnostic category.

The consequence for the individual seems disastrous: "The authority that turned the person Portnoy into a patient also turns him into a diagnosis—a human being into a text" (Frank 73). The textualization of Portnoy, however, can be read in several ways. First of all, Portnoy desires such a text—an essay, a word; he demands an interpretation of his suffering from Spielvogel, and one that goes beyond what he can achieve himself: "a more interesting, more satisfying, more *sophisticated* diagnosis of his complaint" (Brauner, "Masturbation" 81). If Portnoy is enraged by the psychoanalytic interpretation, it is only because it yields so little satisfaction (Frank 73). Portnoy may oppose this text with his own "more inclusive narrative of self-identity" (79), but this too is, after all, just another text—Portnoy's "complaint." If understanding the self is the goal, then there seems to be no escape from interpretation and subsequent textualization; optional are only the mode of discourse and the results. As much as one might criticize the limits and the reductiveness of analytic and literary interpretation, *Portnoy's Complaint* eventually underlines one insight: the desire for meaning is hard to quench. And although Spielvogel is the target of this critique, he eventually provides an alternative to the interpretive trap. His invitation at the end to return to the beginning points to the hermeneutic necessity to confront an experience thoroughly, repeatedly, and jointly before pinning it down.

Conclusion

Although at first there does not seem to be any therapeutic relationship in *Portnoy's Complaint* at all, Portnoy is clearly indebted to his silent analyst in every sentence he utters. He seeks Spielvogel's attention, his trust, and his admiration, begs him for redemptory enlightenment, and continually fights for equality by playing with, attacking, and trying to surpass his analyst. With Spielvogel, Portnoy explores the relationships with his family and the women in his life, but at the same time he works through both his Jewish identity and the historical and cultural limitations that play into his relational matrix. Expertly, he also faces a version of Freud that is simultaneously revered and travestied. But by turning his psychoanalytic powers of imagination and interpretation into an end in itself he eventually fails in his cathartic endeavor, due to his own analytic virtuosity.

The novel takes up this virtuosity to hone its own literary format. The freedom of expression demanded by the psychoanalytic setting allows Roth to elaborate a distinctive language and protest against remaining taboos like obscenity and open sexual content. The fundamental rule provides the model for the construction of *Portnoy's Complaint*, establishing a language and a structure for the remote and the exaggerated and for the dialogic transformation of the monologue. Due to this mixture of psychoanalytic inspiration and literary stylization, the novel retains a high degree of readability despite its experimental quality.

At the same time, the psychoanalytic setting enables the novel to discuss the parameters of its own literary constitution. For the main part, inspiration is not drawn from the neurosis of the protagonist but from the process of psychoanalysis. By putting the reader into the analyst's chair, *Portnoy's Complaint* showcases the relational analogy between reader and psychoanalyst in a prototypical way and allows readers to reconstruct the novel's conclusions by observing their own behavior. They are turned into the transference objects of the novel and are thus subject to all of the temptations but also to all of the dangers implied in Portnoy's relational bid to his analyst. From this entanglement in relationships and in one's own desires (including the desire for explanation), there is no straightforward way out through interpretation, as Portnoy and Spielvogel illustrate. Interpretation only eludes stiff reductivism if it remains open for a tentative and perhaps endless play with meaning and for constant new "beginnings."

Portnoy's Complaint accomplishes much more than a parody of psychotherapy, especially since its critical insights into the limits of interpretability are to be taken very seriously. But with his loquacious hero, Roth also reveals something else: the creative, ludic potential of psychoanalysis that releases Portnoy's wit and Roth's novelistic innovation. Thus, the novel may serve as a comprehensive model for literature's aesthetic engagement with psychoanalysis and its premises. And indeed, many other novels that play with psychoanalysis, such as Graham Swift's *Out of This World* (1988), Robert Menasse's *Don Juan de la Mancha* (2007), and Leon de Kock's *Bad Sex* (2011), draw on Roth's model with similarly exuberant patient narratives in free associative style. In the following chapter, however, we will encounter an entirely different exploration of psychoanalytic aesthetics in the work of J. M. Coetzee.

6

"A Gap, a Hole, a Darkness": Epistemic Desire in J. M. Coetzee's *Life & Times of Michael K*

Introduction: Therapeutic epistemology

The need to recognize the Other, explore and lay down the meaning of that person's existence, drives many of J. M. Coetzee's protagonists, who are often involved in dyads that threaten to tear apart because of this epistemic desire. The magistrate in *Waiting for the Barbarians* (1980) tries to read the scars of the Barbarian girl, Susan Barton in *Foe* (1986) searches an explanatory story for Friday's lost tongue, and David Lurie in *Disgrace* (1999) hopes to gain insight into his daughter Lucy's behavior after the brutal attack they have both suffered through. Bordering on therapeutic endeavors, their efforts to explore life stories, rewrite them, and create new meaning for the speechless Other as much as for themselves point to a longing for spiritual healing, but they are also marked by failure.

In *Life & Times of Michael K* (1983), a similarly ambivalent therapeutic relationship is the focus of the second part of the novel, which allows us to explore this vulnerable relationship between epistemic and therapeutic endeavors. In the dystopian world of the novel, the South African government fights a civil war against the resistance movement, detaining anyone without permanent abode and work as a potential rebel. The eponymous K, a simple-minded former gardener, roams the war-ridden hinterland of the country, escapes from an enforced labor camp, and spends a few secluded months on an abandoned farm growing vegetables before he is captured and interned as an insurgent in Kenilworth Rehabilitation Camp. A Medical Officer, a pharmacist with a rudimentary medical education (162), tends to the almost famished K after he has collapsed during one of the camp drills. Since K refuses any kind of medical intervention, the doctor has to resort to linguistic intervention, attempting to get to know K's story and convince him to eat. But again, the struggle for knowledge and healing fails, and despite his physical weakness, K manages to escape the camp.

It may seem that the relationship between doctor and patient is less determined by therapy than by captivity, and the novel may be read as a critique of (therapeutic) relationships, casting doubt on their capability of producing insight. This is certainly reflected in many readings of the novel, which imply that K cannot be figured out, and the more general warning formulated by postcolonial critics that, ultimately, the Other cannot be understood.[1] Coetzee's thrust is still more complicated, for however tenuous it is, there is a relationship between Medical Officer and K, which is the driving force of an entire section in the novel. Bearing the warranted postcolonial critique in mind, this chapter thus seeks to analyze this depiction of the therapeutic relationship as a complex inquiry into the relational *possibilities* of knowledge.

Classical psychoanalysis has been understood as a hermeneutic project geared toward interpreting a human being and sharpening her understanding of herself. However, even psychoanalysts often doubt, as Adam Phillips stresses, this project's validity: "*Knowing people in language is either impossible and/or no good*" ("Poetry" 34). In his view, psychoanalysis turns to literature because it is interested not just in epistemological questions but also in language, which is an inevitable feature of the psychoanalytic and the literary process. Coetzee's novel reverses this search pattern and employs the structure of the therapeutic relationship as an experimental space to examine language and relationship as epistemological factors, arguing that there is much to be said and explored, even in the face of analytic and narrative failure.

Imprisonment: Michael K and Medical Officer

K has been a victim of institutions his entire life. Due to his limited mental capacities, he spent his childhood in Huis Norenius, a home for "variously afflicted and unfortunate children" (*Life* 4). His "stupidity" (60) and his cleft lip designate him as someone who has limited access to and control over knowledge, which, in the context of the novel, marks his subaltern status. Coetzee never addresses skin color in *Life & Times of Michael K*, but K's "charge sheet" lists him as "CM—40—NFA—Unemployed" (70), a sign that K is considered a "coloured male" (Gallagher 144). Coetzee's rejection of any overt reference to K's physical appearance may be read as a "denial of apartheid's obsessive system of classification" (Head, *Cambridge* 56), and it forces us to read the asymmetry in the relationship with the Medical Officer simultaneously as the result of an obscurely hierarchical political system and, independent of K's putative skin color and the context of apartheid, on its own ambivalent terms.

In the course of the novel, the Medical Officer's attention to K shifts from distanced indifference via careful attention to religious veneration—and precisely because this might seem like an unlikely development, it is necessary to explore why this therapeutic relationship changes its meaning. At the beginning, the Medical Officer treats K according to his usual abstracted routines. His diagnosis—"prolonged malnutrition" (129) and "degeneration of the intestinal wall" (134)—suggests treatment with "a graduated diet, gentle exercise, and physiotherapy, so that one day soon he can rejoin camp life" (133). These therapeutic intentions, however, lack meaning. The camp is neither equipped nor designed to provide for such care, even if a return to camp life were a desirable goal. The doctor sees K as a mentally disabled man who got mixed up with the enemy, obtaining his information from the records instead of taking K's history. That the doctor at first refuses to believe K's story is best illustrated by his persistent use of the name "Michaels," despite K's protests that he is called Michael (131). His lack of respect for K's perspective is also betrayed by the language of his case notes:

> Have been struggling with the new patient Michaels. He insists there is nothing wrong with him, he only wants something for his headache. Says he is not hungry. In fact he cannot hold his foot down. Am keeping him on a drip, which he fights against feebly. Though he looks like an old man, he claims to be only thirty-two. Perhaps it is the truth. (130)

Words like "insists," "claims," "though," and "perhaps" signal his doubts about K's testimony, which he contrasts with his own, supposedly objective observations of the "in fact." Thus, he sticks to the rules of the institution where people are "marks in a book, objects in a system" (Gallagher 150). As his inability to believe K's words indicates, the Officer is not capable at this point of accepting K as an independent individual. Instead, he treats him as an object that can be overwritten and corrected with external labels (Kossew 147).

This is due to the fact that the doctor can only see K's deficiencies at first. He regards him as a "person of feeble mind" (131), as a "poor idiot who doesn't know his arse from his elbow" (142). Such repeated efforts to denigrate K, however, seem to testify to a desire to dispel the threatening feeling that K's presence could somehow question his own position. And indeed, in his very simplicity, K begins to pose a riddle that cannot be solved: "One tries to imagine him running a staging post for insurgents and one's mind boggles" (130). To render K intelligible, the Medical Officer produces a striking series of similes. Mostly, he compares K with small animals—"like a lizard basking" (132), "like a stick insect, . . . whose sole defence against a universe of predators is its bizarre shape" (149), and "a mouse who quit an over-crowded, foundering ship" (136)—and with lifeless puppets—"like one of those toys made of sticks held together with rubber bands" (133), "a figure of fun, a clown, a wooden man" (149). Sue Kossew identifies the Medical Officer's tactics with the discursive colonial tradition of "Othering," which demarcated the colonial subject as an inferior animal (132). Minimalization, objectivization, and dehumanization speak out of these comparisons, which makes Duncan Chesney suspect that the doctor attempts to rob K of his threatening irreducibility: "The officer refuses to place K within a human, social context in which his unsuitability can have critical meaning" (314). However, placing K outside humanity and human understandability seems to be the doctor's only chance of recognizing K's individuality and of perceiving him as "a destabilizing, outside force" (Wittenberg 306). Thus, the similes are actually a means to approach K as something other than a medical object—an individual with a unique story.

As a result, the comparisons cannot be entirely rejected as misinterpretations of K. And, surprisingly, K uses similar imagery when he thinks about himself as "more timorous than a mouse" (105), "like an ant" (83), or "like a lizard under a stone" (116). Even dehumanizing similes are in K's repertoire, as he compares himself to the "stony ground" and describes his limbs as "stick[s] protruding from his body" (121). Yet despite their similar approaches, K's and the Medical Officer's evaluations never cohere. Even when they use the same animal similes, they signify different states of being—enjoyment versus concealment, being lost versus being anxious. Most importantly, however, the comparisons differ in their ultimate purpose. K's existential comparisons are designed to capture his self-experience at a particular moment: "He thought of himself as a termite boring its way through a rock. There seemed *nothing to do but live*" (66, my emphasis). The Medical Officer, in contrast, seeks to endow K with a personal or political meaning: "A hard little stone, barely aware of its surroundings, enveloped in itself and its *interior life*. He passes through these *institutions* and *camps* and *hospitals* and God knows what else like a stone. Through the intestines of the *war*" (135, my emphasis). Their observations may be similar, but the doctor's elaborate interpretation jars with K's existential minimalism. Gilbert Yeoh describes this hermeneutic association between K and Medical Officer as an "asymptotic" relation: "While his interpretations appear to approach an accurate reading of K, they never fully identify the evasive K. The medical officer and Michael K . . . are suspended in a relation of irreconcilable difference" (135). Rather than emphasizing only the difference that remains between asymptote and line, however, I want to focus on the gradual approach described by the asymptote. What is the crucial experience that puts the Officer on this course? Why does he even want to enter a relationship with and learn something about K?

Gradually, in tandem with friendly efforts to care for K, the doctor stops regarding K as a mere object. He makes allowances for K, "not wanting to hurt him" (131), prepares his food, talks to him, and keeps thinking about him. This is reflected in his paternalistic yet tender perception of K as a child: "I took the packet out of his hand and tucked it under the pillow 'for safety.' When I passed an hour later he was asleep, his mouth nudging the pillow like a baby's" (135). However, this added attention does not soften the relationship, as both regard it as a burden. "What am I to this man?" asks K (148), brushing off the Medical Officer's concern for his well-being. The doctor admits, "I do indeed pay too much attention to him" (136); K seems like an "albatross around my neck" (146).[2] And still, he always returns to K's bed to care for him and study him—a significant combination of therapeutic and epistemic devotion that characterizes the changed "attention" the doctor develops in their relationship.

It may seem that K does not contribute anything to this shift in attention, as he resists the treatment and keeps silent for much of the time. K has often needed to fight against another's claims on him, repeating a "pattern of leaving any time he finds himself in circumstances that require his participation in the master/servant dichotomy" (L. Wright 87). His silence and the ambiguity of his terse comments also have a distancing force, causing "frustration and anger" in others (L. Wright 86). In this way, K's resistance has often been read as a sign of his complete aversion from the relationship. Crucially, however, K does not obstruct the formation of a relationship and volunteers plenty of information. Almost self-ironically, he comments on the camp's location in an old racecourse, "I could become a jockey too, at my weight," and on the impediments caused by his cleft lip: "I was never a great one for the girls" (130). He presents his precious pumpkin seeds to the Medical Officer and tells him about his dreams: "I used to stretch out my arms and think I was flying over the fences and between the houses. I flew low over people's heads, but they couldn't see me" (133). This brief story testifies not only to K's readiness to disclose personal details but also to the involuntary suggestive force of his words: with their unusual and bizarre imagery, they invoke the image of an enraptured being craving freedom. K's behavior and his language, which express a puzzling combination of resistance and cryptic self-revelation, evoke questions about the meaning of imprisonment and freedom, and create a provocative force that attaches the Medical Officer—like many others before him—to the puzzle of K and makes him want to figure out his story.

The official search for K's story begins with the investigation into his affiliation with the resistance movement, in which K refuses to testify. The doctor tries to make him talk with reassurances ("Some of us are not even sure you had anything to do with the insurgents" [138]), promises, and threats ("And if you don't co-operate you will go to a place that is a lot worse than this!" [138]). For this reason, Sarah Dove Heider compares the Medical Officer with a torturer who "badgers K with words, his torture-machines of meaning" (88–89). However, sadism is not what motivates the doctor; instead, his emotions express personal frustration over K's resistance against providing the narrative the doctor desires. K's assertions, "I am not in the war" (138) and "I am not clever with words" (139), produce irritation in a man for whom the war is inescapable and truth exists independent from its linguistic construction: "We don't want you to be clever with words or stupid with words, man, we just want you to tell the truth!" (139). Soon, it becomes apparent that the doctor searches for a different kind of truth—not a political truth about K's involvement in the resistance movement, but a psychological truth about his life. He suspects the origin of K's problems in his relationship with his mother, "who sounds like a real killer" (150), observing "how distressed he becomes when he has to talk about his mother. His toes curled on the floor, he licked at the lip-cleft" (139). As much as this close reading of K's body language may point to the Officer's attempts at gaining insight into K, he just as soon turns the story into another distorting myth: "I also think of her sitting on your shoulders, eating out your brains, glaring about triumphantly, the very embodiment of great Mother Death" (150).[3] This suggests the doctor is in need of a story that provides meaning in addition to knowledge.

His attempts to coax K into talking do indeed testify to a belief in the redemptive qualities of storytelling. "Where else in the world are you going to find two polite civilized gentlemen ready to listen to your story all day and all night, if need be, and take notes too?" (140), he asks, as if the listener's attention and his willingness to put the story into writing were existentially important. In fact, the Medical Officer believes that stories can ground an identity, seal memory, and secure one's existence through texts that transcend the bureaucratic record: "Give yourself some substance, man, otherwise you are going to slide through life absolutely unnoticed. You will be a digit in the units column at the end of the war . . . , nothing more" (140). Because he cannot elicit that story from K, he decides to tell the story *for* K by inventing a plausible report about K's political activities. This narrative act enables him to see himself as K's savior and protector, which shows that it is in fact he himself who tries to gain "substance" through the narrative connection to K (Engélibert 52). The idea that he might have saved K "by [his] eloquence"

(142) confirms his identity as a member of the helping professions and reassures his conscience. As K's protector, he can be a conservator of memory, for "no one is going to remember you but me" (152), and an exceptional human being who knows how to appreciate K: "I am the only one who sees you for the original soul you are" (151).

In truth, then, the doctor's efforts turn around his own desire for K's story. When he insists, "I want to know your story" (149), an obsessive need not just for any story, but K's story speaks out of his words. K triggers the doctor's yearning for freedom and meaning because of his own position in the world and the war. The novel's South Africa is riddled with institutions and camps. Every step is monitored, and K's life, "a life lived in cages" (181), is marked by imprisonment, from his youth in Huis Norenius to hospitals, forced labor battalions, and rehabilitation camps. The Medical Officer may not learn much about K's history, but with his resistance and his death-defying refusal of "camp food" (146), K becomes a symbol of the escape from a totalitarian system and the guiding light of the doctor's critique of the camp machinery. The fact that K is actually ambivalent about fences—he seeks "the forgotten corners and corridors between the fences" (47) but has "a feel for wire" (95) and wishes for a fence to protect "the privilege of so much silence" (47)—suggests that the doctor's overestimation of K is largely a projection of his own desire for redemption. For the Officer, K represents "a surrogate for a vicarious quest for freedom . . . ; a space that he craves to fill with meaning . . . ; and an index to his own inadequacies" (D. Wright 10). At the same time, however, these projections are *triggered* by K's strange presence in his care, which makes the Medical Officer question his own role in the war. While the camp system superficially aims at the psychological rehabilitation and reintegration of its inmates, the resources the military is given—discipline and violence—reveal more sinister motives and shake the camp doctor's conviction in his benevolent mandate:

> Do any of us believe in what we are doing here? . . . We are given an old racetrack and a quantity of barbed wire and told to effect a change in men's souls. Not being experts on the soul but assuming cautiously that it has some connection with the body, we set our captives to doing pushups and marching back and forth. . . . At the end of the process we certify them cleansed and pack them off to the labour battalions. (134)

K's presence brings something to the surface that has eaten away at the doctor for a long time. He suddenly sees himself as "living in suspension," "a castaway marooned in a pocket of time, the time of waiting, camp time, war-time. . . . Even the concussion case . . . lives in dying more intensely than

I in living" (158). Thus, the camp doctor has, almost unnoticeably, lost every justification for his existence.

To make up for this sudden lack in meaning, the Medical Officer invests K with mythical significance. K's disabilities, his cleft lip and the ensuing language difficulties—common attributes of mythical figures (Lierop 44)—develop from markers of incomprehensible difference to signifiers of exceptionality. The doctor stylizes K as a singular being in danger, whose worship would also provide a distinction for himself:

> I alone see you as neither a soft case for a soft camp nor a hard case for a hard camp but a human soul above and beneath classification, a soul blessedly untouched by doctrine, untouched by history, a soul stirring its wings within that stiff sarcophagus. . . . You are precious, Michaels, in your way; you are the last of your kind, a creature left over from an earlier age, like the coelacanth or the last man to speak Yaqui. We have all tumbled over the lip into the cauldron of history: only you, following your idiot light, . . . have managed to live in the old way, drifting through time, observing the seasons, no more trying to change the course of history than a grain of sand does. We ought to value and celebrate you. (151–52)

Since the Medical Officer yearns for freedom and meaning, he invests K with defiant exceptionality. The refusal of food becomes a focal point of his mythologization. "Maybe he only eats the bread of freedom" (146), the Medical Officer is soon ready to believe, interpreting K's behavior as passive resistance:

> I slowly began to see the originality of the resistance you offered. You were not a hero and did not pretend to be, not even a hero of fasting. In fact you did not resist at all. . . . Then as I watched you day after day I slowly began to understand the truth: that you were crying secretly, unknown to your conscious self (forgive the term), for a different kind of food, food that no camp could supply. . . . The body, I had been taught, wants only to live. . . . Yet here I beheld a body that was going to die rather than change its nature. (163–64)

This body, which cannot be explained from a medical point of view, unsettles the beliefs of the Medical Officer, charging K with further meaning. For the doctor, K symbolizes an immutable essence, an entity with a deep-seated physical resistance, which scorns death with its tenacity and peacefulness.

The doctor's imagination turns K into a saint, even more so when it envisions K's garden as a paradise beyond the war and the all-encompassing camp structures:

> Let me tell you the meaning of the sacred and alluring garden that blooms in the heart of the desert and produces the food of life. The garden ... is nowhere and everywhere except in the camps.... It is off every map, no road leads to it that is merely a road, and only you know the way. (166)

K's lack of appetite seems to have been caused by his experience in this paradisiacal state. Soon, the doctor spends much of his time observing K, "puzzling over the mystery" (164), becoming aware of "this sense of a gathering meaning" (165). His initial indifference has developed into religious worship and service.

This feverish spiritual attention is undercut and at the same time strengthened by K's eventual disappearance. K's escape from the camp seems like a "miracle" (156) to the Medical Officer and makes him engage even more intensely with K's meaning as a potential but lost savior: "I yet stood dithering over which way lay salvation.... The night that Michaels made his break, I should have followed" (161). Although their relationship is merely a feat of the Officer's imagination from now on, it intensifies further. Like a disciple, he imagines following K everywhere, in order to be led to paradise: "I have chosen you to show me the way" (163). Staging a ritual confession of his sins—"At first I thought of you, I will confess, as a figure of fun" (163)— he designates himself as a "foot-follower" and confesses that "before seeing the light," he had merely been a military man who had ordered K about and made fun of him (162). Now he begs him fervidly: "Michaels, forgive me for the way I treated you" (162). However, as his persistent reference to K as "Michaels" indicates, even this last, imaginary attempt at understanding K remains dubious. The fantasy ends with K's flight from the doctor, who is chased away by children, the more fitting followers of the savior. This anagogic fiction demonstrates the Medical Officer's changed attitude toward his patient: "This literalization of the doctor's metaphorical chasing after significance reinforces the image of K as a reluctant messianic figure" (Kossew 148–49). The officer's worship and his desire for knowledge are thus intimately connected.

Although the Medical Officer misunderstands and fails to explain K's "essence," their encounter is not entirely a failure. With his resistance, K, who at first appears as just another case, forces the doctor to engage, not with his body, but with his psyche—his stories, needs, and desires. This change in attention produces insight not only into the patient but also into the doctor. Instead of meeting the Other in K, he is confronted with the Other in himself—his self-doubts and his complicity in an unjust civil war. Although he tries to assuage his guilt and displace these insights by mythologizing K, the doctor reaches a greater awareness toward the end of their encounter. Indirectly, a role reversal is achieved, in which K, through his silence, serves as the transference object and analyst of the Medical Officer, mirroring what the doctor projects: "K's presence forces the doctor to confront a 'truth' . . . about himself" (Wittenberg 307). In this encounter, the Medical Officer understands that he is not the savior but in need of saving; his therapeutic efforts ultimately find their true object in himself. And yet, he cannot give up his desire for an insight into K—a crucial desire that complicates the aesthetic and poetic epistemology suggested by the novel.

Gaps in experience: The diary as apostrophe and reverie

When readers first encounter the Medical Officer's interpretation, they are already a decisive step ahead of the doctor. Throughout the first part of the novel, in which a heterodiegetic narrator focalized through K guides the story, they have been able to follow K's life almost as if they were in his head. In fact, the focalization is so strong that the language of the narrator often seems to reflect K's consciousness. Simple, short phrases as well as a paratactic syntax without explicit causal connections could indeed be linked to K's childlike, limited perspective, which bars readers from thoroughly penetrating the text (Kern 157–58). For instance, when K witnesses several detonations and loses orientation, the purely phenomenological mode of narration refuses to provide any clarification of the events: "There was a heavy explosion, and at once a second explosion. The air shook, there was a clamour of birds, the hills rumbled and echoed. K stared around wildly" (124–25). But although K's thoughts are often rendered in direct or free indirect speech, readers may suspect the narrator's intrusion. "He thought of himself not as something heavy that left tracks behind it," the narrator reports K's thoughts, "but if anything as a speck upon the surface of an earth too deeply asleep to notice the scratch of ant-feet, the rasp of butterfly teeth, the tumbling of dust" (97). Derek Attridge observes that in sentences like these neither the linguistic rhythm nor the philosophical speculation can be attributed to K. In this way the narrator manages to involve the reader in K's mental processes and make her feel distanced from K's experience at the same time (76). So how much readers really learn about K with the help of this narrator is highly questionable. Coetzee characterizes this style as a "limited omniscient point of view.... That is to say, there is someone who is telling the story about Michael K, who looks like an omniscient narrator, but he doesn't actually tell you very much. And ... there is no guarantee that he knows very much" (qtd. in Penner 94, second ellipsis in original). These uncertainties about narrative authority are increased in the second part of the novel.

The Medical Officer's story presents a noticeable rupture in the text's fabric. The sudden appearance of an unknown autodiegetic narrator irritates the reading process because it disrupts the internal perspective on K readers have attained through the heterodiegetic narrator. This narrative device has been criticized as "ineffective and disruptive" (Gallagher 164). Cynthia Ozick's review of the novel is typical of this reading, but unwittingly points to the strengths of this device.

> If "Life & Times of Michael K" has a flaw, it is in the last-minute imposition of an interior choral interpretation. In the final quarter we are removed, temporarily, from the plain seeing of Michael K to the self-indulgent diary of the prison doctor.... But the doctor's commentary is superfluous; he thickens the clear tongue of the novel by naming its "message" and thumping out ironies. (1)

In defense of the narrative construction I would argue that it is precisely this disruptive and overdetermined quality that gives the doctor's report its significance.

In its apparent superfluity, the section reproduces the dilemma of the Medical Officer: his attempt to explain something even if that explanation remains elusive. It is related to the first part of the novel like the interpretation of an analyst to the story of the patient, inasmuch as it adds another perspective to what has already been said. A message is not just named and repeated but supplemented with an external view, which, by not fitting perfectly with the view of K offered in the first part, creates new meaning through difference. It adds critical contexts to the process of reading, to the reader's relationship with K and to her relationship with the narrators. The presence of a second, doubtful narrator who tries to usurp K's story problematizes the reliability of the first narrator. The narrative of the Medical Officer highlights how difficult it is to speak for another, and the two opposing narrative models serve to question the novel's form and the omniscient perspective on which it relies in part (Head, *Cambridge* 57). Thus, the reader is encouraged to "renegotiate his or her position in relation to the text" (Kossew 140). With the precarious relationship between doctor and patient, *Life & Times of Michael K* stages a dialogue between narrative levels and includes its readers in these dialogues, whose limited access to K is mirrored in both narrators' limitations.

After all, aside from the apparent oversupply of interpretation, the insertion of the second part also creates a rupture in our understanding. Due to the change in perspectives, K's story is suddenly riddled with gaps. What happens between his arrest at the end of the first part and his breakdown at the beginning of the second? How does K manage to escape the camp? Throughout the Medical Officer's narrative, the reader loses his mediated access to K's perspective. How K experiences his imprisonment in the rehabilitation camp and what thoughts plague him throughout that time remains as unknown to the reader as to the Medical Officer. Even in the short third part, this gap in experience is never resolved. K never thinks about the time in the camp explicitly; it seems to be another "pocket outside time" (60) for him.

* * *

The narrative of the Medical Officer abandons this timelessness, however. While the heterodiegetic narrative locates the events of the first part in a vague preterit, the second part counters this experience with numerous small narrative sections written in the present tense. This indicates that we are dealing with a kind of diary. The segmentation and the daily routines of writing point to the structured temporal experience of the camp, but they also serve to exhibit the transformation of the protagonist. However, the diary does not only reflect the doctor's development, as Teresa Dovey argues (306); it also traces the changes in his relationship to K, who turns from the object to the addressee of the text.

This becomes more and more apparent in the changing textual quality of the diary. At first, the doctor only records short observations about his patients. His syntactically minimalistic, elliptic style, as in "Says he is not hungry" (130), suggests the form of case notes. However, the more he engages with K, the more personal his remarks get. They are increasingly polished, rich in metaphors, and, aside from case observations, start to contain narrative passages and subjective reflections about his situation in the camp and his relationship to K. After K has left the camp, his style appears completely transformed:

> I doubt that Felicity pictures to herself currents of time swirling and eddying all about us, on the battlefields and in the military headquarters, in the factories and on the streets, in boardrooms and cabinet chambers, murkily at first, yet tending ever towards a moment of transfiguration in

which pattern is born from chaos and history manifests itself in all its triumphant meaning. (158)

The terse memorandum style has disappeared behind metaphors, accumulations, and a "swirling" syntax, reflective of the officer's enriched yet troubled inner life. To resolve this confusion, the Medical Officer intermittently gives up the form of the diary and turns to K in different modes of writing. When he realizes that K resists him and his treatment, he writes a letter to K, trying to convince "Dear Michaels" (149) to accept the treatment and divulge his story. And after K has disappeared, his self-reflection becomes even more pervasive and enveloped in a direct appeal to K. They lead to the fantasy of his discipleship and a direct confrontation with K, written in a conditional style that has nothing in common with the earlier collection of facts: "And here, in the light of day, you would at last have turned and looked at me" (162). With this "enlightenment" and the exchange of a glance, both signaling a hope for insight, the fantasy facilitates a last encounter with K. Thus, the diary changes from a text focused on the diarist to an apostrophe: "It . . . *apostrophizes* K: i.e. it addresses an absent entity. . . . Although it cannot render K present, the diary is *at the same time* unable to accept his absence" (Marais, *Secretary* 55).

An apostrophe is traditionally directed at a dead or absent person and is thus associated with the conventions of the ode or the elegy (Baldick 17). After K's escape, the Medical Officer's words do indeed speak of veneration and mourning; the absence and elusiveness of his patient are the condition for his reflections. Paradoxically, K's refusal to enter the interrogative dialogue the doctor asks for is a requirement for his dialogic apostrophe to K in his diary. Here—and Coetzee thus provides a salient counter-model to Roth—the silent patient, and not the silent therapist, establishes an asymmetrical analytic dialogue in which he is turned into an imaginary addressee, prompting the reflections of the doctor and giving them a space to unfold. With this dynamic, the second part of the novel illustrates how the relationship between Medical Officer and K is not just reflected in but is the very foundation of the doctor's—and ultimately Coetzee's—writing process.

* * *

The records of the camp doctor testify to his inability to elicit K's story to his satisfaction: K obstructs the anamnesis as much as the therapy, and thus refuses him the desired closure. The diagnosis may be correct from a medical point of view, but his evaluation of K's general condition rests on constructions and allegorical interpretation, which call his judgment into question. Due to their lack of actual facts, his case notes are not even prime examples of a medical narrative, and their scientific aspirations are invalidated by the subjectivity of his narrative.

The longer the doctor tells his story, the more it turns around his own reverie. His thoughts, associations, and fantasies determine his entries. From a formal point of view, his observations resemble the writings of contemporary psychoanalysts, who focus on the countertransference of the analyst as a tool to perceive the conflicts of the analysand; the reverie of the analyst is turned into the medium of the analysand's story. However, the notes of the doctor lack the last critical step, in which self-reflection is interrelated with the perception of the Other. Instead, the doctor is driven by his despair over being unable to approach K. In this behavior, however, he unwittingly mirrors essential elements of his relationship with K, which turns him into a relay for us to gain a limited access to K. A connection to K, it seems, must be mediated through the fantasy of another narrative agent— be it the heterodiegetic narrator or the doctor.

Since the relationship between doctor and K is based primarily on these imaginative acts, the doctor cannot reveal or reconstruct K's story, he can only imagine it. In his diary, the conditional form and the apostrophe indicate this quasi-artistic, imaginative projection. Nevertheless, his report has an analytic component and ties in with the Oedipal motif of involuntary self-revelation. The silent, imaginary relationship with K reveals more about the doctor than about his patient. In an interview, Coetzee doubts that the oral narrative situation in confession and psychotherapeutic practice leads to truth: "To me . . . truth is related to silence, to reflection, to the practice of *writing*" (Coetzee and Attwell 65–66). The self-analysis of the doctor does indeed take place in the medium of diary writing, but its analytic patterns require an Other that propels and contains the search for truth.

Author, physician, conquistador: K's escape from the story

The encounter between K and Medical Officer has often been read as a *mise en abyme*, in which the Medical Officer represents the writer and reader (Dovey 298; Hayes 79). Coetzee does indeed use the therapeutic constellation to expose the problematic components of authorship and interpretation, but he does so through the relationship rather than a single character. K is not just a "text" subject to the revision and interpretation of the physician; instead, the novel is very much concerned with his own telling of the story.

Much has been made of K's reticence with the doctor and others. This silence cannot just be explained with his disability even if the cleft lip and "the old hopeless stupidity" (60) may impair open and comprehensible communication. We do not know much about K's actual intelligence, but his supposed stupidity is constructed as far more than a limiting disability. K employs it strategically to avoid getting arrested: "If I look very stupid, he thought, perhaps they will let me through" (40). K resists a narrative and interpretive fixation within institutions that seek to capture and define him (Marais, "Languages" 36; Attwell 98). But like his starvation, his silence cannot only be read as a voluntary form of resistance. In the face of "systematic and dehumanizing violence" in an apartheid state, K cannot speak. As a member of the disempowered majority of the South African public, Chesney argues, he is systematically refused a voice of his own (311). Marking K with his cleft lip as linguistically disabled symbolically reflects his voiceless political position (Huggan 97). Therefore, Dominic Head reads his silence as much as a sign of his resistance as of his disenfranchisement (*J. M. Coetzee* 98). In a system in which K's patienthood implies imprisonment, there is apparently no such thing as "therapeutic" storytelling.

However, reading K's disability as a political metaphor short-circuits the much more complicated construction of the novel. In fact, K does not outright refuse to tell stories. In the company of friendly people he even feels "the urge . . . to speak" (48). He returns from his seclusion in the mountains because he is afraid "that his story might end" (69). So he is searching for meaning (Hayes 100–01), for explanations, for guiding voices or for educational experiences: "Is that the moral of it all, he thought, the moral of the whole story?" (183). But whenever K struggles with his story, he meets with difficulties. He believes, for example, that "the story of his life had never been an interesting one" (67), and attempting to tell his tale, he realizes that he does not have "the whole story" (79) at his disposal. Other people seem similarly impenetrable to him: "There might be a thousand explanations, he could not read their minds" (107). K does not take interpretations of the behavior of others or even his own actions and thoughts for granted: "Would he have to say that the thought was Robert's and had merely found a home in him, or could he say that though the seed had come from Robert, the thought, having grown up inside him, was now his own?" (95). In this way, K becomes aware of something strange residing within himself. There seems to be a gap between himself and his words whenever he tries to give himself a coherent story:

> Always, when he tried to explain himself to himself, there remained a gap, a hole, a darkness before which his understanding baulked, into

which it was useless to pour words. The words were eaten up, the gap remained. His was always a story with a hole in it: a wrong story, always wrong. (110)

Following a psychoanalytic understanding, narratives are designed to bridge the gaps in life history, to fill them with constructions and thus establish coherence. K, however, has not learned "how to tell a story, how to keep interest alive" (176). This incapability to tell a story could, as Derek Wright argues, be attributed to K's subaltern status and his resistance against the institutions' claim on his story (10–11). But K's difficulties also point to a more fundamental problem. His thoughts turn around the impossibility of matching words with original experience: The story will always be "wrong" because he cannot overcome an experience of internal alterity (Helgesson 191), an unbridgeable gap, a darkness in himself. The gulf he experiences between himself and his self-understanding is similar to the gap that the Medical Officer recognizes in himself and in his relationship with K. While not ignoring political reasons for narrative unattainability, the novel also shows that storytelling always involves the bridging of gaps of inner and outer alterity. In K and the Medical Officer, it presents us two protagonists who, for different reasons, become fundamentally "disabled" by that alterity.

K's inability to tell his story prevents him from constructing the cathartic and grounding biographic narrative the Medical Officer desires. But his silence also protects him from narrative exploitation:

They want me to open my heart and tell them the story of a life in cages. They want to hear about all the cages I have lived in, as if I were a budgie or a white mouse or a monkey. And if I had learned storytelling at Huis Norenius instead of potato-peeling and sums, if they had made me practise the story of my life every day, standing over me with a cane till I could perform without stumbling, I might have known how to please them. . . . When my story was finished, people would have shaken their heads and been sorry and angry and plied me with food and drink. (181)

K recognizes that he would be asked to tell "stories of victimization" to appease the conscience of his audience (Kossew 128). Being able to tell his story would have repercussions. K associates the process of learning a story with violence and telling it with disappointment and exploitation. Whatever catharsis storytelling provides, the novel attributes the curative potential of narrative to a desire in potential listeners rather than to the storyteller's actual abilities.

Nevertheless, K develops a myth about himself: "The truth is that I have been a gardener" (181). Such a coherent narrative fills him with satisfaction, which shows that, despite everything, he desires self-knowledge: "It excited him, he found, to say, recklessly, *the truth, the truth about me*" (181). But the gardener myth is immediately called into question: "I am more like an earthworm, he thought. . . . Or a mole, also a gardener, that does not tell stories because it lives in silence" (182). Since K remains trapped in colonial discourse and resorts to the animal similes that were used to capture him by the Medical Officer, Stefan Helgesson doubts that this could be K's true story: "His true story can never be told; the story that we read is always the wrong story" (233). Helgesson assumes that every narrative K could come up with would always be someone else's, fictional to a certain degree, and thus wrong. But this critique pertains to all personal stories. They can never escape from discourse, be entirely "own" and "true"; they can only be judged by the value the construction has for a particular situation. In the same vein, Coetzee explains to psychoanalyst Arabella Kurtz: "I think we can entertain the notion that we are continually engaging with constructions (fictions) of others, rather than with their 'real' selves, without feeling we are at the edge of an abyss" (142–43). He argues for a psychology that accepts the fictionalization of self and others as a part of life. That is why the, undoubtedly limited, satisfaction K feels in the face of his "truth" is important. It evolves as an opposition to the claims of others but is inevitably shaped by them; it is a paradoxically relational construction of narrative resistance.

* * *

Renouncing the need for a story altogether is as unthinkable for K as for the people who desire it. Most urgently, the Medical Officer probes for this story, and when he fails to obtain it, he inserts his own story instead. But whether as listener, interpreter, or as the "author" of K's story, the doctor cannot capture his patient since most of his thoughts are determined by wishes and frustrated projections. His self-assessment as "persecutor, madman, bloodhound, policeman" (167) shows that the Medical Officer is aware of the problems of his pursuit after K. With his desire to reach K medically and narratively, he sees himself as a part of the colonial authority that persecutes K. From the Officer's impression of doing violence to K, Marais deduces an analogy between domination and persecution on the one hand and authorship and interpretation on the other: "The camps become the equivalent of the text in which the author imprisons his/her characters" ("Languages" 34). K's escape represents his escape from authorial control. For this very reason, Marais sees K as the signified that cannot be captured by the signifiers at the Officer's disposal ("Literature" 119). The more the Medical Officer tries to apprehend him, the more he seems to get away. Michela Canepari-Labib also describes the "doctor/coloniser" as "paternalist and patronizing" and does not believe that he can ever reach a valid interpretation of K (245). Kossew links this with Coetzee's own wish not to "coloniz[e]" the text by "imposing meaning upon it" (139).

In the novel, this analogy between colonizer, author, and critic is extended by adding the physician or psychoanalyst as another figure in the equation. In doing so, Coetzee implicitly draws on a long-standing discursive tradition in psychoanalysis. After all, Freud saw himself as one of the conquistadors and explorers who investigate the dark continent of the unconscious (Grubrich-Simitis 30; Matt 134). Antonino Ferro has criticized this suspicious, subjugating hermeneutics with the same analogy, arguing that the psychoanalyst cannot conquer the unconscious and should not employ interpretation to disempower or "coloniz[e]" the Other (*In* 32). Despite this self-critique within psychoanalytic practices, the analogous treatment of colonial structures, poetics, and therapy is a frequent feature of postcolonial and literary critique as well as novels such as Lewis Nkosi's *Mating Birds* (1986) or Nawal El Saadawi's *Woman at Point Zero* (1975)—quite possibly because of its particular ethical strength. Therapists assume responsibility and take care of living, suffering beings, which increases the moral depth of the analysis and provides a model of care ethics for postcolonial and literary studies.

In *Life & Times of Michael K*, the link between colonizers, analysts, and authors is embedded in a plot development that complicates the analogy. The Medical Officer is neither psychologically educated nor completely loyal to the regime. The more he engages with K and criticizes his own position, the less he actually acts as a Medical Officer. As I have shown, the diary traces a similar development through its formal arrangement. The reveries and apostrophes of the doctor are significant because they emphasize the presence of a relationship in the narrative that is not that dissimilar to a psychoanalytic understanding of the therapeutic relationship—a relational interaction coupled with asymmetry and absence. Thus, authors have an alternative to the conquest of their subject when they speak about the Other. By creating a resistant text that eludes the constructions of the Medical Officer and, potentially, the readers, Coetzee stages a narrative self-critique through formal means.

In this respect, Marais's observation that the Medical Officer gains a kind of access to K through his failure is important: "The moment of the other's escape, of its excession, is the moment of the self's awareness of an otherness that cannot be reduced to a correlate of intentionality" ("Literature" 119).

The Medical Officer is often reproached for his pursuit of K, but such a critique does not take into account the fantastic character of this pursuit. Even within this imaginative projection, the doctor realizes K's inevitable escape. Thus, the diary does not only represent the loss of K: "It is also the *trace* of that loss. So, although K is not, and cannot ever be, present in the diary, he is not entirely absent from it either" (Marais, "Literature" 116).

In the dialogic refraction of narrative perspectives between the different parts of the novel Kossew recognizes an alternative for speaking for another, because it problematizes the relationship between the storyteller and his object (151). What is happening on a textual level may thus be elevated to a creative principle. Coetzee characterizes writing as a dialogic process, "a matter of awakening the countervoices in oneself and embarking upon speech with them. It is some measure of a writer's seriousness whether he does evoke/invoke those countervoices in himself, that is, step down from the position of what Lacan calls 'the subject supposed to know'" (Coetzee and Attwell 65). Positing a relationship between authors and their creations, Coetzee describes how he makes contact with the characters of the novel: "If I was conducting any dialogue in *Life & Times*, it was with Michael K" (qtd. in Kossew 139). Lacan's concept of transference, its instantiation through the elevation of the analyst to a *sujet supposé savoir*, a structure of supposed knowledge (256), is thus insufficient to describe the function of the author. Coetzee's author, as criticized and questioned in the Medical Officer, is more akin to the receptive analyst who struggles with countertransference, rejects a position of knowingness, and seeks to enter a dialogue with his patient. Such an author/analyst, however, would not be a mere function, a neutral blank space, but a being driven by his own desire—a drive that may lead him astray but also lets him seek the confrontation in the first place.

In the multiply determined historical and social context of a colonial civil war and an institutionalized therapeutic encounter, the Medical Officer does not reach a satisfactory narrative about K. This failure nevertheless contains a progressive perspective. The gradual transformation of the doctor would be unthinkable if he had received an answer to his desire immediately, in the shape of a cathartic narrative that discharges the conflict. His transformation comes about through frustration and deferral that propel the continued confrontation with K and his history (Durrant 50). Authorship emerges as a process that is based on an interminable, asymmetric dialogue.

* * *

In *Life & Times of Michael K*, such a dialogue is not possible without interpretation. No character in the novel can ever just *be* with K; everyone always needs to *know* him. K himself is constantly struggling to understand an environment that seems to be encrypted and full of hidden but inaccessible meaning. In medical institutions, in particular, meaning is collected and systematically kept from K, and although he is confronted with the unreadability of this world, he keeps studying it: "He inspected the charts at the foot of the bed but could not make out whether they referred to his mother or someone else" (29). Still, the central character used to discuss this pervasive epistemic desire is the Medical Officer. His desperate pursuit of K is the perfect image for this unquenchable desire. Hungry for insight, he can only shout his reading at his patient who "would break into a run" at the sight of him:

> Your stay in the camp was merely an allegory, if you know that word. It was an allegory—speaking at the highest level—of how scandalously, how outrageously a meaning can take up residence in a system without becoming a term in it. Did you notice how, whenever I tried to pin you down, you slipped away? (166)

With this interpretation, the doctor enters a paradoxical situation. If he is wrong, K has escaped him—and he was therefore actually right. If, however, he is right from the start, he has finally captured K. But that would mean that he was wrong or that he has destroyed K's substance with his interpretation. Still, for all its paradoxical circularity, at first glance, this interpretation seems to be supported by the novel.

K really does not reveal much about himself; he remains an unreadable disturbance for the doctor, who designates him as "the obscurest of the obscure, so obscure as to be a prodigy" (142). Accordingly, Dovey reads him as "that which *eludes* representation," as a figure of the unrepresentable unconscious, "which resurfaces and undermines the conscious meanings of each successive reading" (301, 311). Similarly, Dominic Head believes that "the elusiveness of K is a grand-scale enactment of the poststructuralist idea of infinitely deferred meaning" (*J. M. Coetzee* 4). K's interpretive volatility is not absolute, however, as is shown in his already cited desire for tracelessness. Even if he leaves behind no more than "the scratch of ant-feet, the rasp of butterfly teeth" (97), a "text" remains that is just too fleeting and subtle to be perceived. So it might be difficult but not impossible to "trace" K. Clearly, those who try to read K as a symbol of irreducible meaning become involved in the Medical Officer's paradoxical situation. Marais admits: "Owing to its irreducibility, then, K's otherness inspires what it interrupts. By extension, this alterity, of course, ironizes *my* explanation of its irreducible and therefore ineliminable nature, a reading which has been partly prompted, and therefore ironically qualified, by the officer's final, despairing reading of K" (*Secretary* 52). That is why David Attwell acknowledges that he steps into a metafictional trap when he adopts the interpretation of the Medical Officer (Coetzee and Attwell 204). Our doubts concerning the doctor's interpretations are thus transferred to the critic's interpretation—which is why we have to understand exactly how the Medical Officer fails and how he may still partially succeed within that failure.

Chesney describes the Medical Officer as "a well-intentioned, thoughtful man whose structural position and imperial will to narrate preclude a real understanding of Michael K" (313), thus summarizing what most commentators agree upon: inevitably, the doctor misses K's essence with his interpretive attempts because from his political vantage point he cannot close the gap to K. Whatever he constructs about a nonexisting "Michaels" remains a fiction. Chesney blames the doctor's position in the colonial system for his failure. But the novel suggests there are other factors. "Do I understand that part of the story correctly? That is how I understand it anyhow" (149), is one of the doctor's many appeals to K. He reaches out for an answer from K, but in its absence, he supplies it himself, failing to identify their relationship, rather than his own mind, as the proper locus of insight.

All interpretations thus remain subjugated to his structure of needs. His precarious situation in the camp system has the officer crave meaning, and thus he hopes: "Michaels means something, and the meaning he has is not private to me" (165). He has to fight against the idea that this need might just be "a lack in myself, a lack, say, of something to believe in" (165), because if his thoughts were just a projection and caused by his own deficiencies, he might have reason for suicidal despair. K's difference, the "gaps" (176) that even K is incapable of surmounting, K's silence, and the "lack" of the doctor all taken together create plenty of imaginary space for his projections. As a reader of K he is almost forced to fill the gaps in the text and, for lack of information, he needs to return to his own impressions. As Iser and many psychoanalytic critics have posited, these gaps are the very thing that propels his transference (284). But even when he turns "my bleakest stare in upon myself" (165), he does not manage to analyze himself systematically and face his "lack."

Susan Gallagher thus sees the apparently doomed attempts of the doctor-critic to approach K as a warning for all readers and commentators against the "dangers" of assigning meaning to Others and inventing stories for them (164). Gillian Dooley thinks that readers might laugh about the doctor, given his "contortions . . . to wrest a meaning from Michael" (46). And Heider criticizes the doctor for his empty allegories: "It is all in an imagined speech to K; K is not present. He is a critic haranguing an absent auditor" (91).

But is he not in the same strait any critic of the novel finds herself in, whose interpretations will be just as precarious? Is the reader, stuck in a similar situation, really in a place to laugh about the officer? And is an interest in K not also a precondition for responsibility and care (Marais, *Secretary* 61–62)? To read the behavior of the Medical Officer exclusively as a warning, an allegory of the impossibility of understanding, or even of the laughable or damnable desire for an explanation, prevents us from understanding the similarities between the reader and the Medical Officer. And we must not forget that the doctor manages to gain some insight into himself and turn his medical aloofness into observant care—a path of ethical transformation that is worth looking at.

Before dismissing the Medical Officer's approach entirely, we should take note of the fact that he is given plenty of room to support his position, and that Coetzee comes to his defense:

> He heals people, he helps people, he protects people. Does it matter that his actions don't satisfy him? Maybe the world would be a better place if there were more people like him around. Maybe. I put the question, anyhow. . . . First of all he seems to me a person who believes (or wants) Michael K to have a meaning. I don't think that K believes (or wants) the doctor to have a meaning. (Morphet 457)

According to this reading, the doctor is mainly characterized by his unquenchable thirst for understanding. Even when he is already being attacked by the children in his fantasy, he calls out to K: "Have I understood you? If I am right, hold up your right hand; if I am wrong, hold up your left!" (167). Surely the Medical Officer misses K with this "simplistic system" (Kossew 149); but his desire is comprehensible and mirrors not just the reader's desire for meaning but also K's for self-understanding. This desire for meaning stands in the way of recognition, but the novel also alerts us to the fact that it is inevitable if any understanding is to be had.

The first part of the novel allows readers to entertain the illusion that they have access to K's consciousness. But this access has limits, for we remain "fundamentally unable to share his own experience of that world" (Buelens and Hoens 163). As Attridge has shown, the reader never actually participates in K's emotions: "Although we learn in moving detail of his thought processes and emotions, we never feel that we have assimilated them to our own. The language in these accounts is not necessarily that which K would use in articulating his thoughts—indeed, we often suspect that what are represented as thoughts scarcely exist in an articulated form" (74). Instead, the text is "a narrator's statement *about* K's state of mind" (75).

That means that even at the beginning of the novel, access to K is only possible through a third subject, a fusion of K and the narrator. In the second part, this access is taken away from the reader and K's "gaps" (*Life* 176) become hers—they are transferred onto her via the formal strategies I have outlined earlier. Left with the Medical Officer's mediated reading of K, the reader is almost forced to share the doctor's desirous position in the text. At the same time, this makes her understand K even less than before. Thus, an alienation from K is imposed on her that resembles the incomprehension of the doctor and creates an interpretive suction. The reader, used to being able to follow K, will perceive the sudden rupture in her connection to the protagonist as a "gap" that she wishes to close. By making it impossible to know what K feels during his time in the camp, the question becomes even more pressing. Aside from leaving the reader no other role model than the doctor, the text also produces a structural rupture, which makes the reader as eager to figure K out as the Medical Officer. With its external perspective and the shared need to understand K, the second part of the novel not only represents "an allegory of our reading of it" (Hayes 79) or "an allegory of the escape of the text . . . from the reader" (Marais, "Languages" 37), but an invitation to first become a part of the allegory and participate in the struggle to make sense of K before taking it apart and giving the reader the opportunity to question her own participation. The text allows her to reflect on the impossibility of fusing horizons in the hermeneutic tradition, but she will also see that the Medical Officer moves along an asymptotic line of approach toward K. But it is not through historical or allegorical interpretation that he progresses in his understanding. If he learns anything about K, it is through his devotion and the attention he pays to the resistance reflected in K's words and gestures. Although there is no increase of reliable knowledge about K, his relationship to K changes. And the manifestations of this relationship are very much accessible as a source of information about K. If the reader not only observes but also participates in the interpretive dynamic of the therapeutic relationship, she also learns that this dynamic is the only way to understand anything about K, the doctor, and his investment in K.

Although the therapeutic relationship in *Life & Times of Michael K* does not open toward a complete understanding of the Other, its perspective allows for a more nuanced critique of hermeneutic action than the refusal of any kind of interpretive attempt. Psychoanalysts have long been alerted to the need for an interpretive technique that causes no harm to the Other, but does not lose itself in sterile neutrality either. Ralf Zwiebel points out that the desire for knowledge, understanding, and healing, which Freud called the *furor sanandi*, may become an obstacle to understand the psychic reality of the Other, which is why Bion called on psychoanalysts to bring "no memory, no desire" to therapy (Zwiebel, "Position" 43). Epistemic desire, however, is also what constitutes the psychoanalytic encounter, and it is often the foundation of any kind of engagement with another. Zwiebel's solution to remain open to the immediate moment of intersubjective experience (45) resonates with Ferro's aspiration to concentrate on the emanations of the relationship instead of searching for an interpretation in the past. These psychoanalytic tenets are surprisingly similar to the hermeneutic models Helgesson and Attridge develop for their reading of Coetzee's texts. Helgesson seeks to conceive of "reading as relation," which involves continued reflections on the alterity of the text (188). Instead of imposing a meaning, he wants to care for and enter a relationship with the text. This is also the basis of what Attridge calls "reading as an *event*": "I do not treat the text as an object whose significance has to be divined; I treat it as something that comes into being only in the process of understanding and responding that I, as an individual reader in a specific time and place, conditioned by a specific history, go through" (67). In other words, Attridge recommends taking the individual relationship between reader and text seriously and making that relational experience the foundation of one's work with the text. This orientation of reading, "a living-through or performing of the text" (77), would find its starting point not in knowledge, but in a new experience, in "the contingent, the processual, the provisional that keeps moral questions alive" (76). Thus, both psychoanalytic and literary criticism converge in paying attention to the presence of a relational experience, trying to avoid the ethical pitfalls of desirous reading. Coetzee's novelistic elaboration on these questions is particularly insightful. He not only alerts us to the dangers of desire but also highlights it as an inevitable ingredient of understanding, thus not invalidating the search for meaning but opening it for fluid, *careful* self-critique.

Conclusion

At first glance, all that *Life & Times of Michael K* offers is an insight into the failure of a therapeutic relationship. Despite all his efforts, the Medical Officer cannot convince Michael K to tell his story or even eat and save his life. Behind this story, however, we discover the complex interplay of K's minimal communicative contributions and the development of the camp doctor's mind-set from medical distance via frustration to epistemic desire and a wish for redemption through his patient. Nevertheless, these highly problematic relational gestures bring about a transformation of the ethical consciousness of the doctor and an approach between doctor and patient.

In neglect of this relational dynamic, the encounter between Medical Officer and Michael K has often been read as a commentary on the impossible attempts at controlling colonial subjects by colonizers, patients by doctors, characters by authors, and texts by critics. K's silence and the recognition of his own alterity call into question the possibility of self-knowledge and therapeutic narration, just as the shaky efforts of the doctor for an interpretation of K call into question his attempt at speaking for others and understanding them. However, K does not give up his search for meaning, the doctor's interpretations are not entirely wrong, and if the reader shares any position in the novel, it is the Medical Officer's. Thus, the therapeutic relationship, in which the reader is made to participate, turns out to be an effective instrument to explore how this desire and its interpretive excesses might be criticized effectively without succumbing to silence, and how they might even facilitate a careful variant of narration and comprehension.

What makes this possible is, among other things, a critique of the narrative and interpretive processes embedded in the form of the novel. The opposition between two different narrative modes reveals the function of overinterpretation and creates ruptures in understanding and gaps in experience that can be held accountable for the desire of the reader. The gradual transformation of the diary of the camp doctor from distanced case notes to apostrophizing reverie also enables readers to reconstruct his development, his self-critique, and his misjudgments through his language. Moreover, this structure shows how much a relationship determines the narrative and interpretive devices employed in its frame. The novel thus takes up a typically psychoanalytic framework, insofar as the therapeutic relationship also rests on asymmetrical interpretive and appellative structures that cannot be taken out of their relational context.

Life & Times of Michael K is not a plea for renouncing the desire for explanation and understanding in the face of social or psychological, postcolonial or therapeutic alterity, even if political, historical, and psychic circumstances set clear limits for dialogue in this novel. Coetzee calls the possibility of intersubjective understanding and curative storytelling into question, but he also shows that a meaningful encounter may be encapsulated even within an impossible relationship.

7

"To Keep the Sultan Amused": Scheherazadian Narration in Margaret Atwood's *Alias Grace*

Introduction: Puzzle pieces

In Margaret Atwood's novel *The Robber Bride* (1993), Roz Grunwald rewrites her life's story with her psychotherapist:

> Together the two of them labour over Roz's life as if it's a jigsaw puzzle, a mystery story with a solution at the end. They arrange and rearrange the pieces, trying to get them to come out better. They are hopeful: if Roz can figure out what story she's in, then they will be able to spot the erroneous turns she took, they can retrace her steps, they can change the ending. They work out a tentative plot. (460)

This vision of a mutual narrative process, a puzzle like a "mystery story," which must be turned toward a better ending, corresponds perfectly to the basic tenets of narrative therapy. Roz's goals are pragmatic: "to see if she can improve herself, make herself over into a new woman" (460). Her therapist is "nice" (460), and what she suggests "very reasonable" (461), but the passage is suffused with irony because the powerful emotions that have driven Roz into therapy—hatred, jealousy, and longing—cannot be accommodated in a reasonable plot.[1]

By contrast, the relationship between Grace Marks and Dr. Simon Jordan in *Alias Grace* (1996) could be described as a nonrational search for the missing pieces of a life's puzzle. Atwood's historical novel set in mid-nineteenth-century Canada tells the story of servant girl Grace, who has allegedly participated in the murder of her employer and his housekeeper and has been imprisoned in Kingston Penitentiary for these crimes.[2] A group of rich benefactors is convinced of her innocence and hires Dr. Jordan, a young American neurologist with excellent references, to examine her in the hopes of proving her innocence or preparing for an insanity defense.

The stakes are high. For Grace, this is her only hope of getting out of prison; Jordan depends on solving this case to establish himself professionally—and he becomes increasingly infatuated with his patient.

Jordan, along with other doctors in the novel, eventually contemplates the possibility that Grace suffers from multiple personality disorder (MPD). Disguised in its historical setting, *Alias Grace* capitalizes on the popular debates related to the increase in MPD diagnoses in the United States and Canada between the 1970s and the 1990s. Atwood's inquiry into identity and storytelling in the novel clearly engages with the concerns raised by this condition, which questioned personality models based on unalterable, unitary, and stable identities and highlighted the cultural constructedness of psychological disorders (Porter, "Introduction" 12–13; Merskey 281). Grace's alleged psychological disorder, however, is not the only reason why she becomes an unsolvable puzzle. She uses all her narrative skills to make herself impenetrable for the doctor; she develops intricate plots but omits the conclusion, rearranges the brittle pieces of her story to inveigle Jordan and keep him at a distance, strengthening their relationship as much as she destabilizes it.

In this way, *Alias Grace* keeps bringing up questions about the relational and interrelated construction of identities and narratives. How can we build a sustainable basis for storytelling and self-understanding from antagonistic relational forces and disparate narrative puzzle pieces? Who controls the relationship and the construction of narratives? Atwood has repeatedly linked writing and reading with a range of intra- and interpersonal processes that she associates with historical reconstruction, therapy, criminality, and madness. *Alias Grace* is located firmly in the middle of this metaphoric nexus of associations. My reading of the therapeutic relationship between Grace and Jordan shows that therapy, transference and madness are employed as metaphors to think through the links between knowledge, gender, and sexuality. It highlights how Atwood uses narrative devices such as fragmentation, multiple perspectives, and seriality as well as imagery derived from quilting, MPD, and the Scheherazade myth to create a reading experience that is just as complex and driven by desire as Jordan's attempts to gain analytic knowledge. Atwood extends these metaphors of desire, madness, and therapy into a critique of authorship, the reader's participation in the text's construction, and the impossibility of fixing interpretations to a single meaning—linking historiographical, psychological, and narrative discourses within the image of the therapeutic relationship. Atwood thus promotes a pragmatic, relational approach toward literature, history, and identity.

Folie à deux: Grace Marks and Dr. Simon Jordan

Dr. Jordan's therapeutic motivation is subordinated to a scientific and juridical project—solving the murder case. The young doctor has visited several research institutions in Europe, is well versed in contemporaneous psychological theory, and seeks to develop new therapeutic methods. His ambitions do not only recommend him to the philanthropist circle around Reverend Verringer but also make him ideally suited to the purposes of Atwood, who uses Jordan as a mouthpiece to impart knowledge about nineteenth-century psychology.

Jordan's faith in medical progress and the coming "Age of Enlightenment" to the "study of Mind" (348) is not shared by his patient, whose position in the therapeutic relationship is extremely vulnerable. In general, Grace's emotions toward doctors oscillate between contempt, mistrust—"When there's a doctor, it's always a bad sign" (31)—and fear. With Jordan, the situation is exacerbated because she meets him under the threat of losing her privileges in prison, "locked into" a room of the prison governor's house (42). Despite Jordan's efforts to create "an atmosphere of relaxation and calm" (71), their encounter remains based on force and suspicion, not unlike the encounter between K and the Medical Officer in Coetzee's novel. Grace's imprisonment is not the only factor increasing the asymmetry in the therapeutic dyad. As a suspected lunatic, as a woman, and as a part of the Irish working class, she is not used to being allowed to speak her mind. Grace is multiply and interdependently marginalized because of her conviction, her patienthood, and her psychosocial position. Her alleged crime stigmatizes her as much as contemporaneous assumptions about a woman's propensity to hysteria. Jordan may be critical of the objectification of women in general, but his critique remains indebted to a system built on prejudice and social barriers. His scientific training has taught him that the differences between men and women are discursively constructed, but he holds on to these differences nonetheless: "So he is under no illusions as to the innate refinement of women; but all the more reason to safeguard the purity of those still pure. In such a cause, hypocrisy is surely justified" (100). Limited by his comfortable illusions of moral and intellectual superiority, Jordan fails to see how many of his assumptions about Grace are based on her comparative powerlessness, thus further reinforcing the asymmetry between the two.

The rigid setting and the powerful asymmetry hamper the establishment of a productive working relationship, so Jordan's first efforts are turned toward gaining Grace's trust. In this way, they strike a proper working alliance, a "bargain" (77): "I give you my word that as long as you continue to talk with me, and do not lose control of yourself and become violent, you shall remain as you were" (46–47). Jordan suggests a simple rule for their conversations: "If you will try to talk, . . . I will try to listen" (46). Of particular interest to him is not "what he wanted [Grace] to say, but what [she] wanted to say" (77). He demands that she tell him everything, as "the small details of life often hide a great significance" (187). With this openness for details, incoherence, and the patient's control over the narrative, Jordan seems to anticipate the psychoanalytic fundamental rule. However, his methods lack the radical openness toward the patient's story that psychoanalysis would later institute. With small gifts like apples and turnips, he seeks to trigger associations to the day of the murder. According to Jordan's theory, vegetables stored in the cellar should, via suggestion, activate an associative "chain of thought" (97) from the crime scene to the progression of events, excavating "the memories that must perforce lie buried there" (153). Jordan is caught up in his own interpretive patterns, searching for a specific story. With a simulated lack of comprehension, Grace resists his attempt at controlling her story. She forces him to change his technique and ask her for her "family history" (219), steering the therapy from guided association to free narration, her very own "talking cure."

Jordan's associative method may be reminiscent of C. G. Jung's early associative experiments, but his professional and personal development is clearly based on Sigmund Freud. Sigmund and Si(g)mon(d) are both driven from research to medical practice by financial considerations and the desire to start a family. Jordan started studying medicine "out of a young man's perversity" (63), not wanting to enter the family business at once. His father's bankruptcy and death, however, forced him to earn a living with medicine. He dreams of founding a private institution, but to realize this project he needs a scientific breakthrough. In the meantime, he lives in narrow circumstances, which force him to postpone any thoughts of marriage: "First . . . he must accomplish something of value, discover something of note" (101). His efforts to break through Grace's amnesia are conducted under the pressure of his benefactors as well as his own ambitions, exacerbated by existential fears and libidinal desires. To cater to their own ambitions, both Jordan and Freud experiment with hypnosis but search for other ways to discover or, better yet, conquer the "*terra incognita*" of the unconscious (*Alias* 60); and both resort to free narration as an entryway into the psyche. Despite their fascination, the other sex remains an enigma for them, or, as Freud put it, a "dark continent" ("Question" 212, English in the original). Moreover, Freud's patient Dora provides an intertextual model for Grace's clinical condition, with her recurring bouts of unconsciousness and amnesia ("Fragment" 23; Staels 433). But whereas Freud uses his failure with Dora to revise his theory and practice, turning his defeat into progress, Jordan does not manage to solve the problems of his method. In this respect, he resembles Freud's colleague and mentor Josef Breuer, who is supposed to have fled from the transference love of his patient Anna O. when it threatened to expose him (Freud, "Observations" 159). Freud repeatedly criticized Breuer's behavior as well as his colleagues' frequent love affairs with patients. To read the Freudian motifs in the novel as a generalized critique of psychoanalysis (Niederhoff, "How" 86) thus falls short of Atwood's more intricate patterning. Freud learned from his mistakes with Dora and would emphasize the significance of the fundamental rules of communication and the transference in his later work, whereas Jordan fails to turn his difficulties with Grace into theoretical and technical progress. What reads like a critique of psychoanalytic history is at the same time an illustration of the importance of Freud's most central discovery—the pervasive influence of the therapeutic relationship on the analytic endeavor.

Atwood portrays Jordan as a deeply conflicted, self-reflective but ultimately self-deluded character. At first glance, Jordan's scientific stance seems to be more advanced than Freud's. Jordan discards his teachers' quasi-Freudian attitude that "for a good surgeon, as for a good sculptor, the ability to detach oneself from the business at hand was a prerequisite" (216). Jordan opposes this version of the surgeon's stance, criticizing its "deadening" implications: "Men and women are not statues, not lifeless like marble" (217). However, Jordan's advocacy of the involvement of the doctor is soon revealed as an expression of his deeply conflicted relationship with his patients, and women in particular. Psychological curiosity is used as a rationale for sexual and monetary gains. Jordan justifies his visits to prostitutes ("To heal humanity one must know it, and one cannot know it from a distance" [86]) and his "propensity to view each new acquaintance as a future paying inmate" (60) with his contribution to scientific progress. In addition, his diagnostic gaze serves to degrade women in medical as well as human categories: "The woman must be a ghoul as well as a hypochondriac" (99; Wilson, "Blindness" 185). Ultimately, however, Jordan's attitude shows that he is unable to separate medicine and sexuality. During medical treatments, he cannot rein in his sexual fantasies, while his scientific thinking seems to dominate in his lovemaking, where he conceives of a kiss as an "alternative to taking her pulse" (409). The sexualization of medicine becomes particularly apparent in Jordan's relationship with Grace.

Like the Medical Officer, Jordan is tempted to make his patient understandable through the creation of new imagery, but his comparisons never fail to include an erotic component. Before their first meeting, Jordan imagines Grace as a "heroine of a sentimental novel" (67) and as "a maiden in a towered dungeon" (68). The allure of these dramatic images is evident, as they offer Jordan the roles of hero and savior and correspond with contemporaneous artistic and social constructions of madness and womanhood (Tolan, *Margaret Atwood* 238–39). Jordan is not the only one prone to romantic fantasies. Dr. Bannerling calls Grace a siren (82), and her lawyer compares her with Scheherazade: "Perhaps Grace Marks has merely been telling you what she needs to tell in order to accomplish the desired end. . . . To keep the Sultan amused, . . . to keep the blow from falling" (438). Jordan may spurn the comparisons of others, but he is as "desperate to define her" as the other men (Tolan, *Margaret Atwood* 247). He tries to fight his inclination to project, "I must stick to observation. . . . I must resist melodrama" (69), but his attempts at objectivity are soon revealed as yet another way of trying to pin Grace down in psychological and sexual terms.

As an "object of my investigations" (61) and "an interesting study" (85), Grace seems to him like a clock mechanism, in which "any twitch" (338) is meaningful only insofar as it pertains to the solution of the case. Grace notes his "measuring look" with suspicion (42). Rightly so, for Jordan regards her not only as a scientific object but also as his property: "Grace is his territory; he must repel poachers" (350). The spatial metaphor is adequate, as his examinations are increasingly perceived as an intrusion into her psyche. Jordan sees Grace as an object that must be opened or deciphered: "I approach her mind as if it is a locked box, to which I must find the right key" (153). The violence of his fantasies increases, mirroring, first and foremost, the anxiety of not being able to withstand her attractions: "Some days he would like to slap her. . . . But then she would have trapped him" (421). Grace's own experience of his expeditions into her mind links tenderness with violence, thus also hinting at the sexual overdetermination of his scientific endeavor: "A feeling like being torn open; not like a body of flesh, it is not painful as such, but like a peach; and not even torn open, but too ripe and splitting open of its own accord" (79). These fantasies of hollow bodies and imprisonment point to a desire for sexual and linguistic disclosure, but as Grace's impressions show, they are tied to mutual anxieties and attractions in their relationship. Fearful of losing control, Jordan clutches to a "position of all-knowing authority" (335), medical concepts, and methodical procedures. Thus, he misses important factors in their relationship, the "immeasurable . . . manifestations of her unconscious" (Staels 439), as well as his own loss of professional distance. His adherence to scientific objectivity is increasingly revealed as a defense against his uncontrollable inner world.

His attention quickly moves to Grace's body. He notices that she is "more than pretty" and responds to her sensual presence: "Her scent is a distracting undercurrent. . . . He is in the presence of a female animal; something fox-like and alert. He senses an answering alertness along his own skin" (103).

It is remarkable that Jordan links his sense of attraction with the animal kingdom, both through animal imagery and the activation of other sensory organs besides the ear. This suggests that Jordan tries to disassociate these sensations from his scientific endeavor and fails to see how they have already affected his professional perception. Accordingly, Fiona Tolan observes: "The narrative . . . begins to conflate the psychoanalytic process . . . with an explicitly sexualised desire to physically expose Grace" (*Margaret Atwood* 244). Like the Medical Officer, Jordan is driven by his desire to understand his patient, which also stands in the way of actually "capturing her." By adding a sexual component, Atwood allows us to see how this desirous involvement is also structured by specific, historically determined, and gendered imaginary structures, which draw on stereotypes that construct women as helpless, hysterical, less-than-human, closer to and less able to control their physical desires.

Jordan is aware of the transference he might inspire in patients and its link to the desire for secret knowledge, but he is not equipped with a similar knowledge about his own entrapment in the relationship. He believes that his patients are often drawn to him, "longed to entice him into shadowy corners," "to confide in him . . . with quavers, because he also inspired fear. . . . He has been where they could never go, seen what they could never see" (94). In a similar vein, transferential desires are attributed to Grace: "The poor creature has fallen in love with you. . . . You are doubtless the object of her waking daydreams" (438), her lawyer MacKenzie tells Jordan. When he adds that she was also infatuated with him, Jordan jealously regards MacKenzie as a "conceited little troll" (439), which once more demonstrates Jordan's unconscious involvement with Grace. By displacing their own desires and anxieties, both men reveal themselves as cultivating their own transference: "Simon Jordan and others offload onto women, here specifically Grace, their own desire, disgust, and terror at sex and their sexual longings and needs" (Wisker 47). Rose Lucas suspects that Jordan is blocked from seeing the complexity of Grace's narratives by his unrecognized sexual desires and professional furor, "by his failure to grapple with the complexities of his own position within the gridlock of transference/counter-transference exchange" (182). That Jordan is compelled by the idea of Grace's transference, that he desires "this trembling and clinging," "though, he now sees, in a suspiciously theatrical way" (474), shows most clearly how much he is caught up in the countertransference. He wants to obtain power and recognition through her helplessness but is alerted to the unreality of his fantasies by their theatricality.

Alias Grace provides a particularly revealing study of the therapeutic relationship because Atwood also allows us to see Grace's perception of the treatment. Grace, as she presents herself, is far from transfixed by Jordan.

Instead, she often feels attacked or mocked by his questions; his intrusion into her privacy displeases her. She criticizes his lack of sensitivity—"He has not noticed my tone or else he has chosen not to notice it" (114)—and responds with obdurate silence. Due to Jordan's desire-driven blindness to the asymmetrical relational dynamics and his inability to contain Grace's poetic language in his scientific jargon (March 74), there are many grounds for misunderstanding. In addition, out of mistrust about Jordan's role in a potential acquittal, Grace never allows Jordan to advance too far into her psyche. Crucially, then, she controls his (mis)understanding through a conscious employment of narrative strategies, meeting his efforts at decipherment with targeted cover-up tactics such as "a good stupid look" (43) or a refusal to reveal memories and dreams "to keep something for myself" (116). Jordan's efforts remain fruitless due to these strategies: "She manages to tell me as little as possible" (153).

Her manipulation of the conversation involves such resistance and reticence as well as controlled compliance. One of her techniques to steer the dialogue is the strategic implication of the doctor in her narration. Thus, she caters to Jordan's fantasies when she turns therapy into a confessional, distinguishes Jordan as confidant, "I am telling this to no one but you" (533), and employs submissive phrases like "if you'll forgive me" and the respectful title "Sir" (134). In a maneuver that flatters his professional vanity, emphasizes the singularity of her story, and criticizes the prudery of society at the same time, she calls on Jordan's medical knowledge to defend the wealth of intimate detail in her stories: "I would not tell you about this, Sir, except that you are a doctor and doctors know about it already, so you will not be shocked" (189). In this rhetorical control of the conversation, Grace is guided by Jordan's desire: "I will tell Dr. Jordan about this, as he likes to hear about such things, and always writes them down" (413). In this way, Grace gradually attains more control over the relationship than Jordan. Her powers of observation allow her to turn the tables on Jordan from the start: "It was as if she were contemplating the subject of some unexplained experiment; as if it were he, and not she, who was under scrutiny" (68). Here, her own diagnostic gaze, which surveys his social status, his physical and mental state, serves to turn him into the patient in need to be studied. With her attempts to secure her position through manipulation, Grace thus effects a complete role reversal (Niederhoff, "How" 79).

The conscious employment of all her narrative powers distinguishes Grace from Jordan's clueless surrender to his countertransference. She is pleased by the distracting new structure given to her days by Jordan's regular visits (111) and she enjoys their talks, as Jordan notes with irritation, "much as one enjoys a game of any sort, when one is winning" (422). But none of her utterances allows us to assume that she has fallen in love with Jordan. He is most important to her as a sympathetic listener—as testified to by the letters she writes to him after her release (Lovelady 39)—and not as a lover. It is his attention, the hope and power she gains through his presence, and the possibility to speak that attach her to him (Tolan, *Margaret Atwood* 233; Zimmermann 407–08). However, the seductive quality of her behavior is not lost on Grace; indeed, she herself begins to enjoy this routine. Being written about has a sensual quality for her, which differs from the explorative intrusion of the medical thirst for knowledge by its focus on surfaces:

> I feel as if he is drawing me; or not drawing me, drawing on me—drawing on my skin—not with the pencil he is using, but with an old-fashioned goose pen, and not with the quill end but with the feather end. As if hundreds of butterflies have settled all over my face, and are softly opening and closing their wings. (79)

Partly to secure this almost tender form of writerly attention, partly to increase her chances for a pardon, and partly to thank Jordan for his kindness, Grace adapts her stories to his expectations: "I set to work willingly to tell my story, and to make it as interesting as I can, and rich in incident, as a sort of return gift to him" (286). Grace's willingness to expose herself extends to the physical level: "I could show him the scar" (420), she muses as she contemplates presenting her body as another piece of evidence. Uncovering and shaping her story is thus in some ways analogous to seducing Jordan. Their (narrative) relationship contains erotic components that cannot only be attributed to Jordan's heated fantasy; they are co-produced by Grace's compliance, which employs seduction as an ambiguous strategy for resistance and survival (Löschnigg and Löschnigg 448). Grace appears as a Scheherazade who spins her stories to sustain Jordan's interest in her case (Darroch 117) and, at the same time, save herself from him. Thus, her story emerges as one of the few aspects of her life over which and through which she still wields power. However, by closing herself off from Jordan, she also loses an opportunity to share her concerns with someone; as Tolan recognizes, she remains "trapped between silence and representation" (*Margaret Atwood* 234).

Increasingly, however, Grace's unattainability destabilizes Jordan. It haunts him even in his dreams, in which he is engaged in a futile search for a woman under the sheets: "frantically he rummages. But no; the last sheet is a bedsheet, and there's nothing under it but a bed" (408). His frustration begins to undermine his physical and psychological condition:

> For a moment he thinks he's gone deaf, or suffered a small stroke: he can see her lips moving, but he can't interpret any of the words. . . . The

> trouble is that the more she remembers, the more she relates, the more difficulty he himself is having. He can't seem to keep track of the pieces. It's as if she's drawing his energy out of him—using his own mental forces to materialize the figures in her story. (338)

In a narrative act of transference, Grace materializes her story through him. He becomes the medium of a narrative that can only take full effect in the presence and through the emotional involvement of another. Instead of penetrating her and pinning down a scientifically valid result, he is affected by Grace's supposed madness: "I . . . have come near to addling my own wits, in my assiduous attempts to unpick those of another" (490). Again, the tables between Grace and Jordan have turned; his frustration turns to madness and his life into another version of Grace's story.

In fact, Jordan's struggle with Grace begins to reveal ever more problematic structures in his own behavior. "It is not Grace Marks who uncovers *her* secrets but Simon Jordan *his*: his salacious and repressed past, dreams and thoughts catching up with him," Gina Wisker observes (56). Jordan's frustration is finally discharged in a careless affair with his landlady Rachel Humphrey. As Burkhard Niederhoff notes, this behavior aligns Jordan with the other men in Grace's life who exploit women for their own gains ("How" 79). But as the relationship progresses, Jordan's lot begins to mirror his patient's. Rachel tries to solicit him to kill her husband and elope to the United States, eerily replicating the crime Grace has been accused of. Jordan strikes camp and abruptly returns to the United States, fleeing as much from Rachel as from Grace. But Jordan's supposed escape is also a repetition of Grace's story, as Michelle Roberts argues: "Atwood distinguishes her account of the transference game by creating Jordan as a distorting mirror to Grace" (47). Due to an injury he suffers in the hastily joined American Civil War, Jordan loses his memory of Kingston. His mother hopes to cure him from his amnesia with an associative method similar to his own. Jordan is defeated by Grace's story, losing, much like her, his access to his biography and the power over his future. This, however, does not mean that Atwood destroys any sympathies the readers may have for him, as Barbara Rigney claims (158). Instead, her analysis of the therapeutic relationship considers the historical development of psychology, the social construction of gender roles, and the influence of sexual desire as factors that inevitably create the asymmetry in the dialogue between Jordan and Grace and cause misunderstandings within the dyad. Thus, she succeeds in representing Jordan's difficulties as a result of his socially and personally determined blind spots and as a consequence of the entanglement of both partners' needs and desires in the therapeutic relationship. And finally, his defeat is a defeat by the superior powers of a storyteller, whose performance is reflected and examined in the construction of the novel.

Alias Scheherazade: Multiple perspective disorder and stitching serial evasion

Upon opening the novel, readers of *Alias Grace* encounter a dense, multimodal patchwork of epigraphs from literary and historical sources, drawings, poems, letters, and narratives by different narrators, which are further interrupted by the segmentation of the novel into different parts, named after and illustrated by a variety of different quilt patterns. In thus assembling the material for the historical reconstruction of Grace's story, quilting, which is so essential to Grace's activities, determines the narrative configuration of the entire text. Grace's quilt stitching and simultaneous storytelling suggest a link between the two activities. Both, according to Earl Ingersoll, are aimed at producing larger textures from disparate fragments (385). The quilt thus works as a "metaphor for the literary artifact itself," but it also illustrates the process of reading and making sense of the disparate parts of the story (Rogerson, "Reading" 5, 9).

For many women in the nineteenth century, a female handicraft circle was often the only opportunity to speak freely (Wilson, "Quilting" 125). Thus, there is also a close thematic link between therapy and handicrafts, as quilting enables Grace to follow Jordan's proto-psychoanalytic fundamental rule: "Her stitching gives her a focus and, apparently, relaxes her sufficiently to converse freely with her interrogator" (Rogerson, "Reading" 7).[3] The way in which Atwood collects and links the parts of her novel also has an associative character. It resembles the quilt, "an object of unity in spite of fragmentation" (Murray 78), as much as psychoanalytic work. To speak with Freud, Atwood's historical novel digs in the past in its attempt to reconstruct Grace's story with "remains found in the débris" (Freud, "Constructions" 259)—only here, the remnants are drawn from the case documentation and contemporaneous literature. The multimodality of the novel points to the variety of sources—memories, fantasies, associations, cultural and scientific material—that must be consulted for this kind of (re-)construction. In their disparateness, the fragments of the novel are analytically disassembled; reading the novel is synonymous with synthesizing them. Atwood's metaphor of choice, however, is not Freud's archaeology but a form of textual or textile assembly—and we will see later why this is so.[4]

The construction of a psychoanalytic case involves not just the assembly of the preserved remnants but also their completion and supplementation (Freud, "Constructions" 259). "Where mere hints and outright gaps exist in the records, I have felt free to invent," Atwood admits in her "Author's Afterword" (542). Uncertainties, gaps, and contradictions determine the compilation of documents. In order to make the problems of historical narration visible, Atwood has recourse to the "proliferation of narratives with no ultimate points of fixity" that Peter Brooks associates with psychoanalysis (*Reading* 278). Fiction—Atwood's and that of the authors cited by her—fills up the construction, but it cannot close all gaps. The accumulation of genres and differing narratives relativize their respective validity, but at the same time, the dissolution of teleological narrative structures emerges as the only possibility of approaching the past (Löschnigg and Löschnigg 46; Michael 421–22). In this way, patchworks and psychoanalysis are more than metaphors for the text. They emerge as textual strategies that enable us to imagine historical and biographical storytelling as expansive and nonlinear constructions.

* * *

With regard to the fictional narratives in the novel, this associative effect is supported by the super- and juxtaposition of a range of narrative perspectives: Grace's, Jordan's, and an unknown narrator's. This multiperspectivity allows for a variety of analytic effects—effects that mirror psychoanalysis and at the same time open the text for narratological analysis.

Grace's voice is present in the novel in two autodiegetic narrative modes. She tells Jordan about her life in their therapeutic sessions in the past tense and she tells us about her experiences in prison in the present tense. These two voices reflect the theme of multiple identities, but they also exemplify the split between narrating I and narrated I in therapy—there is a Grace in the present of the relationship and a Grace that is being searched for in the past. However, her self-analysis is not employed in the service of therapy, as Freud would have it. Instead, she uses elaborate stylistic techniques to disguise her present self in the story of her past self. On the one hand, the text we read is reminiscent of oral narration. Jordan, as Grace's partner in dialogue, is woven into her narrative. Grace keeps addressing him, pointing out important events, or apologizing for the way she presents things to him. In this way, she creates the illusion of Jordan's inclusion in her narrative. On the other hand, her story is shaped by a systematic organization and an unusual richness in detail that is typical of written texts and serves to unsettle Jordan: "The very plenitude of her recollections may be a sort of distraction" (215–16). In a similar manner, the present tense narrative that, in the absence of another tangible "listener," is presumably addressed to us, the readers, serves to irritate the relationship between narrator and addressee. Maria and Martin Löschnigg note that Grace's thoughts reach a reflexivity and poeticality beyond the scope of a young maidservant (445). Taken together with the ambiguous narrative situation—can Grace really be aware of her readers?—her narrative destabilizes what we knew about her and her background. Yet another way to read these passages may be in explicit exclusion of an addressee. Readers may only be witnesses to Grace's dialogue with herself, which posits Grace's self-analysis against Jordan's attempts at therapy. Whereas she turns to Jordan with rhetorical tools that are supposed to manipulate their relationship, she turns inside with a poetic and reflective gaze that allows her to analyze her experiences. In proper psychoanalytic fashion, Grace's real "listener" seems to be herself.

With respect to the doctor, the text stages a reverse analysis from an external perspective. Jordan is an avid letter writer, and he may try to analyze himself, but he is not always honest to himself. His story is told by a heterodiegetic narrator, who is focalized through the doctor but analyzes his thoughts and his language, exposing and commenting on daydreams and blind spots from an ironic distance. We are, for example, told that Jordan wishes no closer relationship with his landlady, but the narrator adds, "despite an image that leaps into his mind, unbidden . . . of Mrs. Humphrey . . . being savaged by a hulking figure that bears no resemblance to himself; although . . . the quilted dressing gown looks identical" (163). Highlighting the objections "despite" and "although," the syntax here exposes wishes Jordan seeks to deny. Dissected by the heterodiegetic narrator, the doctor who takes Grace as his object of psychological observation thus becomes an object of analysis himself (Staels 445).

Atwood's perspectival multiplicity allows for a simultaneous but asymmetrical access to both sides of the therapeutic dyad, which are engaged in fraught examinations of their selves and of the Other. The concurrent internal and external dialogues that take effect in and beyond psychoanalysis are transferred to the narrative construction of the novel. None of the protagonists appears as a mere mirror for the needs of the other because their interdependence also comes to light on a formal level, and only a combination of all perspectives affords an insight into the therapeutic relationship. A complete overview, however, remains impossible because at decisive moments Atwood rebuffs her readers, reminding them that their privileged access to Grace's thoughts can be retracted at any moment. Grace's narrative flourishes are "a sort of distraction" and a mode of seduction. Eventually, the therapy session and the hypnosis scene in which Grace talks about the murder are told from Jordan's perspective, yielding no insight into Grace's thoughts. "After several hundreds of pages of gradual revelation, readers may have cause to feel excluded and misled when their intimate access to Grace is denied in this crucial scene," Heidi Darroch protests (116). Thus, readers are robbed of any trust they may have had in the characters' narratives. Jordan disqualifies himself with his compromised neutrality and his excessive fantasies. Grace is also an unreliable narrator because she either suffers from amnesia and MPD, which would cast doubt on her knowledge, or she does not, which would call her honesty into question. She notes herself that she cannot always distinguish between reality and dream (343) and describes memories as fragments, "like a plate that's been broken. There are always some pieces that would seem to belong to another plate altogether; and then there are the empty spaces, where you cannot fit anything in" (118–19). Thus, Grace questions the possibility of meticulous archaeological reconstructive work. A multiplicity of perspectives and a richness in detail alone do not guarantee the construction of a "complete" narrative.

* * *

In many ways, *Alias Grace* is constructed as an analytic crime novel. Although Jordan resists the role of a "judge" (357), he is nevertheless employed to find out the truth about the circumstances of the murder and compile a psychogram on Grace. In many popular novels from all over the world, the psychoanalyst is a successful detective—Wessel Ebersohn's *Divide the Night* (1981), Batya Gur's רצח בשבת בבוקר (*The Saturday Morning Murder*) (1988), or Jed Rubenfeld's *The Interpretation of Murder* (2006), in which Freud himself aids the detective, are prime examples. And yet, whatever promise *Alias Grace* extends to recover a truth via psychoanalytic detection, it is eventually disappointed. "Atwood uses the detective genre as subtext while challenging its conventions," Hilda Staels argues: "Whereas the traditional detective story starts with the desire to know and ends with the discovery of the offender and with the reconstruction of the history of the offence, *Alias Grace* describes a psychoanalyst's epistemological attempts to arrive at absolute knowledge through reason and ends in epistemological fallibility" (432). Jordan does indeed take over the role of detective when Grace's story does not yield the answers he desires, but his search for external evidence and his interviews with witnesses lead nowhere. "What are such physical tokens worth? A magician produces a coin from a hat, and because it's a real coin and a real hat, the audience believes that the illusion too is real" (451). The analytic-detective procedure is exposed as a theater of illusions—maybe because it is related to storytelling, which, for Atwood, is the "medium of the illusionist, the trickster" (Stein 169). At the end, Jordan admits to his investigative failure: "Nothing has been proved. But nothing has been disproved, either" (451). Once more, the analyst-detective runs up against the troublesome instability of analytic truth.

Atwood, however, produces this failure by pitting one model of analytic procedure—Oedipus's analysis—against another—Scheherazade's seriality. Grace's resistance against Jordan's analytic efforts relies, at least in part, on serial storytelling. It is quite telling that Sarah Polley's project of adapting the novel to film eventually came to fruition as a Netflix miniseries that exploits the inherent complexity and seriality of the novel (Onstad). Grace's intradiegetic narration is perceived as a serial narrative because of the session structure of the narrative frame and the fragmented form of the novel. This implicit seriality is closely linked to the motifs of quilting and therapy. The first professional narrators who used serial forms, the rhapsodes, derived their name not without reason from ῥάπτω = sewing ("Rhapsode"). Serial narration, sewing, and therapy all assemble disparate pieces out of puzzles, textiles, and narratives and navigate the tensions between continuity and discontinuity that pervade *Alias Grace*. Repeatedly, Grace's narrative is interrupted by other narrators, section endings, and the following illustrations and epigraphs. These caesuras are reflected on the diegetic level, as the protagonist knows how to play with them. At Jordan's invitation— "Shall we continue with your story where we left off?"—she pretends to have forgotten her clue and explains: "This is not quite true; but I wish to see if he has really been listening to me" (228). The disruption is thus taken as an occasion to test if Jordan has been paying attention to the serial narrative. In this manner, the novel provides clues to the important connection between personal attachment and serial form.

Grace and the novel that bears her name need to bestow upon their story enough allure to make their audience *want* to continue listening or reading. Part of that enticement is created by promising a solution to the case. However, such a solution cannot actually be provided if the attachment is to be continued. A simple explanation of Grace's guilt or innocence would immediately destroy the magic she needs to bind Jordan to herself and her story. In many ways, Grace is successful; she creates so much desire for a story in Jordan that he can no longer act as a proper analyst-detective (Staels 433). And yet, the progression of the narrative thus gains a frightful dynamic of its own: "Today I must go on with the story. Or the story must go on with me, carrying me inside it ... ; although I hurl myself against the walls of it ... and beg God himself to let me out" (345). Scheherazade gets tangled up in a narrative that was designed to enfetter the audience. She has set a narrative dynamic in place that cannot be stopped if the relationship based on that narrative is to remain in place.

In order to detect the pattern of deferral and detail, with which Grace and the novel stave off the end, one must pay attention to this relationship rather than to its putative results. This is Jordan's mistake; he never notices that the progression and the form of the narrative process are more significant and more powerful than its outcome. With Brooks, Grace's technique might be described as a feature of every plot construction: "The desire of the text (the desire of reading) is hence desire for the end, but desire for the end reached only through the at least minimally complicated detour, the intentional deviance, in tension, which is the plot of narrative" (*Reading* 104). Deferral and distraction, "tension" and "deviance," however, can only work and fuel the narrative desire if the reader is attached to the narrative. Otherwise, she would not tolerate the deferral tactics. "Desire is the wish . . . for fulfillment, but fulfillment delayed so that we can understand it in relation to origin and to desire itself," Brooks adds, and declares: "The story of Shahrazad again suggests itself as the story of stories" (111). Seduction and obstruction, attachment and interruption, promise and deferral are thus the connected double movements of the serial plot. Jordan and the readers desire denouement, but with every interruption, with every negotiation about continuation, the narrative returns them to their relationship with Grace, which stands in the way of and makes up for the lack of closure. Readers find themselves confronted with their own desire to continue the relationship with Grace and the novel—or to terminate it. With its references to Scheherazade, *Alias Grace*, too, is a story of stories, or, rather, of storytelling, highlighting the relational component in narrative desire.

Storytelling à deux: Split authorship and entangled readers

Although Grace is presented as a self-aware narrator, her official story is authored by others:

> I can remember what I said when arrested, and what Mr. MacKenzie the lawyer said I should say, . . . and what the others said I must have said, for there are always those that will supply you with speeches of their own . . . ; and that sort are like the magicians who can throw their voice, at fairs and shows, and you are just their wooden doll. . . . My true voice could not get out. (342)

Her lawyer wants "a story that would hang together, and that had some chance of being believed" (415), while the newspapers are interested in believing "the worst; they can sell more papers that way" (412). All of them construct Grace according to their own goals, so that she remains imprisoned in medical and social discourses as well as "a variety of fantasy scripts" (Howells 36). Grace identifies these scripts as public performances, performed *through* her doll-like persona, but since their authors hold more discursive power than Grace and have a stage for their performance at their disposal, they may turn their fantasies into the public story.

Because of the multiplicity of these constructions, Grace notes a proliferation of her story:

> I think of all the things that have been written about me—that I am an inhuman female demon, that I am an innocent victim . . . , that I have blue eyes, that I have green eyes, . . . that I am a good girl with a pliable nature and no harm is told of me, that I am cunning and devious, that I am soft in the head and little better than an idiot. And I wonder, how can I be all of these different things at once? (25)

The diversity of prescribed roles creates an irritation that threatens to bury Grace beneath foreign ascriptions, but it also gives her a chance to hide behind them. Grace observes, organizes her perceptions, and turns herself into an empty screen for such projections: "I've learnt how to keep my face still" (29). Aware of the power of language and performance, she controls her speech carefully (Siddall 95) and adapts to the expectations of others: "I could see that she felt some tears were in order, and I shed several" (512). Through her own theatrical performance, Grace subverts the scripts of others. Her knowledge about the constructedness of narratives allows her to obtain agency in the relationship with Jordan (Siddall 91–92). As I have shown in my analysis of their relationship, Grace defies Jordan's therapeutic management of her story with a range of manipulative devices. Refusing to commit to any one version of her story and only adding more variants to the multiplicity of "Grace," she eludes a judgment of her truthfulness, gains more control over her story, and divests Jordan of the same amount of control (Löschnigg and Löschnigg 446, 449). A multiplication of stories is here presented as both the result of an interpretive desire and as its highly effective antidote.

Nevertheless, Darroch wants to understand Grace's story as a therapeutic restructuring of her past rather than as a manipulation of her doctor; for her, Grace's narration of traumatic experiences is "a way of comprehending what actually occurred and of evaluating what can safely be revealed to others"

(117). In this reading, Grace's narration helps her overcome her passivity and may lead to healing; it is "a means of recuperating a fragile and fragmented self" (104). However, the novel is highly ambivalent about the therapeutic function of narrative. Although Grace clearly benefits from storytelling, it is never revealed whether she ever tells the truth or recuperates anything from a traumatic past. Like Scheherazade, Grace uses storytelling primarily to sustain a strategic relationship (Löschnigg and Löschnigg 448) and increase her influence on the audience. This control over narration leads Ingersoll to interpret her as a metafictional character who represents the "storyteller, or author" (394). Her status as author, however, is precarious because despite all her efforts at manipulation, she is still subject to external constraints and lacks complete control over her stories. And with Grace, authorship falls under the suspicion of criminality, madness, schism, and polyphony.

For Atwood, the most important similarity between the work of the author and the psychoanalyst lies in their attention to the fictions people use to organize their lives: "So, everybody is involved in narrative and to that extent, everybody is involved in fiction. Because people fictionalize themselves. . . . They project onto other people roles that they carry around inside their heads, probably left over from their childhoods and families, and they see other people in their lives as those roles" (Metzler 283–84). Through a self-reflexive process in which fictionalizations become visible, literature can participate in the task of the psychoanalyst: "Then you can see to what extent you yourself are inventing, so you can demythologize the way you're connecting your life and divest yourself of dangerous illusions which you have invented yourself. Some psychoanalysts describe what they are doing with their patient is they are 'working on the patient's narrative'" (Metzler 284). In this explicit analogy, psychoanalyst and writer both delve into fiction to loosen fixations, "demythologize" them and return back from the depths. Atwood, however, is interested in the darker aspects of authorship that cannot be contained in therapy's rational practices. Jordan's failure at objectivity suggests that the crucial aspects of authorship become visible through the irrational undercurrents of psychoanalysis. As his motto in *The Interpretation of Dreams* showed,[5] Freud searched for the unconscious in some kind of underworld: in the "mad" netherworlds of the dream and mental illness. Atwood describes storytelling in general as "demonic, a function of possession, a practice akin to witchcraft" (Rigney 162). In *Negotiating with the Dead*, she characterizes writing as a labyrinthine struggle with emptiness and "darkness," "and a desire or perhaps a compulsion to enter it" (xxiii–xiv), "a desire to make the risky trip to the underworld" (156). Atwood's author is thus a figure who mediates between the psychoanalyst and the madwoman.

For Atwood, authors inevitably suffer from a schism, "for the mere act of writing splits the self in two" (*Negotiating* 32):

> By two, I mean the person who exists when no writing is going forward—the one who walks the dog, eats bran for regularity, takes the car in to be washed, and so forth—and that other, more shadowy and altogether more equivocal personage who shares the same body, and who, when no one is looking, takes it over and uses it to commit the actual writing. (35)

The medial structure of the written document, outlasting the moment of composition, brings about this split because the "author" is forever tied to the ephemeral act of writing while the real person lives on. Thus, writing seems to have little in common with the oral storytelling of Grace's therapeutic encounters. But with her split personality, Grace illuminates Atwood's schizoid poetics. If read in the context of the novel, the possibility that a hidden part of a personality commits the crime means that the crime of the author who "commit[s] the actual writing" can never be fully determined, not least because, like Grace, she envelops herself defensively in her own constructions (53). As long as it remains unclear who speaks, the author cannot be analyzed, and all interpretations simply bounce back. The presence Atwood gives her is an illusion, too: "We have the impression that [the writer] is right here, in the same room with us—we can hear the voice. . . . Or so it seems" (148). Grace's is such a voice, here with us but not, never to be localized. This conception of the author's voice, however, withdraws the text from any kind of control, be it the author's or the reader's, and puts it into a dialogic, relational context; without multiple authorship, multiple positions and stories, there is no text. Accordingly, writing is linked to a susceptibility to others and an openness to their constructions, which, again, fits Grace's performative resistance and her description of madness: "When you go mad you don't go any other place, you stay where you are. And somebody else comes in" (37). In Atwood's conceptualization of writing, this unwitting receptiveness for "somebody else" is replaced by a susceptibility to "something else": "It is opening yourself, discarding your self, so that the language and the world may be evoked through you" ("End" 348). Atwood's poetics—in its obsession with absent Others, journeys to the underworld, theatrics, and internal dialogues—thus merges authorship with madness and its exploration through the structure of psychoanalysis.

* * *

Aside from a madwoman, Atwood's author is also a criminal who leaves clues and seeks to hide them from the reader. Jordan, as he tries to decipher Grace's text, has emerged as yet another version of the reader as analyst-detective. His inability to resolve Grace's story, however, invites, even urges the reader to take over the role of the investigator: "In *Alias Grace*, the author is the criminal. The psychoanalyst-detective becomes the victim or patient, and the role of detective is assigned to the reader," Staels observes (436). Jordan's position is clearly inferior. Readers know more about Grace, and through the heterodiegetic narrator, they are also told what Jordan does not know, even about himself (Darroch 112). Compared with Jordan, the readers are twice privileged since they have more insight into the therapeutic dyad and know how much he lags behind modern psychology. This constellation may easily lead to a condescending attitude toward the doctor. Hannelore Zimmermann, for instance, describes her growing impatience with Jordan during his clumsy attempts at understanding Grace (411). Darroch reads Jordan's failure as a satisfying act of revenge against male presumptions regarding the analysis of women: "There is a peculiar pleasure in knowing more than Jordan, the expert, and for post-Freudians perhaps an additional satisfaction in retracing the common narrative trajectory of the ambitious male analyst's misunderstanding of, and overinvolvement in, his female patient's story of seduction, violence, and betrayal" (114). As in Coetzee's novel, however, this hostile attitude blocks any insight into the similarity between Jordan and the readers, who, despite their superiority, are also seduced by Grace. By the time they start criticizing Jordan, they have already been made a part of the relationship and its power structures.

In fact, the readers are deceived by Grace often enough. After the description of a beautiful sunrise, for example, she tells them: "In fact I have no idea of what kind of sunrise there was. In prison they make the windows high up" (275). The novel withholds important information from readers at crucial moments. The hypnosis scene, in particular, shows that they have been deceived about their privileged relationship to Grace's intimate thoughts. When a second personality suddenly speaks for Grace and takes responsibility for the crime, the audience cannot decide whether what they see is reality or a performance. What should be a climax that finally provides the desired knowledge only leads to further insecurity and a need for further explanations (Lucas 185). Jordan is thus a disillusioning mirror of the reader's fantasy of gaining intimate access to Grace's thoughts and cracking the case: "We recognize ourselves as gullible, ready to accept versions in which we can invest, which reinforce our beliefs and expectations," Wisker admits (38).

If readers criticize Jordan but do not criticize themselves in turn, they run the risk of likewise getting entangled in the relationship without recognizing how they contribute to it. Grace uses Jordan's desires, his tendency to turn into a "voyeur" in his investigations (449), to manipulate him. But is the reader not, as Atwood believes, also a "spy, a trespasser, someone in the habit of reading other people's letters and diaries" (*Negotiating* 126)—especially in this novel, which gives her access to the characters' intimate thoughts and messages? Accordingly, Tolan believes that "the reader's desire to know what really happened becomes conflated with Simon's attempts to unlock Grace's memory" ("Psychoanalytic Theme" 103). This may even be necessary. Without the desirous attachment of the reader/listener, literature cannot sustain itself. Atwood describes reading as a part of the process of writing, "the necessary completion without which writing can hardly be said to exist" ("End" 345). Thus, Jordan also has an important function for Grace. She stresses repeatedly that she tells and adapts her story *for* him, much like Atwood believes that an author always addresses a reader (*Negotiating* 151). Jordan's interventions change the progress of the narrative at important junctures. Indeed, he functions as a "medium," through which Grace's story is materialized and mirrored in his reflection and unwitting repetition.

Nonetheless, Jordan is not Atwood's ideal reader: "The act of reading a text is like playing music and listening to it at the same time, and the reader becomes his own interpreter" (*Negotiating* 50). Atwood demands a high degree of interpretive and observational skills as well as a self-reflexive attitude in her reader that resembles the stance of the ideal analyst, who acts in the transference and observes it at the same time. Jordan, however, is not interested in the music, "the tune played by the musical box," but in "the little cogs and wheels within it" (98). Atwood warns us against concentrating exclusively on form and technique: "We all know that a book is not really a person. . . . But if you . . . ignore the human element in them—that is, their voices—you . . . will be an idolator, or else a fetishist" (*Negotiating* 145). For Atwood, the connection between text and reader is a proper, emotionally charged relationship. As long as Jordan is only interested in the "mechanics" of his object, he remains a fetishistic reader who does not recognize the relationship established by the act of analyzing and thus underestimates his own personal part in the process of understanding. "Reading . . . changes you," Atwood explains. "You aren't the same person after you've read a particular book as you were before" ("End" 345). The reader, like Jordan, may be deceived, disappointed, and confronted with her anxieties, but never does the confrontation with the text leave the reader untouched and unchanged.

* * *

Jordan is not the only reader who strives to put an interpretive label on Grace. Dr. Bannerling does not grow tired of emphasizing that Grace is "an accomplished actress and a most practiced liar" (81). Her lawyer entitles her as "Our Lady of the Silences" (433) and "Scheherazade" (438). These interpretations quickly become readable as consequences of the reader's desire and expose the "mechanisms" that drive the men to these conclusions (Müller 242).

The rootedness of interpretations in individual structures of need and the joint construction of narratives call into question what Jordan holds up as "truth." "He can't state anything with certainty and still tell the truth, because the truth eludes him. Or rather it's Grace herself who eludes him" (473). He understands that she hides parts of her story intentionally to protect herself: "If she has anything to hide, she may want to stay in the water, in the dark" (374). For Niederhoff, the novel's critique of interpretation therefore amounts to "an attack on psychoanalysis" and its belief that insight leads to healing ("How" 86). In light of the previously discussed correlations, however, this conclusion becomes dubious. Grace never allows for interpersonal insight to be produced, and the novel is not interested in what would happen if she did. Instead, it tackles the problem of narrative constructions, which are the actual focus of modern psychoanalytic practice (not, as is still often assumed, the excavation of knowledge). Thus, the critique of the therapeutic process hinges on its institutionalization, and, as Tolan explains, on Jordan's problematic methods, designed to explain Grace at all costs ("Psychoanalytic Theme" 102). If, however, psychoanalysis is a relational process in which narratives are jointly produced, neither Grace's evasive storytelling nor Jordan's misguided scientific narrative is entirely without value: "Grace's narrative can be judged as neither true nor false but instead is a reflection of both characters' desires: Dr. Jordan's for medical authority, Grace's for pardon, for a personal story, and for a listener" (Fiamengo 55).

Having reached the limits of his therapeutic inventiveness, Jordan agrees to have Grace hypnotized. But the conclusion of this "theatrical" performance (462) is a further multiplication of interpretations through the emergence of a second personality. Verringer sees in her behavior "a clear case of possession," and DuPont supplements Jordan's guess that it might be "a neurological condition" with a precise diagnosis, "*double consciousness*" (470–71). However, what remains open to debate is not just the explanation of her behavior but also the reality of the experience: "Was Grace really in a trance, or was she play-acting, and laughing up her sleeve?" (472).[6] Once again, the suspicion of theatrics creeps into a medical performance, but, as opposed to its employment in psychoanalytic discourse, playacting is not a cathartic alternative to telling what cannot be told, but a form of resistance against catharsis. The novel never reveals a solution to Grace's case and her behavior: "Indeed, there are hints throughout the novel to support every one of these interpretations," Coral Howells observes (34). Maybe Grace finally meets a hidden part of her self on DuPont's "stage"; but maybe both of them play a comedy in which Grace confounds the roles that have been imposed on her with her own performance. Atwood confronts us not with narrative truth but with theatrical truth, which is performative, ambiguous, playful, and resists interpretation.

If we accept the consequence of this insight, that there are only "versions of truth," Grace eludes any kind of final interpretation (Tolan, *Margaret Atwood* 228). Her deeds cannot be explained (anymore). This may not, as Atwood remarks, call into question historical truth itself, but it certainly affects its attainability: "I am not one of those who believes there is no truth to be known; but I have to conclude that, although there undoubtedly was a truth—somebody did kill Nancy Montgomery—truth is sometimes unknowable" ("In Search" 1515). As long as the truth remains unknowable and the only alternatives are constructions that owe their status to the power and skill of the actor and interpreter, historiography, psychoanalysis, and fiction are all aligned as "discursive constructs" (Staels 431). All partake in the "realm of storytelling" and are linked to artistic work, "design, artifice, construction, and discretion" (Tolan, *Margaret Atwood* 225). In her historical novel, which, as a genre, is certainly concerned with historical truth, Atwood challenges this aspiration for her own project of "historiographic metafiction" (Murray 66) as much as for the treatment of history in general. By combining several texts and perspectives, she avoids the necessity of giving Grace a final story: "Atwood's novel engages in a curious leveling out of the authority of all the texts it presents" (Michael 421). It questions a traditional understanding of history and of the "one and true" story, emphasizes the textuality of history, and allows for multiple, overdetermined, incomplete, and contradictory versions (421). The juxtaposition of various narratives defies a teleological conception of historical sequence, and instead leads to a planar tapestry that can be read in more than one direction at once. Atwood thus replaces an essentialist understanding of history with a pragmatic use of historical tradition:

> We have to be listening first, before [the past] will say a word, and, even so, listening means telling, and then re-telling. It's we ourselves who must do such telling, about the past, if anything is to be said about it; and our audience is one another. . . . The past no longer belongs only to those who once lived in it; the past belongs to those who claim it, and are willing to explore it, and to infuse it with meaning for those alive today. The past belongs to us, because we are the ones who need it. ("In Search" 1515–16)

Interestingly, Atwood embeds this use of history in a quasi-therapeutic frame of listening and retelling, in which history is not evaluated by epistemic accuracy but by need. History can thus be transformed to fulfill a cathartic purpose in constructing the self and its relationships.

Atwood's identity politics also follows this narrative pragmatism. Reverend Verringer might be indignant that "we cannot be mere patchworks!" (471), but in Atwood, identities are indeed patchworks, constructed and manipulated like histories, in order to develop useful narratives (Tolan, *Margaret Atwood* 224). The fictionalizing tendency is thus extended, as mentioned before, to one's own self: "What we consider real is also imagined: every life lived is also an inner life, a life created" (Atwood, *Negotiating* 7). This dissemination of fictionalizations of the self, however, is a provocation for feminist politics. Darroch criticizes the novel because it leaves open the possibility that Grace invented her trauma. The feminist project of returning a voice to the victims of abuse might certainly be hampered by an emphasis on the fictional aspects of personal histories (Darroch 118). However, what if there is no such *one* voice to be returned? Irrespective of whether Grace suffers from MPD or not, the novel presents her as a patchwork, split into multiple stories and identities (Löschnigg and Löschnigg 456). MPD thus actively symbolizes the plural core of every personality, reflecting the change of psychological and psychoanalytic theories of the self that Atwood grapples with. Roy Schafer, for instance, calls for a recognition of the multiplicity of narratives about the self. A unitary identity is an illusion constructed by language but not confirmed by the individual's psychic reality (*Retelling* 53–54). Atwood's novel meticulously traces and reveals this process of self-construction via narration. Concomitantly, the novel makes use of the same technique: "Atwood too reveals herself to be an expert seamstress for, when (re)creating the fluid past of her characters, she quilts the disparate bits and pieces into an aesthetic whole" (Vevaina 94). The associative, "quilting" function of narration mitigates the rifts without completely eliminating them. By combining splitting and deferring with the synthesis of analytic fragments, Grace and the novel do eventually cater to a need for understanding and coping (Vevaina 95). The part and the whole thus find each other in the process of narration, but the seams of desire and indeterminacy will remain visible all the same.

Conclusion

In contrast to Philip Roth and J. M. Coetzee, Margaret Atwood allows us access to both sides of the therapeutic relationship. Thus, it becomes apparent how antagonistic needs and desires generate the foundation of the relationship between Grace Marks and Dr. Jordan—a scientific and erotic interest on the one hand, and a desire for attention and self-determination on the other. In *Life & Times of Michael K*, we saw how the desire of the doctor destabilized the relationship while allowing for personal insight; in *Alias Grace*, the patient uses the desire of the doctor to manipulate the relationship with strategic narration, thus foreclosing the possibility of insight. It is not just Jordan's growing sexual desire that obfuscates his view of Grace. Grace is a Scheherazade who has realized that power—in the nineteenth century almost inevitably concentrated in male hands—can be attained through narrative means, and she plays off this power against Jordan. But storytelling also involves a loss of control, not just for the inept and infected listener but also for the narrator herself.

This is also suggested by the form of the novel. A patchwork of textual genres and perspectives deprives the reader of the desired facts while simultaneously overwhelming her, even more so because associative techniques are used, not just to establish contexts but to fill gaps with dubious constructions and conduct an analysis of historical material that forecloses a solution of the case. Narrative abundance and deferral emerge as strategies for seduction, in order to link story segments, attach the audience, and still deny them a solution at the very end.

From this point of departure, it is almost impossible not to reevaluate the (self-)control of the author. In *Alias Grace*, the author is akin to the criminal and the madwoman, who plays with the analyst. According to the novel, authorship is a practice of splitting the self, of conducting an internal dialogue, exercising power, and staging a play—a practice that is necessarily confronted with the constructions of others and the loss of control over one's own narrative. In turn, readers are enticed to criticize the doctor and his interpretive desire only to realize that they share his susceptibility to the narrators' chicaneries. In the end, they cannot control the narrative any more than they can attain a final truth or the "true" identity of Grace. Historiography and psychoanalysis, and with them truth, identity, and narrative forms of communication, all appear polyphonic and indeterminable. As a consequence, the narrator must proceed pragmatically, according to a particular structure of needs, and, if need be, fall back on fictions.

In the novel, psychoanalysis is defined as one narrative process among many. In order to do so, Atwood assembles motifs from psychoanalytic history, methodical precursors, and fragments from the biographies of their founders, creating another pragmatic, fictionalized variant of the past. Despite the fallibility of the proto-psychoanalyst Jordan, this does not lead to a generalized critique of the practices of psychoanalysis but serves to outline problems psychoanalysis shares with literature—the elusiveness and the relational construction of (historical) truth.

8

"Act It Out, If You Like": Anti- and Stage-Psychiatry in Peter Shaffer's *Equus*

Introduction: Anti-psychiatry

Having blinded six horses in a religious frenzy, seventeen-year-old Alan Strang is sent to child psychiatrist Martin Dysart's clinic to keep him out of prison. The more the therapist begins to understand his patient, who has created a personal horse cult to escape the intellectual, spiritual, and moral confines of his family, the more he calls his own task, the destruction of the "work" of his patient, into question. Extremely successful, produced all over the world with a spectacular dramatic staging, adapted in a 1977 Sidney Lumet film, and decorated with "every theatrical award available" (MacMurraugh-Kavanagh 8), Peter Shaffer's play *Equus* (1973), which deals almost exclusively with the encounter between the child psychiatrist and his delinquent patient, was also criticized harshly: psychoanalyst Sanford Gifford vented his resentment in the *New York Times* by calling it "a skilful mixture of truth, banality and pretension" (qtd. in Cooke and Page 55). Although Shaffer had a child psychiatrist look over his manuscript ("Author's Notes" xxi), the play was met with much resistance among psychiatrists, who believed that Shaffer attacked their profession. In an interview, Shaffer noted with some amusement: "In England the play was found shocking because it seemed cruel to horses, in America because it seemed cruel to psychiatrists." At the same time, the public outrage made the play successful: "Every remark which could be construed in any way as anti-psychiatric fed the audience's apparent communal fantasy of enjoying revenge on its doctors" (qtd. in Cooke and Page 50).[1]

Since Shaffer does in fact question the objectives of psychotherapy (Burke, "Introduction" xiii), he has often been associated with the Scottish "anti-psychiatrist" R. D. Laing (J. Taylor 27; Plunka 152), who, along with colleagues like David Cooper or Thomas Szasz, exposed the problems of institutionalized psychiatry and experimented with alternative treatments in the 1960s and 1970s. However, aside from some general research into psychoanalytic theories on neuroses and psychosis, Shaffer claims to have based his play mainly on C. G. Jung (Bach 117), and Alan's horse god Equus does indeed seem to derive his numinosity from his archetypal significance (Klein, *Peter Shaffer* 134).² Shaffer dismisses Freud's "little worried package of responses and reflexes, sexual drives and frustrations" (qtd. in Cooke and Page 50), but he is clearly fascinated by Jung's thoughts and their reference to age-old imagery. For Shaffer, this quasi-literary imagination turns Jung into the "poet of psychiatry" (qtd. in Cooke and Page 50). In Jung's work, Shaffer finds plenty of material to substantiate and illustrate his critique of psychiatry. And yet, it will be interesting to see how this anti-psychiatric tendency is undercut by Shaffer's obvious fascination with psychiatry's "poetry." Shaffer avails himself creatively of the methods of psychoanalysis to give his questions a dramatic shape. His recourse to Jung and psychotherapy is motivated by an aesthetic interest, which is apparent everywhere in the play. In my reading of Shaffer's engagement with psychiatry in *Equus*, I will thus not only focus on the depicted therapeutic relationship and the psychiatrist's conflicts, which have obsessed Shaffer's critics, but also look at the methods Shaffer employs to forge dramatic material out of the "poetry of psychiatry." This is the only way to elucidate where, in the context of his concept of creativity, Shaffer's critique begins.

Matters of faith: Alan Strang and Dr. Martin Dysart

In Dysart's children's clinic, severe cases of psychological breakdown and abuse are a part of his daily routine: "A fifteen year old schizophrenic, and a girl of eight thrashed into catatonia by her father. Normal, really . . ." (*Equus* 3). With consistent cynicism, Dysart meets his entire occupation: "One great thing about being in the adjustment business: you're never short of customers" (5). "Take a couch," is his way of offering his visitors a seat in his "torture chamber" (3). But the seemingly light wordplay points to deep dissatisfactions with the implications of his work. Dysart's phrase "adjustment business" emphasizes the banality and commerciality he associates with his work, which is painted in even more somber colors by the association with torture. At the same time, the introduction of the couch into the idiom "take a seat" highlights his routines and the interference of the artificial world of therapy with his social world. Apparently, Dysart suffers from his profession, whose horrors and repressive qualities have become so commonplace that even his ironic critique remains stuck in professional language. Fundamentally unhappy in work and life, he refuses to take any more patients: "I can't even cope with the ones I have" (3).

Despite his reluctance, he is convinced by Judge Hesther Salomon to attend to a patient who refuses treatment himself. Alan stares mutely at Dysart and thwarts his initial questions with the singing of advertising jingles. Even after Dysart has established a communicative rapport with Alan, the boy remains hostile. He challenges Dysart, slanders his treatment methods as "stupid" (27) or as "a con trick" (64), and refuses to recognize results: "It was lies anyway" (64). His resistance is mainly directed against Dysart's psychological intrusion: "*Tell me, tell me, tell me, tell me!* . . . Bloody Nosey Parker! Just like Dad" (43), Alan cries furiously. In doing so, he not only mocks Dysart's intrusive work but also identifies the therapist with his father, where his resistance seems to originate. Crucially, Alan's antagonism is not based on criminological or religious reservations—he neither attempts to escape judicial consequences nor is he worried, as Dysart will be, about preserving his creativity; instead, his resistance results from the instinct to protect his psyche against the surveillance of a father figure.

With his defiance, Alan manages to break through the routines of his doctor. After their first encounter, Dysart is fascinated and knows that the treatment will be "unsettling" (10). However, this motivates him to get through to Alan. Combining methods from psychoanalysis and psychiatry, he seeks to elucidate the problems of his patient through a wild mixture of depth analysis, hypnosis, dream interpretation, medication, and "truth-drug" placebos (70). With tactical ingenuity, he breaks Alan's resistance by employing a combination of valorization and counterirritation. The analysis is most successful, however, when Dysart allows Alan to get involved in the therapeutic game of question and answer. Provocatively mimicking the therapist, Alan answers Dysart's questions with questions of his own so that Dysart is forced to explain the rules of therapy again: "It's my job to ask the questions. Yours to answer them." Alan answers with a counterproposal: "I'll answer if you answer. In turns." Dysart agrees to this adjustment of the therapeutic setting, under one condition: "Only we have to speak the truth" (20). This negotiation signals that Dysart is willing to adjust the treatment to Alan's needs. In the process, he loses his exclusive power over the therapeutic action, as Alan takes control: "We're playing what I say" (43). The patient thus manages to upend the therapeutic hierarchy, becoming an inquisitor who does not offer therapy but, with trenchant remarks about Dysart's childless and sexless marriage, arouses the therapist's anger: "Wicked little bastard— he knew exactly what questions to try. . . . They aim unswervingly at your area of maximum vulnerability" (44). Dysart must accept Alan's questions and, to a certain extent, become a patient himself (Lengeler 278) if he wants to continue playing the therapeutic game. Alan does not overcome his fear of Dysart's intrusion until he can himself become an intruder and replace the asymmetry between uneducated delinquent patient and older analyst with equitable interaction (Zapf 216).

In this way, mutual trust and respect is slowly established in their relationship. When he speaks about the sexual content of his horse cult, for example, Alan opens himself for precarious topics (32). Dysart can resolve conflicts with Alan and concedes part of the control over the treatment to his patient: "You don't have to do it, if you don't want to" (48). Soon, Hesther becomes aware of this intimacy. Jokingly, she suggests Alan could be searching for a "new God," only to add in earnest: "Maybe he just wants a new Dad" (68). Alan's anxiety and defense against his authoritarian father and his desire to surrender himself to an idealized father unite in an ambivalent father transference onto Dysart. What Hesther does not recognize is Dysart's involvement in the situation. He has already accepted the father role, which becomes apparent when he defends Alan against his mother Dora (62). In psychotherapy with adolescents it is quite common that therapists serve as a substitute for the parents, and this transference leads to strong bonds that resist analysis (Lehmkuhl and Lehmkuhl 615–18). Alan and Dysart are quickly involved in a collusion: "Alan and Dysart share a mutual dependency . . . : Alan is looking, if not for a god to worship, at least for a father to love and respect. Dysart is looking for a son, someone whom he can instruct" (Klein, *Peter Shaffer* 124). The play stages this transferential relationship as a mirror of their mutual need for a good father-son relationship—compensating for the lack of meaning and love.

These relational forces become visible in the mutual development of the protagonists. Even at the beginning of the play, Alan and Dysart are constructed as a paradoxical pair of opposites and doubles: "They are opposite and complementary in some ways. . . . But their basic similarities repeatedly impress us. Both are motivated by desires to destroy . . . . Both have sexual difficulties" (Glenn, "Anthony" 275–76). Through their similarities, the merging of roles, and mutual transferences and identifications, Alan and Dysart close in on each other in an inverse development, in which Alan starts to appreciate Dysart's therapeutic work and Dysart to admire Alan's horse cult (Zapf 217). Whereas for Alan, the possibility of improving his life emerges now, Dysart is pulled deeper into his crisis. The questions raised by Alan show that Dysart's problem is not exhaustion but existential dissatisfaction. This discontent seems closely connected to his sterile marriage and his profession as a "shrink": "I shrank my *own* life" (67). Dysart feels trapped in a dead-end situation: "All reined up in old language and old assumptions, straining to jump clean-hoofed on to a whole new track of being I only suspect is there" (2). His world seems limited by conventional cognitive models and his inability to find meaning and passion beyond his routines. Dysart believes that his patient has triggered these reflections: "It's that lad of yours [Alan] who started it off" (9). Alan's horse cult, in which Dysart recognizes an enviable capacity for passion, confronts him with a desirable way of being alive and a unique creativity that prompt a strong countertransference reaction. The passion he ascribes to Alan makes him envy the boy and wish to participate in the experience vicariously (Quigley 28). However, this does not solve his crisis, and the longer he is preoccupied with Alan's ardent horse cult, the more he is forced to recognize his mediocrity and his exclusion from passionate experience (Greiff 71).

Despite his desires, Dysart seems paralyzed. Madeleine MacMurraugh-Kavanagh believes that Dysart's scientific education prevents him from devoting himself to a religion: "Dysart longs for worship emotionally but his access to it is blocked intellectually" (80). His own profession—psychiatry—cannot provide him with a similar source of meaning (Bach 145). Therefore, in the course of the play, the stocktaking of the psychiatric business coincides with a generalized critique of institutionalized belief systems. Dysart realizes, of course, that Alan's religion is a symptom-formation that causes him plenty of distress. Trapped between a mother who clings to Christian dogma and a father who sneers at religion but seems no less totalitarian and repressed, Alan's only way out is his *own* religion, which, however, cannot break him away from the subjugation and self-chastisement of its Christian origins. "A boy spends night after night having this stuff read into him: an innocent man tortured to death," Alan's father recounts, and declares: "If you want my opinion, it's the Bible that's responsible for all this" (18). And yet, with its sensuality and the secrecy of its worship, Alan's religion rebels against the parents' values—the mother's religious fanaticism just as much as the father's uptight hypocrisy. Undoubtedly, Dysart has to see Alan's religion as an expression of his conflicts. At the same time, he also understands it as a creative production that allows short-term release to Alan and nourishes Dysart's hope of being saved through vicarious participation. Since his patient with his ecstatic experience stands in for something completely "Other," Dysart starts idealizing him and turns him into a "potential savior" (Stacy 330).

Professionally, Dysart is clearly aligned with the Freudian persuasion, in which religion is viewed as a neurotic symptom that can be explained and overcome with the help of psychoanalysis (Freud, "Future" 53). In contrast, C. G. Jung is an advocate for the compatibility of religion and therapy. For him, all religions are therapeutic and supposed to treat the sufferings of the soul ("Grundsätzliches" 15). Freud also recognized an affinity between therapy and religion, comparing psychoanalysis to confession. However, whereas Freud preferred therapy over confession because it forces the analysand to say even more—namely what he does not know ("Question" 189)—Jung is willing to exploit the suggestive forces in both practices and, in some cases, to recommend religious devotion as a surrogate for psychotherapy ("Grundsätzliches" 15-16). Dysart, however, is caught up in the opposite problem. Conventional psychiatry is incapable of being a surrogate for religion. Therefore, he starts to question the very foundations of his profession: "What am I doing here? . . . These questions, these Whys, are fundamental—yet they have no place in the consulting room" (61). Alan's case initiates a critique of psychiatry and society, symbolized in a dream in which Dysart is a priest who dissects children for sacrificial purposes:

> I've started to feel distinctly nauseous. . . . Of course, I redouble my efforts to look professional—cutting and snipping for all I'm worth: mainly because I know that if ever those two assistants so much as glimpse my distress—and the implied doubt is that this repetitive and smelly work is doing any social good at all—I will be the next across the stone. (8)

As Una Chaudhuri explains, dream analysis is hardly necessary to sense Dysart's skepticism and guilt (57), but the particular form his doubts assume deserves more attention. At first, Dysart merely expresses his qualms about his patients' well-being. However, by establishing a connection between psychiatry, sacrifice, and the violation of souls, his part in the dream ritual makes his doubts seem much more sinister. Manfred Beyer reads Dysart's intrusion into children's bodies as a symbol of the intrusion into the patient's intimate world, and the extraction of their entrails as a symbol of the destruction of individual vitality (161). As its etymological origins suggest, analytic work is here associated with dissection, which no longer liberates but destroys creativity. Dysart's disgust with this injurious activity finds a physical expression in his dream. The repetitiveness and the stench of the sacrificial practice mirrors his attitude toward psychiatry, which, for him, consists in the serial processing of cases with a bitter aftertaste. The most important feature of the dream, however, is its reference to religious practices. From Dysart's point of view, a connection between psychiatry and religion is established, in which repressive therapeutic and belief systems are an obstacle to personal development: "Both revolve around destruction in the dubious interests of social control" (MacMurraugh-Kavanagh 94).

Dysart diagnoses his environment in terms of the sterility from which he suffers himself: "I'll give him the good Normal world where we're tethered beside him" (92-93). He is convinced that psychiatry is complicit in the consolidation of this situation. In this assessment, he agrees with the anti-psychiatrists, who identified subtle mechanisms of social control even in the most humane techniques of psychiatry (Crossley 878). The fabrication of normalcy—in Freud's critical opinion just a construct, an "ideal fiction" ("Analysis Terminable" 235)—and the destruction of individuality, however, are not necessarily the goal of therapy. Freud believed psychoanalysis had a revolutionary potential: "[Society] is bound to offer us resistance, for we adopt a critical attitude towards it; we point out to it that it itself plays a great part in causing neuroses" ("Future Prospects" 147). Dysart still sees psychiatry as complicit in the process of normalization because, in his view, it has long adopted the directives of society and implants them in individuals. Everything that psychiatry might achieve when it acts as a social control mechanism would serve to secure a highly doubtful normalcy and functionality. Appealing to Dysart's reason, Hesther's advice is to compromise and return Alan to normal life: "You know what I mean by a normal smile in a child's eyes, and one that isn't—even if I can't exactly define it. . . . Then we have a duty to that, surely?" (47). Dysart, however, is worried about the treacherous nature of normalcy, to which his profession seems dedicated with religious ardor:

> The Normal is the good smile in a child's eyes—all right. It is also the dead stare in a million adults. It both sustains and kills—like a God. . . . The Normal is the indispensable, murderous God of Health, and I am his Priest. . . . I have honestly assisted children in this room. . . But also—beyond question—I have cut from them parts of individuality repugnant to this God. (49)

Jung has devoted extensive thought to this conflict between adjustment and individuality. He differentiates between "ill-adjusted individualists" and people with an underdeveloped individuality, who must by no means be normalized ("Grundsätzliches" 6, my translation). With patients who are sick because they are "too normal," the doctor must help them develop their personality on the path of individuation:

> The doctor has to leave the individual path to a cure open, and then the cure will not lead to a change of the personality, but it will be a process that is called *individuation*, i.e., the patient becomes who he really is. At worst, he will even put up with his neurosis because he has understood the meaning of his illness. ("Grundsätzliches" 9, my translation)

Shaffer presents Alan as an ill-adjusted individualist and thus in need of therapy. However, by pointing out the relation to Jung's thought, I do not want to suggest an alternative course of treatment for this fictional character.

Instead, the comparison highlights a creative component in Freud's and Jung's concept of therapy—a possibility for productive criticism and personal development aided rather than hindered by the psychiatrist. Thus, Dysart's conflict emerges as a highly self-referential construct. For Dysart is not just a psychiatrist, he is also a suffering human being, for whom the treatment he is about to prescribe to Alan would be intolerable. For himself, not necessarily for Alan, the idea or the obligation of being nothing but normal would, in Jung's words, be "the pinnacle of a Procrustean bed" and a "sterile, hopeless hell" ("Probleme" 75, my translation).

Living in a sterile hell of his own making, Dysart is afraid of destroying Alan's most distinguishing trait. That his religion is mostly an expression of his suffering, and not just of creativity and individuality, is something that Dysart, with his admiration, can hardly recognize: "All right, he's sick.... But that boy has known a passion more ferocious than I have felt in any second of my life. And let me tell you something: I envy it" (67). Dysart sees Alan's situation only from his own point of view: He admits that his personal needs, brought to light by his envy, affect his idealization of Alan and his critique of psychiatry. Thus, his only escape seems a personal one: "I'd like to leave this room and never see it again in my life.... I've been in it too long" (72). Critics have strongly objected to this attitude. Hélène Baldwin claims that "[not] many psychiatrists feel that their profession is a failure and wish to abandon it" (125), and John Simon, even more apodictically, declares: "No one with this attitude would have become a psychiatrist, or, having developed it on the job, have persisted in that profession" (101). These judgments, however, do not recognize the emotional difficulties psychotherapeutic work entails for all participants. Ralf Zwiebel speaks of a "fight for survival," emphasizing that the psychoanalyst's work is always accompanied by dissatisfactions, doubts, feelings of incompetence, exhaustion, and lack of courage ("Position" 37, my translation). A therapist needs to endure these feelings because they enable him to analyze his own work productively. Thus, the "questions I've avoided all my professional life" (60) start from a critique of Dysart's own life and involve psychiatry as a whole.

Shaffer reported, "The play, as it grew under my hands, came more and more to question the ultimate uses of psychiatry" (Burke, "Introduction" xiii). However, *Equus* does not argue entirely against psychiatry. Hesther's opposite point of view, "He's been in pain for most of his life.... And you can take it away" (66), remains valid, and Alan's deeds are, as Michael Quigley attests, hardly made light of: "Ambivalence is precisely the kind of response Shaffer expects from us. We are not expected to approve of Alan Strang's actions.... Shaffer expects us to understand as well, however, the potential horrors of a life devoid of extreme passion and worship" (29). Despite his irresolvable predicament and not without qualms, Dysart decides to treat Alan: "I'm going to make you well, I promise you" (91). Although such a prospect of complete recovery and catharsis might seem implausible from the point of view of contemporary psychoanalysis (Ellenzweig 50), Shaffer's main concern is not the authentic representation of a curative process but the creation of a dramatic effect. Dysart concedes: "He won't really go that easily. . . . When Equus leaves—if he leaves at all—it will be with your intestines in his teeth." Thus, the play's emphasis is not on the possibility of failure but the dangers of success: "My achievement . . . is more likely to make a ghost!" (92). Apart from relief from his symptoms, he cannot promise Alan a good life. Since he identifies therapy with a sterile society, cure and vitality seem incompatible. Dysart is far away from the Jungian idea of individuation or personality development through therapy; he fails to preserve the poetic—literally, creative—force Shaffer identifies in Jung's writing. But since he is in the middle of a dilemma, acknowledging the need to ease Alan's pain as well as the threat to his creative energy, his attitude is more complicated than an idealization of Alan's disorder or a demonization of psychotherapy. Shaffer uses him to illustrate a predicament, in which every way out leads to new difficulties: "Tragedy obviously does not lie in a conflict of Right and Wrong, but in a collision between two different kinds of Right" (Burke, "Writer" vii). By recognizing this conflict between the potential and the dangers of treatment, Dysart has changed a great deal at the end of the play: "I need . . . a way of seeing in the dark. . . . There is now, in my mouth, this sharp chain. And it never comes out" (93–94). Dysart assumes Alan's role as a person in need of help, who imagines himself aptly as a horse in harness, because he has questioned his life choices so fundamentally that he cannot avoid the consequences. As a result, *Equus* is mostly a report on *Dysart's* process of analysis. The therapeutic relationship with Alan is the medium on which his crisis of faith is played out, and thus allows for an analysis of his critique of psychiatry and society as a consequence of his own failures.

Dysart's therapeutic stage: Acting out in epic therapy

Given the importance of the therapist's crisis of faith, it is not surprising that *Equus* focuses on the developmental process of Dysart. The play achieves this effect by having Dysart present the events. "I'm not making much sense. Let me start properly: In order" (2), he says at the end of his first monologue. With this gesture, he establishes himself as a narrator who controls the course of the action. His idea of "order" determines the plot when he tells Alan's and his own story to Hesther and the audience. According to Adrian

Burke, the audience thus get the impression that Dysart's case study is actually a report on his own condition: "One of the play's ironies is that Dysart is made to comment more on himself and his actions than on those of his patient" ("Introduction" viii). In light of his deep-seated doubts, it is imperative that Dysart turns the analysis back on himself, becomes his own patient and narrative object—he is commentator and director, narrator I, and narrated I (Černy 159). As a therapist, he is supposed to work with the relationship and steer narratives in which he takes over a variety of roles and illuminates a variety of ideas. In therapy there is never a complete separation between narrator and actor since the action of the analyst consists primarily in storytelling. In this way, Dysart controls all essential structural elements of the play—perspective, plot structure, character development, and dialogue construction. Even the audience depends on him for their access to the action. They have to assume that everything they see has already been filtered by Dysart.

The presence of a narrator, who is the only character directly addressing the audience, has frequently led critics to identify Shaffer's with Brecht's epic theater. Supposing that the text creates distance through its narrative structure, Hubert Zapf argues that the resulting alienation effect encourages a consistent interpretive-reflective attitude toward the play (219). He assumes that the narrative representation mirrors the distance Dysart feels toward his own actions and emphasizes that, for Dysart and the audience, Alan's experience is always mediated through therapeutic reconstruction (206). However, Dysart's narrative is not just a case study but an analytic confession. He engages the audience in his therapeutic difficulties and makes them participate emotionally in his moral and epistemic failure to reach Alan. Even if Shaffer takes up specific devices from epic theater, such as narrative distancing effects, he clearly differs from Brecht because he dispenses with sociopolitical education and an abstract narrative stance—in favor of identification:

> Instead, he intends (and achieves) a balance between mental attentiveness and emotional engagement. . . . [Shaffer's narrators] not only unify and comment on each episode, they also condition our intuitive responses *to* them through their participation *in* them. Emotional and psychological identification, so despised by Brecht on ideological grounds, naturally arises as a result leading us to respond more to character than to context or situation: . . . it is Dysart's existential disintegration that penetrates our consciousness more than the implications of a socially-imposed (and thus arbitrary) definition of psychosis. (MacMurraugh-Kavanagh 28-29)

Dysart addresses the audience not to enlighten them but to relieve himself and to ask for their understanding: "The thing is, I'm desperate" (2). Due to this focus on personal problems it is also hardly possible to read the play as a straightforward critique of psychiatry.

The therapist admits his own lack of neutrality and simultaneously embroils the audience in his subjectivity. Dysart's character "is revealed exclusively through his own words" (Klein, *Peter Shaffer* 117), which makes him the most complex but also the least objectively characterized figure in the play. But the play goes further than simply placing all attention on Dysart. The psychoanalytic situation serves to concentrate the action on the reciprocal dynamics between therapist and patient. The relationship of these twin protagonists is the actual center or protagonist of the play (Greiff 72), a third entity that changes Dysart *and* Alan. All the other characters that appear in their narratives, such as Alan's parents or Dysart's wife, remain one-dimensional (Burke, "Introduction" x), mere functional devices within the process of meaning-making between Alan and Dysart. Accordingly, they appear only when they are needed, as indicated in Shaffer's "Author's Notes": "They get up to perform their scenes, and return when they are done to their places around the set" (xxii). These actors can be likened to Antonino Ferro's "characters"; they appear in the therapeutic process only to illuminate the relationship between Alan and Dysart.

The play's focus on the therapeutic relationship is strengthened further by enveloping the dialogues in Dysart's narrative: "The play expands its structure by placing a duet within a frame of narration, observation, or comment" (Beckerman 205). Investigation, resistance, and reaction determine the therapeutic pair's communicative behavior, which is subsequently elucidated in Dysart's commentary. Alan's and Dysart's conversations appear to be analytic because they are structured by an internal dynamic of resistance and because they are accompanied by the therapist's interpretations. And while the therapeutic dialogue is thus edited into a narrative case study, Dysart's retelling is actually dialogic in nature: "His monologues are, in effect, special kinds of dialogue. Despite their apparent single-sidedness, they are only variants of the primary model of action—the scene between two people. That scene may narrow to an exchange between actor and audience in which the audience is both a passive actor and an active observer" (Beckerman 203). Influenced by Alan and eager to reach Hesther and the audience with his speech, Dysart's narrative cannot be described as one-dimensional or monologic. *Equus* is not a classic "memory play," "a partially enacted homodiegetic narrative in which the narrator is also a participant in the events he or she recounts and enacts" (Richardson, "Voice" 682). Instead, it might be described as a "therapy play," in which memory is triggered within a relationship and followed up with therapeutic strategies. Dysart's story can only be followed up through Alan, and Alan can enact his story only with Dysart's help; both reach certain aspects of their experience only through being challenged by the other. This is encapsulated in a theatrical form in which narrative and dialogue are consistently intertwined and mutually illuminating.

A similarly dialogic interaction is established between narrated past and present. Dysart's desire to narrate "in order" is never really achieved. Martin Brunkhorst describes how the play's fictional levels multiply as the plot moves inward (231). In the play's present, Dysart tells the story of the immediate past (his therapeutic encounter with Alan), in which they explore the distant past (Alan's childhood and his crime). These layers become strategically juxtaposed under Dysart's control, who employs analepsis and prolepsis as therapeutic and narrative techniques. Particularly with regard to the most distant past, the narrative is structured not according to chronology but necessity—to elucidate Alan's childhood, invoking and commenting on parts of the story as needed. Forging a coherent case or, rather, a dramatic narrative from these discontinuous events and locations is the therapeutic task of Dysart and the synthetic task of the audience (Chaudhuri 50).

Due to the play's apparent focus on the story of Alan's crime, *Equus* looks both like a case study and an analytic drama. The play can be read in the tradition of the analytic myth of *Oedipus Rex*, to which it adheres through stylistic elements from Greek tragedy (Klein, "Peter Shaffer's *Equus*" 175), the motif of (failing) vision (Bach 119), and the Oedipal structure of Alan's family. Neil Timm believes that Oedipus and Dysart are engaged in a similar search for themselves: "Oedipus wants facts and truth; Dysart searches for motives, the way. Yet each becomes the object of his own search through a pattern of reversal" (129). The case analysis simulates a detective plot: dialogues that sound like interrogations (Beckerman 206), the juridical premise, and Dysart's role as "Nosey Parker" (43), as detective who investigates outside of the clinic and seeks out witnesses—all these elements might very well be the features of a detective story (Burke, "Introduction" viii), with Dysart playing the conservative role of the detective "as society's agent in order to . . . bind the criminal again to the constraining rules of society" (Hühn 460). Despite Dysart's protests against this role, this plot construction tends to override the anti-psychiatric critique; the suspense of the detective plot strives for a resolution of Alan's madness rather than for its preservation. However, on the one hand, in contrast to *Oedipux Rex*, the social dilemma, unlike the private one, remains unresolved in Shaffer's play. On the other hand, the starting point for the analytic drama is not Alan's crime but the existential crisis of the psychiatrist, whose analysis is effected through the analysis of Alan (Černy 158). It is, as I have already emphasized, first and foremost the story of their relationship. Alan, too, becomes a detective when he questions Dysart's marriage. Thus, the investigation does not proceed unilaterally but simultaneously in both directions. In this play, analysis is not the analyst-detective's work on the plot of the patient but their shared work on the plot of the analysis. Dysart's commentary refers every reported event back to his relationship with Alan and its emergence in analysis. The complex web of time periods and levels of meaning becomes recognizable and understandable as something to which neither Alan nor Dysart can hold their distance. Dysart emerges as a narrator who controls the events only in tandem with his patient.

* * *

Alan's case, like Oedipus's, cannot be solved without the participation of other characters. The reports of witnesses play an important role for Dysart in reconstructing Alan's history. First and foremost, however, the boy's childhood experiences are represented for the audience through jointly enacted flashbacks. Including all necessary members of the ensemble, what is discussed in therapy is made visible on the stage.

In the first act, Alan's memories are narrated or reported under hypnosis, while being illustrated by a simultaneous staging of the remembered event. This leads to ruptures and a juxtaposition of the therapeutic scene and the scene narrated therein. In the hypnotherapy session that concludes the first act, Dysart steps into the scene by assisting Alan in envisioning his past: "Sssh. . . Quietly. . . Good. Now go in" (53), he instructs Alan during the imaginative return to the stable. In the second act, this dramatic enactment reifies itself in Dysart's analytic technique. With the help of a placebo, he convinces Alan to reenact his crime in the therapist's office: "And not just *tell* me—*show* me. Act it out, if you like . . . . I want you to feel free to do absolutely anything in this room" (73). In addition, he supports the enactment by goading Alan on, by asking questions or taking over roles. By making the play a part of the treatment, he enables Alan himself to confront the scene, reflect and comment on it, question it, and live through it again. At the same time, Dysart's desire for a less intellectual access to ritual experience finds expression in this technique; his effectiveness seems to heighten when he can replace an abstract narrative with a tangible enactment. Metadramatically, the dramatic narrator thus seems to question his own purpose.

With these various enactments Alan changes the way he acts in these flashbacks. Most of the time, he turns directly to Dysart when the therapist challenges his play. In a couple of cases, however, Dysart is just an outside observer while Alan acts with the people from his memories: "*During these scenes Alan acts directly with [Jill], and never looks over at Dysart when he replies to him*" (74). In other scenes, Alan speaks with Dysart as if the therapist were involved in the action. Through these visual and ludic axes, transference connections are established between the characters. When Alan looks at his father while talking to Dysart, he performs a visually mediated father transference, which allows him to introduce a family conflict into the therapeutic context (Beckerman 205). Telling his story and simultaneously speaking for his past self, Alan is positioned as narrator, observer, and actor, who rewrites the role he plays in his own life. Like Dysart, he is involved in the mutual narrative process in many different functions.

When Dysart leads us through the time periods, he becomes, as Bach notes, the director of their past (159). As we have seen, however, the patient is always a part of this direction. The scenes Dysart stages with Alan provide a commentary on his own case report (Černy 159) and the multitude of roles they take on substantiate a reflective process, in which both are allowed to be observers and actors. The result is much more than the implementation of a play within the play. In *Equus*, the theatrical metaphor that has been used to describe the therapeutic relationship is concretized in Dysart's and Alan's employment of the as-if space of the hospital—the stage shows a clinic that is turned into a stage. The interrelation between both places is delineated by Otmar Seidl and Michael Ermann, who view the psychiatric hospital as a space between internal and external reality, a transitional space, which can become "the stage of the patient's internal world" (181, my translation). The patient reacts to the experiences in the institution with diverse scenic figurations, which, at the same time, represent an offer for the therapist or other patients to play along (182). As a safe haven, the clinic thus creates a space for play. This motif runs through *Equus*, from the playful negotiation of the rules of the therapeutic process up to Alan's enactment of the past. Through the staging of Alan's flashbacks, every level of his memory is turned into the dramatic present and reconstructed in scenic representation (Brunkhorst 231). In this way—in material translation—the stage is revealed as a transferential space in which past and present are superimposed. Functioning as a stage, the therapist's office is transformed into a variety of historical settings (Lengeler 275), so that the here and now of analysis may represent any then and there of their story. When Dysart speaks of "acting out," he does not refer to the modern psychoanalytic concept—the destructive acting out of unspoken impulses within the therapeutic relationship (Bateman and Holmes 194–95). His notion is closer to Freud's "*act[ing] out*," a reenactment of memories and fantasies related to transference ("Fragment" 119). In Freud's terms, then, the therapist in *Equus* stages a past conflict to make it available for treatment.

According to Lothar Černy, the employment of this mechanism in the play suggests a fundamental affinity between the dramatic and the analytic task. He argues that *Equus* engages productively with psychoanalysis not because it dramatizes a psychoanalytic case but because it knows how to make use of the "dramatic potentiality" of the analytic process (160–61, my translation). Shaffer consciously materializes the metaphorical understanding of the theatrical qualities of psychoanalysis in the theatrical representation. Thus, he creates an additional self-reflexive dimension, which further unlocks the dramatic potential of the analytic process. In fact, the play reveals the very foundations of the theater metaphor by showing how drama and analysis both depend on performance to address absent content. However, immanent and immediate performance alone does not have an effect in the play—there is a need for narrative evaluation in dramatic and analytic play-acting.

In *Equus*, ludic scenes are embedded in a narrative continuum through epic mechanisms like announcements, comments, or logical arguments (Brunkhorst 231–33). The mutual dependence of diegetic and mimetic techniques in psychoanalysis is spelled out here in the play. Černy argues that Shaffer connects the psychoanalytic process with Alan's experience through this simultaneous memory work and analytic commentary, bringing memory to life and interpreting it at the same time (159). The drama provides a transitional space that can be likened to the space of analysis, a space that sits not just between experiential but also between representational worlds. Ludic elements are enclosed in narrative structures to make them more effective, and vice versa, as the play depends on the narrating gamemaster for its coherence. The simultaneity of therapy and biography is supplemented by a simultaneity of enactment and narration.

* * *

The particular form in which this narration was enacted for the first time remains important for the reception of the play as published editions of *Equus* preserve the directions for John Dexter's original stage production.[3] Shaffer explains in his "Author's Note": "Their visual action is to me as much a part of the play as the dialogue" (xix). Indeed, many of the effects of *Equus* are created by ritual elements like light, pantomime, and masks (Zapf 168).[4]

Alan's imaginative world becomes palpable through these stage devices: "[The audience's] absorption in and understanding of the drama is intensified by the penetration of Alan's mind through amplified noises and changes of lighting that condition representation and clarify meaning" (MacMurraugh-Kavanagh 16). Ryan Claycomb goes so far as to relate all avant-gardist elements of the play to Alan's illness:

> The logic of time is disrupted only because Strang's story cannot come out coherently: the pathologized narrative must be teased out by Dysart as the reluctant agent of narrative coherence; the dream sequences and fantastical flashbacks result from the same pathologized narrative incoherence. . . . This heightened theatricality, including the mask work and ritual features . . . , are almost exclusively the means of representing Strang's heightened sense of the horses. (106)

If this were true, the play would have a problem. Since Alan is psychiatrically "corrected" at the end, the related formal devices would be questioned along with his creative disorder, and a play that may have seemed innovative would actually take on a conservative attitude toward psychiatry and theatrical form (106–07). Claycomb grants *Equus* a certain degree of ambivalence because the loss of creativity is at least met with regret: "While this individual play may labour to contain, pathologize, and recuperate a queer and resistant avant-garde back into productive middle-class culture, the theatrical images of madness linger" (118). And still, the play ends with the containment of Alan's madness and is thus, according to Claycomb, both anti-psychiatric and anti-avant-gardist.

However, to attribute all stylistic elements exclusively to Alan's disorder neglects the fact that some of them are recurrent elements of Shaffer's dramatic technique and theatrical aesthetics, independent of the topos of madness. They are, instead, intimately related to the strategy of reconstructive narration, which is employed in a number of Shaffer's plays. In rudiments, it can be found in *The Royal Hunt of the Sun* (1964), in which Old Martin reflects his questionable participation in Pizarro's expedition in Peru. Similarly, Salieri's "confess[ion]" in *Amadeus* (1979) uses the perspective of the old man to illuminate his relationship with Mozart. In *Equus*, this constellation is intensified through the simultaneous therapeutic reconstruction of Dysart's and Alan's conflicts. Alan and Dysart tell their stories in the way they do— with narrative incoherence and fantasy enactments—not because they are mad but because they are part of a reconstructive therapeutic process that demands this kind of storytelling. The therapy that Claycomb criticizes as conservative is thus the catalyst for the progressive narrative form.

The setup of the stage supports this orientation toward the therapeutic encounter. The ritualistic atmosphere is infused with medical and psychiatric elements of the analytic setting, which reflects Dysart's entanglement in the therapeutic relationship and his crisis of faith on the level of the production. At the center of the stage, a square of wood, resembling a "railed boxing ring," is placed on a larger circle (Shaffer, "Author's Notes" xxii). This arrangement suggests that the relationship is characterized by intense, combative altercations. A boxing match, with its focus on two fighters and their battle, is in some ways analogous to the therapeutic encounter, in which individuals are pitted against each other and in which a serious confrontation is playfully reenacted. The square represents the therapist's office; in here, Dysart holds the sessions with Alan and receives visitors. It is the room from which all scenes are initiated and to which they return at the moment of climax, as Dysart takes on an outside observer's position. In this way, the stage directions reflect how the therapeutic process entails a blurring of boundaries between inside and outside, between what happens in the therapeutic encounter and the memories reflected therein.

On the square and around the ring, benches serve as props or as seats for the actors when they do not play and serve as "witnesses, assistants—and especially a Chorus." Moreover, a part of the audience is placed on the stage, "on tiers of seats in the fashion of a dissecting theatre" (Shaffer, "Author's Notes" xxii). This inclusion of the audience—or, rather, the framing of the actors—creates a quasi-scientific effect, which is emphasized by the use of medical imagery in Harold Clurman's set descriptions: "The stage is as bare as a surgical arena. Around it are several tiers of seats on which student members of the audience are placed, as if observing a lecture demonstration. . . . A battery of powerful lights shine down on the platform to lend the proceedings an atmosphere of scientific precision" (qtd. in Cooke and Page 52). In this way, "successive rings of scrutiny" are created, as Beckerman argues (204). The actors on the stage are at the same time spectators of the scene, while a group of spectators become actors, a presence on the stage for the other spectators, so that spectators always watch other spectators. This is not just closely linked to the fact that every enactment is also a "performance for other characters, actors, or spectators" (Beckerman 206). In conjunction with the clinical setting, this also generates an atmosphere of analytic observation and dissection, which characterizes the psychiatric institution. Zapf believes that the spectators are thus made familiar with Dysart's state of mind, wondering whether human experience is only accessible from a reflexive distance and in experimental simulation (206). And yet, in this way, the spectators actually become involved. In contrast to a conventional stage arrangement, they are made aware of their function as spectators and become participants in the therapeutic process through Dysart's apostrophes.

Dysart's artistic doubts: Spectatorship as supervision and interpretive side effects

The potential endangerment of Alan's creativity is a major part of Dysart's doubts about the treatment. He ascribes an individual, creative component to Alan's pain: "His pain. His own. He made it" (66). With the pain, Dysart's therapy might also eliminate the creation; for him, the suffering patient is the artist of his disorder. As a complex syncretistic system of ancient, Christian, and idiosyncratic features, Alan's religious mania does have some striking creative streaks. That is why Greiff declares that Alan, as the creator of his horse cult, is a "poet and mystic" (66) and identifies him as a typical artist figure, who is isolated from society by "something exceptional within [himself] which elevates and confers uniqueness" (72). Despite his recognition that Alan's creation is regressive, Zapf also finds something creative and artistic (*Ursprünglich-Kreatives, ja Künstlerisches*) in Alan's cult (213). Dysart, however, has no part in this. His name, Dys-art, alludes to the decay of his therapeutic art and his general artistic deficiency: "He finds that he lacks the spiritual power of art, that power which generates creation" (Walls 320). Dysart may recognize art, but he cannot practice it. As a therapist, his only task seems to destroy it: "Passion, you see, can be destroyed by a doctor. It cannot be created" (93).

In this way, *Equus* participates in the debate on the compatibility of creativity and therapy. Artists have long feared that psychoanalysis might curtail or extinguish the creativity they wring from their psychological pain (Schönau and Pfeiffer 3). "The view that madness may be the price of ecstasy or the mark of penetrating wisdom is as old as Plato," Chaudhuri notes (52). In *Equus*, Dysart sees a danger in psychotherapy and reveres Alan's madness: "To the psychiatrist, the boy's delusional rituals are a fascinating work of art" (Gifford, qtd. in Cooke and Page 55). This is clearly a one-sided perspective on the problem. In interviews, Shaffer has insisted that he does not believe in a link between art and madness: "I do not believe that Art and insanity have anything to say to each other. The greatest Art—the symphonies of Haydn or the paintings of Bellini—virtually defines sanity for me" (qtd. in Stacy 326). Alan's art is not "great"; his creation is a compensation for suffering that is incapable of overcoming the limitations of a rigid religious and sexual education. *Equus* is far from glamorizing Alan's creativity;

instead, it demonstrates how Dysart's admiration derives from *his* deficits. Nevertheless, Dysart, like the anti-psychiatrists, points to an important insight. Alan's production contains remarkable elements; "the so-called mad had something to say, and . . . it was worth listening to and taking seriously" (Phillips, *Going* xiv).

David Cooper, with R. D. Laing part of the anti-psychiatric movement, believes that poets and schizophrenics have access to a realm of experience beyond language: "If poets are athletes of the extra-verbal, so are many people called schizophrenic" (120). Only the poet, however, is capable of mediating this experience through the compromise of language. Like Dysart, Cooper is afraid that therapy might destroy a patient's creative potential and reduce his complex communication to a simple verbal formula. However, Cooper's thoughts also imply that there is the possibility of successful analysis. Through acting out and transference, the preverbal is, as it were, poetically reintroduced into linguistic mediation. Thus, Alan and Dysart are not just sick and impeded artists, but become creative in therapy, by returning enactments and sensations to language. With Dysart as a therapeutic participant, Alan develops a play out of his life story that has numerous curative effects. It allows Dysart to deploy interventions, it strengthens the therapeutic relationship, and it brings about an immediate cathartic release when Alan collapses with exhaustion after his final enactment. In these enacted narratives, Dysart becomes a co-author. He goads his patient on, stages his own scripts, and performs as an actor; and in the representation of his own conflicts, he becomes the director of the actions within the play and the narrator of Alan's case history, rearranging it according to his own insights and presenting it to the audience in a changed and subjectively colored light. Therapy and narrative art thus do not remain separate, even if and especially when Dysart utters his doubts, for he uses the narrative methods of psychoanalysis to try and heal himself (Bach 160). The play undercuts Dysart's notion of the therapist's destructive force; in *Equus*, playful reenactment and passion for the patient *can* be created by a doctor.

* * *

Alan is introduced as an object for the study of his therapist, who understands himself mostly as an observer in their relationship—and he is immediately fascinated by the case. Bach, however, describes Dysart's spectatorship as an obsession and a loss of control because it brings to light his own insecurities (148). Dysart tries to see and read Alan, to piece together the particulars of his case, but what he finds wears him down. Described in this way, his experience resembles the impact Shaffer wants a play to have on the audience.

It should "startle and absorb an audience," and he believed that "people come to the theatre to be surprised, moved and illuminated," receiving the play "viscerally," as it were. MacMurraugh-Kavanagh comments: "In other words, for Shaffer, theatre should not necessarily involve itself with the territories of experience concerned with logic or rationality, but should satisfy audience needs associated with instinct and intuition. The theatre thus becomes a site of mystery where levels of experience denied access in daily life attain expression" (17). Dysart encounters this theatrical experience with Alan; his captivating appearance in the clinic jolts the therapist out of his lethargy. In the course of the treatment, experiences in the relationship cause Dysart to recognize doubts he used to perceive only vaguely and to get in touch with new areas of self-experience. And yet, as a representative for the spectators, Dysart also exposes the limitations of Shaffer's ideal theatrical experience. His access to the patient's mystic experience is vicarious, and intensifies his own conflicts but offers no catharsis.

Dysart mirrors the spectators, and, at the same time, he transforms their spectatorship. With imploring apostrophes, "You see, I'm lost.... You see, I'm wearing that horse's head myself" (1–2), he seeks the help of the audience. As doubting psychiatrist who reports his dreams and questions himself in front of witnesses he turns himself into a patient, asking the audience for their help and understanding in his process of self-analysis (Bach 125). This stance is reinforced by the placement of the audience in the "dissecting theatre"; it creates the impression of "assisting at a lecture-demonstration" and actively partaking in a "scientific experiment" (Chaudhuri 50). The audience is thus urged to take over the therapist's role, so to speak, and compelled to relate to the difficulties of the job. The reenactment of Alan's treatment allows Dysart to watch himself as an observer of Alan and involves the audience in these reflections. While they serve as sounding boards in Dysart's self-observation (much like Hesther), they also puzzle over Alan's case: "The audience here is effectively identifying with Dysart since it is equally eager to discover the explanation for Alan's crime: we too analyse the boy's responses" (MacMurraugh-Kavanagh 31). Due to the arrangement of the set, they are forced to keep their eyes on both Dysart's practice and their own observer's position. Thus, they actually assume the role of a supervisor who supports a psychoanalyst in a case without being able to interfere.

This is distinctly reflected in the flow of commentary dedicated to Dysart's therapeutic endeavor in literary and psychoanalytic criticism—regardless of the fact that *Equus* does not depict a real case. Jeffrey Berman criticizes Dysart's blindness toward Alan's need for treatment and recommends a different therapist ("*Equus*" 421–22). Anthony Corello accuses Dysart of a whole array of professional errors and concludes with pointing out alternative courses of treatment (196–203). Samuel Shem is especially concerned by the speed with which Alan is cured through abreaction. "Good psychiatrists," he counters, "sit in their chairs for long periods of time and make mutual relationships that help sick people to grow in that relationship until the person can move on. It is, by and large, quiet, intense, slow work" (55). With his appeals for help, Dysart seems to entice these "supervisors" on the sidelines of the play to extend the analysis into infinity. As far as these critics' recommendations are from recognizing Alan's treatment as a fictional construction set up for personal failure, they may at the same time be a predictable reaction to the effects of the play, to Dysart's enlistment of the audience as supervisors.

* * *

Organized by Dysart's search for Alan's story and by his own self-reflective process, the structure of the play follows the development of his understanding and seems to adhere to the rational interpretive model of psychology, in which the discovery of the origin of a disorder leads to a cure (Zapf 202). However, according to Una Chaudhuri, this Freudian riddle is just the surface of the play: "If the [Freudian narrative] disappoints (critics), it does so necessarily, revealing the ultimate inadequacy of intellectual schemes in accounting for human experience" (59). The play may thus confirm the importance of analytic interpretation only to refute it.

Dysart voices his doubts about the psychiatric power of interpretation early on in the play: "The only thing I know for sure is this: a horse's head is finally unknowable to me. Yet I handle children's heads—which I must presume to be more complicated" (2). He seems to be occupied with an object that cannot be fully understood, and for the exploration of the "black cave of the Psyche," all he has is a "dim little torch" (60)—his professional methods do not provide enough "light" to illuminate the inside world of his patients and solve the questions raised in treatment.

Dysart may reconstruct the psychological circumstances of the crime, but these circumstances do not lead to the crime with logical necessity. In this sense, Alan's mother criticizes his—and the play's—psychoanalytic assumption that the parents are to blame: "If you added up everything we ever did to him, from his first day on earth to this, you wouldn't find why he did this terrible thing" (63). Her own, hardly convincing attempt to blame Alan's deeds on the devil demonstrates how both doctor and family impose an interpretive scheme on Alan: "a complex" or "the Devil." Thus, Zapf concludes that instead of an objective psychological profile, all Dysart can accomplish is interpretive reconstruction (203). The theory of interpretation that underlies the play conceives of understanding as an act of identification with the perpetrator, emulating the doctor eager for understanding (*nach dem Vorbild des um Verständnis bemühten Arztes*) and presenting empathy as the leading dramaturgic principle (Brunkhorst 232). In this way, another parallel between Dysart and the audience is established in their experience of the events of the play: "Both are processes of discovery, journeys into the unconscious, encounters with irrational parts of the self" (Chaudhuri 59).

Dysart has to grapple with the epistemological doubts endemic to his discipline. However, in contrast to J. M. Coetzee's Medical Officer or Margaret Atwood's Dr. Jordan, he gains substantial knowledge about his patient and his past. Measured by psychoanalytic standards, he delivers a good interpretation that convinces Alan, particularly since he allows his patient to contribute in its realization. The problem that is actually at the core of *Equus* is not the impossibility of interpretation but its side effects. Based on questionable methods, the interpretation threatens to normalize and destroy the patient's creativity instead of facilitating it. The problematic gap between method and result is clearly indicated in Dysart's warning and promise: "Everything I do is a trick or a catch. That's all I know to do. But they work" (70). Surveillance, control, even deceit characterize Dysart's therapeutic style. He sees his techniques as tricks, which generate insight under false pretenses and with the authoritarian methods of an inquisitor. This critique of the interpretive process of psychiatry is reinforced by the dream in which he serves as a sacrificial priest:

> Then, with a surgical skill which amazes even me, I fit in the knife and slice elegantly down to the navel, just like a seamstress following a pattern. I part the flaps, sever the inner tubes, yank them out and throw them hot and steaming on to the floor. The other two then study the pattern they make, as if they were reading hieroglyphics. (9)

In Dysart's vision, the elegance of the explanation only serves to veil its potential for violence. Interpretation comes with an injury to or the death of the object of analysis without a guarantee that the "hieroglyphics" are even worth reading. Just as Dysart is afraid he might destroy Alan's creativity, the critic may dissect a text until only the shredded entrails remain. With Dysart's professional doubts, interpretation and therapy are called into question more generally. Both seem possible and necessary but also fraught with aesthetic and ethical difficulties. The more Dysart invests in the relationship with Alan, the more his conflicts and anxieties intensify, for he might not be able to meet Alan's interpretive and therapeutic requirements. Dysart's appeal to the audience is a plea for understanding and a warning that every critic loath to destroy his object must wear "this sharp chain" (94), the necessary doubts about their professional conduct.

Conclusion

In *Equus*, the therapeutic relationship reflects the crises of both protagonists. The analysis of the patient's religious mania becomes the medium for the analysis of the therapist's crisis of faith. Dysart is in danger of growing desperate in the futile search for meaning in his life and in his profession. It is not a contradiction that this becomes manifest in a vivid relationship, in which Dysart breaks through the resistance of his patient with playful means, creating an atmosphere of mutual affection and dependence. Apparently, he needs the change in his treatment routine to uncover his deep-seated doubts. Only with Alan's help does he manage to utter his critique of religion, society, and psychiatry and their joint complicity in the destruction of individual development.

Dysart's inner turmoil is reflected in the structure and style of the entire play. Ritualistic elements in the production are placed in a clinical setting, which turns spectatorship into supervision. As therapist and patient act on the stage, their means of representation oscillate between narration and enactment, commentary and dialogue, flashback and present action, all of which are deployed as complementary and interwoven elements of a psychoanalytic aesthetics in order to reveal the acts of self-revelation and self-exploration as relational processes. The "therapy play" that unfolds emphasizes the interactional dynamics of the process of remembering, which emerges from a therapeutic motive and which can only be promoted through mutual questioning. Since the play makes such an overt use of the formal elements of therapy, a metaphoric, metadramatic level is established, on which the interplay of diegetic and mimetic processes is reflected. Similar structures of intertwined narrative and play spaces and their metaphoric processing can be found in other therapy plays such as Tom Kempinski's *Duet for One* (1980), John Pielmeier's *Agnes of God* (1982), and Conor McPherson's *Shining City* (2004). They differ from other types of psychoanalytic plays— biographic-speculative pieces like Hélène Cixous's *Portrait de Dora* (1976), Nicholas Wright's *Mrs Klein* (1988), or Mark St. Germain's *Freud's Last Session* (2009)—through their focus on a specific therapeutic relationship, and they find their prototype in *Equus*.

Even if therapy is thus exposed as a playroom with creative potential for narrative enactments, the play itself is centered around the creativity of madness. However, just like Dysart, Alan is not a liberated artist; the therapist's therapeutic and the patient's sick creativity are both about to necrotize. Once again, a psychoanalytic hermeneutic is suspected of bringing about this destruction. Dysart does not have any alternative perspectives, not even the renunciation of his therapeutic creed and practice. The play nonetheless suggests that a critical attitude toward one's work may at least aid in cultivating an ethical awareness for the ramifications of one's actions toward an Other. Fittingly, the audience is asked to act as Dysart's supervisors, allowing him to play out his self-criticism and enticing them to become complicit in his actions and affected by his moral dilemma.

Despite the strong doubts about therapy raised in the play, my analysis has shown that the play cannot be equated with the movement of anti-psychiatry, with which it is so often associated. Dysart's responsibility and his promise to alleviate Alan's pain cannot easily be reconciled with a critique of psychiatry that blames it for the destruction of creativity and individuality. Moreover, Dysart's doubts are not based on political but personal considerations. By exploring the underlying motives of Dysart's critique of therapy, it reminds us that political dissatisfaction may be deeply intertwined with personal dissatisfactions that stand in the way of identifying the actual sources of one's grievances and effecting personal and social change. While thus extending a critique of psychiatry, *Equus* still uses the aesthetic potential of therapy through an effective connection between narration and enactment. On a formal level, it remains indebted to a process whose results it mistrusts. In other words, the play might be anti-psychiatric in content, but it is definitely pro-psychiatric in form. If there is then a way out of the dilemma, it cannot be the outright rejection of psychiatry. Instead, the play's conflictedness suggests that a solution can only be found in the mediation of these positions, scenic re- and co-construction, and (self-)critical awareness in the face of the conflicts arising out of personal, ethical, and aesthetic quandaries.

9

"Locked in a Room, Listening": Talk-Show Therapy and Co-Construction in *In Treatment*

Introduction: Talk-show therapy

At least since the extremely successful HBO production *The Sopranos* (1999–2007), psychotherapy has seen a remarkable surge in popularity on television. Aside from numerous shows that have the occasional recourse to scenes in a therapeutic setting, like *Six Feet Under* (HBO, 2001–05), *Mad Men* (AMC, 2007–15), or *Sherlock* (BBC, 2010–), many television series are completely dedicated to psychotherapists and their patients, including *Bloch* (SWR/WDR, 2002–13), *Huff* (Showtime, 2004–06), *Tell Me You Love Me* (HBO, 2007), *Web Therapy* (LStudio.com/Showtime, 2008–15), and *Necessary Roughness* (USA, 2011–13).[1]

Thus, it is not at all surprising that in Israel, too, a television show was developed that focuses on a therapist's practice. As a therapy series, however, Hagai Levi's *Be'Tipul* (בטיפול; "In Treatment") (HOT3, 2005–08) is exceptional. Whereas *The Sopranos*, *Bloch*, *Huff*, or *Tell Me You Love Me* follow the therapists or the patients into their homes, exploring their private lives in connection with or independent of their therapeutic sessions, the Israeli series takes place almost exclusively in the office of therapist Re'uven Dagan. Intrigued by this concentrated format, Rodrigo García adapted *Be'Tipul* for a US-American audience in close collaboration with Levi. The result, *In Treatment* (HBO, 2008–10), is based mostly on its Israeli model (Levi et al.), departing from it only in the final third season. In the HBO series, most of the action is also located in the office of therapist Paul Weston (Gabriel Byrne), giving his private life no precedence over his patient's stories as they are told in therapy. *In Treatment* does not send its therapist on detective adventures, as *Bloch* does, nor does it allow him to intervene actively in his patient's lives—a technique used, for instance, in *Necessary Roughness* to introduce more variety into the therapeutic plot. And unlike *Huff* or *The Sopranos*, it does not illustrate the sessions with visual effects, flashbacks, or fantasy sequences. Instead, every episode of *In Treatment* consists simply of a conversation between Paul and his respective patient. In essence, the series is a fictional talk show in a therapeutic setting.

In Treatment is doubtless the most well-known offshoot of *Be'Tipul*, but by far not the only one. In many other countries, local HBO divisions and other channels decided to repeat this form of reproduction and adaptation: in Canada (*En thérapie*, TV5 Québec Canada, 2012–14), in the Netherlands (*In Therapie*, NCRV, 2010–11), in Italy (*In Treatment*, Sky Italy, 2013), in Serbia, Croatia, and Slovenia (*Na terapiji*, Fox TV Srbija, 2009; Croatian HRT, 2013; POP Brio, 2011), in Romania (*În derivă*, Engl. "Drifting," HBO România, 2010–12), in the Czech Republic (*Terapie*, HBO Česká republika, 2011–13), in Poland (*Bez tajemnic*, Engl. "Without Secrets," HBO Polska, 2011–13), in Russia (Без свидетелей, Engl. "Without Witnesses," Первый канал, 2012), in Hungary (*Terápia*, HBO Magyarország, 2012–14), in Brazil (*Sessão de Terapia*, GNT, 2012–14), in Argentina (*En Terapia*, TV Pública, 2012–14), and in Japan (心療中/*Shinryouchuu -in the Room-*, Nippon Television, 2013). In these adaptations, not only did the producers translate the dialogue and cast new actors, they also adapted the show to their cultural contexts. Despite these changes on a local level, however, the basic narrative structure remained the same in every case.[2]

How did this curious transcultural success of a serial come about, which, with its small cast, limited setting, and actionless plot, seems to hold few attractions for a television audience? In countries like the United States and Argentina, where psychotherapy is part of the everyday life of many people, it is easier to explain why an audience might be interested in such a pure representation of therapy than in Eastern European countries or even in Russia, where, for political reasons, a therapeutic culture that could support the peculiar premises of the series has never developed (Bronfen and Levi). Therefore, the reasons for the dispersion of the show must be located beyond the therapeutic motif—in the aesthetic and self-reflexive potential of the psychotherapeutic structure for the medium of television. In order to examine this structure more closely, I will focus on the most widely distributed US-American variant *In Treatment*. Apart from the United States, it was broadcast in other English-speaking countries and, in translations, in France, Germany, Austria, and Switzerland. Despite the supposedly simple setting, *In Treatment* emerges as a highly complex series, which allows me to extend the discussion of the shape of therapeutic relationships and of the narrative and aesthetic benefit of therapeutic structures. This is clearly stressed by the titles of the various adaptations, which hint at a focus on intimate dialogue and a room that is closed to others. What happens between Paul, his patients, and his supervisors in this room will thus be my first concern.

Supervision: Dr. Paul Weston, Dr. Gina Toll, and Dr. Adele Brouse

Trained in psychoanalysis, Paul Weston offers a modern psychodynamic talk therapy with once-weekly sessions (Kahr 1054). In his practice, his focus lies in the therapeutic relationship, which, as Thomas Klein notes, generates the psychological suspense in the series (190). In the show's close attention to the relationship and its nuanced representation of Paul's differing alliances with his patients, the setting never remains the same. In the first season, Paul counsels the anesthesiologist Laura, the military pilot Alex, the young gymnast Sophie and the married couple Jake and Amy—a group of patients that will be replaced in each of the following seasons.[3] At the end of the week, Paul visits a therapist himself. During the first two seasons he goes to his old mentor Gina Toll (Dianne Wiest), who, because of their common history, serves as a friend, supervisor, and individual and couple's therapist. In the third season, Paul turns to the younger analyst Adele Brouse (Amy Ryan). Their conversations focus on Paul's difficulties with his patients and his personal problems—a broken marriage, the conflicted relationships with his parents, and his worries about suffering from Parkinson's disease. The series thus uses Paul's supervisions not just to address his therapeutic work; they also represent therapeutic encounters in their own right, in which relational experience and reflection are constantly intertwined. Since the themes of the entire series are dealt with in these sessions, I will here concentrate on Paul's relationships with Gina and Adele.

In the fifth episode, Paul visits Gina for the first time after many years. He seeks help because he feels "anxious" and "wiped out" before his sessions and is afraid of losing control (1.05). Gina had long acted as Paul's supervisor when both were working at the psychoanalytic institute in Baltimore. Both joyful and tense, Paul immediately acts out his anxiety about opening up to Gina by taking a seat in her chair instead of the couch reserved for patients. In the course of their talks, it becomes clear why they have not seen each other in a while. Not only had Paul witnessed how Gina abandoned a patient who had fallen in love with her; Gina's "professional assessment" of his therapeutic practice also once destroyed his chances at directing the institute: "That letter pissed on eight years of my work. Despite it, though, I became an excellent therapist. And some people might say that . . . I became a better therapist than you" (1.10).

No wonder that their relationship is still marred by the old power plays—evident in Paul's occupation of Gina's chair, his desire to surpass her, and his perpetual attacks on her analytic technique. The atmosphere is so tense because Paul is afraid Gina still sees him as an "intern" (1.15) and a failure: "And you thought, 'Here he comes again, "Paul, the failure."' And I thought, she's been sitting here like a sleepy old spider, just waiting, waiting for something like this to happen" (1.05). Uneasy, he leaves a session early, swallows pills as if they provided magic protection against Gina's interpretations (1.10), and repeatedly attacks her: "Would you . . . drop the fucking catlike smile, the bullshit Buddha pose of yours and just tell me for once what you really think?" (2.30). In Paul's imagery, the cat, the spider, and even Buddha apparently represent treacherous calmness—a treachery he suspects behind Gina's neutrality, which seems violating, dangerous, and false to him. This reflects his disappointment at Gina's "treason" as well as his doubts regarding the psychoanalytic technique Gina stands for.

But why does Paul visit Gina at all if he harbors that much suspicion and rage? With time, it becomes clear that he depends on her as an antipode: "You've created this cold version of me that's limiting and castrating because when you're arguing with me you want to see yourself as battling the forces of repression" (1.40). As his sharpest critic and expert in erotic temptation, Gina allows Paul to justify himself and to work on his doubts about the meaning and the limits of his therapeutic work—doubts that have become acute with his patient Laura. Her sudden admission of being in love with him engulfs Paul in a crisis. With his marriage in pieces, he also feels attracted to her, but he knows that the rules of therapy do not allow a relationship between analyst and patient. The authors of *In Treatment* thus turn toward a central concern of psychoanalysis, the transgressive potential of transference love. Jürg Willi recognizes that patients often fall in love with the therapists for whom they have opened their innermost beings; however, by engaging in a sexual relationship with a patient, the analyst destroys the therapeutic working relationship and compromises his role as a therapist. Therefore, most patients, even if they were trying to seduce their therapists, are actually disappointed and angry when they realize the therapists were not strong enough to keep them safe in the therapeutic setting (71). In a classic case of "erotic transference" (1.05), Laura wants to win Paul over. She tries to invade his apartment and thus his privacy (1.10) or to make Paul jealous with a detailed account of an affair with his other patient Alex (1.20). Nevertheless, Paul remains wary of crossing this boundary. He knows that Laura believes she must win men with sex; an affair would only confirm this relational pattern, as Gina warns: "Here's a girl with damaged self-esteem. . . . If you fall for these advances, she won't be grateful. She'll be shocked, rightly so" (1.20). When Paul decides to declare his love to Laura despite everything, she does indeed appear irritated and suspicious: "I don't wanna be the . . . cure to a marriage that ran out of steam, or a job that became routine" (1.43).

The meetings with Gina are dominated by Paul's battle with himself and his supervisor, an attempt to sort through his feelings for Laura and find a way to treat her, resulting in a protracted debate about transference love. Paul advocates an open engagement with transference and countertransference as a therapeutic tool: "What better way is there to air this than to bring it to the surface and put it out there? This room is supposed to be a safe zone where we can open things up and talk about things in a controlled way" (1.05). Gina, however, worries that the needs of the therapist will then take precedence, voicing criticism that has often been launched against the Relational School of psychoanalysis: "This is transference plain and simple. Of course, you and Mitchell and your New York Gang have idealized it" (1.05). The relationship between Paul and Gina is thus constructed on the basis of the theoretical quarrel between modern theory and more rigid therapeutic standards. Their debates become a form of imparting information on psychoanalytic theory: "Paul and Gina reproduce and reargue the entire historical discussion surrounding the normative evaluation of, and taboo concerning, transference love in psychoanalysis in narrative form" (Lang 204). With much theoretical verve, Paul begins to campaign against the exclusion of the erotic: "Freud, Messler Davies, all the big guys, they all talk about how attraction is inevitable, it's part of therapy. But if you brush it under the rug, the message that you're giving to the patient is that their feelings are perverse, are dangerous" (1.10). Gina, however, resolutely opposes Paul's justifications: "Every time we go deeper, you reach for some theory, these male therapists tormented by lust for their patients" (1.10).[4] Gina recognizes that Paul feeds his entanglement in his countertransference with theoretical positions in order to hide causative emotions and conflicts. For Gina, the debate is not about theory or orthodoxy. Protecting the patient is always her first priority: "It's not a law, it's beyond a code of ethics. It's essential. It's something you carry inside you" (1.20). Slowly, Gina breaks Paul's theoretical resistance and advances on his countertransference. He is reluctant to admit that he has succumbed to the "cliché" of having fallen in love with a patient, but, throwing all caution to the winds, he eventually visits Laura to declare his love. On the threshold of her bedroom, however, he has a sudden panic attack, which Gina explains as follows:

> That anxiety attack was yours. It wasn't external. It was you. What restrained you was the very best of you, your deepest standards, personal, and professional, and moral. . . . You saved yourself from being hurt and from hurting a woman that you cared about. What, do you think that . . . that moral decisions are always made in the absence of temptation, that

they're made easily, that they're made gracefully? Give yourself some credit. . . . You wanted her so very badly. So badly that you had an anxiety attack in order to stop yourself. (1.43)

Only with Gina's interpretation do we recognize a dimension of Paul's desire that had been hidden behind his angry resistance—his earnest qualms about his decision and his fear of hurting Laura. The moral decision indeed turns out to be something that, as Gina had said, "you carry inside you" (1.20). Ethical action is here not realized in an abstract resolution but in an embodied relational act.

Paul is primarily dissatisfied with the limits of his involvement and power in the therapeutic relationship. He quickly establishes intense relationships with his patients—"I identify with them, I put myself out for them" (1.20)—but he also lays a personal claim to them (Greenberg 123) and gets too involved. When his patient Alex dies in a flight training accident, Paul realizes that his jealousy about Alex's affair with Laura may have led him to ignore his patient's pain: "I guess I was too involved, so I didn't get the message" (2.10). Despite this acknowledgment that his involvement may cause harm, he still keeps arguing for more personal immersion in therapy—perhaps because he depends on the emotional bonds he establishes in therapy. In the second season, after he has been left by his wife, Paul admits that he uses his patients as surrogates: "I'm not getting anything from my family, so I try to get it from my patients. I know it's wrong, but who else do I have?" (2.20). Paul deplores not being able to support and influence his patients beyond interpretation. Repeatedly, he talks about what patients do when they are "out the door" (1.40; 2.30). Paul knows that his emotional encroachment on his patients' lives is a consequence of his powerlessness, which is mirrored in the series by the fact that the audience, just like Paul, are not shown what happens with the characters outside of his room. But whereas Paul is worried that he cannot satisfy his patients' needs, Gina warns against intervening in their lives: "You cause them to become dependent on you. You cripple them" (2.30). Paul is thus denied the close relationships he so desires.

Although Paul makes many mistakes as an involved therapist, he is extremely effective as soon as he can establish a sustainable relationship. His success with Sophie, for example, makes him wonder: "Maybe Yalom is right: Maybe it is the relationship that actually heals" (1.40).[5] Paul's own contribution to this personal bond is strongly determined by his personality, his family situation, and his past (Barnett). However, we do not learn anything about this until the second season when Paul confronts the imminent death of his father, who had left the family in Paul's teenage years. As a consequence, he had to take care of his bipolar mother up until her traumatic suicide. Gina guesses that his helplessness and his desire to bond with his patients is rooted in his inability to cure his mother (2.15). His feelings of guilt have become intertwined with the separation from his own children and influence the treatment of his patients. This is especially apparent with Oliver, a child of divorce. Due to his own experiences of loss, Paul identifies with the boy: "And it's taking everything I have not to invite him to come live with me. I know what he needs and I want to give it to him" (2.15). These developments are especially intriguing given Paul's and Gina's theoretical disagreement; they support Paul's argument that therapy consists of an interaction that the therapist cannot escape. By means of this detailed discussion of therapeutic theory, *In Treatment* becomes a platform on which Gina and Paul pit orthodox against relational psychoanalytic perspectives. In the course of the plot development, however, the potential pitfalls of both therapeutic approaches are exposed. Again and again, the therapeutic relationship emerges as all-important, and Paul's empathic strategies are often especially effective when he feels strongly for a patient. At the same time, the series agrees with Gina's warning that acting out Paul's countertransference with Laura would harm her and that his passionate dedication to his patients also harms him, as it admits no room for a life outside of his office.

In the face of Paul's difficulties with Laura, Gina often steps over the boundaries of her role as supervisor. As a student, Paul romanticized her— "You were brilliant. And we believed . . . everything you said" (2.35)—but by now she is more of a mother figure for him. She worries about Paul and cares for him during their sessions, offering him tea (1.10) or rearranging a chair so he can put up his feet (1.40). Her steadfast convictions offer Paul a foothold in the precarious situation with Laura: "Whatever you tell me, I'm here for you. I won't abandon you, no matter what" (1.20). This is the promise of absolute security associated with the ideal mother; Gina thus creates a Winnicottian holding environment for Paul. In this way, their relationship oscillates between aggression, rivalry, comradeship, attraction, and maternal care, friendship, counseling, couples therapy, psychoanalysis, and supervision, and thus always along "blurred lines" (2.05). Juggling so many professional and personal roles, Gina sometimes fails to endure Paul's attacks and uphold her neutrality:

> I really think you're acting like an asshole. I really think that you're a therapist who has remarkably little insight into your own behavior. . . . You get to be the innocent victim, doing your best. And I'm just like everyone else, I'm out to fuck you over. . . . You're tortured by what you see as your failures with your parents, with your patients, with your father, so you're destroying all your careful work, and mine. (2.30)

Paul and Gina have to balance too many roles, and the personal feelings from their shared past are too strong to be kept out of the therapeutic framework. As early as the first session, Gina asks: "What role have you assigned to me?" (1.05), but she cannot successfully negotiate her functional position with Paul. The ambivalence in their relationship is never overcome because, on the one hand, Gina appears as a "mentor who's prevented you from having anything you ever wanted," and, on the other hand, Paul sees her as "my sanctuary": "All of my parts of myself that I don't like . . . I could bring them here and it was always okay" (2.35).

However, even after the termination of this relationship, the conflicted bond with Gina persists. Asked about Gina's novel, which he brings to his first session with his new therapist Adele, he praises his former supervisor effusively. Soon he recognizes that this idealization is supposed to serve as a protective device against Adele: "It's like a shield or a security blanket" (3.04). Having read on in the book, Paul comes to believe that one of the unsympathetic characters is based on him and his old rage resurfaces: "She's revealed herself to be completely indiscreet, utterly selfish" (3.08). Adele, however, is not convinced by Paul's protestations: "I think I'm beginning to understand how the dynamic between you and Gina developed, how she came to play so many roles in your life. . . . How is it you say she represented you in the novel? Needy, childish, poor husband, deficient father? Is it possible that you convinced her that you were, in fact, incapable?" (3.12). The boundary violations and the myriad of roles taken over by Gina have often been criticized among psychoanalysts—her double role as therapist and supervisor is unprofessional and prevents real progress (Mitscherlich and Leuzinger-Bohleber; N. Köhler 52). It is remarkable that, by introducing a new therapist, *In Treatment* adopts this critique and thus comments on itself. With her interventions, as both a mirror and a foil, Adele helps us criticize Paul's relationship with Gina retroactively.

As is made instantly apparent to us, Paul attempts to repeat these old patterns with Adele. Once again, he connects the denigration of a rival and resistance against change with idealization and the search for a friend and mother. Paul mocks Adele's interpretations and charges her with dogmatism: "You sound like a textbook" (3.12). Soon, however, he starts admiring her empathy and her professional devotion: "And I've imagined that you might understand something of my life, my loneliness. I know, I know, textbook transference. I know it's ridiculous, a fantasy" (3.16). The "textbook" events are clearly something Paul judges as conventional and thus somehow unreal. Adele refuses to dismiss transference love as absurd, but she also does not permit its realization. She tolerates Paul's feelings and encourages him to explore them. Thus she allows him to enter deeper into his wishful fantasy: "I imagine us having dinner at the end of a day of work, . . . talking about our minor triumphs with patients, helping each other to sort through difficult cases" (3.16). When he notices the slight rounding of her belly, however, he realizes that his romantic fantasies run up against a different reality and attacks her as a "Freudian ice queen." Calmly, she talks about her pregnancy and "how your noticing it earlier might be affecting our discussion" (3.24). In this way, Adele lets Paul see that he is again enacting one of his "unhealthy relationships" (3.28).

This relationship is played out against Paul's worries about suffering from Parkinson's. Adele suspects that Paul's anxiety is linked to a fundamental incapacity to act. Paul himself complains about a lack of passion for life outside of the therapeutic relationship: "I've got this pattern I seek out people who have, who have, themselves, a passion for life and I feed off them instead. I allow them to feel for both of us" (3.16). This is precisely the function of a therapist—to serve as a resonating body for the emotions of others and reduce one's own reactions. Hence, Paul is afraid of having become unable to feel, which is reflected in a dream:

> I'm running along the outside of this tall wrought-iron fence. . . . The fence starts to curve and I can sense this opening up ahead, gates. And I have this tremendous feeling of excitement. . . . And then my legs just . . . get heavy and I'm slowing down as if I'm stuck in quicksand. And I can't move. I sense something behind me, and I turn my head, and it's my father. (3.08)

Paul's first interpretation is that the dream forces him to recognize the symptoms of Parkinson's, the disease that killed his father. Adele, however, notices a different detail: "I'm struck by the fact that you become stuck . . . before you turn and see your father approaching . . . . I'm wondering if you have some agency in stopping yourself from moving forward" (3.08). Despite Paul's predictable anger at her suggestion, Adele manages to distill new meaning from his lost childhood, the family's emigration from Ireland, and his mother's depression: "I think caring for your mother was also a way of saving yourself. It was miserable, yes, but it was also safe and familiar." Even today, Adele adds, he searches for safe but artificial relationships in his "burrow-like office" (3.16):

> I think up until this point you've sought out relationships that are safe, where the risk to yourself emotionally is a small one. Outside the office you keep your distance, inside you do the opposite, you overinvest. You seek out intimacy. But . . . your patients, they're all substitutes of a kind,

allowing you to avoid actually engaging in the world, experiencing life in any real way. (3.28)

With a professional distance from Paul that Gina never achieved, Adele develops a new perspective on Paul's earlier behavior and becomes the series' self-analytic voice, by which the third season sheds light on the previous two. She believes that his attempts to enlist her as his girlfriend or supervisor are part of a strategy to prevent insight into his behavior: "You do anything you can to push our relationship past its prescribed time and purpose.... [A]nything except for what you came to me for, to be your therapist, to get me to challenge you to look at yourself" (3.20). Thus Adele helps Paul recognize that transference can be a way to protect oneself against personal relationships, which also explains why Paul ultimately got stuck with Gina. Accordingly, Paul increasingly sees himself as trapped in the safety zone of analysis, in which a relationship is established but robbed of its consequences:

> Because I can't tell what's real. How can I go on seeing you, looking at you, keep coming here, when you epitomize the conflict? ... You just said "relationship." But the point is that it isn't one. It's been created in this room by the artifice of therapy.... You're sitting across from me and you're pregnant and I still think you are meant to be with me. (3.28)

The artificiality of the relationship with Adele, which is emphasized by the fact that it repeats elements from the relationship with Gina, resonates with Paul's long-held skepticism about psychotherapy when he hits a wall with another patient.

Sunil, a Bengali professor of mathematics, who came to live with his son in the United States after the death of his wife, increases Paul's doubts about the desired connection with his patients. When Sunil starts displaying violent tendencies, Paul defends his patient against Adele's concerns about the safety of his family. Due to their similar age and their "somewhat isolated lives" (3.24), Paul identifies with his patient. Like Sunil, he seems "trapped" (3.04), suffering from an immigrant's isolation in America, and thus Paul believes he understands Sunil: "I know exactly how he feels, why he locks himself off in that room" (3.12). Ultimately, however, he is forced to tell Sunil's family about his violent fantasies, and Sunil is deported. He learns only later that he was unwittingly enlisted by Sunil, who had made up his fantasies to escape the entrapment in his son's family and be allowed to return home to India. Although it turns out that Paul's initial doubts about Sunil's violent tendencies were right, he feels deceived in every other respect. In the fictional space of therapy, he cannot trust anything anymore: "I just find myself questioning the whole thing" (3.28). Even before, he had berated his profession as "completely and utterly divorced from real life" (1.40). With his patients and his therapists, Paul lives through a myriad of transference phenomena that are thoroughly worked through and questioned regarding their influence on the therapeutic relationship: transference love, rivalry, disappointment, responsibility. Several relationships on several layers seem to be superimposed. Paul's relationships with his parents, his wife, and his children are repeated in the relationships with his patients and Gina, to which the third season adds yet another self-reflexive layer through Paul's sessions with Adele. The artificial quality of transference is thus particularly emphasized, and the limitations Paul feels also affect the audience. Although they are increasingly aware of the constructedness of the therapeutic situation, it remains the only visible experience and therefore, despite all artificiality, more "real" than the action outside of analysis. There is thus an inevitable ambiguity between real and fictional experiences in the structure of therapy and *In Treatment*.

Television treatment: Serial settings and talking heads

Television, like therapy, is structured serially (Cavell 79). Therefore, Jane Feuer believes that the television series is the best medium for representing therapy:

> The idea of scheduling by the hour is not the only thing television and psychotherapy have in common. Both are, so to speak, serialized. They unfold over time with gaps in between each session. They are intimate and lend themselves to a two-person dialogue. For all these reasons, television is a better medium than film for portraying the "reality" of psychoanalysis.

In Treatment carries this structural similarity to extremes by concentrating almost exclusively on the representation of therapy and making the sessions available through a modular serial structure (Strauß 156). Every patient visits Paul at a fixed date. In the first season, Laura is on Paul's schedule on Mondays, at ten o'clock, while Sophie visits him Wednesday afternoons at four. Originally, the corresponding episode could also be seen on the assigned weekday. Viewers could choose freely from the modular sessions on offer; if they tuned in only on Mondays, they could concentrate on Laura's story. A viewer who wants to see all episodes of the series is not free at all, however. During the first season, HBO aired the episodes at the matching weekday at 9:30 p.m. Viewers who wanted an even more rigid attachment to the series could watch the episodes on HBO Signature, where they were aired not only on the day but also at the exact time they take place in the diegetic world (Umstead 24). The therapist's schedule was thus mirrored on the level of the television program (Blanchet 47–48). From the second season onward, HBO refrained from this elaborate programming and showed the episodes in two weekly blocks (Vernadakis 54). The experiment of linking the therapist's and the viewer's schedule had apparently failed, but its failure points to the narrative challenges television viewers were asked to confront in *In Treatment*.

Usually, in contemporary television series, several narrative threads are interwoven in a single episode, but through its modular episodic structure, *In Treatment* presents them as separate from each other (Lang 199). Supervision is the only place where all of the storylines are connected with each other, albeit just in cursory reflection. The stories of the patients are not developed further but simply retold and critically examined. The distribution of the characters to their set weekdays thus means that members of the audience who stick to the broadcasting rhythm meet a specific character only every five episodes. Dorothy Rabinowitz criticizes the ensuing wait as "something of a drag." With all its subjectivity, this reaction points to an essential element of the narrative structure of *In Treatment*—the confrontation of the audience with the rigidity of a temporal framework on which they have no influence. Suspense, eagerness, and impatience but also boredom may be the result of the regular interruptions and the slow progression of time (Hatchuel 196–97). At the same time, *In Treatment* illustrates the double formal structure of the series (Hickethier, *Fernsehserie* 10)—the tension between its parts and the whole. While the sequence of single episodes allows for flexibility, the series as a whole makes extreme demands on the time management of the viewer. Clare Birchall praises this structure: "What made the original scheduling so inspired was the way in which it mirrored the pace of real life." Just like the patient, the viewer waits an entire week for the next session in a particular treatment, and like the therapist, she sees every patient at a fixed date that she cannot change once she has committed to the schedule. Thus superimposing the therapist's on the viewers' schedule, the series invites them to identify with the therapist. For television and the television series in particular, such an attachment of the viewer has long been a typical programming strategy. However, when *In Treatment* was launched, the relationship between audiences and television had already changed. In the age of "*post-broadcast-television*" (K. Köhler 23), DVD, streaming, and download have liberated the viewer from a specific airtime. With its attempt to strengthen the audience's attachment to a specific time slot, *In Treatment*, in its first season, thus points self-reflexively to the inherent seriality of its medium and its subject matter—interruptions, waiting time, and continuation are important features of serial narratives and of therapy. In their course, viewer and patient are tied to a fixed narrative time and forced to adopt routines. That HBO abandoned the original scheduling attests to the challenge this posed to the tolerance of the audience and the strong commitment that is taken on by viewer and patient to get involved in a therapy/series that ties all participants to an appointed time every day.[6]

Even beyond its programming, *In Treatment*'s aesthetic strategies depend on the progression of time, which provides room for the process of working through. The parallel arrangement of viewing time and diegetic time incorporates the series structurally and functionally in the everyday life of the audience (Mikos, *Es* 398). *In Treatment* stages how, in therapy and in the television series, the life of the analyst-viewer goes on between the narrative building blocks provided by every single patient, and how the narratives of other patients and the events and reflective moments of the analyst-viewer's life change the reception of every single continued storyline. Over a certain length of time, repetitions and interpretations accrue and make working through possible. Similarly, the waiting period between patient-specific episodes allows for an enrichment of the narrative through the progression of time, which necessarily entails new and repeated experiences and paves the way for a gradual change in how viewers assess the protagonists. The juxtaposition of narratives is not achieved, as for example in a series like *The Sopranos*, by interweaving them in the structure of a single episode but by creating a space for their reflection, which is concretized in the supervision sessions. Thus, a dialogue between patient histories is created within the dialogue of psychoanalyst and supervisor.

The special progression of time in a therapeutic encounter is also mirrored on another level. At first glance, *In Treatment* suggests that narrative time and narrated time are nearly congruent; watching a dialogue takes just as much time as the protagonists need to talk to each other. However, although it is mentioned several times that Paul offers a classic fifty-minute hour, no episode is longer than half an hour.[7] This dramatization and acceleration of the therapeutic process is apparently deemed necessary to make the series bearable. Like many other psychoanalysts before him, Glen Gabbard does not believe that an audience would accept the detailed representation of a therapy session in real time: "A videotape of an actual therapy session, replete with silence, evasion, and idiosyncratic references to people and places, would bore the average viewer in approximately 18 seconds." Thus, he echoes Freud, who believed: "An unauthorized listener who hit upon a chance [session] would ... be in danger of not understanding what was passing between the analyst or the patient, or he would be bored" ("Question" 185). For a long time, representations of therapy seemed tolerable only if they were packed with action or filled with melodramatic undertones (Gabbard). Though striving for realism in so many of its formal features, *In Treatment* subjects the therapeutic dialogues to a "narrative streamlining" (Bem 28) so that the viewer is spared mental leaps, unclear references, or lengthy silences. With its "shortness," the series seems to imply that a fifty-minute episode focusing on two people in dialogue would oversaturate the audience.

* * *

Not just time but space, too, is determined by the therapeutic setting in *In Treatment*. Paul's offices in Baltimore and Brooklyn and the offices of his therapists Gina and Adele are the focal points of the series. It ventures outside in only a few episodes—and sometimes the cold open or the last scene allows us a glance at the arrival or the departure of a patient. This decision to focus the series spatially on therapy lends it aesthetic coherence but also creates a claustrophobic effect, which is addressed in Paul's attitude toward his office. Adele recognizes this immediately:

> You used very similar language when you spoke both about the possibility of having Parkinson's as well as your experience of being a therapist. You talked about Sunil being stuck up in the spare room, about feeling trapped like mice in a glue trap with your patients. That same language of escape and entrapment came up when you spoke about Gina. (3.04)

"Entrapment" thus emerges as the aesthetic principle of the series (Hatchuel 195), evocatively interweaving the two facts that patients may regard the treatment room as a prison (Intelmann 21) and that many popular series focus on one such setting. Interestingly, the series adopts a similarly ambivalent attitude toward its own entrapment as Paul does. Ceaselessly concerned with Paul's being "sick of sitting in a chair day after day after day listening to people's problem's" (2.05) and the limitations this also sets for the series, *In Treatment* nevertheless fully exploits the affordances of the closed space of the therapist's office.

First and foremost, space serves as a carrier of meaning. Paul's office is stuffed with books, ship models, and other artifacts that provide plenty of information about his personality but also create a variegated background to balance out the minimalist reduction of the setting. Due to the concentrated scenery, little changes become meaningful straightaway. When Alex insists that Paul accept the gift of a coffee maker, he inscribes himself in Paul's room just as much as Sophie does when she presents Paul with a new ship model (1.12; 1.13). His room is the battlefield that patients have to conquer, that Sophie makes her own by repurposing the couch as a balancing beam, or that Laura seeks to transgress by using the bathroom in Paul's private apartment (1.18; 1.06). The office thus becomes a reflective surface for the therapeutic relationship. The bi-personal field that creates an invisible tension between two individuals in therapy is thus visualized spatially—in approach and repulsion, in intervention and retreat. As Thomas Klein observes, the distance between Sophie and Paul becomes a signifier for their personal relationship. A physical approach between them signals an imminent breakthrough and her free movements in his office represent her sense of security in his space (194). Room and relationship are coupled to a degree that they seem to work through each other. When Paul asks his patient April why therapy enables her to think different thoughts—"What is it about this room that makes things seem different?"—she answers: "I don't know. The isolation, the detachment. You" (2.17).

Paul's office as the room dedicated to the therapeutic relationship is thus the room in which thinking and storytelling become possible, though only in the characteristic minimalist style of the series. Whereas other representations of therapy, such as *The Sopranos* or *Tell Me You Love Me*, seem to take filmic devices like the flashback or the fantasy sequence for granted, *In Treatment* renounces them almost completely. Only in a single scene is the audience allowed to experience a short fantasy of Paul's during a session with Laura (1.16), which, however, is significantly located in his office and immediately linked back to the therapeutic dialogue with a pan shot. In contrast to *The Sopranos*, where the therapy scenes, though dominated by the therapeutic dialogue itself, still rely on flashbacks, it becomes apparent how far *In Treatment* takes this minimalist principle. Although neither the characters nor the camera leave the room, it changes with every patient and his or her individual ways to appropriate it through body and narrative. Present and past spaces overlap, as Madeleine and Willy Baranger explain: when patients tell stories in *In Treatment*, these are "superimposed or mixed situations" (799), as the present analytic dyad reflects a myriad of narrated events and spaces. The patients' stories are thus liberated by the room, but they are also "trapped" because they cannot go beyond it in terms of their visual presentation in the series.

Increasingly, Paul sees this ambivalence as a problem. The experiences in therapy seem unreal and false to him: "Isn't it time that I go outside and experience reality, step beyond the office doors and see the difference for myself?" (3.28). Although it becomes clear that neither his understanding of Sunil nor his feelings for Adele are fictitious, the room, in which Paul feels trapped, is built on artificial rules and creates something that is just as artificial—the therapeutic relationship. Everything Paul experiences here is, in the words of Leo Bersani, "suspended in virtuality" (28). The therapeutic space, as an artificial medium between therapist and patient, produces art(ifice) and fiction, but it also creates a sustainable relationship for a complex juxtaposition of real emotions and newly formed mental connections that cannot always be measured against reality. However, the more Paul begins to doubt the sincerity of his patients and the truthfulness of his relationship with Adele, the less he considers the therapeutic relationship as a proper carrier for the narratives of his patients and the more he feels cramped: "All I know is that I can't spend the next ten or twenty years like this, locked in a room, listening" (3.28). His incessant doubts about his profession mirror the inherent problem of the series—whether and how long it can sustain the exclusive setting, being "locked in a room." At the end of the final season, Paul leaves behind his patients and his therapist. Regarding the door marking the borders of this room, he concludes: "You can close it behind me" (3.28).

* * *

On the other side of that door, all action is concentrated on the dialogue between therapist and patient. Christine Lang describes the staging of conversations in *In Treatment* as fairly conventional: "It is all presented in muted colors, soft lighting, and a classical mise-en-scène, with alternating shots and reaction shots ranging from medium shots to close-ups; we always see the characters at eye level" (201). The shot/reverse shot pattern, the close-ups, and the medium shots allow viewers to follow the dialogue without any irritations. This mode of staging a dialogue, with its focus "on the smallest eye movements, that gazes into the soul of one person talking," is, as Feuer states, common in televisual genres like the soap opera. Lang also identifies the "talking heads" as very typical of television, but she observes: "Virtually no other TV series is reduced to the spoken word to this extent. The diegesis unfolds entirely through the dialogues" (201). With its minimalism and its reduction to the therapeutic situation, *In Treatment* thus seems to epitomize and even radicalize a classic television aesthetic (Feuer). Everything is focused on dialogue and language to such an extent that even the cliffhanger of the first season points self-referentially to the continuation of the dialogue. To Paul's question "What's left for me now, Gina, hm?" she answers: "We'll have to talk about that" (1.43). In the following shot, the viewers watch both of them through Gina's window—they are, for now, released from the analytic space whose prisoners Paul and Gina remain. This metatelevisual hint at the "talking heads" leads us to conclude that *In Treatment* examines the relationship between dialogue and television series and thus the link between the talking cure of psychoanalysis and the "talk-medium" of television (Bem 29).

In contemporary television, this concentration on dialogue may seem almost anachronistic. Timotheus Vermeulen and Gry Rustad have described how television series appear to have turned away from the "rhetorics" of narrative, which privileged the spoken word to a degree that "watching" television seemed almost unnecessary, and have embraced a "cinematic style," which privileges the filmic image (341). *In Treatment*, however, abandons the cinematic principle of "show, don't tell" (Oren). In fact, nothing much seems to happen in the therapist's office except talk. This is especially apparent in Sunil's case; the descriptions of his violent fantasies create the sense that something is about to happen, maybe even a murder. But Sunil's fantasies are indeed "just talk." The abstinence demanded in psychoanalysis is thus transferred to the aesthetic formula of the series. Once, Paul deplores that he cannot fulfill the wishes of his patients: "They want to be loved, even by me, they want a child, or they want to be my child, . . . they want attention, they want affection, they want hope, they want pills and they want sex. . . . But I don't give them those things" (2.30). *In Treatment* does not give viewers those things either—they are merely talked about. Paul's continued discontent with his limited possibilities, his repeated desire to support his patients beyond his doors suggest that the question turns not just around the limitations of psychoanalysis but around the limitations of spectatorship and whether such a concentrated dialogue is capable of captivating the audience even if television is no longer bound to the spoken word. Or, in other words: What does a televised dialogue have to accomplish in order to fascinate an audience?

All patients tell Paul about their lives and slowly go back to their past. At first glance, *In Treatment* thus seems committed to an analytic plot pattern. Christoph Dreher and Christine Lang argue that since the series depends on the retrospective investigation of past events, it is essentially an analytic drama. By making sure that the discovery of information takes place at the right pace to attach the audience to the series, analytic and serial dramaturgy are, in fact, linked here (Lang 202). Alessandra Stanley also notes an artistic pattern of brokering information: "In every session the patients' words are veined with allusions and elusions, clues to problems or patterns that are invisible to them but absorbing for the viewer." Does the allure of the series thus reside in its riddle structure? The critical impressions certainly testify to *In Treatment*'s affinity with archaeology and the art of detection. However,

Paul never investigates outside of the therapeutic space, as, for example, Simon Jordan or Martin Dysart do. His detective work is reduced to the dialogue.

Therefore, the comparison with the detective is not entirely convincing; everything that can be discovered manifests itself in the presence of the relationship. Even if there are hidden motives or repressed events to recover, the series derives its true dynamic not from the past but from the here and now of the therapeutic dyad. This is shown in Paul's supervisions. Gina and Paul discuss how a patient's past—Laura's tendency to seal relationships with sex, Alex's power struggle with his father, Sophie's mistrust of her parents—resurfaces in their interaction with Paul and how Paul, in turn, injects his own history—the conflict with his wife or the depression of his mother—into every therapeutic encounter. This transference allows viewers to imagine the past even if they only see the present. This becomes particularly evident in Paul's interaction with Gina. Seldom do they have to talk about their past controversy because both know about it. At the same time, their conversation is infused with the story of their relationship, oscillating, as it does, between trusting affection and passionate professional dispute. Since the actual suspense of the series is thus transferred to the time and space of the therapeutic dialogue, it does not need any flashbacks or exterior scenes.

This special spatial and temporal structure, with the concentration on dialogue and language, paradoxically forces viewers to watch the series with great concentration. Following the dialogue by listening is not enough, for it is made visible in a particularly sparse but meaningful way. Music or camera movement are rarely employed, and only to indicate the intensification of a conflict (T. Klein 201). Mostly, these conflicts become manifest in the behavior of the characters. Even if the protagonists remain silent, their gaze, their gestures, and their use of the room mirror the development of insight and intimacy in the therapeutic relationship (T. Klein 200). All these subtle elements of communication can only become meaningful because they are built into the mechanics of the series. Through repetition and variation a matrix is developed with which these signs can be analyzed and understood (T. Klein 190), and the conversation is exposed as an embodied action that gains depth with its serial continuation. The minimalism of the setting with its simultaneous richness in visible details forces viewers to be especially attentive and use their imagination to add on to what the protagonists say. The series thus provides a challenge to viewing and listening at the same time. Lang believes that, being challenged in that way, viewers gain an understanding of the structure of psychotherapy and adopt its goal, "to discover what lies hidden beneath the surface" (201). However, what *In Treatment* actually encourages is not so much to go beyond or under the surface but, instead, to begin perceiving the surface as meaningful, to pay attention to the smallest particulars of a communicative process, to remain in the presence of the therapeutic session and appreciate its dynamic richness in details without having to take recourse to the explanatory benefits and diverting effects of the flashback.

Co-treatment: Analysis as co-production

Paul is surprised when he learns that Gina has started writing a novel. Fervidly, he questions her ability to be a writer: "A novel is about complexity. It's about contradictions, foibles, human folly. Not absolutes. For you, complexity is a problem, some kind of pathology that needs to be treated" (1.20). For him, Gina, too, seems to be limited by her analytic attitude and the therapeutic space: "You've never lived outside this room. . . . You write fiction, about how life could have been, should have been. . . . [C]an you really help anybody if you live in a bubble?" (1.40). Implicitly contradicting Paul's opinion, *In Treatment* shows that complexity is actually made possible by this secluded but shared "bubble," which is used by the series to reflect its narrative process.

Paul, Gina, and Adele see therapy as a chance to retell one's own life. Adele explains: "At a certain point, you have to move past the stories that you've assigned to your life, these steadfast explanations you've settled on years ago" (3.16). Far from steadfast, in analysis, memories turn out to be unreliable and are continually revised, as Gina notes: "We like to think of them as indelible records of our past, but every time we pull out a scene we fiddle with it a little before we put it back in" (2.15). Although Paul knows this, he resists Gina's implication that he may not have understood his own history properly. Even for a trained professional, it is apparently difficult to resolve set narratives, look at them anew and reformulate them. Thus, Gina has to work not just on the story but also on the hostile feelings stirred up by analysis. She insists on the difference between real feelings and fictional elements in his life story: "I'm not questioning your feelings about your childhood. They're absolutely accurate. I'm just wondering . . . that maybe some of the facts aren't what you think they are" (2.15). Without Gina's insistence, Paul wouldn't work on these gaps; his retelling depends on her intervention. In this dyadic procedure, the story is automatically transferred to a present relational context, in which the past is renegotiated.

In this way, the analyst becomes a co-narrator in a complicated process of co-narration. Paul's sessions with Sophie are particularly revealing in this respect. At first, the young gymnast does not seek therapy, just his professional opinion about an accident that her insurance provider suspects may have been a suicide attempt. However, when Paul promises to give her his report, "without any more . . . shrink-like questions," she gets angry: "Doesn't sound like you're interested . . . . Maybe I have something to say about what it says in [the report]" (1.03). In other words, she demands that they co-produce her story. The basis for this mutual process of negotiation is a good relationship, and at the beginning of the treatment, Sophie tests Paul repeatedly, for example by asking him to help her strip off wet clothing (1.08)—he prudently assigns this task to his wife—or by committing another suicide attempt in his bathroom (1.20)—where he catches her just in time. After Paul has won her trust by protecting her privacy and life, he can offer Sophie a safe space, "here, in this room," where she can open up (1.28). He promises her that she may determine the course of the treatment herself: "The person who's in therapy controls the gas, so to speak. And the wheel, for that matter" (1.13). Paul's influence on the narrative process is still immense. His interventions change the course of the story, emphasize turning points, or uncover details that could not be told before. Sensitively, Paul reacts to the hidden signals his patient sends out. The decisive turning point in Sophie's therapy comes about when Paul responds to a cue from their very first session. Sophie had pointed out a pile of books, one of which, he later discovers, was published by her father—a volume with nude art photographs. When Paul confronts her with his discovery, Sophie believes he accuses her father of sexual abuse and, in turn, accuses Paul of "abusing" her with the distortion of her words (1.28). However, by following her own hints, his intention is not to force a narrative on her but to discover new aspects of her story together: "What I'm trying to do is to help you find your own answers!" (1.38). In order to do so, he must first question Sophie's story and put up with her resistance before they can reach a new, co-constructed story.

These complex narrative processes are embedded in another mutually constructed context in the series. Paul's private circumstances also influence the stories he can tell with his patients. The connections between Paul's family and his patients are linked by a dramaturgic strategy used in many narrative series, in which a storyline A is mirrored and commented on by a storyline B (Newman 18). Here, this strategy is hardly ever used in structuring a single episode, but it is important in structuring therapy as a narrative project, which is based on the establishment of connections and the interpretation of relational experiences. In every season, Paul's central problem—his love for Laura in season one, his conflict with his father in season two, and his supposed Parkinson's disease in season three—influences the relationships with his patients. At Gina's, he relates important events from his practice, which are decisively revised by his relativizing remarks as well as by the interpretation of his supervisor. Thus, the series creates a complicated palimpsest of stories. Every patient tells Paul about his or her life. Throughout the week, four different patient narratives are collected, which, through their very difference, emphasize conflicts as well as narrative and interactive styles, reflect Paul's different interventions into their narrations, and begin to extend and elucidate each other by way of contrast. In the presence of Gina and Adele, Paul repeats the stories of his patients, retells the therapy sessions from his point of view, and contextualizes them with his own experiences and memories from outside the therapeutic encounter. This makes the previous therapy sessions appear in a new light, as Paul reveals hidden thoughts, but also sometimes refuses to tell the truth or produces interpretations of the events we have seen that may surprise us. The supervision sessions create, as Lang argues, a "counterplot," which adds on to the patients' stories. At the same time, however, we are dealing with an exchange among experts, who, with their discussions about contemporary psychoanalytic theory, turn toward an informed and interested viewer to increase the self-reflexive content of their dialogue (Lang 200). Gina and Adele question Paul's point of view and his narrative style, as he had previously done with his own patients, reflect them with the help of psychoanalytic theory, and thus weave in additional levels of complexity. The multiplicity of superimposed stories and narrative processes offers an opportunity to reflect on the narrative event itself and its dependence on perspective, narrative stance, and relational context.

In this bundle of co- and counter-narrations, neither patient nor therapist is an empowered author of his or her self. "Look, any shrink will tell you that a patient is the author of his own life" (3.08), Paul reflects at one point, but this supposed authorship is represented as precarious and shared. As single narrators, the patients are stuck to facts they cannot change, to damages and deficits a new narrative cannot erase, and to a version of their story with which they have arranged themselves. The challenge through a co-narrator is essential to start the process of reappraisal, but it also changes the status of one's authorship. The patient is no longer the sole author of his life. And yet, the therapist does not just become the new author either. Indeed, Paul regrets that he has not more control over the stories of his patients: "You know who I envy? Writers. They create these characters that they want to spend time with and then they decide whether they're gonna let them live or die, or let them be happy or unhappy." Gina, however, sets Paul's romanticized idea of therapy straight: "But we don't run the show, Paul. . . . We help people understand" (1.40). *In Treatment* thus rejects the analogy between therapist and author/artist; the therapist's responsibility toward the patient robs him of artistic freedom. Observers, critics, analysts, and supervisors can become creative narrators in a shared process, but they lack absolute control. While it must fight the possibility that the therapist seizes the story of the patient, abuses and changes it to his own liking, a thoroughly balanced therapeutic process respectful of the needs of the patient does not empower her to be the independent author of her life story either. The resulting narrative belongs neither to the patient nor to the therapist but is a co-production for which both share responsibility. To develop a story "of one's own" is impossible when it is always juxtaposed with and changed by other narratives, but without such an independent "original" it becomes impossible to detach the story from outside influences. An effective narrative ethics that prevents the occupation of the story by an Other is only possible through a relational process of negotiation that continually tests the status of the narrative against the standards of both co-narrators.

* * *

In the analytic context, mutual narration is based on mutual listening. To pay close attention to what the other says is not just the task of the therapist but also the task of the patient if she wants to change her story. Psychoanalysis and *In Treatment* actually consist of a series of interrelated reading or listening processes, which take the viewer-analyst beyond evenly suspended attention.

Gina can tell at least one thing from Paul's narratives: "It's clear to me how carefully you listen. You have a great ear. You have a great sense of empathy" (2.30). For Gina, Paul's listening can be grasped via the recounting of his therapeutic encounters, which emphasizes the link between both activities. Paul, however, is unhappy that his attention has no more than a narrative effect: "And then he goes back into the world, the real world . . . . And the work that we've done together is just . . . gone" (3.04). Adele's protest that "even the act of listening has value" (3.04) suggests there may be other benefits of his work, which Gabriel Byrne recognizes in a comparison between therapy and confession: "We need to be listened to and understood. We need a sacred place to do it. . . . When you go to confession you unburden yourself of your so-called sin and are forgiven. In therapy you are not forgiven but you are listened to. The therapist's office is also a sacred place" (Raphael). Listening does not need to have an immediate effect; it has a value of its own. That is true even for the therapist. In his first session with Gina, Paul muses: "I remember you said once that one of our biggest problems was that we don't have an audience. . . . Somebody that you can go to and say: Did you see how I maneuvered that person into that situation?" (1.05). Paul's wish for an audience that is, ironically, granted to him by the television audience, emphasizes the privacy and seclusion of the therapeutic situation. Paul craves for a listener who validates his achievements, who, so to say, cultivates an aesthetic appreciation of Paul's therapeutic artwork. However, in the role of supervisor and listener, Gina sees herself as a critical agent: "What I meant was, is that we have no one to criticize us, no one to review us" (1.05). Paul and Gina thus clash with their desires for a neutral and criticizing supervisor versus an engaged and empathic listener.

Paul builds listening relationships with his patients based on his own need for intimacy: "I can't help but connect with the person.... That's my reward" (1.20). He even admits to a longing for the families of his patients: "Sometimes I dream about the family members of patients that I'm treating, people I've never met" (1.40). Gina is able to link this desire with Paul's fear of losing his own family, highlighting again that Paul's abilities as a listener are bound to his emotions and his relational history. However, this preoccupation might also limit his abilities to listen. "Even without outright lying people only hear what they really want to hear or what they're capable of hearing," Paul notes (3.28). Transferring this insight to the therapist should perhaps lead to Freud's demand for evenly suspended attention. But Paul believes that his desire is a prerequisite for his work. Without fascination, without desire, and without love, it is impossible, at least according to Paul, to be a therapist: "I have to find something in each of my patients that I love, otherwise I won't be able to treat them" (1.23). Attention must be based, as we have already seen in Coetzee, on a balanced desire that stimulates interest but does not cause too much distraction. Gina admits:

> You want to know what I struggle with? It's not that I'm too reserved, too detached. It's that I'm too emotional. I'm impulsive and emotional and I give myself over right away and passionately.... Can't you see that I'm protecting myself because I'm afraid I'll get carried away? I won't be able to think, I won't be able to analyze, I won't be able to work. (1.40)

Listening is a relational act that comes with the possibility of getting lost in delicate interpersonal predicaments and desires. These must be treated as responsibly as the stories that emerge from them. Paul tells Gina after Alex's suicide: "I was like a repository, really, a trustee. There were things that he never told anyone else, his private thoughts, and they've stayed with me" (1.40). Storytelling and listening thus create a connection based on witnessing and the ability to hold and protect a part of the Other.

On many levels, the structure of *In Treatment* encourages viewers to share the position of the therapist. They adopt his schedule and his task of understanding the patients' stories. They listen to them and pay attention to the minute signs conveyed on Paul's couch through facial expressions and gestures. The information management of the series turns the viewer into a detective or a "virtual" therapist: "(S)he listens carefully and interprets; (s)he tries to decipher the veiled and indirect utterances of the characters, attempts to read what lies hidden beneath the surface of faces and gestures, ... and speculates about the outcome of the drama" (Lang 204–05). The viewer is asked to become a reader of the smallest signs and symbols, who must pay evenly suspended attention without knowing which movement or which word may suddenly acquire a special meaning.

The relationship that is established between patient, therapist, and viewer, however, does not just consist in the viewer's adoption of the therapist's role. Byrne believes that the allure of the series resides in the voyeuristic opportunities it provides for viewers: "They get to empathise with the patient, to criticise and judge the patient. They have the same relationship with the doctor, too. It's a three-character play: the doctor, the patient and the audience" (Raphael). Viewers may indeed oscillate between different roles— they may analyze like the therapist, feel like the patient, trying to build a relationship with the therapist, or observe this dyad like the supervisor. The daily repetition of the therapeutic interaction only serves to strengthen the identification with the characters and to make them a part of the viewer's everyday life (Sterngast).

Aside from the serial structure, gaps in the narrative also urge viewers to adopt the role of the supervisor. Paul may be present in every episode, but he usually holds back his opinions; he is a riddle that becomes less and less readable. With the contradictory knowledge viewers gain over time, he is exposed as an unreliable narrator whose words cannot be trusted (Lang 204). Even his own sessions or the short sequences out of his family life do not cohere to complete the puzzle of his inner life or his experiences. In the psychoanalytic frame of the series, in which Paul is constantly interpreted by himself and his therapists and in which only the audience has an overview of all sessions, they are implicitly asked to analyze not just the patients but also the therapist (Hatchuel 204). To do so, they have to collect the fragments of Paul's story and assemble an interpretation.

* * *

In Treatment's invitation to participate in the interpretive process does not mean that interpretation remains unproblematic. In their everyday business, the therapists in the series are quite aware of a psychoanalytic tendency to overinterpret. They try to avoid biased interpretations by listening and concentrating on the patient. Thus, Gina reminds Paul not to analyze too much—"just describe" (1.15)—to prevent them from missing important details of his experience. She uses a variety of techniques to force Paul to pay attention to what he says. When they speak about Laura, Gina notices: "Suddenly it's all about genitals, gynecologists and urologists and . . . You know, it seems to me that you're taking all of this to an extremely intimate realm, and you're saying to me, 'I'm extremely vulnerable here'" (1.15). Thus, Gina does not take Freudian sexual interpretation at face value but realizes that Paul talks about a different form of intimacy—the relationship between Paul and herself, and the ways they talk about it. She may sound like a Rogerian talk therapist when she mirrors Paul's words: "I know it's irritating, but I just want to make sure that I understand" (2.15). However, as these words lead us to understand, this repetition works not just because it assures Gina's full comprehension of Paul's meaning but precisely because it irritates his position as a storyteller. Paul gets to listen to his own words in the way Gina's paraphrase has transformed them. Thus, she emphasizes a feature of all interpretations: they repeat and rearrange, they reveal patterns and significant language use. With the same technique, Adele manages to detect surprising links in Paul's idiom, such as a "language of escape and entrapment" (3.04). The therapists in *In Treatment* are thus engaged in painstaking philological work, redirecting us from ready-made interpretive patterns to paying detailed attention to the patient's acts of self-expression.

Although this technique is often surprisingly accurate, Paul is extremely resistant against interpretation and charges Gina with reductionism. He believes she only sees patterns that confirm her prejudgments: "You're so caught up in your little theories" (1.05). He is also afraid that "a fully conscious human being would be paralyzed." Gina argues: "And when anxiety and fear and pain bubble up from below, how can that be dealt with except by looking at it?" (1.40). None of the patients in the series is in treatment without being troubled by serious problems. For Gina, interpretation is not the creation of new, superfluous content but a way of dealing with inevitable conflict, a way of living and being in the world. "But you can't observe yourself through your own binoculars" (2.25), she adds, emphasizing the need for relational structures in analysis. For her, however, the process remains distanced, limited to clinical observation, and dependent on technical support, as her binocular metaphor suggests.

Paul desires a more intuitive strategy of dealing with patients: "I think we'd be far more effective if we relied less on instruments, theories and books and more on our own instincts" (1.40). But his instincts do not change just his capacity for attention but also the evaluation of his patients. Paul recognizes that he cannot override the gap between narrative and external reality:

> What's also interesting is seeing the relatives of patients that you've treated. The participants in the stories that you've heard dozens of times. ... We think we know them, but we don't really know them at all. We know reactions to them, or versions of them idealized or vilified. ... I ask myself all the time if I actually know what I think I know about

my patients' lives. . . . Amy, I don't think she can ever really be known. I mean, there are certain patterns that identify themselves from her past, but I cannot shrink her. She's too complicated. And then I say to myself, "Do I really know any of these people, or are they all just one big fiction that I've constructed in my head?" (1.40)

He is afraid that every impression he gains in therapy is just a one-dimensional, fictional construction on his part. Thus, his interpretations do create something new. However, the characters that inhabit the narratives of therapy have not been invented by him; they are mutual constructions. Paul's impression of Amy is influenced by her stories just as much as Amy's version of herself is scrutinized and expanded by Paul; and yet, neither variant is congruent with the "real" Amy. *In Treatment* allows viewers to participate in this construction of insight and come to the same realization as Paul. Like the therapist's, the viewer's image of the patients and their families is based on their stories and enhanced by their own imagination (Richter). Many an encounter with supposedly known family members may thus surprise the audience. This reaction, like the interpretations in Paul's or Gina's analyses, is co-produced and pre-shaped by the hints and gaps of the series, which are filled by the viewer.

Paul, however, remains dissatisfied with co-construction because it does not involve any form of action. He reproaches Gina: "You sit in that goddamn chair, and your patients are falling apart in front of you, but instead of reaching out to help, you study them as if they were pieces of a puzzle!" (2.30). Paul differentiates a good treatment from solving a mere (quasi-literary) puzzle by pointing to the therapeutic mandate, from which interpretive work cannot be detached and which includes the responsibility to do more than decipher the patient's "text." However, when he imagines how he might counsel his patient Mia as a life coach—"I would tell her to quit her job, I would tell her to grow her hair, . . . I would tell her to take up biking, not wear heels for a year, and I'd tell her, 'Get a dog'" (2.30)—the problem is obvious. With his paternalistic attitude, Paul would instruct Mia to cultivate a supposedly more natural femininity to resolve her doubts—whether it was right to choose her career over a family—according to his own ideals of womanhood. Paul's recommendations would not contain any co-construction, they would merely be a unilateral interference. The limitation of the interpretive power of the therapist is justified by his responsibility to preserve the integrity of the patient and her text in the face of all kinds of interventions, to help compose but not impose a story. That is why it all comes back to listening:

> These people come to me, they want me to fix their problems, and the truth is, I think all I can do is . . . keep them company during a rough

patch. I don't think anybody's life can be figured out, but it is in our nature to keep trying to make sense of it, and sometimes we can use help. That's when, if we're lucky, there's somebody in the room who can listen. (2.35)

Conclusion

The relational nexus woven by *In Treatment* over three seasons and thirteen therapeutic relationships is staged in multiple ways. Every relationship stands for itself but is always mirrored in adjacent familial and therapeutic constellations, spread out in supervision, and examined with the help of orthodox and contemporary psychoanalytic theories. All this is connected to the conflicts Paul brings into the sessions—his countertransference love, his jealousy, his paternal affection for his younger patients, his yearning for maternal care, and his rivalry with his supervisors. Dealing with the relationship and navigating between intense, real emotions and artificial constructions is still the "most difficult [portion]" of the psychoanalytic work (Freud, "Fragment" 13). Paul fights with both supervisors about his countertransference and his longing to throw off the shackles of his profession, but whether he will find an alternative for himself and his patients remains doubtful.

Through the dialogue of two analysts, *In Treatment* not only stages controversies of psychoanalytic theory but also reflects the critique viewers with a psychoanalytic background have launched against the series. In this debate, the series itself takes up a mediator's position by calling for and still problematizing the engagement of the therapist. Thus, a critical discourse on *In Treatment*, debating treatment technique and its fictional representation, has developed in journals and on television. What has rarely been acknowledged, however, is that the show's claim does not consist only in presenting psychoanalysis adequately or providing a narrative access to its theory. What has also become evident in this chapter is that *In Treatment* works through therapy, as it were, to explore the limitations of the analogy between psychoanalysis and television.

By translating the psychoanalytic setting into a television series, *In Treatment* manages to transfer the problem of the "limitations" of the therapeutic situation into the form of the series. The attachment created through the session structure as well as the show's concentration on the therapist's office and the spoken word emphasize the artificiality and virtuality of therapy. In a format thus strongly oriented toward narrative, the as-if character of the analytic dialogue becomes apparent and may create the desire to break out of the prison of the consulting room and its linguistic boundaries. However, with the focus on the present relationship and its smallest gestures, the series also draws its suspense and its aesthetic appeal from the mutual involvement and the multifaceted, multichannel communication in therapy. At the same time, *In Treatment* points to the limitations of the formal inspiration provided by psychoanalysis; the show does not attempt to create a perfect equivalent to psychoanalysis, even though emulating the latter often serves to enhance its "televisuality." Thus, it points to a basic problem of the formal exchange—psychoanalysis lacks an orientation toward spectators. As an aesthetic experience, it is only available to its immediate participants. *In Treatment*, however, still accepts the challenge to adapt psychoanalytic forms and use them as a stimulant for self-reflection.

In this framework, the narratives between patients and therapists are presented as co-constructions between several agents in dyads and even triads. Thus, the series demonstrates that an analyst cannot control his characters like an author, showcasing the problems of the classic analogy. Instead, it demands that the analyst participate in a process of co-narration, even if that changes the story only to a minimal degree—a perspective on authorship that may not surprise us so much given the communal production process behind a series like *In Treatment*. All participants have to take up responsibility for the shape of the narrative and have to negotiate the result between themselves, which also leads to a relational perspective on listening and interpreting. Both cannot be achieved from a distance but demand involvement. This participation, however, may not be taken so far as to endanger the integrity of the co-constructed text. By inviting the audience to identify with the positions of patients, therapists, and supervisors and to train their attention on the minutest details of communication, gaps in the narrative text, and changes in perspective, viewers are turned into co-producers asked to supplement the minimalist series with their own interpretations and fantasies. This explains the international attraction of the series—through a self-reflexive analogy with psychoanalysis, it challenges the audience by taking the medium of television to its limits. Thus, it not only reveals the audience's limitations but also opens a new space for communicative expansion and imaginative co-construction.

Part Four

Conclusion

Even after the complicated success of *In Treatment*, therapeutic relationships have remained a curiously recurrent constellation in literature, theater, film, and television. With apparently unabating energy, they have kept fascinating writers and audiences, as testified to in recent years by such diverse releases as E. L. Doctorow's novel *Andrew's Brain* (2014), Richard Appignanesi's graphic novel series *Graphic Freud* (2012–), Mark St. Germain's play *Freud's Last Session* (2010), and television series like the Hulu production *Chance* (2016–17) and numerous Netflix originals like *Gypsy* (2017), *Atypical* (2017–), and *Wanderlust* (2018). There is a mutual attraction between therapy and the arts, which, as this study has shown, is not based solely on the themes and theories of psychology and psychoanalysis, but as much on their methods and the complex aesthetic practice encapsulated in the therapeutic relationship. In psychoanalysis and aesthetic theory, in novels, plays, and television series, therapy and art meet at and benefit from reciprocal thematic, aesthetic, and poetological interfaces for their interrelated projects of self-legitimation and self-reflection.

The relationship between patient and therapist is the topical foundation of these artistic encounters. Psychoanalytic theories describe the therapeutic relationship as a complex transference-countertransference structure that is filled with experiences, emotions, and fantasies from past and inner worlds. While in early psychoanalytic practice this was considered an obstacle to be overcome, transference is now considered the central feature of the therapeutic relationship, which gives it its specificity and its particular functionality. In the transference, the entire world of the patient becomes tangible for the therapist if she succeeds in cultivating a receptive stance through her own countertransference.

In search of the origin of symptoms and in the attempt to get to the bottom of their patients' life stories, the fictional therapists in literature, theater, and television encounter this transference in a plethora of wishes directed at the analyst, be they for power, love, care, or attention, protection or trust, salvation, or knowledge. But analysts are, in turn, embroiled in strong countertransference reactions and often fight against losing their neutrality by falling in love with or in awe of their patients. In *Equus* and *Life & Times of Michael K*, the distress of the therapists, their desire for knowledge and salvation, is actually what sustains the relationship. The cold and distant stance demanded by orthodox psychoanalysis is called into question without, however, discarding it completely. If the partners fail to negotiate between their adversarial wishes and to harness their passions, the relationship breaks down eventually. Out of the tensions between neutrality and involvement, the texts draw productive stories of resistance and transformation. The patients protect themselves against the illumination of their inner life, which might make them vulnerable, just as the therapists are afraid that an intimate relationship with their patient might disturb their risk-free equanimity. The promise of change can be a threat and the asymmetry of therapy an imposition that few analysands are ready to accept, and they seek interaction to overturn conventional therapeutic hierarchies. Portnoy strives to become his own psychoanalyst; unwittingly, Michael K triggers a transformation of the interpersonal and ethical consciousness of the Medical Officer; Grace "infects" Dr. Jordan with her alleged madness because his eroto-scientific desire cuts across her need for self-protection; and Alan plays a therapeutic game that rattles Martin Dysart's routinized defenses. With utmost consistency, *In Treatment* implements the reversal of the treatment hierarchy by concretizing the recurrent theme of therapists in need of therapy. Dr. Paul Weston tries to escape the artificial limitations of his role as a therapist—and he is in treatment himself. Thus, with their depictions of reciprocal transference-countertransference reactions and mutual treatment, all texts push toward interactional models of the therapeutic relationship.

In other words, the protagonists establish a bi-personal field that serves as a matrix for narration. Inasmuch as their asymmetric interaction is a third entity created by both, the texts acknowledge that everything that happens between patient and therapist, including the narrative dynamic produced by their encounter—which often equals the texts' own narrative dynamic—depends on their orientation in the conflict between resistance and relatedness. With the help of this close link between relational and narrative action, the therapeutic dyad provides a framework in which the texts can treat other topics. The depiction of a therapeutic relationship creates a "transferential" space that may be filled with the protagonists' narratives and enactments. In this way, the texts adopt the characteristic relational amalgam of therapeutic present and private past, as a foundation not just to reflect the relational matrix of the characters but also to look beyond the specific dyadic context. The superficially actionless conversation between therapist and patient absorbs other contents—relational matrices, historical and psychiatric developments, political contexts, and social debates—and provides a supporting narrative grid for them.

The psychoanalytic monologue in *Portnoy's Complaint* works so effortlessly because it ties in parodistically with the success of psychoanalysis in the United States of the 1950s and 1960s. It gives Portnoy a basis to speak about his Jewish and sexual identity and their integration into his everyday life and language. The anti-psychiatric movement that gains momentum in the 1970s is reflected in *Equus*. A critique of psychiatry, religion, and society is executed in the therapeutic relationship while Dysart fights his private battle with personal and professional frustrations. The forced therapy in *Life & Times of Michael K* can hardly be read without considering the racist colonial forces of the South African apartheid state of the 1980s, as the therapeutic relationship induces the Medical Officer to inspect his entanglement in an oppressive regime. In *Alias Grace*, we encounter a similar relationship under duress, which allows Atwood to consider gender as a factor in the attainment of social and narrative power and in the control over self-constructions. In the mid-1990s, the novel may hark back to preanalytic times in nineteenth-century Canada, but the engagement with the diagnosis "multiple personality disorder," much in vogue at the end of the twentieth century, also enables it to tie in with contemporary debates about identity politics and psychiatric fictions. At this point, other treatment methods besides the talking cure have long taken over the therapeutic market, and psychoanalysis is considered obsolete by many professionals and by the public. However, with the hit show *The Sopranos* and subsequent therapeutic series like *In Treatment*, it gains new visibility and popularity in benevolent but not uncritical portrayals of psychoanalytic practice. The minimalist *In Treatment* retreats to the intimate realm of the therapist's office; by staging debates about technical difficulties like countertransference it creates a space for the negotiation of personal conflicts and psychoanalytic theory. Thus, the therapeutic relationship turns out to be a flexible narrative platform to break through taboos, criticize political and psychiatric systems, and comment on social and psychoanalytic discourses.

But to view the therapeutic relationship simply as a frame for thematic considerations of current relevance falls short of capturing its full functionality. As I have shown in my readings, the protagonists' narratives are intimately connected with the relationships that frame them; and the topics they touch upon—their critiques of emotional entanglements, identity constructions, or social institutions—are always developed in a contentious dialogue, through the confrontation of the two independent perspectives of doctor and patient. It is the relationship as a third space that dialogizes ethical issues and complicates political debates such as gendered and racial Otherness. The texts also intervene at a theoretical level, transforming two-dimensional oppressor-victim narratives into complex, three-dimensional relational conflicts that rule out curative prospects, silence, and nonintervention as an escape from the commitment to and the responsibility for an Other. From *Portnoy's Complaint* to *In Treatment*, the therapeutic relationship has thus proven to be an essential linchpin of the narrative action and the evaluation of the texts' key themes. It is both battlefield and playground for interpersonal conflicts, a yearned-for place of connection on which the protagonists project their hopes, and a platform for social and artistic debates. With its help, it is possible to work through highly diverse, forbidden, or difficult topics without limiting them to a single perspective—not least because of the fundamental rule's requirement of absolute openness and the dialogic structure of therapy. The mediating function of the therapeutic dyad is thus supported by formal features that the novels, plays, and television series derive from the psychoanalytic aesthetic. The thematic function of the therapeutic relationship is thoroughly interlocked with its formal execution.

* * *

With the fundamental rule, evenly suspended attention, and the hermeneutic techniques developed by Freud and his disciples, psychoanalysis sets itself up as a narrative practice providing specific guidelines for storytelling, listening, and interpreting. For many psychoanalysts, however, this does not describe the aesthetic experience of their work precisely enough. My analysis of their self-descriptive strategies has shown that psychoanalytic discourse resorts to a comparison with the arts to construct an aesthetics of psychoanalysis: viewed from this perspective, transference creates ambiguous, "mixed" characters and spatiotemporal experiences; its representational forms oscillate between the story and the stage; and language gains poetical significance. Asymmetrical dialogues allow patient and therapist to be alone in the presence of another and be in touch with inner voices. Structurally, psychoanalysis fluctuates between the tendency to work its way backward into hidden depths—an analytic strategy that has since Freud been associated with the myth of Oedipus—and a tendency to work serially on the present relationship and commit to the myth of Scheherazade. Confronting texts from literature, theater, and television with this psychoanalytic involvement in aesthetics elucidates both the psychoanalytic discourse and the texts that draw on it. They use the formal elements of the setting to find patterns for an artistic confrontation with the therapeutic relationship, contradicting the postulated unrepresentability of psychoanalytic experience. Their goal in taking up and experimenting with these formal rules, however, is not the faithful representation of psychoanalysis but a reflection on and a transformation of their own expressive potential.

In literature, theater, and television, the asymmetry of the psychoanalytic setting and the fantasy character of the psychoanalytic personnel is clearly seen as an inspiration to experiment with narrative perspective and reliability. The narrator in psychoanalysis is often the only complex character while secondary characters are mere fantasy constructions of that central consciousness. With strategic changes in perspective, *Life & Times of Michael K* and *Alias Grace* demonstrate that even the partners in the relationship often remain a fantasy character and a surface for the projections of the other. In this way, however, the depicted therapies are turned from analyses of a single character to an examination of inner realities and bi-personally constructed relational matrices. They emphasize the multiple ways in which characters may be assembled and employed, unmasking the unreliability of all personal narration and the fictionalizations of self and other.

The therapeutic setting also impinges on the formal construction of time and space. The relationship is established in a therapist's office or a therapeutic institution; narrated time is structured by sessions and narrative time emulates the therapeutic passage of time, turning readers and viewers into witnesses of the immediate process of narration. *In Treatment*'s minimalism takes the limitations of the psychoanalytic setting most seriously, uncompromisingly reducing its space to Paul's office and translating the therapeutic session structure into serial episodes. However, to some extent, all of my examples tend to reduce space and structure time in that way, and, crucially, embed further narratives within that framework. These embedded narratives create a sense of spatiotemporal ambiguity, so that entire life stories are projected into the boundaries of therapy. By employing direct appellations and apostrophes, play-within-play, and variants of the therapeutic dialogue, all texts find a form to keep both levels of psychoanalytic experience discernable at all times. As we move into the past, the present relationship does not get lost, just as the room, the couch, or the chair are never left behind. Thus, a perspective beyond the therapeutic situation is opened up. Wherever the patients' or the therapists' narratives may go, they find their anchor and formal determination in the spatiotemporal, relational context of their narration.

An inevitable, yet apparently dubious aspect of the psychoanalytic frame is the necessity for interpretation. A veritable excess of interpretation looms in *Portnoy's Complaint* and determines a major part of the protagonist's text. In the other examples, interpretations are also ubiquitous and fulfill a structural function. The entire second part of *Life & Times of Michael K* is "superfluous" interpretation; *Alias Grace*, with its associative structure, challenges readers to build their own constructions; Dysart's monologues in *Equus* create a reflective space where his therapeutic material can be explored with the audience; and *In Treatment*'s supervision sessions also serve the purpose of providing additional interpretation and elucidation. These interpretations help verbalize internal experience that could not otherwise be represented in theater or television. But what is more, interpretation is revealed again and again as overinterpretation and interpretive doubling, which, surprisingly, is seen not as superfluous but as creating interpretive diversity or enabling an interpretation *of* interpretation. These constructions thus exploit the self-referentiality of psychoanalysis and work toward an evaluation of its inherent interpretive attitude.

This extends to the simultaneous recourse to mimetic and diegetic representational forms, which find their foundation in the psychoanalytic tension between storytelling and reenactment. The ludic, even comic, potential of psychoanalysis that is exemplified in the comparison with theater is taken up by Roth, who uses the rules of psychoanalysis to liberate his language in a comedic performance. Most texts, however, focus on a conflict between telling and showing. Coetzee's and Atwood's therapists are so eager for an elaborate, straightforward narrative that they do not recognize they are in the process of enacting what they seek to know. The texts of their relationships provide a counterpoint to the narratives they demand from their patients. In Shaffer's play, the stage metaphor of psychoanalysis is taken literally when Dysart turns the enactment of Alan's past into the main technique of his work even as he envelops the treatment in his own narrative. Freud's directive to privilege the story over the enactment, however, is reversed, and the stage triumphs over the story, enabling insight through playful representation. The theatrical production of the play takes this connection into account by using stagecraft to create a therapeutic observational space and make this stage within the stage visible to the audience. In television, the therapeutic relationship also figures as a narrative stage, but while most television series about therapy use flashbacks to help illustrate the narrative, *In Treatment* concentrates on the narration itself. All enactments remain limited to the therapeutic situation, which is just what orthodox psychoanalytic technique demands. Thus, the theatrical metaphor once again emphasizes the virtuality of therapy, which allows for the reenactment of the past through playful narration and narrative play. The dimensions of this narrative play space seem suspended from reality and artificially constructed; and yet, they do not produce pure fiction but a complex mixture of interior and exterior experience. This creates an appealing blend of fictionality in which fantasy content fuses with emotional reality, allowing both to unfold their full effects. This virtual, multidimensional relationality of the transference ultimately serves to reflect on artistic experience in general—inasmuch as art is conceived as a medium for virtual relationships.

The multitude of nonverbal communicative modes represented in *In Treatment* shows how much narrative and enactment intersect. But the verbal formats of psychoanalysis also hold inspirational potential for the fictional texts. The strongly regulated but radically open oral narration of psychoanalysis facilitates the breaking of taboos and the dialogic transformation of the written monologue in *Portnoy's Complaint*. Since K refuses to produce the desired narrative, the Medical Officer falls back on written case notes and reverie, thus determining the form of the second part of *Life & Times of Michael K*. Psychoanalytic associative experiments, drama therapy, and the case study inspire the composition of *Alias Grace* and *Equus*. In addition, Portnoy's hysterical excesses, K's silence, and Grace's memory gaps are infused with the verbal styles associated with specific mental conditions. But in none of these cases does this serve only to characterize a "sick" character. The critical practice of diagnosing a character is called into question in all of these examples, and instead, the diagnosis given by the text itself is exploited in its formal composition—a formal experiment with these verbal styles changes the communicative structure of the text as well as the possible relationships between text and reader.

Psychoanalysis is not based solely on rules for speech and actual dialogue, which is quite apparent in *Alias Grace*, *Equus*, and *In Treatment*. It also establishes a particular dialogic relation between therapist and patient, in which interpersonal *and* internal conversations are made possible by the paradoxical absent presence of another. Thus, Spielvogel as well as K, despite their limited linguistic presence, are constantly apostrophized in their respective therapeutic relationships, asymmetrically and asymptotically woven into the novels. Relatedness, which also occurs in seemingly monological passages in Shaffer and Atwood, does not necessarily need the equal presence of an interlocutor in the text; it can be reconstructed linguistically and imaginatively by characters and readers.

The structure and content of these conversations is often inspired by psychoanalytic tropes as well. None of the texts manages without at least attempting to reach for the past or solve a riddle in tentative detective plot structures. Regular analytic narratives or dramas, however, do not materialize. The multiperspectivity of *Alias Grace* or the fragmentariness of *Life & Times of Michael K* problematize the feasibility of straightforward analysis on a formal level, while also pointing to contradictions within the psychoanalytic narrative itself. For the therapeutic narrative setup, be it fictional or real, the orientation to the present relationship and the interrelatedness of perspectives seems equally as important as turning to the past, exposing the unassailability of riddles—mysteries and gaps that cannot be filled or resolved but point to the endlessness of analytic work. Analysis is thus necessarily serial, and not just where this formal structure is established by a television series and imitated up to the scheduling of sessions and the termination. Serial narration also features in *Alias Grace* and repetitions haunt the structure of *Portnoy's Complaint*. The sense that therapy needs "to be continued" determines the texts, as any kind of resolution is either debunked or deferred to the future. Dysart's investigation stops with doubts about the possibility of succeeding with therapy, and Paul's with his ambivalent statements about the closing of his and Adele's doors. Grace's letter is never answered, and neither is the last question of the Medical Officer or Spielvogel's suggestion "perhaps to begin" at the end of *Portnoy's Complaint*. The mythical figures linked with analysis and seriality, Oedipus and Scheherazade, are called up, problematized, and balanced against each other. They point to a tension between resolution and deferral, narrative profit and narrative pleasure in all storytelling.

The texts thus adhere closely to the formal constraints suggested by psychoanalysis. They are therapy plays, therapy novels, and therapy series not just because they address therapy but because they use it to distill artistic material and transform it as a means of experimenting with unusual modes of expression. Thus, they test and expand the limitations of their own media while simultaneously shedding new light on the therapeutic relationship, its formal and medial properties, and the tendency in psychoanalytic discourse to compare psychoanalysis with the arts. On the one hand, the intersections between psychoanalytic aesthetics and the seemingly unlimited possibilities for textual composition and metafictional reflection support the notion that psychoanalytic and artistic experience are somehow alike. On the other hand, the psychoanalytic aesthetic demonstrates its autonomy in novels, plays, and television series, for the forms that are created depend on their respective media as much as the engagement with psychoanalytic experience pushes them to overcome these formal constraints. So, in other words, the productive relationship between psychoanalysis and the arts, which drives them to refer to each other in comparisons, analogies, and formal exploitation, is fueled as much by their differences as by their likeness.

* * *

In contrast to much of the previous research, which has limited its focus to the thematic representation of the therapeutic relationship, this study has shown that psychoanalysis, literature, theater, and television create a canvas out of the thematic and formal features of the therapeutic relationship to reflect on themselves with analogies that negotiate between psychoanalytic and aesthetic theory. In psychoanalytic discourse, these analogies emerged as common figures of reflection for hypotheses about creativity and authorship, reader-response theory, and hermeneutic and therapeutic considerations. Based on the assumption that authors and actors, texts, characters, readers, spectators, and critics build transference relationships with each other, authors have often been compared to patients and therapists, readers and critics to analysts, or texts to analysands. The contradictory multiplicity of analogies does not necessarily invalidate these attempts at comparison but highlights the shared problem areas that are relevant for psychoanalysis, literature, and media studies, and thus reappear in fictionalized accounts of therapy. The novels, plays, and television series, however, establish an additional level of reflection on aesthetic relationships by creating particular conditions for reading and viewing. They find manners of employing the analogy that interrogate the tenets held up in theory. Whereas psychoanalytic and critical discourse seeks to employ the analogy as a model for self-understanding, I am concerned with the ways in which the formal, aesthetic, analogical, and self-reflexive dialogues of psychoanalysis and art prepare and question each other.

Frequently, the relational analogy between therapy and art is used to explore the connections among illness, health, therapy, and creativity. In psychopathographic studies, in the Medical Humanities, and in psychoanalytic theories of creativity, the artist often appears as a neurotic who draws her strength from her deficiencies and treats herself with her stories. *Equus*, however, is the only text discussed here in which the idea of a mad or sick artist is earnestly considered at all, and even Shaffer eventually discards the idea—Alan is too disturbed to be an actual artist. However, the promise of healing through narrative that is linked to Oedipus and Scheherazade is also interrogated. If patients like Grace Marks profit from therapeutic dialogues, the reason is not a cathartic effect or the construction of a "better" narrative, but the secondary gains of narration. Through stories, they establish a relationship, in which narration provides pleasure or relief, without the resolution of the conflict being in sight or even desirable. However, the contrary idea that the analyst might become the prototype of the author, as other versions of the analogy suggest, is also called into question in *Life & Times of Michael K* and *Alias Grace*. The attempt to tell the story *for* someone else leads to impotence rather than narrative empowerment. If anything, it is the therapeutic relationship that emerges most clearly as a foundation for artistic production. Its therapeutic and research practice—in tandem with the use of its aesthetic forms—is appreciated as a creative process, for example when Roth harnesses the fundamental rule for literary use. Therapy here does not appear as the goal of art but as a creative process in its own right, as an incentive for creative production and a source of formal inspiration.

The relational analogy has also been used to ask how actively the author is integrated into narrative processes and relationships. Since the texts are primarily concerned with oral narrative relationships, the characters that may be read as author figures always seem involved in interactive relationships, and their overall functionality as "authors" is consistently challenged. The patient in Coetzee's novel can hardly speak at all; with Atwood's protagonist Grace, authorship appears as a stance of high formal control, but also as split, shady, and thus located in the associative field of play-acting, crime, and madness. In the examples discussed here, the author as narrator is not dead but very much present and alive; she inscribes herself into narrative and relational texts, but she is also questioned in her function as the sole creator of the text. She is not ill or dead but doubled. Narration evolves in the therapeutic process as a co-construction—a perspective that inspires new possibilities in the tentative analogy between therapy and artistic production. If authorship is understood as a relational and not as a narcissistic process, however, different concerns arise, such as narrative responsibility, authorial control, and the mutual negotiation involved in authoring and reading artistic products.

In the fictional examples, the role of the present yet absent co-constructor is usually assigned to the reader. But most characters who could symbolize readers or viewers in novels, plays, and television series appear far from reliable; they cannot muster the evenly suspended attention psychoanalysis demands from the analyst. Without neutrality, the analysts and therapists may be flawed, but they emerge even more clearly as figures of a relational analogy used to investigate the process of reading. Their countertransference, their longing for relationships, and their love for their patients, their curiosity, their attachment, and their desire for a meaningful connection are the focus of these texts. In all therapeutic constellations discussed here, the relationship emerges as a premise for the establishment of narration and attention. Thus, the ideas promoted by the texts do not differ much from recent understandings of psychoanalytic technique, which call for involved and engaged therapists who do not exclude their passions from the treatment. The texts argue that the reader cannot avoid a similarly involved, passionate stance, and some might even suggest that such a stance is preferable to the alternative. Thus, this side of the analogy ties in with the Scheherazade model. The attachment of the reader is established through her desire, that is, an act of seduction, which, as *Alias Grace* shows, may be almost exclusively accomplished by narrative means. Unfortunately, this claim does not actually sketch out the ideal conditions of reading. Even though reading relations seem to work better if their relational component is acknowledged, the possibilities of mutual understanding remain limited and the reader is always portrayed as in danger of losing control, like Dr. Jordan or the Medical Officer. Nevertheless, the conclusion drawn by the fictional texts resonates with psychoanalytic theory. Subjectivity and paradoxality, which introduce uncontrollability into the process of relating and understanding, cannot, for their own good, be eliminated from art or psychoanalysis.

The fact that the "texts" of all these potential readers are alive, stand in front of them as embodied interlocutors, allows the novels, plays, and series to tackle fundamental problems of reading and interpretation that could not be discussed with a "mute" text. Just as psychoanalysis profits from the text metaphor to understand aspects of its own experience, so literature, theater, and television embrace the metaphor of conversation for their own explorations of narrative possibilities. The existence of a dissenting and actively resisting counterpart intensifies the consequences of the analyst-reader's desire. Engagement and subjectivity remain a problem for all endeavors seeking insight, especially if the object of epistemic desire eludes the investigator. The question of the possibility of insight worries all disciplines embroiled in the relational analogy—psychoanalysis, art, philology, and hermeneutics. In my examples, the therapeutic relationship is used as a theoretical laboratory to experiment with and examine these epistemological doubts. Portnoy, the Medical Officer, Jordan, Dysart, Paul and his clients—psychoanalysts as much as analysands—all of them are greatly invested in understanding what lies behind a person, a story, a deed, or a symptom. Their task lies not just in the excavation of trauma and its exterior sources but in a quest into the interior, which unearths secret fantasies, desires, and guilt. Therefore, like Oedipus, the investigators always learn something about themselves they did not want to know. In contrast to the myth, however, the riddles are only multiplied by such an insight into the self. Silence, lost pieces of the puzzle, and the reticence of the Other ensure that a final resolution fails to materialize, but the categorical need to know and the related emotional entanglements of the analyst/interpreters often intensify the problems. Without these relationships, however, storytelling and listening, author- and readership cannot be imagined either. Insight and desire are *not* diametrically opposed. Insight is adulterated by desire, but this desire (for knowledge) is also its condition.

In light of these problems, the classic interpretive techniques of psychoanalysis, which are geared toward explicating biography and providing a diagnosis, are criticized as models for understanding human beings and art. Due to their lack of neutrality, the protagonists in my examples cannot separate their interpretations from the relationship, their desire for a relationship, or the claims of the Other. Where these entanglements are simply disregarded, as in Portnoy's or Spielvogel's unilateral interpretations or in the fantasies of the Medical Officer, the interpretation has grotesque or repressive features. *Equus* also calls the classical medical interpretive techniques, such as "surgical" analysis and concept-based interpretation, into question. However, as soon as the interpretation involves interactive co-construction, it appears extraordinarily powerful. *In Treatment*, in particular, discusses reading and interpretation as practices that demand engagement but are threatened by unilateral intervention. Not unlike modern psychoanalytic theory, its fictional renditions argue for an interpretive technique that focuses on the fabric of the relationship and not so much on external material. Thus, the texts all criticize hierarchical structures in reading and interpretation and prefer dialogical relationships, even if they come with their own epistemological and relational pitfalls.

The consequence is a different form of responsibility, which is addressed by many texts. The destructive potential of an interpretation may affect the patient in *Equus*, and like *Life & Times of Michael K*, the play inquires whether interpretation can be an ethical and curative act at all if there is always the danger of imposing meaning on the Other, destroying his "voice," or getting lost on one's own wrong-headed interpretive tracks. Renouncing judgment or intervention, however, can also create a moral dilemma. Psychoanalysis thus appears as a space for the negotiation of ethical difficulties without offering moral guidance. *In Treatment* is an example of how the mutual work elevates these concerns to a different level. If the relationship is a production site for meaning and jointly constructed narratives, there is no "authentic" narrative that could be preserved; both narrators have a responsibility for their own contributions to a joint story. The texts recognize that relationships, therapy, and narrative cannot exist unless the participants agree to make themselves vulnerable to each other. They locate possible ethical concerns not in this vulnerability itself—indeed, this vulnerability becomes the precondition for an ethical stance toward each other—but in the desire for intervention and action *beyond* the relationship and mutual storytelling. The artificial, fictional plane of a (psycho)analytic space always poses the danger of creating too much distance, but it is also a safe space, in which interpretation can work as a relational experiment and which enables the fellow player, be it patient or analyst, reader or critic, to try out the proffered interpretations in the protected frame of their shared relationship.

The relational analogy and its self-reflexive aspirations pervade these texts through a proliferation of metalevels, in which thematic and theoretic dimensions become readable in multiple directions beyond the immediate story of a therapeutic encounter. In their analogical operations, however, literature, theater, and television employ different procedures than theoretical texts, which negotiate their conclusions discursively. The novels, plays, and series also do this, through explicit comparisons, discussions staged between characters, and subtle similarities between reading, interpreting, and analyzing shining through between plot and formal construction. Explicitly or implicitly, the characters are aligned with the changing functions of narrators, authors, texts, readers, and critics. Crucially, however, the texts also offer their audience an opportunity to participate in the play with these analogies. They allow readers and spectators to *be* patient, analyst, and supervisor, so that they can experience and examine themselves whether there are any similarities between their position and the role offered by the text. Thus, *Portnoy's Complaint* almost pushes the reader in the analyst's position with its simultaneous appellation and exclusion of Spielvogel. In *Life & Times of Michael K*, an epistemic desire is created in the reader by transferring the experiential gaps of the Medical Officer to the reader. Here, as in *Alias Grace*, readers are tempted to reject the analyst until they are made to realize that they are closer to the problematic doctor figures than they like to think. In *Equus*, Dysart turns the spectators into his supervisors by confessing to failures and tempting them to "know better" than the therapist. *In Treatment*, finally, urges the audience to adopt Paul's schedule and to identify with the therapist who, at the same time, remains the biggest riddle for them to analyze. Thus, conclusions by analogy are implemented performatively, turning the audience, via a form of textual transference, into their own objects of analysis. Psychoanalysis and the arts meet in one shared potential. They not only turn their attention to a topic but also rely on its enactment in a relationship. The immediate interaction between text and reader provides a basis for the reflection and discussion of possible correlations and differences between therapy and art.

In one surprising respect it is difficult to follow the analogy into the fictional examples. The question of art's potential therapeutic effects remains oddly obscure. Indeed, the texts question the promise of healing even when they engage with actual therapeutic practice; they do not depict successful cures, and if they do, these successes are small and unspectacular. Moreover, it becomes evident that the story—if it gets told at all and does not remain inaccessible as in *Life & Times of Michael K*—is far from a reliable therapeutic medium. It is too polyphonic, too fragile, too easily invaded by constructions, too distorted by anxiety and resistance, and finally too powerless to articulate the unspeakable or provide a solid access to truth or healing. The "true" or the "good" story exists as a need, not as a solution.

Parodistic and earnest critique of the premises of psychoanalysis is thus often palpable in the texts—critique of its techniques, its powers, and its ethical suppositions. At the same time, Roth and Shaffer display a considerable fascination with the creative and aesthetic potential of psychoanalysis, while Atwood and Coetzee delineate common fields of interest in the therapeutic structures of desire. Through intertextual and psychoanalytic interpretive procedures, the results and techniques of psychiatry and psychoanalysis are exploited as mechanisms of production, and in *In Treatment*, theoretical discussions such as the treatment of countertransference become central ideas that drive the plot. With the therapeutic relationship and its self-reflexive potential, the texts thus revisit the differences between art and psychoanalysis as well as the conundrums uniting their fields, always looking toward the aesthetic and theoretical stimuli produced in this encounter with the other discipline.

* * *

The novels, plays, and television series I have discussed here use the therapeutic relationship as a device to transform themselves in content and form and reflect these transformations as well as their aesthetic foundations through the establishment of a fictional metalevel. Thus, they engage critically with ideas like co-authorship, relation through narration, passionate reading, and the ethics of interpretation. On both sides of the analogy, however, the challenge and the potential it represents for the two disciplines have not always been recognized. In artistic discourses and literary scholarship, psychoanalysis is still often thought of as a threat and its compulsion to explain is considered to be irreconcilable with the removed world of fiction. In turn, psychoanalysts have mostly seen representations of therapy as a critique, satire, or misrepresentation of their work instead of engaging with the suggestive forces inherent in the texts' concentration on aesthetic concerns. The interconnections, the distortions, the artistic overexpansion of psychoanalytic constraints could serve to explore the aesthetic dimensions of psychoanalysis, which theorists have struggled to describe with comparisons of their own invention.

My study has shown that an interdisciplinary exchange takes place in psychoanalytic texts, aesthetic theory, and artistic works not just via ideas and theorems but also (and particularly) via figures of thought and speech, forms, methods, and procedures. The goal of this exchange is not necessarily the application of insights or methods from one discipline to another. The aesthetic created in psychoanalysis and the specific medium it cultivates in the therapeutic relationship interface with literature, theater, and television and cannot be described with a comparison of their central questions alone. In their exchange, psychoanalysis and the arts have created specific forms of interdisciplinary interaction that produce specific insights into their disciplines and their dependence on each other.

My investigation, which has paid attention to these interrelated thematic, formal, and self-reflexive modes of interaction, would also find considerable material in other media like poetry, comics, or film. Nonfictional genres like case histories and psychoanalytic studies could also be examined with regard to their recourse to the aesthetic foundations of therapy. Beyond that, the procedure could be extended to other scientific disciplines and their specific aesthetics and analogies. Stimulating forms and methods, in which the arts are particularly interested, could be found in disciplines that do not understand themselves primarily as an art; and exploring the dialogues they may nevertheless entertain with the arts might open our eyes for the aesthetics of their disciplinary methods.

So why are the arts so interested in psychoanalysis? Why is psychoanalysis fascinated by the arts? Psychoanalysis undoubtedly gains insight into itself through this comparison. Its relationship with art is fueled by the belief that artists have a unique insight into particular forms of experience (Phillips, "Poetry" 17). But there is more: the analogical relationship with the arts helps the discipline grasp its own aesthetic dimension—a quality that is not opposed but intimately related to its therapeutic function. Psychoanalysis is an effective practice because it induces its participants to enter into the specific aesthetic experience that is psychoanalytic storytelling and interpretation. In turn, the comparison allows artistic texts to use the inherently self-reflective therapeutic relationship, in which all events and all narratives are always referred back to the relational framework between therapist and patient, as a laboratory. Here, they can develop their own models about relational aesthetics and poetics and implement them performatively. Quite often, these interdisciplinary exchanges turn around reciprocal self-legitimation. If psychoanalysis is an art, it has an intrinsic value; if art (and, by implication, scholarship that deals with art) is a process that provides insight and therapy, it surpasses the accusation of being a useless and idle pastime. In the process, both sides emphasize shared methods and raise shared questions. At least a part of the unchecked popularity of psychoanalysis in the arts can be explained by this possibility for self-reflection and legitimation, which may be connected to more obvious explanations, such as the representation of therapeutic cultures, the usefulness of the psychoanalytic session as a plot device, and the easy generation of profound and zany patient and therapist characters. At the same time, it has become apparent that the popularity and the prevalence of therapeutic constellations cannot be explained with thematic advantages and social contexts alone. The attraction of such a figure is also based on aesthetic, theoretical, and strategic features.

How can the relationship be described that is thus established between the arts and psychoanalysis? Is it the dialogue that Shoshana Felman has called for between psychoanalysis and literature ("To Open" 6)? This would not be entirely appropriate, for in this encounter the disciplines seldom meet as equal partners. As I have shown, psychoanalysis and the arts speak through and to, but seldom with, each other. Meanwhile, the dialogue that develops here, unilateral but always turned toward the other, has much to do with the psychoanalytic dialogue. Psychoanalysis and the arts use the other field as an interactional canvas to analyze themselves and each other. This (self)reflexive confrontation is far from being completed. The renaissance of psychoanalysis in countless television series since *The Sopranos* and its continued presence in drama, poetry, and prose indicates that literature, theater, and television have not yet taken everything from the psychoanalytic art of the relationship, its dialogic patterns, and its narrative action that waits to be discovered.

Notes

Chapter 1

1 I will use "psychoanalysis" as a broadly defined term, which may be extended to a range of therapeutic practices informed by psychoanalysis or depth psychology—as long as they adopt the psychoanalytic understanding of the therapeutic relationship and its narrative practices as defined in the following chapter. I follow Roy Schafer in this broad definition of psychoanalytic work (*Retelling* 266).

2 Jacques Lacan is an important exception to this agreement. He excludes the real therapeutic relationship almost completely from his theory and sees the analyst's function primarily in his impersonal structural position: "The analyst for Lacan represented above all what is absent and missing, a position fostered by therapeutic abstinence. The austere technical approach he advocated, however, worked against attention to what most analysts call the analytic relationship and its affective dimension" (Kirshner 343). Since for this very reason Lacan provides no insight into the central questions of this study, the psychoanalytic school influenced by him will not be discussed any further.

3 In line with Freud's writing practice, I will use terms like "doctor," "analyst," and "therapist" as well as "patient" and "analysand" interchangeably. When I employ these terms (and other generic terms like "author" and "reader") without a specific person or character in mind, I will alternate between masculine and feminine pronouns.

4 In this study, I will use "text" as a transmedial term to designate the artistic product, a term that is well established in literary, theater, and television studies (Balme 78; Fiske 14).

5 When I speak of "dialogue," two different levels must be kept in mind: at a higher level, the disciplines of psychoanalysis and art enter an intertextual exchange that is often referred to as a "dialogue." This is not to be understood as a mutual and harmonious interaction; instead, it is characterized by the differences of the two disciplines, which often ignore the other's arguments if they call their own methods into question and use the patterns and insights of the other discipline for their own purposes, often by way of criticism, distortion, or caricature. Within the scope of this relationship, the texts themselves employ the term "dialogue" as a key term and metaphor to describe what is going on between analyst and therapist as well as between different entities in narrative relationships. It is not, perhaps, surprising that the disciplines reflect their own interaction via a concept that also describes the communicative patterns they employ within their own boundaries. Although this will sometimes lead to overlaps between my critical vocabulary and the metaphors the texts

employ themselves, I prefer to stick to the terms—precisely because the intradisciplinary dialogues do not exist independently from each other and are involved in a process of mutual metaphoric enrichment.

6 Hanif Kureishi gained his knowledge about psychoanalysis in three distinct ways: via psychoanalyst friends, reading psychoanalytic literature, and psychoanalytic treatment (Kureishi and Koval).

7 The other writers considered in this book have been similarly open about their relationship to psychoanalysis. Philip Roth writes about his psychoanalytic treatment in his autobiography (*Facts* 137), and Peter Shaffer and Hagai Levi talk about it in interviews (Berman, "*Equus*" 421; Melville, "TV Interview"). Atwood also explains her views on psychoanalysis in an interview (Metzler, "Creativity" 284). And Coetzee, while having "no experience from either side of the clinical dialogue" (Coetzee and Kurtz 12), has been open about the inspirations he has drawn from Freud. This knowledge, however, does not add anything essential to an understanding of texts that talk openly about motivations for and resistances against treatment—texts that find inspiration not just from personal experience but also from the wide dissemination of psychoanalytic theory and therapeutic narratives in the United States, England, and Israel.

8 The dream sequences in Pabst's and Hitchcock's films certainly testify to an aesthetic interest in psychoanalytic theory (Hitchcock had them designed by Salvador Dalí). However, a dream sequence that is not shown as changed by interpretation is a representation of an event that occurs outside of the psychoanalytic frame, and is thus, strictly speaking, not linked to the psychoanalytic process.

9 England and the United States, as well as countries like Canada and South Africa, were refuges for psychoanalysts who were forced to emigrate during the rise of fascism in Central Europe in the 1930s and 1940s (Steiner 589; Book). The most important theoretical developments in psychoanalysis concerning the therapeutic relationship, such as object relations theory and relational treatment models, have their roots in the United Kingdom and in the United States.

10 Rose describes the change in self-care behavior in the context of the "psy"-revolution without judging its quality. Many commentators go further: for example, by blaming therapeutic cultures for the egocentrism in modern societies. Frank Furedi criticizes therapy culture mostly because it unduly emphasizes the vulnerability of the self: "It posits the self in distinctly fragile and feeble form and insists that the management of life requires the continuous intervention of therapeutic expertise" (21).

11 To give just one example, the public performance of the private that has become the mainstay of "therapeutic" talk shows is not intended in psychoanalysis. On the contrary, it provides a particularly protected, dyadic space, whose goal is not the publication of personal secrets but a confrontation with experiences that the patient keeps hidden even from herself—experiences that still cannot be expressed, even in a "therapy culture."

12 Furedi emphasizes that his target is not clinical practice but therapy as a cultural phenomenon (22).
13 Examples are *Annie Hall* (1977) or *Deconstructing Harry* (1997). In *Another Woman* (1988), psychoanalysis has a more comprehensive structural function, but the protagonist is not in therapy. She is inspired to analyze herself by accidentally overhearing another woman's analytic sessions (Scheurer, "Think" 275).
14 It is noteworthy that artistic engagements with the therapeutic relationship are particularly prominent in the Anglophone world—unlike representations of other psychoanalytic tenets, like dreams or psychotic thinking, which can easily be found in a variety of national traditions. One reason for this concentration may be the historical development of psychoanalytic theory, in which relational thinking has been especially prominent in the United Kingdom and the United States. Francophone representations of therapy such as Hélène Cixous's *Portrait de Dora* (1976) react much more strongly to impulses from Lacanian psychoanalysis than Anglo-American developments. In addition, many noteworthy German examples like Robert Menasse's *Don Juan de la Mancha* (Austria, 2007) and Annette Hug's *In Zeleny's Zimmer* (*In Zeleny's Room*; Switzerland, 2010) lag behind similar texts like *Portnoy's Complaint* or *In Treatment* and deal with their subject matter less radically. It is possible to attribute the greater popularity and intensity of the therapeutic narrative in Anglophone cultures to the history of the global distribution of psychoanalysis. Bernhard Handlbauer notes that, as a consequence of the mass emigrations before and during the Second World War, the discipline was virtually transplanted from the German- to the English-speaking world (152).
15 Gladys Schmitt's *Sonnets for an Analyst* (1973), John Updike's short story "My Lover Has Dirty Fingernails" (1980), Alison Bechdel's autobiographic comic *Are You My Mother?* (2012), and the numerous films dedicated to therapeutic action, such as Robert Redford's *Ordinary People* (1980) and Arnaud Desplechin's *Jimmy P.* (2013), show that these elements can also be found in other arts and genres.

Chapter 2

1 Andersen and Berk have shown that transference is an everyday experience in relationships that is supposed to assist in the interpretation of social situations. Demonstrably, transference influences memory, affect, motivation, and expectation as well as judgments and conclusions drawn from specific interactions (112).
2 In contrast to other analysts, Ogden does not use the "third" to talk about a person outside of the therapeutic dyad or a symbolic third component in the relationship. Cultural determinants, like language or professional standards, can influence the interactions in the analytic

dyad (Gerson, "Relational Unconscious" 77). Ogden, however, explicitly distinguishes his analytic third from other such thirds, including Lacan's symbolic third, in which the Law of the Father and language form a third that prevents the dyad from collapsing (Ogden, *Subjects* 64; Benjamin, "Beyond Doer" 11–12).

Chapter 3

1 It is difficult to grasp the specific fictionality of transference. According to a semantic definition, in which fictionality is defined by a missing reference to reality (Schaeffer), transferential phenomena are hybrids because they always retain a reference to reality. A pragmatic definition of fictionality is also problematic. The agent of transference usually has no intention of speaking or acting without an actual referent. Transference, it seems, involves a hybrid, accidental form of fictionality.
2 Spence's definition of "narrative truth" reads as follows: "It depends on continuity and closure and the extent to which the fit of the pieces takes on an aesthetic finality. Narrative truth is what we have in mind when we say that such and such is a good story, that a given explanation carries conviction, that *one* solution to a mystery must be true" (31).
3 Nünning and Sommer define mimetic narrativity as "the representation of a temporal and/or causal sequence of events," hinging "upon the degree of eventfulness," and diegetic narrativity as the "verbal transmission of narrative content" (206).
4 Striking examples include the title of the Relational School's journal *Psychoanalytic Dialogues* or the translation of Stephen Mitchell's *Influence and Autonomy in Psychoanalysis* (1997) under the programmatic German title *Psychoanalyse als Dialog* (2005). The word "dialogue" also appears in titles by Thomas Ogden, Roy Schafer, and Hermann Argelander.
5 Matthias Sträßner disagrees, arguing that the psychoanalytic drama is only a marginal type of the analytic drama because its riddle resides in a person, not a fact, and because diagnostic procedures replace investigative procedures (66, 68). Even this argument, however, highlights some common structures of psychoanalysis and analytic drama.

Chapter 4

1 Ovid describes Pygmalion's passionate relationship with his statue as follows: "Often he lifts his hands to the work to try whether it be flesh or ivory; nor does he yet confess it to be ivory. He kisses it and thinks his kisses are returned. He speaks to it, grasps it and seems to feel his fingers sink into the limbs" (83).

2 Similar analogies can be found in Bal, who compares the analysis of literature with the psychoanalytic process (146), Jones, who criticizes the tendency of doctors to treat the patient as a text (192), or Priel, who wants to reconceptualize the analytic process by comparing it with the interpretation of art ("Psychoanalytic Interpretations" 135).
3 The emphasis on narrative, reflection, insight, and the use of the "changeable" human being as object of analysis, as well as the opposition against suggestion that Brecht inscribes in the epic theater (112–13), resonate with contemporaneous versions of psychoanalytic therapy. The link can also be found in the discussion surrounding Peter Shaffer's *Equus*, whose analytic aesthetic draws, at least in part, on elements of the epic theater.

Chapter 5

1 Even earlier, whimsical allusions to psychoanalysis can be found in Roth's work. In his short story "Eli, the Fanatic" (1959), the protagonist finds a note written by his wife, containing the following information: "I had a sort of Oedipal experience with the baby today" (190).
2 This interpretation is backed up by Spielvogel's continuous presence in Portnoy's rhetoric as well as Spielvogel's "perhaps." This reservation sounds ironic, considering Portnoy's torrent of words, and would seem less plausible if Spielvogel used it to initiate the encounter rather than to segue from a preliminary phase to proper analytic work.
3 Shostak also argues that Jewishness "constitutes the neurosis that brings Portnoy to Dr. Spielvogel's couch. Roth confirms this diagnosis when Alex constructs *Americanness* as health" (87). Hagenmeyer notes that viewing their Jewish identity as an illness was a common defensive mechanism among many American Jews at the time (127).
4 Bettelheim assumes that Portnoy's choice of a Jewish psychoanalyst reveals "that deep down he does not want to transcend his own background" ("Portnoy" 4). As will become apparent later, this also facilitates the fantasy of a symmetrical relationship between Portnoy and Spielvogel.
5 With König, one could read Portnoy's abrogation of the analyst as a maneuver to present himself as knowledgeable and powerful (111), which would confirm Spielvogel's diagnosis of narcissism. However, leaving aside the fact that such a diagnostic reduction would not do justice to the intricate criticism of psychoanalytic interpretation in the novel, Portnoy's needs are more complex: he desires equality with the psychoanalyst, acts out his fascination with psychoanalytic interpretation, and fends against the threat of its hermeneutic power to his individuality.
6 Contemporary psychoanalysts insist that the therapist who rarely intervenes may also trigger strong transferences (König 76). The novel plays with the idea that the silent analyst cannot be erased from the analytic

narrative—if only because he produces the constant need to make sense of his silence.

7 Spacks ascribes Portnoy's limited point of view to his resistance against intimacy (634). Tanner interprets Portnoy's comical exaggerations as an attempt to free himself from debilitating emotional baggage (67).

8 "Shame isn't for writers," Roth explains (Karel), underlining the importance of full disclosure in his poetics.

9 Note, for instance, Portnoy's incidental negation of Freud's concept of family romance: "I don't remember that I was one of those kids who went around wishing he lived in another house with other people" (94–95).

10 While the length of the novel is counted among the biggest weaknesses of the text by critics like Irving Howe, who believes that "brief as it is, the book seems half again too long, since there can be very little surprise or development in the second half, only a recapitulation of motifs already torn to shreds in the first" (240), the perceived excessive length and the repetitions are actually what makes *Portnoy's Complaint* adhere to a psychoanalytic aesthetics, as they convey the long and grueling effects of working through the same material over and over again.

11 Claudia Roth Pierpont reports: "People continually accosted [Roth] in the street, apparently convinced that they knew him intimately" (65).

12 Here, Winnicott's notion that play is "inherently exciting and precarious" seems most pertinent to Roth's aesthetics (*Playing* 70). The allure and the transformative potential of fantasy are greater when it interacts with reality. Accordingly, in *Deception*, Philip tells his wife: "What heats things up is compromising me" (177).

13 Roth recounts a "masked" version of this story in *Zuckerman Unbound* (1981). Zuckerman, who undergoes similar experiences with his scandalous novel *Carnovsky* as Roth did with *Portnoy's Complaint*, is clearly another product of artistic transference.

Chapter 6

1 Drawing on Levinas and Blanchot, Mike Marais, for instance, concludes "that the other can never be accommodated or known" (*Secretary* xii). Postcolonial theory has been concerned with the inaccessibility of the perspective of the Other since Spivak's essay "Can the Subaltern Speak?" Ashcroft, Griffiths, and Tiffin contrast Spivak's doubts "whether or not the possibility exists for any recovery of a subaltern voice that is not a kind of essentialist fiction" with Parry's critique, which posits that the emphasis on the absence of this voice obfuscates its "profoundly disruptive presence" (Ashcroft et al. 10–11).

2 The allusion to Samuel T. Coleridge's "The Rime of the Ancient Mariner" points to the Medical Officer's growing feelings of guilt since the Mariner's

burden is a consequence of shooting the albatross: "Instead of the cross, the Albatross / About my neck was hung" (6).

3   The fantasy that K rescued his mother from the burning city is reminiscent of the rescue of Anchises from Troy on his son Aeneas's shoulders (Franssen 455).

Chapter 7

1   In Atwood's earlier, contrasting short story "The Sin Eater" (1977), therapist Joseph understands how to attach his patients with passion: "Some of them were *devoted* to him. If he'd told them to shoot the Pope or something, they'd have done it just like that" (219).
2   Atwood rewrites an authentic case: the murder of Thomas Kinnear and his housekeeper Nancy Montgomery on July 23, 1843. Their servant James McDermott and housemaid Grace Marks were convicted for this murder after they had been arrested during their attempted flight to the United States (*Alias* 537).
3   In the nineteenth century, handicrafts were often used for medical and social rehabilitation (Rogerson, "Reading" 6).
4   Freud uses a textile metaphor in his speech for the Goethe prize, where he describes the complex relationship between an artist's drives, his experiences, and his works as a "weaver's masterpiece" ("Goethe Prize" 212). However, it never appears as a systematic metaphor for the therapeutic process.
5   "Flectere si nequeo superos, Acheronta movebo" (Freud, "Interpretation" ix). Transl.: "If I cannot bend the will of the Gods above, I will move the underworld."
6   Niederhoff believes that Grace is not play-acting because it would not be "in her interest" ("Return" 76). However, by attempting to pin down the event to one version, he commits the same mistake as Jordan of reducing an ambiguous situation to a single interpretation.

Chapter 8

1   Shaffer's own experience with psychotherapy was not entirely positive: "I've always wondered . . . how much good psychiatry and all the rest of it was doing those of my acquaintances who were in treatment. . . . I began to wonder some time ago whether it might not be a false religion with a lot of worshipers." Accordingly, he aborted his own treatment: "I can't say I enjoyed the experience. . . I didn't expect to find it fun, but it didn't seem to be. . . well. . . very nourishing. I decided to soldier through on my own" (qtd. in Berman, *Equus* 421, last three ellipses in original).

2   For C. G. Jung, the horse is an archetype of the instinctual world, representing the nonhuman, animal psyche ("Praktische Verwendbarkeit" 169–70).
3   In terms of stage design, Dexter was an important co-author of *Equus*. According to Klein, he is responsible for the flashbacks, the stylization of the set, the use of light, and the nude scenes ("Peter Shaffer's *Equus*" 179–80).
4   Plunka deals extensively with the ritual elements in Shaffer's theater (168). For a discussion of Shaffer's indebtedness to Aristotle and Artaud, see Klein, "Peter Shaffer's *Equus*" 175; MacMurraugh-Kavanagh 27; Baldwin 122.

Chapter 9

1   Other examples and the reasons for this popularity are discussed in Scheurer, "Erzähler."
2   Hagai Levi explains that every version was adapted to the specific cultural context and to the local psychotherapeutic ethos. In Russia, for example, the producers decided to turn the male psychoanalyst into a female consultant with personal bonds to her clients. According to Levi, in Russia, the therapeutic profession is perceived as effeminate and no one would, as a rule, speak with a stranger about private problems (Bronfen and Levi).
3   In the second season, we meet Mia, a successful lawyer longing for a family, April, an architecture student with cancer, CEO Walter, who suffers from insomnia, and Oliver, who struggles to come to terms with his parents' divorce. In the third season, Paul treats the Indian mathematician Sunil, who feels out of place in the United States, the reeling actress Frances, and the rebellious adolescent Jesse, who suffers from tensions with his adoptive parents.
4   Jody Messler Davies's article "Love in the Afternoon," which was used by the writers of *In Treatment* (Lang 208), deals with the sexual fantasies of a female therapist about her male patient (Messler Davies 153), contradicting Gina's intervention here and hinting at a countertransferential component of her own resistance against relational approaches to transference.
5   Paul alludes to "existential" psychologist Irvin Yalom, who has emphasized the importance of the therapeutic relationship in many books, including his collection of case studies *Love's Executioner* (13).
6   The trend, as Netflix, Amazon Prime Instant Video, and other Watch on Demand options show, is actually toward greater independence and sovereignty of the viewer. It is thus reasonable to assume that HBO's experiment failed because the modes of viewing television series had just begun to change (Bem 29).
7   In a few episodes, this can be explained by patients arriving late or leaving early, by entering in the middle of a session or by the title credits replacing a larger chunk of the session. In most sessions, however, no such explanation can be construed.

Works Cited

Therapy in Literature and Theater

Appignanesi, Richard, and Sława Harasymowicz. *The Wolf Man: Graphic Freud*. SelfMadeHero, 2012.
Appignanesi, Richard, and Oscar Zarate. *Hysteria: Graphic Freud*. SelfMadeHero, 2015.
Atwood, Margaret. *Alias Grace*. 1996. Virago, 1997.
Atwood, Margaret. *The Robber Bride*. 1993. Virago, 1994.
Atwood, Margaret. "The Sin Eater." 1977. *Dancing Girls*, Vintage, 1996, pp. 213–24.
Bechdel, Alison. *Are You My Mother? A Comic Drama*. Jonathan Cape, 2012.
Cixous, Hélène. *Portrait de Dora*. Editions des femmes, 1976.
Coetzee, J. M. *Life & Times of Michael K*. 1983. Vintage, 2004.
Doctorow, E. L. *Andrew's Brain*. Abacus, 2014.
Ebersohn, Wessel. *Divide the Night*. 1981. Gollancz Crime, 1990.
Gur, Batya. *The Saturday Morning Murder: A Psychoanalytic Case*. 1988. Translated by Dalya Bilu, HarperPerennial, 1993.
Hug, Annette. *In Zelenys Zimmer*. Rotpunktverlag, 2010.
Hustvedt, Siri. *The Sorrows of an American*. 2008. Picador, 2009.
Kempinski, Tom. *Duet for One*. 1980. Samuel French, 1981.
Kock, Leon de. *Bad Sex*. Umuzi, 2011.
Kureishi, Hanif. *Something to Tell You*. 2008. Faber and Faber, 2009.
Mann, Thomas. Der Zauberberg. 1924. Fischer, 2008.
McPherson, Conor. *Shining City*. Nick Hern, 2004.
Menasse, Robert. *Don Juan de la Mancha oder Die Erziehung der Lust*. 2007. Suhrkamp, 2009.
Munro, Alice. "Dimensions." *Too Much Happiness*, Vintage, 2009, pp. 3–33.
Nkosi, Lewis. *Mating Birds*. East African Publishing House, 1983.
Pielmeier, John. *Agnes of God*. 1979. Samuel French, 1982.
Roth, Philip. *American Pastoral*. 1997. Vintage, 1998.
Roth, Philip. *The Anatomy Lesson*. 1983. Vintage, 2005.
Roth, Philip. *The Breast*. 1972. Vintage, 1994.
Roth, Philip. *Deception*. 1990. Vintage, 2006.
Roth, Philip. "Eli, the Fanatic." 1959. *Goodbye Columbus*, Vintage, 2006, pp. 185–221.
Roth, Philip. *The Facts: A Novelist's Autobiography*. 1988. Vintage, 1997.
Roth, Philip. *Goodbye Columbus*. 1959. Vintage, 2006.
Roth, Philip. *The Human Stain*. 2000. Vintage, 2005.
Roth, Philip. *Letting Go*. 1962. Vintage, 2007.
Roth, Philip. *My Life as a Man*. 1974. Vintage, 1993.
Roth, Philip. *Operation Shylock*. 1993. Vintage, 1994.

Roth, Philip. *Patrimony: A True Story*. 1991. Vintage, 1999.
Roth, Philip. *Portnoy's Complaint*. 1969. Vintage, 1994.
Roth, Philip. "The Psychoanalytic Special." 1963. *Penguin Modern Stories 3*, edited by Judith Burnley, Penguin, 1969, pp. 7–30.
Roth, Philip. *Reading Myself and Others*. 1975. Vintage, 2001.
Roth, Philip. *Sabbath's Theater*. 1995. Vintage, 1996.
Roth, Philip. *Zuckerman Unbound*. 1981. Vintage, 2005.
Rubenfeld, Jed. *The Interpretation of Murder*. Headline Review, 2006.
Saadawi, Nawal El. *Woman at Point Zero*. 1975. Zed Books, 1998.
Schmitt, Gladys. *Sonnets for an Analyst*. 1973. Carnegie Mellon UP, 2004.
Shaffer, Peter. *Equus*. 1973. Longman, 1993.
Sinclair, Jo. *Wasteland*. Harper & Brothers, 1946.
St. Germain, Mark. *Freud's Last Session*. 2009. Dramatists Play Service, 2010.
Svevo, Italo. *Zenos Gewissen. La coscienza di Zeno: Zweisprachige Ausgabe*. 1923. Zweitausendeins, 2007.
Swift, Graham. *Out of This World*. Penguin, 1988.
Updike, John. "My Lover Has Dirty Fingernails." 1966. *The Music School: Short Stories*, Vintage, 1980, pp. 164–74.
Wright, Nicholas. *Mrs Klein*. 1988. Nick Hern, 2009.

Therapy in Film and Television

Allen, Woody, director. *Annie Hall*. United Artists, 1977.
Allen, Woody, director. *Another Woman*. Orion Pictures, 1988.
Allen, Woody, director. *Deconstructing Harry*. Fine Line Pictures, 1997.
Ball, Alan, creator. *Six Feet Under*. HBO, 2001–05.
Chase, David, creator. *The Sopranos*. HBO, 1999–2007.
Desplechin, Arnaud, director. *Jimmy P. (Psychotherapy of a Plains Indian)*. IFC Films, 2013.
Fröhlich, Pea, and Peter Märthesheimer, creators. *Bloch*. SWR/WDR, 2002–13.
Gatiss, Mark, and Steven Moffat, creators. *Sherlock*. BBC, 2010–.
Hitchcock, Alfred, director. *Spellbound*. United Artists, 1945.
Kruger, Liz, and Craig Shapiro, creators. *Necessary Roughness*. USA, 2011–13.
Kudrow, Lisa, creator. *Web Therapy*. LStudio.com/Showtime, 2008–15.
Levi, Hagai, creator. *Be'Tipul*. HOT3, 2005–08.
Levi, Hagai, and Rodrigo García, creators. *In Treatment*. HBO, 2008–10.
Lowry, Bob, creator. *Huff*. Showtime, 2004–06.
Lumet, Sidney, director. *Equus*. Winkast Film, 1977.
Mort, Cynthia, creator. *Tell Me You Love Me*. HBO, 2007.
Nunn, Kem, and Alexandra Cunningham, creators. *Chance*. Hulu, 2016–17.
Pabst, Georg Wilhelm, director. *Geheimnisse einer Seele*. Ufa, 1926.
Payne, Nick, creator. *Wanderlust*. Netflix, 2018.
Polley, Sarah, creator. *Alias Grace*. Netflix, 2017.
Rashid, Robia, creator. *Atypical*. Netflix, 2017–.

Redford, Robert, director. *Ordinary People*. Paramount Pictures, 1980.
Rubin, Lisa, creator. *Gypsy*. Netflix, 2017.
Weiner, Matthew, creator. *Mad Men*. AMC, 2007–15.

Other Works Cited

Alcorn, Marshall W., and Mark Bracher. "Literature, Psychoanalysis, and the Re-Formation of the Self: A New Direction for Reader-Response Theory." *PMLA*, vol. 100, no. 3, 1985, pp. 342–54.

Altmeyer, Martin, and Helmut Thomä. "Einführung: Psychoanalyse und Intersubjektivität." *Die vernetzte Seele: Die intersubjektive Wende in der Psychoanalyse*, edited by Martin Altmeyer and Helmut Thomä, Klett-Cotta, 2006, pp. 7–31.

Andersen, Susan, and Michele Berk. "Transference in Everyday Experience: Implications of Experimental Research for Relevant Clinical Phenomena." *Review of General Psychology*, vol. 2, no. 1, 1988, pp. 81–120.

Anderson, Charles M. "Editor's Column: Writing and Healing." *Literature and Medicine*, vol. 19, no. 1, 2000, pp. ix–xiv.

Angeloch, Dominic. *Die Beziehung zwischen Text und Leser: Grundlagen und Methodik psychoanalytischen Lesens; mit einer Lektüre von Flauberts 'Éducation sentimentale.'* Psychosozial-Verlag, 2014.

Angeloch, Dominic. "Die Beziehung zwischen Text und Leser: Methodik und Problematik gegenübertragungsanalytischen Lesens." *Psyche*, vol. 67, no. 6, June 2013, pp. 526–55.

Anz, Thomas. "Psychoanalyse und literarische Moderne: Beschreibungen eines Kampfes." *Psychoanalyse in der literarischen Moderne. Eine Dokumentation: Band I. Einleitung und Wiener Moderne*, edited by Thomas Anz, LiteraturWissenschaft.de, 2006, pp. 11–60.

Aristotle. *Poetics*. Translated by Stephen Halliwell, Duckworth, 1987.

Arndt, Peer. "Therapie und Theater." *Forum der Psychoanalyse*, vol. 20, no. 4, 2004, pp. 379–90.

Aron, Lewis. *A Meeting of Minds: Mutuality in Psychoanalysis*. Analytic Press, 2001.

Ashcroft, Bill, Gareth Griffiths, and Helen Tiffin. "Issues and Debates: Introduction to Part One." *The Post-Colonial Studies Reader*, edited by Bill Ashcroft, Gareth Griffiths, and Helen Tiffin, Routledge, 2006, pp. 9–13.

Atterton, Peter. "'The Talking Cure': The Ethics of Psychoanalysis." *The Psychoanalytic Review*, vol. 94, no. 4, August 2007, pp. 553–76.

Attridge, Derek. "Against Allegory: *Waiting for the Barbarians*, *Life & Times of Michael K*, and the Question of Literary Reading." *J. M. Coetzee and the Idea of the Public Intellectual*, edited by Jane Poyner, Ohio UP, 2006, pp. 63–82.

Attwell, David. *J. M. Coetzee: South Africa and the Politics of Writing*. U of California P, 1993.

Atwood, Margaret. "An End to Audience?" *Second Words: Selected Critical Prose*, Anansi, 1982, pp. 334–57.

Atwood, Margaret. "In Search of *Alias Grace*: On Writing Canadian Historical Fiction." *The American Historical Review*, vol. 103, no. 5, 1998, pp. 1503–16.

Atwood, Margaret. *Negotiating with the Dead: A Writer on Writing*. Cambridge UP, 2002.

Auerhahn, Nanette C. "Interpretation in the Psychoanalytic Narrative: A Literary Framework for the Analytic Process." *The International Review of Psycho-Analysis*, vol. 6, 1979, pp. 423–36.

Avishai, Bernard. *Promiscuous*: Portnoy's Complaint *and Our Doomed Pursuit of Happiness*. Yale UP, 2012.

Bach, Susanne. *Grenzsituationen in den Dramen Peter Shaffers*. Lang, 1992.

Bakhtin, Mikhail. *Creation of a Prosaics*. Edited by Gary S. Morson and Caryl Emerson, Stanford UP, 1990.

Bakhtin, Mikhail. *Problems of Dostoevsky's Poetics*. Translated by Caryl Emerson, Manchester UP, 1984.

Bal, Mieke. *On Story-Telling: Essays in Narratology*. Polebridge P, 1991.

Balbert, Peter. "Configurations of the Ego: Studies of Mailer, Roth, and Salinger." *Studies in the Novel*, vol. 12, no. 1, 1980, pp. 73–81.

Baldick, Chris. *Oxford Concise Dictionary of Literary Terms*. Oxford UP, 2004.

Baldwin, Helene L. "*Equus*: Theater of Cruelty or Theater Sensationalism?" *West Virginia University Philological Papers*, vol. 25, 1979, pp. 118–27.

Balint, Michael. *The Basic Fault: Therapeutic Aspects of Regression*. Taylor and Francis, 2013.

Balint, Michael. "The Doctor's Therapeutic Function." *The Lancet*, June 5, 1965, pp. 1177–80.

Balme, Christopher. *Einführung in die Theaterwissenschaft*. Erich Schmidt, 2003.

Baranger, Madeleine, and Willy Baranger. "The Analytic Situation as a Dynamic Field." Translated by Susan Rogers and John Churcher. *The International Journal of Psychoanalysis*, vol. 89, no. 4, 2008, pp. 795–826.

Barnett, Laura. "How Realistic Is *In Treatment*? We Ask Real British Psychotherapists What They Think of the Hit TV Show." *The Guardian*, April 26, 2011, http://www.guardian.co.uk/society/2011/apr/26/in-treatment-british-psychotherapists.

Barthes, Roland. "De l'oeuvre au texte." *Le bruissement de la langue: Essais critiques IV*, Éditions du Seuil, 1984, pp. 71–80.

Barthes, Roland. "La mort de l'auteur." *Le bruissement de la langue: Essais critiques IV*, Éditions du Seuil, 1984, pp. 63–69.

Barthes, Roland. *S/Z: Essai*. Éditions du Seuil, 1970.

Bateman, Anthony, and Jeremy Holmes. *Introduction to Psychoanalysis: Contemporary Theory and Practice*. Routledge, 1995.

Bayard, Pierre. "Is It Possible to Apply Literature to Psychoanalysis?" *American Imago*, vol. 56, no. 3, Fall 1999, pp. 207–19.

Beckerman, Bernard. "The Dynamics of Peter Shaffer's Drama." *The Play and Its Critic: Essays for Eric Bentley*, edited by Michael Bertin, UP of America, 1986, pp. 199–209.

Bem, Caroline. "Of Talk and Silence on Television: Notes on *In Treatment*." *Seachange*, vol. 3, 2012, pp. 25–39.
Benjamin, Jessica. "Beyond Doer and Done to: An Intersubjective View of Thirdness." *The Psychoanalytic Quarterly*, vol. 73, 2004, pp. 5–46.
Benjamin, Jessica. "An Outline of Intersubjectivity: The Development of Recognition." *Psychoanalytic Psychology*, vol. 7, 1990, pp. 33–46.
Benjamin, Walter. "Die Aufgabe des Übersetzers." *Gesammelte Schriften Bd. IV,1*, Suhrkamp, 1972, pp. 9–21.
Bennett, Toni L. "Drama: Transforming the Pathology of Compulsive Repetition." *Journal of Poetry Therapy*, vol. 11, no. 4, 1998, pp. 205–13.
Berman, Jeffrey. "*Equus*: After Such Little Forgiveness, What Knowledge?" *The Psychoanalytic Review*, vol. 66, no. 3, 1979, pp. 407–22.
Berman, Jeffrey. "Revisiting Roth's Psychoanalysts." *The Cambridge Companion to Philip Roth*, edited by Timothy Parrish, Cambridge UP, 2007, pp. 94–110.
Berman, Jeffrey. *The Talking Cure: Literary Representations of Psychoanalysis*. New York UP, 1985.
Berns, Ulrich. "Der Rahmen und die Autonomie von Analysand und Analytiker." *Forum der Psychoanalyse*, vol. 18, no. 4, 2002, pp. 332–49.
Bernstein, Jeanne W. "Countertransference: Our New Royal Road to the Unconscious?" *Psychoanalytic Dialogues*, vol. 9, no. 3, 1999, pp. 275–99.
Bersani, Leo. "The It in the I." *Intimacies*, by Leo Bersani and Adam Phillips, U of Chicago P, 2008.
Bettelheim, Bruno. *The Uses of Enchantment: The Meaning and Importance of Fairy Tales*. Knopf, 1976.
Bettelheim, Bruno. "Portnoy Psychoanalyzed." *Midstream*, vol. 15, 1969, pp. 3–10.
Bettighofer, Siegfried. *Übertragung und Gegenübertragung im therapeutischen Prozess*. Kohlhammer, 2004.
Beyer, Manfred. "Peter Shaffers *Equus* und die Paradoxie vom gesunden Kranken und kranken Gesunden." *Forum modernes Theater*, vol. 2, no. 2, 1987, pp. 154–69.
Bion, Wilfred R. *Attention and Interpretation*. Jason Aronson, 1995.
Bion, Wilfred R. *Learning from Experience*. Rowman & Littlefield, 2004.
Birchall, Clare. "In Treatment: Why Can't UK Networks Commit to the Hit Show?" *The Guardian*, June 11, 2009, http://www.guardian.co.uk/culture/tvandradioblog/2009/jun/11/in-treatment-uk-tv?INTCMP=ILCNETTXT3487.
Black, Max. "Metaphor." *Proceedings of the Aristotelian Society*, vol. 55, 1954/5, pp. 273–94.
Blanchet, Robert. "Quality TV: Eine kurze Einführung in die Geschichte und Ästhetik neuer amerikanischer Fernsehserien." *Serielle Formen: Von den frühen Film-Serials zu aktuellen Quality-TV- und Online-Serien*, edited by Robert Blanchet, Schüren, 2011, pp. 37–70.
Blättler, Christine. "Überlegungen zu Serialität als ästhetischem Begriff." *Weimarer Beiträge*, vol. 49, no. 4, 2003, pp. 502–16.

Bohleber, Werner. "Editorial." *Psyche*, vol. 53, no. 9/10, September 1999, pp. 815–19.

Bohleber, Werner. "Intersubjektivismus ohne Subjekt? Der Andere in der psychoanalytischen Tradition". *Die vernetzte Seele: Die intersubjektive Wende in der Psychoanalyse*, edited by Martin Altmeyer and Helmut Thomä, Klett-Cotta, 2006, pp. 203–26.

Bohleber, Werner, Peter Fonagy, Juan P. Jiménez, Dominique Scarfone, Sverre Varvin, and Samuel Zysman. "Für einen besseren Umgang mit psychoanalytischen Konzepten, modellhaft illustriert am Konzept 'Enactment.'" *Psyche*, vol. 67, no. 12, December 2013, pp. 1212–50.

Book, Andrew. "Psychoanalysis in Canada: Brief History." *Canadian Psychoanalytic Society*, http://www.en.psychoanalysis.ca/about-cps/psychoanalysis-in-canada.

Boothe, Brigitte. "Begegnung als Verwandlung: Psychoanalyse der Übertragung." *Intermedien: Zur kulturellen und artistischen Übertragung*, edited by Alexandra Kleihues, Barbara Naumann, and Edgar Pankow, Chronos, 2010, pp. 269–87.

Boothe, Brigitte. "Editorial." *Schwerpunktthema: Erzählen, Träumen und Erinnern: Erträge klinischer Erzählforschung*, edited by Brigitte Boothe, Special Issue, *Psychoanalyse—Texte zur Sozialforschung*, vol. 2, 2009, pp. 101–09.

Boothe, Brigitte. "Erzählen im medizinischen und psychotherapeutischen Diskurs." *Wirklichkeitserzählungen: Felder, Formen und Funktionen nicht-literarischen Erzählens*, edited by Christian Klein and Matías Martínez, Metzler, 2009, pp. 51–80.

Boothe, Brigitte. *Der Patient als Erzähler in der Psychotherapie*. Vandenhoeck & Ruprecht, 1994.

Boothe, Brigitte, and Bernhard Grimmer. "Die therapeutische Beziehung aus psychoanalytischer Sicht." *Die therapeutische Beziehung*, edited by Wulf Rössler, Springer, 2005, pp. 37–58.

Boothe, Brigitte, and Agnes von Wyl. "Einleitung." *Erzählen als Konfliktdarstellung: Im psychotherapeutischen Alltag und im literarischen Kontext*, edited by Brigitte Boothe and Agnes von Wyl, Lang, 1999, pp. 7–43.

Boothe, Brigitte, Agnes von Wyl, and Res Wepfer. *Psychisches Leben im Spiegel der Erzählung: Eine narrative Psychotherapiestudie*. Asanger, 1998.

Brandell, Jerrold R. "Introduction." *Celluloid Couches, Cinematic Clients: Psychoanalysis and Psychotherapy in the Movies*, edited by Jerrold R. Brandell, SUNY P, 2004, pp. 1–17.

Brauner, David. "'Getting in Your Retaliation First': Narrative Strategies in *Portnoy's Complaint*." *Philip Roth: New Perspectives on an American Author*, edited by Derek Parker Royal, Praeger, 2005, pp. 43–57.

Brauner, David. "Masturbation and Its Discontents, or, Serious Relief: Freudian Comedy in *Portnoy's Complaint*." *Critical Review*, vol. 40, 2000, pp. 75–90.

Bräutigam, Walter. "Realistische Beziehung und Übertragung." *Die psychoanalytische Haltung: Auf der Suche nach dem Selbstbild der Psychoanalyse*, edited by Peter Kutter, Raúl Páramo-Ortega and Peter Zagermann, Verlag Internationale Psychoanalyse, 1993, pp. 165–86.

Brecht, Bertolt. "Anmerkungen zur Oper 'Aufstieg und Fall der Stadt Mahagonny.'" *Schriften über Theater*, edited by Werner Hecht, Henschelverlag, 1977, pp. 108–18.

Breuer, Josef. "Beobachtung I. Frl. Anna O…" *GW: Nachtragsband*, pp. 221–43.

Bronfen, Elisabeth, and Hagai Levi. "Is Television Series the New Psychological Treatment?" *Youtube*, uploaded by Mosse Lectures, July 8, 2012, https://www.youtube.com/watch?v=l_EzaysXkJ8.

Bronstein, Catalina. "On Free Association and Psychic Reality." *British Journal of Psychotherapy*, vol. 18, no. 4, 2002, pp. 477–89.

Brooks, Peter. *Body Work: Objects of Desire in Modern Narrative*. Harvard UP, 1993.

Brooks, Peter. *Psychoanalysis and Storytelling*. Blackwell, 1994.

Brooks, Peter. *Reading for the Plot: Design and Intention in Narrative*. Clarendon Press, 1984.

Bruner, Jerome. *Making Stories: Law, Literature, Life*. Farrar, Straus & Giroux, 2002.

Brunkhorst, Martin. "Der Erzähler im Drama: Versionen des Memory Play bei Fry, Shaffer, Stoppard und Beckett." *Arbeiten aus Anglistik und Amerikanistik*, vol. 5, no. 2, 1980, pp. 225–40.

Buber, Martin. *Das dialogische Prinzip*. Lambert Schneider, 1973.

Bucci, Wilma, and Norbert Freedman. "The Language of Depression." *Bulletin of the Menninger Clinic*, vol. 45, no. 4, July 1981, pp. 334–58.

Buchholz, Michael B. "Die Metapher im psychoanalytischen Dialog." *Psyche*, vol. 52, no. 6, June 1998, pp. 545–71.

Buelens, Gert, and Dominik Hoens. "'Above and Beneath Classification': Bartleby, *Life and Times of Michael K*, and Syntagmatic Participation." *Diacritics: A Review of Contemporary Criticism*, vol. 37, no. 2/3, 2007, pp. 157–70.

Burgoyne, Robert. "The Cinematic Narrator: The Logic and Pragmatics of Impersonal Narration." *Journal of Film and Video*, vol. 42, no. 1, 1990, pp. 3–16.

Burke, Adrian. "Introduction." *Equus*, Longman, 1993, pp. viii–xiv.

Burke, Adrian. "The Writer on Writing." *Equus*, Longman, 1993, pp. iv–vii.

Campbell, Patrick. "Introduction." *Psychoanalysis and Performance*, edited by Patrick Campbell and Adrian Kear, Routledge, 2001, pp. 1–18.

Canepari-Labib, Michela. *Old Myths—Modern Empires: Power, Language, and Identity in J. M. Coetzee's Work*. Lang, 2005.

Capps, Lisa, and Elinor Ochs. *Constructing Panic: The Discourse of Agoraphobia*. Harvard UP, 1995.

Carlson, Marvin A. *Places of Performance: The Semiotics of Theatre Architecture*. Cornell UP, 1989.

Cavell, Stanley. "The Fact of Television." *Daedalus*, vol. 111, no. 4, 1982, pp. 75–96.
Černy, Lothar. "Peter Shaffer; *Equus*." *Englische Literatur der Gegenwart*, edited by Rainer Lengeler, Bagel, 1977, pp. 157–70.
Charon, Rita, Joanne T. Banks, Julia E. Connelly, Anne H. Hawkins, Kathryn M. Hunter, Anne H. Jones, Martha Montello, and Suzanne Poirer. "Literature and Medicine: Contributions to Clinical Practice." *Annals of Internal Medicine*, vol. 122, no. 8, April 1995, pp. 599–606.
Charon, Rita, and Maura Spiegel. "Editor's Preface: Narrative, Empathy, Proximity." *Literature and Medicine*, vol. 23, no. 2, Fall 2004, pp. vii–x.
Chaudhuri, Una. "The Spectator in Drama/Drama in the Spectator: Peter Shaffer's *Equus*." *Contemporary British Drama, 1970–90*, edited by Hersh Zeifman and Cynthia Zimmerman, U of Toronto P, 1993, pp. 41–61.
Chesney, Duncan M. "Towards an Ethics of Silence: Michael K." *Criticism: A Quarterly for Literature and the Arts*, vol. 49, no. 3, 2007, pp. 307–25.
Clark, Hilary A. "Introduction: Depression and Narrative." *Depression and Narrative: Telling the Dark*, edited by Hilary A. Clark, SUNY P, 2008, pp. 1–12.
Clarke, Brett H. "Hermeneutics and the 'Relational' Turn: Schafer, Ricoeur, Gadamer and the Nature of Psychoanalytic Subjectivity." *Psychoanalysis and Contemporary Thought*, vol. 20, no. 1, 1997, pp. 3–68.
Clarkson, Petruska. "A Multiplicity of Psychotherapeutic Relationships." *British Journal of Psychotherapy*, vol. 7, no. 2, December 1990, pp. 148–63.
Claycomb, Ryan M. "Middlebrowing the Avant-Garde: *Equus* on the West End." *Modern Drama*, vol. 52, no. 1, 2009, pp. 99–123.
Clemenz, Manfred. "Psychoanalyse und künstlerische Kreativität." *Psyche*, vol. 59, no. 5, May 2005, pp. 444–64.
Coen, Stanley. *Between Author and Reader: A Psychoanalytic Approach to Writing and Reading*. Columbia UP, 1994.
Coen, Stanley. "Introduction: Essays on the Relationship of Author and Reader: Transference Implications for Psychoanalytic Literary Criticism." *Psychoanalysis and Contemporary Thought*, vol. 5, no. 1, 1982, pp. 3–15.
Coenen, Hans G. *Analogie und Metapher: Grundlegung einer Theorie der bildlichen Rede*. De Gruyter, 2002.
Coetzee, J. M. *Disgrace*. 1999. Vintage, 2000.
Coetzee, J. M. *Foe*. 1986. Penguin, 1987.
Coetzee, J. M. *Waiting for the Barbarians*. 1980. Vintage, 2004.
Coetzee, J. M., and David Attwell. *Doubling the Point: Essays and Interviews*. Harvard UP, 1992.
Coetzee, J. M., and Arabella Kurtz. *The Good Story: Exchanges on Truth, Fiction and Psychoanalytic Psychotherapy*. Harville Secker, 2015.
Coleridge, Samuel T. *The Rime of the Ancient Mariner*. Edited by Lincoln R. Gibbs, Ginn & Co., 1898.
Cooke, Virginia, and Malcolm Page, editors. *File on Shaffer*. Methuen, 1987.

Cooper, Arnold M. "Some Persistent Issues in Psychoanalytic Literary Criticism." *Psychoanalysis and Contemporary Thought*, vol. 5, no. 1, 1982, pp. 45–53.
Cooper, David. *The Death of the Family*. Penguin Books, 1972.
Corello, Anthony V. "*Equus*: The Ritual Sacrifice of the Male Child." *The Psychoanalytic Review*, vol. 73, no. 2, Summer 1986, pp. 191–211.
Crapanzano, Vincent. "Text, Übertragung und Deixis." *Psyche*, vol. 41, no. 5, May 1987, pp. 385–410.
Cremerius, Johannes. *Vom Handwerk des Psychoanalytikers: Das Werkzeug der psychoanalytischen Technik. Band 2*. Fromann-Holzboog, 1984.
Crossley, Nick. "R. D. Laing and the British Anti-Psychiatry Movement: A Socio-Historical Analysis." *Social Science & Medicine*, vol. 47, no. 7, October 1998, pp. 877–89.
Dablé, Nadine. *Leerstellen transmedial: Auslassungsphänomene als narrative Strategie in Film und Fernsehen*. Transcript, 2012.
Darroch, Heidi. "Hysteria and Traumatic Testimony: Margaret Atwood's *Alias Grace*." *Essays on Canadian Writing*, vol. 81, Winter 2004, pp. 103–21.
Dennerlein, Katrin. *Narratologie des Raumes*. De Gruyter, 2009.
Derrida, Jacques. *Resistances of Psychoanalysis*. Translated by Peggy Kamuf, Pascale-Anne Brault, and Michael Naas, Stanford UP, 1998.
Dewing, Hilary. "'Remote Control: Psychoanalysis and Television,' London, October 2010." *British Journal of Psychotherapy*, vol. 27, no. 2, May 2011, pp. 214–17.
Diderot, Denis. "Paradoxe sur le comédien." *Oeuvres*, Gallimard, 1951, pp. 1003–58.
Dooley, Gillian. *J. M. Coetzee and the Power of Narrative*. Cambria, 2010.
Döring, Tobias. "Performing Psychoanalysis: The Knots of Freudian Drama and the London Stage." *Psychoanalyticism: Uses of Psychoanalysis in Novels, Poems, Plays and Films*, edited by Ingrid Hotz-Davies and Anton Kirchhofer, WVT, 2000, pp. 155–76.
Dovey, Teresa. *The Novels of J. M. Coetzee: Lacanian Allegories*. Donker, 1988.
Dreher, Christoph, and Christine Lang. "Sie denken immer nur an das Eine? Die Psychotherapie-Serie *In Treatment*." *SPEX*, February 15, 2010, http://www.spex.de/2010/02/15/sie-denken-immer-nur-an-das-eine-die-psychotherapie-serie-in-treatment/.
Durrant, Sam. *Postcolonial Narrative and the Work of Mourning: J. M. Coetzee, Wilson Harris, and Toni Morrison*. SUNY P, 2004.
Eaton, Marcia M. "On Being a Character." *British Journal of Aesthetics*, vol. 16, no. 1, 1976, pp. 24–31.
Eckstaedt, Anita. "Wie Patienten erzählen—Dialogstrukturen: Erfahrungen aus der psychoanalytischen Praxis." *Über sich selber reden: Zur Psychoanalyse autobiographischen Schreibens: Freiburger literaturpsychologische Gespräche 11*, edited by Johannes Cremerius, Königshausen & Neumann, 1992, pp. 25–35.

Eco, Umberto. "Innovation & Repetition: Between Modern & Postmodern Aesthetics." *Daedalus*, vol. 134, no. 4, Fall 2005, pp. 191–207.
Eiland, Howard. "Philip Roth: The Ambiguities of Desire." *Critical Essays on Philip Roth*, edited by Sanford Pinsker, G. K. Hall, 1982, pp. 255–65.
Ellenzweig, Allen. "Domestication and Its Discontents." *Gay & Lesbian Review Worldwide*, vol. 16, no. 1, January/February 2009, p. 50.
Engélibert, Jean-Paul. *Aux avant-postes du progrès: Essai sur l'oeuvre de J. M. Coetzee*. Pulim, 2003.
Entralgo, Pedro Laín. *Doctor and Patient*. Translated by Frances Partridge, McGraw-Hill, 1969.
Ermann, Michael. "Transference Interpretations as Relationship Work." *International Forum of Psychoanalysis*, vol. 3, no. 1, 1994, pp. 25–33.
Esman, Aaron H. "Psychoanalysis and Literary Criticism: A Limited Partnership." *Psychoanalysis and Contemporary Thought*, vol. 5, no. 1, 1982, pp. 17–25.
Faulstich, Werner. "Serialität aus kulturwissenschaftlicher Sicht." *Endlose Geschichten: Serialität in den Medien*, edited by Günter Giesenfeld, Olms-Weidmann, 1994, pp. 46–54.
Feldman, Marvin J. "The Use of Obscene Words in the Therapeutic Relationship." *The American Journal of Psychoanalysis*, vol. 15, no. 1, 1955, pp. 45–48.
Felman, Shoshana. *Jacques Lacan and the Adventure of Insight: Psychoanalysis in Contemporary Culture*. Harvard UP, 1987.
Felman, Shoshana. "To Open the Question." *Literature and Psychoanalysis: The Question of Reading, Otherwise*, edited by Shoshana Felman, Special Issue, *Yale French Studies*, vol. 55/56, 1977, pp. 5–10.
Felman, Shoshana. "Turning the Screw of Interpretation." *Literature and Psychoanalysis: The Question of Reading, Otherwise*, edited by Shoshana Felman, Special Issue, *Yale French Studies*, vol. 55/56, 1977, pp. 94–207.
Felski, Rita. *The Limits of Critique*. U of Chicago P, 2015.
Felski, Rita. *Uses of Literature*. Blackwell, 2008.
Ferenczi, Sándor. "Die Elastizität der psychoanalytischen Technik." 1927/8. *Bausteine zur Psychoanalyse, III. Band: Arbeiten aus den Jahren 1908–33*, Verlag Hans Huber, 1939, pp. 380–98.
Ferenczi, Sándor. "Introjektion und Übertragung." 1909. *Bausteine zur Psychoanalyse, I. Band: Theorie*, Internationaler psychoanalytischer Verlag, 1927, pp. 9–57.
Ferenczi, Sándor. "Zur psychoanalytischen Technik." 1919. *Bausteine zur Psychoanalyse*, II. Band: *Praxis*, Internationaler psychoanalytischer Verlag, 1927, pp. 38–54.
Ferro, Antonino. *The Bi-Personal Field: Experiences in Child Analysis*. Edited by Elizabeth Bott Spillius, Routledge, 1999.
Ferro, Antonino. *In the Analyst's Consulting Room*. Translated by Philip Slotkin, Brunner-Routledge, 2002.

Ferro, Antonino. *Psychoanalysis as Therapy and Storytelling*. Translated by Philip Slotkin, Routledge, 2006.
Ferro, Antonino. "Some Implications of Bion's Thought." *International Journal of Psychoanalysis*, vol. 83, no. 3, June 2002, pp. 597–607.
Feuer, Jane. "Being in Treatment on TV." *Flow*, vol. 9, no. 13, 2009, http://flowtv.org/2009/05/being-in-treatment-on-tvjane-feuer-university-of-pittsburgh/.
Fiamengo, Janice. "Truths of Storytelling: A Response to Burkhard Niederhoff." *Connotations: A Journal for Critical Debate*, vol. 19, no. 1–3, 2009/10, pp. 53–67.
Fish, Stanley E. "What is Stylistics and Why Are They Saying Such Terrible Things about It? Part II." *boundary 2*, vol. 8, no. 1, 1979, pp. 129–46.
Fiske, John. *Television Culture*. Routledge, 1987.
Flader, Dieter, and Wolf D. Grodzicki. "Hypothesen zur Wirkungsweise der psychoanalytischen Grundregel." *Psyche*, vol. 32, no. 7, July 1978, pp. 545–94.
Flores, Teresa. "Women Analyzing Women: The Difficult Patient." *The International Journal of Psychoanalysis*, vol. 91, no. 5, October 2010, pp. 1236–38.
Forrey, Robert. "Oedipal Politics in *Portnoy's Complaint*." *Critical Essays on Philip Roth*, edited by Sanford Pinsker, G. K. Hall, 1982, pp. 266–74.
Foucault, Michel. *L'ordre du discours: Leçon inaugurale au Collège de France prononcée le 2 décembre 1970*. Gallimard, 1971.
Foucault, Michel. "Qu'est-ce qu'un auteur?" *Dits et écrits I: 1954–69*. Gallimard, 1994, pp. 789–821.
Frank, Thomas H. "The Interpretation of Limits: Doctors and Novelists in the Fiction of Philip Roth." *Journal of Popular Culture*, vol. 28, no. 4, Spring 1995, pp. 67–80.
Frankland, Graham. *Freud's Literary Culture*. Cambridge UP, 2000.
Franssen, Paul. "Fleeing from the Burning City: Michael K, Vagrancy and Empire." *English Studies*, vol. 84, no. 5, October 2003, pp. 453–63.
Freud, Sigmund. "Analysis Terminable and Interminable." 1937. *SE 23*, pp. 209–53.
Freud, Sigmund. "An Autobiographical Study." 1925. *SE 20*, pp. 1–74.
Freud, Sigmund. "On Beginning the Treatment." 1913. *SE 12*, pp. 121–44.
Freud, Sigmund. "The Claims of Psycho-Analysis to Scientific Interest." 1913. *SE 13*, pp. 163–90.
Freud, Sigmund. "Constructions in Analysis." 1937. *SE 23*, pp. 255–69.
Freud, Sigmund. "Creative Writers and Day-Dreaming." 1908. *SE 9*, pp. 141–53.
Freud, Sigmund. "Delusions and Dreams in Jensen's *Gradiva*." 1907. *SE 9*, pp. 1–95.
Freud, Sigmund. "The Dynamics of Transference." 1912. *SE 12*, pp. 97–108.
Freud, Sigmund. "Fragment of an Analysis of a Case of Hysteria." 1905. *SE 7*, pp. 1–122.
Freud, Sigmund. "The Future of an Illusion." 1927. *SE 21*, pp. 1–56.

Freud, Sigmund. "The Future Prospects of Psycho-Analytic Therapy." 1910. *SE 11*, pp. 139–51.

Freud, Sigmund. "The Goethe Prize." 1930. *SE 21*, pp. 205–14.

Freud, Sigmund. "Goethe-Preis 1930: Brief an Dr. Alfons Paquet; Ansprache im Frankfurter Goethe-Haus." 1930. *GW XIV*, edited by Anna Freud, Imago, 1948, pp. 543–50.

Freud, Sigmund. "From the History of an Infantile Neurosis." 1918. *SE 17*, pp. 1–123.

Freud, Sigmund. "On the History of the Psycho-Analytic Movement." 1914. *SE 14*, pp. 1–66.

Freud, Sigmund. "The Interpretation of Dreams." 1900. *SE 4/5*, pp. ix–628.

Freud, Sigmund. "Introductory Lectures on Psycho-Analysis." 1916/17. *SE 15/16*, pp. 1–463.

Freud, Sigmund. "Leonardo da Vinci and a Memory of His Childhood." 1910. *SE 11*, pp. 57–137.

Freud, Sigmund. "Lines of Advance in Psycho-Analytic Therapy." 1919. *SE 17*, pp. 157–68.

Freud, Sigmund. "Moses and Monotheism: Three Essays." 1939. *SE 23*, pp. 1–137.

Freud, Sigmund. "On Narcissism: An Introduction." 1914. *SE 14*, pp. 67–102.

Freud, Sigmund. "Notes upon a Case of Obsessional Neurosis." 1909. *SE 10*, pp. 151–318.

Freud, Sigmund. "Observations on Transference-Love." 1915. *SE 12*, pp. 157–71.

Freud, Sigmund. "An Outline of Psycho-Analysis." 1940. *SE 23*, pp. 139–207.

Freud, Sigmund. "Preface to Reik's *Ritual: Psycho-Analytic Studies*." 1919. *SE 17*, pp. 257–63.

Freud, Sigmund. "The Question of Lay Analysis." 1926. *SE 20*, pp. 177–258.

Freud, Sigmund. "Recommendations to Physicians Practising Psycho-Analysis." 1912. *SE 12*, pp. 109–20.

Freud, Sigmund. "Remembering, Repeating and Working-Through." 1914. *SE 12*, pp. 145–56.

Freud, Sigmund. *The Standard Edition of the Complete Psychological Works of Sigmund Freud*. Edited and translated by James Strachey in collaboration with Anna Freud, Vintage, 2000–7.

Freud, Sigmund. "Studies on Hysteria." 1895. *SE 2*, pp. vii–321.

Freud, Sigmund. "Three Essays on the Theory of Sexuality." 1905. *SE 7*, pp. 123–245.

Freud, Sigmund. "'Wild' Psycho-Analysis." 1910. *SE 11*, pp. 219–27.

Freud, Sigmund, and Karl Abraham. *Briefe* 1907–26. Edited by Hilda C. Abraham und Ernst L. Freud, Fischer, 1965.

Freud, Sigmund, and Ludwig Binswanger. *Briefwechsel* 1908–38. Edited by Gerhard Fichtner, Fischer, 1992.

Freund, Elizabeth. *The Return of the Reader: Reader-Response Criticism*. Methuen, 1987.

Friedman, Lawrence. "Modern Hermeneutics and Psychoanalysis." *Psychoanalytic Quarterly*, vol. 69, no. 2, April 2000, pp. 225–64.

Friedman, Maurice. "Martin Buber and Dialogical Psychotherapy." *Journal of Humanistic Psychology*, vol. 42, no. 4, Fall 2002, pp. 7–36.

Frier, Ina. "Objektbeziehungen im literarischen Prozeß: Ein psychoanalytischer Beitrag zur Literatur und Kreativität." *Jahrbuch der Psychoanalyse, Beiträge zur Theorie und Praxis der Psychoanalyse*, vol. 24, 1989, pp. 214–45.

Fröhlich, Vincent. *Der Cliffhanger und die serielle Narration: Analyse einer transmedialen Erzähltechnik*. Transcript, 2015.

Fröhlich, Vincent. "Filling In: Rezeptionsästhetische Gedanken zur seriellen Narration." *Quality-TV: Die narrative Spielwiese des 21. Jahrhunderts?!*, edited by Jonas Nesselhauf and Markus Schleich, Lit Verlag, 2014, pp. 213–25.

Furedi, Frank. *Therapy Culture: Cultivating Vulnerability in an Uncertain Age*. Routledge, 2004.

Furst, Lilian R. *Just Talk: Narratives of Psychotherapy*. U of Kentucky P, 1999.

Furst, Lilian R. "Pairing Literature and Medicine." *Literature and Medicine*, vol. 10, no. 1, 1991, pp. 130–42.

Gabbard, Glen O. "The Shrink Rap: At Last, a Realistic TV Portrayal of Psychotherapy: *In Treatment*." *Slate*, January 28, 2008, http://www.slate.com/id/2182943/.

Gabbard, Glen O., and Krin Gabbard. *Psychiatry and the Cinema*. U of Chicago P, 1987.

Gadamer, Hans-Georg. *Wahrheit und Methode: Grundzüge einer philosophischen Hermeneutik*. J.C.B. Mohr, 1990.

Galgut, Elisa. "Reading Minds: Mentalization, Irony and Literary Engagement." *The International Journal of Psychoanalysis*, vol. 91, no. 4, August 2010, pp. 915–35.

Gallagher, Susan V. *A Story of South Africa: J. M. Coetzee's Fiction in Context*. Harvard UP, 1991.

Gallese, Vittorio. "Mirror Neurons, Embodied Simulation, and the Neural Basis of Social Identification." *Psychoanalytic Dialogues*, vol. 19, no. 5, 2009, pp. 519–36.

Gay, Peter. *Freud: A Life for Our Times*. Little Books, 2006.

Gebauer, Mirjam. "Milieuschilderungen zweier verrückter Monologisten: Philip Roths *Portnoy's Complaint* als ein Vorbild für Thomas Brussigs *Helden wie wir*." *Orbis Litterarum: International Review of Literary Studies*, vol. 57, no. 3, 2002, pp. 222–40.

Gedo, John E. "Working Through as Metaphor and as a Modality of Treatment." *Journal of the American Psychoanalytic Association*, vol. 43, no. 2, 1995, pp. 339–56.

Gerson, Samuel. "Neutrality, Resistance, and Self-Disclosure in an Intersubjective Psychoanalysis." *Psychoanalytic Dialogues*, vol. 6, no. 5, 1996, pp. 623–45.

Gerson, Samuel. "The Relational Unconscious: A Core Element of Intersubjectivity, Thirdness, and Clinical Process." *The Psychoanalytic Quarterly*, vol. 73, no. 1, 2004, pp. 63–98.

Gesing, Fritz. "Annäherungen an eine psychoanalytische Theorie der literarischen Form." *Die Psychoanalyse der literarischen Form(en): Freiburger literaturpsychologische Gespräche 9*, edited by Johannes Cremerius, Königshausen & Neumann, 1990, pp. 33–63.

Giesenfeld, Günter. "Serialität als Erzählstrategie in der Literatur." *Endlose Geschichten: Serialität in den Medien*, edited by Günter Giesenfeld, Olms-Weidmann, 1994, pp. 1–11.

Girgus, Sam B. "Philip Roth and Woody Allen: Freud and the Humor of the Repressed." *Semites and Stereotypes: Characteristics of Jewish Humour*, edited by Avner Ziv and Anat Zajdman, Greenwood, 1993, pp. 121–30.

Glenn, Jules. "Anthony and Peter Shaffer's Plays: The Influence of Twinship on Creativity." *American Imago*, vol. 31, no. 3, Fall 1974, pp. 270–92.

Glenn, Jules. "Freud, Dora und das Kindermädchen: Eine Untersuchung der Gegenübertragung." *Psyche*, vol. 43, no. 6, June 1989, pp. 522–34.

Gooblar, David. "'Oh Freud, Do I Know!': Philip Roth, Freud, and Narrative Therapy." *Philip Roth Studies*, vol. 1, no. 1, Spring 2005, pp. 67–81.

Gordon, Lois G. "*Portnoy's Complaint*: Coming of Age in Jersey City." *Literature and Psychology*, vol. 19, no. 3/4, 1969, pp. 57–60.

Gordon, Paul. "The Celluloid Couch: Representations of Psychotherapy in Recent Cinema." *British Journal of Psychotherapy*, vol. 11, no. 1, September 1994, pp. 142–45.

Gorney, James E. "The Field of Illusion in Literature and the Psychoanalytic Situation." *Psychoanalysis and Contemporary Thought*, vol. 2, 1979, pp. 527–50.

Grebstein, Sheldon. "The Comic Anatomy of *Portnoy's Complaint*." *Comic Relief: Humor in Contemporary American Literature*, edited by Sarah Blacher Cohen, U of Illinois P, 1978, pp. 152–71.

Green, André. "The Double and the Absent." *Psychoanalysis, Creativity and Literature*, edited by Alan Roland, Columbia P, 1978, pp. 271–92.

Greenberg, Harvey R. "*In Treatment*: Doctor Paul Weston—Psychotherapist or Cinetherapist?" *The Psychoanalytic Review*, vol. 98, no. 1, February 2011, pp. 121–34.

Greenson, Ralph R. *Psychoanalytische Erkundungen*. Translated by Hilde Weller, Klett-Cotta, 1982.

Greiff, Louis K. "Two for the Price of One: Tragedy and the Dual Hero in *Equus* and *The Elephant Man*." *Within the Dramatic Spectrum*, edited by Karelisa V. Hartigan, UP of America, 1986, pp. 64–77.

Grolnick, Simon A. "Play, Myth, Theater, and Psychoanalysis." *The Psychoanalytic Review*, vol. 71, no. 2, September 1984, pp. 247–62.

Grubrich-Simitis, Ilse. "Einleitung: Sigmund Freuds Lebensgeschichte und die Anfänge der Psychoanalyse." *"Selbstdarstellung": Schriften zur Geschichte der Psychoanalyse*, Fischer, 1971, pp. 7–33.

Habermas, Tilmann. "Freuds Ratschläge zur Einleitung der Behandlung: Eine narratologische Interpretation der Wirkweise der psychoanalytischen Situation." *Freud neu entdecken: Ausgewählte Lektüren*, edited by Rolf Haubl, Vandenhoeck & Ruprecht, 2008, pp. 204–29.

Habermas, Tilmann. "Who Speaks? Who Looks? Who Feels? Point of View in Autobiographical Narratives." *International Journal of Psychoanalysis*, vol. 87, no. 2, April 2006, pp. 498–518.

Habermas, Tilmann, Michaela Meier, and Barbara Mukhtar. "Are Specific Emotions Narrated Differently?" *Emotion*, vol. 9, no. 6, 2009, pp. 751–62.

Haddawy, Husain, translator. *The Arabian Nights*. Everyman's Library, 1992.

Hagenmeyer, Hubert. "Die Kontroverse über Philip Roths *Portnoy's Complaint*." *Jewish Life and Suffering as Mirrored in English and American Literature*, edited by Franz Link, Schöningh, 1987, pp. 121–32.

Hamburger, Andreas. "Goldne Träume kehrt ihr wieder: Bericht über eine Lektüre." *Methoden in der Diskussion: Freiburger literaturpsychologische Gespräche 15*, edited by Johannes Cremerius, Königshausen & Neumann, 1996, pp. 46–81.

Handlbauer, Bernhard. "Über den Einfluß der Emigration auf die Geschichte der Psychoanalyse." *Forum der Psychoanalyse*, vol. 15, no. 2, July 1999, pp. 151–66.

Hatchuel, Sarah. "Trapped *In Treatment*." *GRAAT On-Line*, vol. 6, 2009, pp. 195–210.

Haubl, Rolf, and Wolfgang Mertens. *Der Psychoanalytiker als Archäologe: Eine Einführung in die Methode der Rekonstruktion*. Kohlhammer, 1996.

Haubl, Rolf, and Wolfgang Mertens. *Der Psychoanalytiker als Detektiv: Eine Einführung in die psychoanalytische Erkenntnistheorie*. Kohlhammer, 1996.

Hayes, Patrick. *J. M. Coetzee and the Novel: Writing and Politics after Beckett*. Oxford UP, 2010.

Head, Dominic. *The Cambridge Introduction to J. M. Coetzee*. Cambridge UP, 2009.

Head, Dominic. *J. M. Coetzee*. Cambridge UP, 1997.

Heider, Sarah D. "The Timeless Ecstasy of Michael K." *Bucknell Review: A Scholarly Journal of Letters, Arts and Sciences*, vol. 37, no. 1, 1993, pp. 83–98.

Heigl-Evers, Annelise, and Hans-Eduard Salfeld. "Lesen als Gegenübertragung: Veränderungen des emotionalen Rezeptionsverhaltens in Transformationsphasen literarischer Texte." *Materialien Psychoanalyse*, vol. 11, no. 1, 1985, pp. 1–49.

Heimann, Paula. "On Counter-Transference." 1949. *About Children and Children-No-Longer*, Tavistock, 1989, pp. 73–79.

Helgesson, Stefan. *Writing in Crisis: Ethics and History in Gordimer, Ndebele, and Coetzee*. U of KwaZulu-Natal P, 2004.

Hermann, Max. "Das theatralische Raumerlebnis." *Raumtheorie: Grundlagentexte aus Philosophie und Kulturwissenschaften*, edited by Jörg Dünne and Stephan Günzel, Suhrkamp, 2006, pp. 501–14.

Hickethier, Knut. "Die Fernsehserie—eine Kette von Verhaltenseinheiten: Problemstellungen für die Seriendiskussion." *Serie: Kunst im Alltag*, edited by Friedrich Salow, Vistas, 1992, pp. 11–18.

Hickethier, Knut. *Die Fernsehserie und das Serielle des Fernsehens*. Faulstich, 1991.

Hoffman, Anne G. "Is Psychoanalysis a Poetics of the Body?" *American Imago*, vol. 63, no. 4, Winter 2006, pp. 395–422.

Holland, Norman N. *5 Readers Reading*. Yale UP, 1975.

Holland, Norman N. *The Dynamics of Literary Response*. Oxford UP, 1968.

Holland, Norman N. "Shakespearean Tragedy and Three Ways of Psychoanalytic Criticism." *Hudson Review*, vol. 15, no. 2, 1962, pp. 217–27.

Holland, Norman N. "Why This Is Transference, Nor Am I Out of It." *Psychoanalysis and Contemporary Thought*, vol. 5, no. 1, 1982, pp. 27–34.

Holmes, Jeremy. "The Language of Psychotherapy: Metapher, Ambiguity, Wholeness." 1984. *British Journal of Psychotherapy*, vol. 21, no. 2, 2004, pp. 209–26.

Holm-Hadulla, Rainer M. "Psychoanalysis as a Creative Shaping Process." *International Journal of Psychoanalysis*, vol. 84, no. 5, October 2003, pp. 1203–20.

Hotz-Davies, Ingrid, and Anton Kirchhofer. "Introduction: Psychoanalysis as Cultural Material." *Psychoanalyticism: Uses of Psychoanalysis in Novels, Poems, Plays and Films*, edited by Ingrid Hotz-Davies and Anton Kirchhofer, WVT, 2000, pp. 11–31.

Howe, Irving. "Philip Roth Reconsidered." *Critical Essays on Philip Roth*, edited by Sanford Pinsker, G. K. Hall, 1982, pp. 229–44.

Howells, Coral A. "Margaret Atwood: *Alias Grace*." *Where Are the Voices Coming From? Canadian Culture and the Legacies of History*, edited by Coral A. Howells, Rodopi, 2004, pp. 29–37.

Huggan, Graham. "Is There a K in Africa? The Modern Parables of Kafka, Laye and Coetzee." *Canadian Review of Comparative Literature*, vol. 17, no. 1/2, 1990, pp. 85–98.

Hühn, Peter. "The Detective as Reader: Narrativity and Reading Concepts in Detective Fiction." *Modern Fiction Studies*, vol. 33, no. 3, Autumn 1987, pp. 451–66.

Hustvedt, Siri. "The Analyst in Fiction: Reflections on a More or Less Hidden Being." *Contemporary Psychoanalysis*, vol. 46, no. 2, Spring 2010, pp. 224–34.

Hustvedt, Siri. "Freud's Playground." *Living, Thinking, Looking*. Sceptre, 2013, pp. 196–219.

Hustvedt, Siri. "Playing, Wild Thoughts, and a Novel's Underground." *Living, Thinking, Looking*. Sceptre, 2013, pp. 37–40.

Hutter, Albert D. "Poetry in Psychoanalysis: Hopkins, Rossetti, Winnicott." *Transitional Objects and Potential Spaces: Literary Uses of D. W. Winnicott*, edited by Peter L. Rudnytsky, Columbia UP, 1993, pp. 63–86.

Illouz, Eva. *Saving the Modern Soul: Therapy, Emotions, and the Culture of Self-Help*. U of California P, 2008.
Ingersoll, Earl G. "Engendering Metafiction: Textuality and Closure in Margaret Atwood's *Alias Grace*." *American Review of Canadian Studies*, vol. 31, no. 3, Fall 2001, pp. 387–401.
Intelmann, Claudia. "Der Raum in der Psychoanalyse: Zur Wirkung des Raumes auf den psychoanalytischen Prozess." Dissertation, LMU München, 2008.
Iser, Wolfgang. *Der Akt des Lesens: Theorie ästhetischer Wirkung*. Fink, 1984.
Ivey, Gavin. "Plying the Steel: A Reconsideration of Surgical Metaphors in Psychoanalysis." *Journal of the American Psychoanalytic Association*, vol. 58, no. 1, February 2010, pp. 59–82.
Jackson, Leonard. *Literature, Psychoanalysis and the New Sciences of the Mind*. Longman, 2000.
Jones, Anne H. "Reading Patients: Cautions and Concerns." *Literature and Medicine*, vol. 13, no. 2, Fall 1994, pp. 190–200.
Jones, Ernest. "The Oedipus-Complex as an Explanation of Hamlet's Mystery: A Study in Motive." *The American Journal of Psychology*, vol. 21, no. 1, January 1910, pp. 72–113.
Jung, C. G. "Grundsätzliches zur praktischen Psychotherapie." 1935. *Praxis der Psychotherapie*, Rascher, 1958, pp. 1–20.
Jung, C. G. "Die praktische Verwendbarkeit der Traumanalyse." 1931. *Praxis der Psychotherapie*, Rascher, 1958, pp. 148–71.
Jung, C. G. "Die Probleme der modernen Psychotherapie." 1929. *Praxis der Psychotherapie*, Rascher, 1958, pp. 57–81.
Jung, C. G. "Die Psychologie der Übertragung." 1946. *Praxis der Psychotherapie*, Rascher, 1958, pp. 173–345.
Jung, C. G. "Ziele der Psychotherapie." 1929. *Praxis der Psychotherapie*, Rascher, 1958, pp. 38–56.
Jung, Irene. *Schreiben und Selbstreflexion: Eine literaturpsychologische Untersuchung literarischer Produktivität*. Westdeutscher Verlag, 1989.
Kahr, Brett. "Dr Paul Weston and the Bloodstained Couch." *The International Journal of Psychoanalysis*, vol. 92, no. 4, August 2011, pp. 1051–58.
Karel, William, director. *Philip Roth, sans complexe*. Cinétévé, 2011.
Kartiganer, Donald M. "Freud's Reading Process: The Divided Protagonist Narrative and the Case of the Wolf-Man." *The Psychoanalytic Study of Literature*, edited by Joseph Reppen and Maurice Charney, Analytic Press, 1985, pp. 3–36.
Kelleter, Frank. "From Recursive Progression to Systemic Self-Observation: Elements of a Theory of Seriality." *The Velvet Light Trap*, vol. 79, Spring 2017, pp. 99–105.
Kern, Susanne. *Das Unsagbare erzählen: J. M. Coetzees ästhetische Strategien zur Darstellung von Gewalt*. Lang, 2010.
Kernberg, Otto F. "The Influence of the Gender of Patient and Analyst in the Psychoanalytic Relationship." *Journal of the American Psychoanalytic Association*, vol. 48, no. 3, Summer 2000, pp. 859–83.

Kernberg, Otto F. "Notes on Countertransference." *Journal of the American Psychoanalytic Association*, vol. 13, no. 1, January 1965, pp. 38–56.

Kirchhofer, Anton. "Stories and Explanations: Therapy and Knowledge in Saul Bellow and Philip Roth." *Psychoanalyticism: Uses of Psychoanalysis in Novels, Poems, Plays and Films*, edited by Ingrid Hotz-Davies and Anton Kirchhofer, WVT, 2000, pp. 88–113.

Kirshner, Lewis A. "Between Winnicott and Lacan: Reclaiming the Subject of Psychoanalysis." *American Imago*, vol. 67, no. 3, Fall 2010, pp. 331–51.

Kittler, Erika. "Zurück zur Talking cure? Koreferat zu Antonino Ferro: Faktoren der Heilung und die Beendigung der Analyse." *Zeitschrift für psychoanalytische Theorie und Praxis*, vol. 21, no. 2/3, 2006, pp. 176–85.

Klein, Dennis A. *Peter Shaffer*. Twayne, 1979.

Klein, Dennis A. "Peter Shaffer's *Equus* as a Modern Aristotelian Tragedy." *Studies in Iconography*, vol. 9, 1983, pp. 175–81.

Klein, Thomas. "*In Treatment*: Talkshow." *Was bisher geschah: Serielles Erzählen im zeitgenössischen amerikanischen Fernsehen*, edited by Sascha Seiler, Schnitt, 2008, pp. 186–201.

Kliman, Bernice W. "Names in *Portnoy's Complaint*." *Critique: Studies in Modern Fiction*, vol. 14, no. 3, 1973, pp. 16–24.

Köhler, Kristina. "'You people are not watching enough television!': Nach-Denken über Serien und serielle Formen." *Serielle Formen: Von den frühen Film-Serials zu aktuellen Quality-TV- und Online-Serien*, edited by Robert Blanchet, Schüren, 2011, pp. 11–36.

Köhler, Nicholas. "Is a Therapist Allowed to Do That?" *MacLean's*, vol. 122, no. 20, 2009, p. 52.

König, Karl. *Übertragungsanalyse*. Vandenhoeck & Ruprecht, 1998.

Kossew, Sue. *Pen and Power: A Post-Colonial Reading of J. M. Coetzee and André Brink*. Rodopi, 1996.

Kunzke, Dieter. "Grundlegende Merkmale interpersonaler, intersubjektiver und relationaler Ansätze als Ausdruck aktueller Entwicklungstendenzen in der Psychoanalyse." *Psyche*, vol. 65, no. 7, July 2011, pp. 577–616.

Küpper, Joachim, and Christoph Menke. "Einleitung." *Dimensionen ästhetischer Erfahrung*, edited by Joachim Küpper and Christoph Menke, Suhrkamp, 2003, pp. 7–15.

Kureishi, Hanif, and Ramona Koval. "Hanif Kureishi on Writing, Psychoanalysis and Relationships." *The Book Show*, September 3, 2008, http://www.abc.net.au/radionational/programs/bookshow/hanif-kureishi-on-writing-psychoanalysis-and/3203626#transcript.

Lacan, Jacques. *Le séminaire, livre XI: Les quatre concepts fondamentaux de la psychanalyse*. Éditions du Seuil, 1973.

Lang, Christine. "The Idea of Love in the TV Serial Drama *In Treatment*." *Screening the Dark Side of Love: From Euro-Horror to American Cinema*, edited by Karen A. Ritzenhoff and Karen Randell, Palgrave Macmillan, 2012, pp. 197–210.

Langenmayr, Margret. *Lese-Erfahrungen im Gruppengespräch· Ein Beitrag zur psychoanalytischen Erforschung literarischer Rezeptionsprozesse.* Lang, 1993.

Laplanche, Jean, and Jean-Bertrand Pontalis. *Das Vokabular der Psychoanalyse.* Suhrkamp, 1973.

Lavine, Steven D. "The Degradations of Erotic Life: *Portnoy's Complaint* Reconsidered." *Michigan Academician: Papers of the Michigan Academy of Science, Arts, and Letters,* vol. 11, 1979, pp. 357-62.

Layton, Lynne. "The Detective and the Princess: Commentary on Paper by Jeanne Wolff Bernstein." *Psychoanalytic Dialogues,* vol. 9, no. 3, 1999, pp. 307-18.

Lehmkuhl, Gerd, and Ulrike Lehmkuhl. "Psychodynamik und Therapieprozess im Jugendalter und die Haltung des Therapeuten." *Psychoanalyse mit und ohne Couch: Haltung und Methode,* edited by Axel Gerlach, Anne-Marie Schlösser, and Anne Springer, Psychosozial-Verlag, 2003, pp. 614-27.

Leikert, Sebastian. "Das kinästhetische Unbewusste: Funktion und Mechanismen des kreativen Prozesses im Feld der Sprache und der Ästhetik." *Psyche,* vol. 67, no. 9/10, September 2013, pp. 962-90.

Lengeler, Rainer. "Peter Shaffer: *Equus*: Der Mythos vom ursprünglichen Leben." *Englisches Drama von Beckett bis Bond,* edited by Heinrich F. Plett, Fink, 1982, pp. 272-94.

Levi, Hagai, Steven Levinson, Rodrigo García, Blair Underwood, Rick Rosen, and David R. Ginsburg. *Israel's Film Industry: Transposing* Be-Tipul *to* In Treatment. UCLA, 2009, http://www.international.ucla.edu/israel/be-tipul?AspxAutoDetectCookieSupport=1.

Lichtenstein, Gene. "A Writer's Journey: (A Literary Essay and, in Part, a Memoir)." *Jewish Social Studies: History, Culture, and Society,* vol. 3, no. 3, 1997, pp. 156-76.

Lierop, Karin van. "Mythical Interpretation of J. M. Coetzee's *Life and Times of Michael K*." *Commonwealth Essays and Studies,* vol. 9, no. 1, 1986, pp. 44-49.

Loewald, Hans W. "Psychoanalysis as Art and the Fantasy Character of the Psychoanalytic Situation." *Journal of the American Psychoanalytic Association,* vol. 23, no. 2, April 1975, pp. 277-99.

Loewenstein, Era A. "The Freudian Case History: A Detective Story or a Dialectical Progression? Reflections on Psychoanalytic Narratives from a Lacanian Perspective." *Psychoanalytic Psychology,* vol. 9, no. 1, Winter 1992, pp. 49-59.

Lorenzer, Alfred. "Der Analytiker als Detektiv, der Detektiv als Analytiker." *Psyche,* vol. 10, no. 1, 1985, pp. 1-11.

Löschnigg, Maria, and Martin Löschnigg. "Eine kanadische Scheherazade: Erzählen und Identität der Protagonistin in Margaret Atwoods *Alias Grace*." *Germanisch-Romanische Monatsschrift,* vol. 49, no. 4, 1999, pp. 441-61.

Lovelady, Stephanie. "I Am Telling This to No One But You: Private Voice, Passing, and the Private Sphere in Margaret Atwood's *Alias Grace*." *Studies in Canadian Literature,* vol. 24, no. 2, 1999, pp. 35-63.

Lucas, Rose. "Narratives, Terminable and Interminable: Literature, Psychoanalysis and Margaret Atwood's *Alias Grace*." *History on the Couch: Essays in History and Psychoanalysis*, edited by Joy Damousi and Robert Reynolds, Melbourne UP, 2003, pp. 177–87.

Lucius-Hoene, Gabriele. "Erzählen als Bewältigung." *Schwerpunktthema: Erzählen, Träumen und Erinnern: Erträge klinischer Erzählforschung*, edited by Brigitte Boothe, Special Issue, *Psychoanalyse—Texte zur Sozialforschung*, vol. 2, 2009, pp. 139–47.

Luif, Vera. "Narrative im therapeutischen Dialog." *Schwerpunktthema: Erzählen, Träumen und Erinnern: Erträge klinischer Erzählforschung*, edited by Brigitte Boothe, Special Issue, *Psychoanalyse—Texte zur Sozialforschung*, vol. 2, 2009, pp. 218–25.

Macé, Marielle, and Marlon Jones. "Ways of Reading, Modes of Being." *New Literary History*, vol. 44, no. 2, Spring 2013, pp. 213–29.

MacMurraugh-Kavanagh, Madeleine. *Peter Shaffer: Theatre and Drama*. Macmillan, 1998.

Mahler-Bungers, Annegret. "Versuch über die Kunst einer psychoanalytischen Aisthesis und einige Konsequenzen für die psychoanalytische Literaturinterpretation." *Psyche*, vol. 67, no. 6, June 2013, pp. 501–25.

Mann, Thomas. "Mein Verhältnis zur Psychoanalyse." *Freud und die Psychoanalyse: Reden, Briefe, Notizen, Betrachtungen*, edited by Bernd Urban, Fischer, 1991, pp. 22–23.

Marais, Michael. "Languages of Power: A Story of Reading Coetzee's 'Michael K'/Michael K." *English in Africa*, vol. 16, no. 2, 1989, pp. 31–48.

Marais, Michael. "Literature and the Labour of Negation: J. M. Coetzee's *Life & Times of Michael K*." *Journal of Commonwealth Literature*, vol. 36, no. 1, 2001, pp. 107–25.

Marais, Michael. *Secretary of the Invisible: The Idea of Hospitality in the Fiction of J. M. Coetzee*. Rodopi, 2009.

March, Cristie. "Crimson Silks and New Potatoes: The Heteroglossic Power of the Object. Atwood's *Alias Grace*." *Studies in Canadian Literature*, vol. 22, no. 2, 1997, pp. 66–82.

Marta, Jan. "Lighting the Way: The Temporal Dimension of Narrative in Psychotherapy." *Literature and Medicine*, vol. 13, no. 1, Spring 1994, pp. 143–57.

Matejek, Norbert. *Leseerlebnisse: Ein Beitrag zur psychoanalytischen Rezeptionsforschung*. VAS, 1993.

Matt, Peter von. *Literaturwissenschaft und Psychoanalyse*. Reclam, 2001.

McCulliss, Debbie. "Bibliotherapy: Historical and Research Perspectives." *Journal of Poetry Therapy*, vol. 25, no. 1, March 2012, pp. 23–38.

Meissner, William W. "Toward a Neuropsychological Reconstruction of Projective Identification." *Journal of the American Psychoanalytic Association*, vol. 57, no. 1, February 2009, pp. 95–129.

Melville, Jonathan. "TV Interview: Hagai Levi, Creator of *In Treatment*." *Adventures in Primetime*, October 10, 2009, http://adventuresinprimetime. wordpress.com/2009/10/10/tv-interview-hagai-levi/.

Mentzos, Stavros. "Nachwort." *Bruchstück einer Hysterie-Analyse*. Fischer, 2007, pp. 123–34.

Merskey, Harold. "Multiple Personality Disorder and False Memory Syndrome." *The British Journal of Psychiatry*, vol. 166, no. 3, March 1995, pp. 281–83.

Mertens, Wolfgang. *Psychoanalyse: Geschichte und Methoden*. C. H. Beck, 2008.

Messler Davies, Jody. "Love in the Afternoon: A Relational Consideration of Desire and Dread in the Countertransference." *Psychoanalytic Dialogues*, vol. 4, no. 2, 1994, pp. 153–70.

Metzler, Gabriele. "Creativity: An Interview with Margaret Atwood." *Margaret Atwood: Works and Impact*, edited by Reingard M. Nischik, Camden House, 2000, pp. 277–86.

Michael, Magali C. "Rethinking History as Patchwork: The Case of Atwood's *Alias Grace*." *Modern Fiction Studies*, vol. 47, no. 2, Summer 2001, pp. 421–47.

Michel, Pierre. "*Portnoy's Complaint* and Philip Roth's Complexities." *Dutch Quarterly Review of Anglo-American Letters*, vol. 4, 1974, pp. 1–10.

Mielke, Christine. *Zyklisch-serielle Narration: Erzähltes Erzählen von 1001 Nacht bis zur TV-Serie*. De Gruyter, 2006.

Mikos, Lothar. *Es wird dein Leben! Familienserien im Fernsehen und im Alltag der Zuschauer*. MAkS-Publ, 1994.

Mikos, Lothar. "Übertragungserleben: Soziale Aspekte des Umgangs mit Familienserien." *Medium*, vol. 17, no. 3, 1987, pp. 28–30.

Miller, Michael C. "Winnicott Unbound: The Fiction of Philip Roth and the Sharing of Potential Space." *The International Review of Psycho-Analysis*, vol. 19, no. 4, Winter 1992, pp. 445–56.

Mitchell, Stephen A. *Influence and Autonomy in Psychoanalysis*. Analytic Press, 2005.

Mitchell, Stephen A. *Psychoanalyse als Dialog: Einfluss und Autonomie in der analytischen Beziehung*. Translated by Theo Kierdorf and Hildegard Höhr, Psychosozial-Verlag, 2005.

Mitchell, Stephen A. *Relational Concepts in Psychoanalysis: An Integration*. Harvard UP, 1988.

Mitchell, Stephen A. *Relationality: From Attachment to Intersubjectivity*. Taylor and Francis, 2014.

Mitscherlich, Margarete, and Marianne Leuzinger-Bohleber. "*In Treatment*— Der Test: Zwischen Handlung und Behandlung." *Scobel Extra*, 3sat, March 21, 2011.

Mittell, Jason. "Narrative Complexity in Contemporary American Television." *The Velvet Light Trap: A Critical Journal of Film & Television*, vol. 58, Fall 2006, pp. 29–40.

Moretti, Franco. *Distant Reading*. Verso, 2013.
Morphet, Tony. "Two Interviews with J. M. Coetzee, 1983 and 1987." *TriQuarterly*, vol. 69, Spring-Summer 1987, pp. 454–64.
Müller, Klaus P. "Re-Constructions of Reality in Margaret Atwood's Literature: A Constructionist Approach." *Margaret Atwood: Works and Impact*, edited by Reingard M. Nischik, Camden House, 2000, pp. 229–58.
Müller-Braunschweig, Hans. "Aspekte einer psychoanalytischen Kreativitätstheorie." *Psyche*, vol. 31, no. 9, September 1977, pp. 821–43.
Müller-Pozzi, Heinz. "Die psychoanalytische Situation als Sprechereignis: Die poetische Funktion der Sprache im psychoanalytischen Diskurs. Ein intertextuelles Spiel." *Luzifer-Amor: Zeitschrift für die Geschichte der Psychoanalyse*, vol. 22, 1998, pp. 41–63.
Murray, Jennifer. "Historical Figures and Paradoxical Patterns: The Quilting Metaphor in Margaret Atwood's *Alias Grace*." *Studies in Canadian Literature*, vol. 26, no. 1, 2001, pp. 65–83.
Nerenz, Klaus. "Zu den Gegenübertragungskonzepten Freuds." *Psyche*, vol. 39, no. 6, June 1985, pp. 501–18.
Neukom, Marius. "Literaturwissenschaftliches Arbeiten mit der Erzählanalyse JAKOB." *Erzählen als Konfliktdarstellung: Im psychotherapeutischen Alltag und im literarischen Kontext*, edited by Brigitte Boothe and Agnes von Wyl, Lang, 1999, pp. 163–80.
Newman, Michael Z. "From Beats to Arcs: Towards a Poetics of Television Narrative." *The Velvet Light Trap: A Critical Journal of Film & Television*, vol. 58, Fall 2006, pp. 16–28.
Niederhoff, Burkhard. "How to Do Things with History: Researching Lives in Carol Shield's *Swann* and Margaret Atwood's *Alias Grace*." *Journal of Commonwealth Literature*, vol. 35, no. 2, 2000, pp. 71–85.
Niederhoff, Burkhard. "The Return of the Dead in Margaret Atwood's *Surfacing* and *Alias Grace*." *Connotations: A Journal for Critical Debate*, vol. 16, no. 1–3, 2006/7, pp. 60–91.
Novak, Estelle Gershgoren. "Strangers in a Strange Land: The Homelessness of Roth's Protagonists." *Reading Philip Roth*, edited by Asher Z. Milbauer and Donald G. Watson, St. Martin's, 1988, pp. 50–72.
Nuetzel, Eric J. "Psychoanalysis as a Dramatic Art." *The Annual of Psychoanalysis*, vol. 26/27, 1999, pp. 295–313.
Nünning, Ansgar, and Roy Sommer. "The Performative Power of Narrative in Drama: On the Forms and Functions of Dramatic Storytelling in Shakespeare's Plays." *Current Trends in Narratology*, edited by Greta Olson, de Gruyter, 2011, pp. 200–31.
Ogden, Benjamin H., and Thomas H. Ogden. *The Analyst's Ear and the Critic's Eye: Rethinking Psychoanalysis and Literature*. Routledge, 2013.
Ogden, Thomas H. "Comments on Transference and Countertransference in the Initial Analytic Meeting." *Psychoanalytic Inquiry*, vol. 12, no. 2, 1992, pp. 225–47.

Ogden, Thomas H. *Conversations at the Frontier of Dreaming*. Aronson, 2001.
Ogden, Thomas H. *The Matrix of the Mind: Object Relations and the Psychoanalytic Dialogue*. Aronson, 1986.
Ogden, Thomas H. *Projective Identification and Psychotherapeutic Technique*. Karnac, 2005.
Ogden, Thomas H. *Reverie and Interpretation: Sensing Something Human*. Karnac, 1999.
Ogden, Thomas H. "Some Thoughts on the Use of Language in Psychoanalysis." *Psychoanalytic Dialogues*, vol. 7, no. 1, 1997, pp. 1–21.
Ogden, Thomas H. *Subjects of Analysis*. Northvale: Aronson, 1994.
Ogden, Thomas H. *This Art of Psychoanalysis*. Routledge, 2005.
Ogden, Thomas H. "This Art of Psychoanalysis: Dreaming Undreamt Dreams and Interrupted Cries." *International Journal of Psychoanalysis*, vol. 85, no. 4, August 2004, pp. 857–77.
Ogden, Thomas H. "What's True and Whose Idea Was It?" *International Journal of Psychoanalysis*, vol. 84, no. 3, June 2003, pp. 593–606.
Olinick, Stanley L., and Laura Tracy. "Transference Perspectives of Story Telling." *The Psychoanalytic Review*, vol. 74, no. 3, Fall 1987, pp. 319–31.
Onstad, Katrina. "'Alias Grace': 20 Years in the Making, but on TV at the Right Time." *The New York Times*, October 25, 2017, https://www.nytimes.com/2017/10/25/arts/television/alias-grace-margaret-atwood-sarah-polley.html.
Oren, Tasha. "Therapy Is Complicated: HBO's Foray into Modular Storytelling with *In Treatment*." *Flow*, vol. 7.05, no. 7, 2008, http://flowtv.org/2008/01/therapy-is-complicated-hbohbo's-foray-into-modular-storytelling-with-in-treatment/.
Ovid. *Metamorphoses: Vol. II*. Translated by Frank Justus Miller, Harvard UP, 1916.
Ozick, Cynthia. "A Tale of Heroic Anonymity." *The New York Times Book Review*, December 11, 1983, http://www.nytimes.com/books/97/11/02/home/coetzee-michael.html.
Penner, Allen R. *Countries of the Mind: The Fiction of J. M. Coetzee*. Greenwood Press, 1989.
Petersen, Peter. "Übertragen und Begegnen im therapeutischen Dialog." *Die Rolle des Therapeuten und die therapeutische Beziehung*, edited by Hilarion Petzold, Junfermann, 1980, pp. 13–36.
Pfeiffer, Joachim. "Literaturwissenschaft." *Freud-Handbuch: Leben, Werk, Wirkung*, edited by Hans-Martin Lohmann, Metzler, 2006, pp. 329–47.
Pflichthofer, Diana. "Performanz in der Psychoanalyse: Inszenierung—Aufführung—Verwandlung." *Psyche*, vol. 62, no. 1, January 2008, pp. 28–60.
Phillips, Adam. *Going Sane*. Harper Perennial, 2007.
Phillips, Adam. *On Flirtation*. Harvard UP, 1994.
Phillips, Adam. "Poetry and Psychoanalysis." *Promises, Promises*, Faber and Faber, 2000, pp. 1–34.

Phillips, Adam. *Winnicott*. Penguin, 2007.

Pick, Irma B. "Working Through in the Countertransference." *The International Journal of Psychoanalysis*, vol. 66, no. 2, 1985, pp. 157–66.

Pierpont, Claudia R. *Roth Unbound: A Writer and His Books*. Farrar, Straus & Giroux, 2013.

Pietzcker, Carl. *Lesend interpretieren: Zur psychoanalytischen Deutung literarischer Texte*. Königshausen & Neumann, 1992.

Pietzcker, Carl. "Literarische Form—eine durchlässige Grenze." *Die Psychoanalyse der literarischen Form(en): Freiburger literaturpsychologische Gespräche 9*, edited by Johannes Cremerius, Königshausen & Neumann, 1990, pp. 64–91.

Pietzcker, Carl. *Psychoanalytische Studien zur Literatur*. Königshausen & Neumann, 2011.

Pietzcker, Carl. "Überblick über die psychoanalytische Forschung zur literarischen Form." *Die Psychoanalyse der literarischen Form(en): Freiburger literaturpsychologische Gespräche 9*, edited by Johannes Cremerius, Königshausen & Neumann, 1990, pp. 9–32.

Pietzcker, Carl. "Zur Psychoanalyse der literarischen Form." *Perspektiven psychoanalytischer Literaturkritik: Johannes Cremerius zum sechzigsten Geburtstag*, edited by Sebastian Goeppert, Rombach, 1978, pp. 124–57.

Pincus, David, Walter Freeman, and Arnold Modell. "A Neurobiological Model of Perception: Considerations for Transference." *Psychoanalytic Psychology*, vol. 24, no. 4, October 2007, pp. 623–40.

Plunka, Gene A. *Peter Shaffer: Roles, Rites, and Rituals in the Theater*. Fairleigh Dickinson UP, 1988.

Porter, Roy. "Introduction." *Rewriting the Self: Histories from the Renaissance to the Present*, edited by Roy Porter, Routledge, 1997, pp. 1–14.

Porter, Roy. *Madness: A Brief History*. Oxford UP, 2002.

Priel, Beatriz. "Bakhtin and Winnicott on Dialogue, Self, and Cure." *Psychoanalytic Dialogues*, vol. 9, no. 4, 1999, pp. 487–503.

Priel, Beatriz. "Psychoanalytic Interpretations: Word-Music and Translation." *International Journal of Psychoanalysis*, vol. 84, no. 1, February 2003, pp. 131–42.

Prugger, Prisca. "Wiederholung, Variation, Alltagsnähe: Zur Attraktivität der Sozialserie." *Endlose Geschichten: Serialität in den Medien*, edited by Günter Giesenfeld, Olms-Weidmann, 1994, pp. 90–113.

Psychoanalytisches Seminar Zürich. "Es nimmt kein Ende! Serie als neues Paradigma." *PSZ*, November 8, 2013, http://www.psychoanalyse-zuerich.ch/news/70.

Quigley, Michael. "'I Stand in the Dark with a Pick in My Hand, Striking at Heads!': Excavations of the Grotesque in Peter Shaffer's *Equus*." *Literature and the Grotesque*, edited by Michael J. Meyer, Rodopi, 1995, pp. 20–30.

Rabinowitz, Dorothy. "Live from New York, a Miracle." *The Wall Street Journal, Eastern Edition*, December 26, 2008, http://www.wsj.com/articles/SB123005314850930467.

Racker, Heinrich. *Übertragung und Gegenübertragung: Studien zur psychoanalytischen Technik.* Reinhardt, 1982.
Raggatt, Peter T. F. "Multiplicity and Conflict in the Dialogical Self: A Life-Narrative Approach." *Identity and Story: Creating Self in Narrative,* edited by Dan P. McAdams, American Psychological Association, 2006, pp. 15–35.
Raguse, Hartmut. "Leserlenkung und Übertragungsentwicklung: Hermeneutische Erwägungen zur psychoanalytischen Interpretation von Texten." *Zeitschrift für psychoanalytische Theorie und Praxis,* vol. 6, no. 1, 1990, pp. 106–20.
Raphael, Amy. "Is Gabriel Byrne a Suitable Case for Treatment?" *The Guardian,* October 17, 2009, http://www.guardian.co.uk/film/2009/oct/17/gabriel-byrne-hbo-in-treatment?INTCMP=ILCNETTXT3487.
Reiche, Reimut. "Kunst und Kunsttheorie." *Freud-Handbuch: Leben, Werk, Wirkung,* edited by Hans-Martin Lohmann, Metzler, 2006, pp. 307–18.
Renik, Owen. "Analytic Interaction: Conceptualizing Technique in Light of the Analyst's Irreducible Subjectivity." *The Psychoanalytic Quarterly,* vol. 62, no. 4, October 1993, pp. 553–71.
Renik, Owen, and Elizabeth B. Spillius. "Intersubjectivity in Psychoanalysis." *International Journal of Psychoanalysis,* vol. 85, no. 5, October 2004, pp. 1053–64.
"Rhapsode." *Encyclopædia Britannica Online,* May 14, 2008, http://academic.eb.com.proxy.ub.uni-frankfurt.de/levels/collegiate/article/rhapsode/63401/history.
Richardson, Brian. "Voice and Narration in Postmodern Drama." *New Literary History,* vol. 32, no. 3, 2001, pp. 681–94.
Richter, Rainer. "Die neue 3sat-Serie 'In Treatment—Der Therapeut': Interview mit BptK-Präsident Prof. Dr. Rainer Richter." *BundesPsychotherapeutenKammer,* February 15, 2010, http://www.bptk.de/aktuell/einzelseite/artikel/die-neue-3sa.html.
Rickard, John S., and Harold Schweizer. "Introduction." *Psychoanalysis and Storytelling,* by Peter Brooks, Blackwell, 1994, pp. 1–20.
Ricoeur, Paul. *De l'interprétation: Essai sur Freud.* Editions du Seuil, 1965.
Rigney, Barbara H. "Alias Atwood: Narrative Games and Gender Politics." *Margaret Atwood: Works and Impact,* edited by Reingard M. Nischik, Camden House, 2000, pp. 157–65.
Rilke, Rainer Maria. *Briefe.* Insel, 1980.
Roberts, Michelle. "Truth's Patchwork." *New Statesman,* vol. 125, no. 4304, 1996, pp. 46–47.
Rogerson, Margaret. "Reading the Patchworks in *Alias Grace*." *Journal of Commonwealth Literature,* vol. 33, no. 1, 1998, pp. 5–22.
Rose, Nikolas. "Assembling the Modern Self." *Rewriting the Self: Histories from the Renaissance to the Present,* edited by Roy Porter, Routledge, 1997, pp. 224–48.

Rousseau, George. "Medicine." *The Routledge Companion to Literature and Science*, edited by Bruce Clarke, Routledge, 2011, pp. 169–80.

Russell, Carla. "What Is the Difference between a 'Psychoanalytic' and a So-Called 'Normal,' Everyday Relationship? The Controversy between Freud and Ferenczi." *British Journal of Psychotherapy*, vol. 13, no. 1, Fall 1996, pp. 37–52.

Sabbadini, Andrea. "Introduction." *The Couch and the Silver Screen: Psychoanalytic Reflections on European Cinema*, edited by Andrea Sabbadini, Brunner-Routledge, 2003, pp. 1–15.

Sacksteder, William. "The Logic of Analogy." *Philosophy & Rhetoric*, vol. 7, no. 4, Fall 1974, pp. 234–52.

Salje, Gunter. *Film, Fernsehen, Psychoanalyse*. Campus-Verlag, 1980.

Sandler, Joseph. *The Patient and the Analyst: The Basis of the Psychoanalytic Process*. Edited by Christopher Dare and Alex Holder, Allen & Unwin, 1973.

Schaeffer, Jean-Marie. "Fictional vs. Factual Narration." *The Living Handbook of Narratology*, September 20, 2013, http://www.lhn.uni-hamburg.de/article/fictional-vs-factual-narration.

Schafer, Roy. "Action and Narration in Psychoanalysis." *New Literary History*, vol. 12, no. 1, 1980, pp. 61–85.

Schafer, Roy. *Language and Insight*. Yale UP, 1978.

Schafer, Roy. "Listening in Psychoanalysis." *Narrative*, vol. 13, no. 3, 2005, pp. 271–80.

Schafer, Roy. "Narration in the Psychoanalytic Dialogue." *Critical Inquiry*, vol. 7, no. 1, 1980, pp. 29–53.

Schafer, Roy. *Retelling a Life: Narration and Dialogue in Psychoanalysis*. Basic Books, 1992.

Schehr, Lawrence R. "Fragments of a Poetics: Bonnetain and Roth." *Solitary Pleasures: The Historical, Literary, and Artistic Discourses of Autoeroticism*, edited by Paula Bennett and Vernon A. Rosario, Routledge, 1995, pp. 215–30.

Scheurer, Maren. "Erzähler in Analyse, Therapie in Serie: Zur produktiven Verbindung von Fernsehserie und Psychotherapie." *Quality-TV: Die narrative Spielwiese des 21. Jahrhunderts?!*, edited by Jonas Nesselhauf and Markus Schleich, Lit Verlag, 2014, pp. 195–209.

Scheurer, Maren. "The Psychopathology of Everyday Women: Psychoanalytic Aesthetics and Gender Politics in *Letting Go* and 'The Psychoanalytic Special.'" *Philip Roth Studies*, vol. 13, no. 1, Spring 2017, pp. 13–28.

Scheurer, Maren. "'Think of Oedipus': Der Mythos der Psychoanalyse in Woody Allens *Another Woman*." *Mythos und Film: Mediale Adaption und Wechselwirkung*, edited by Vincent Fröhlich and Annette Simonis, Winter, 2016, pp. 263–88.

Scheurer, Maren. "'What It Adds Up To, Honey, Is Homo Ludens!' Play, Psychoanalysis, and Roth's Poetics." *Philip Roth Studies*, vol. 11, no. 1, Spring 2015, pp. 35–52.

Schiller, Friedrich. *Werke und Briefe in zwölf Bänden: Briefe; 2. 1795–1805*. Edited by Norbert Oellers, Deutscher Klassiker Verlag, 2002.

Schmidt-Hellerau, Cordelia. "Das Ich, der Analytiker und die analytische Beziehung: Überlegungen zur gegenwärtigen amerikanischen Psychoanalyse." *Psyche*, vol. 56, no. 7, July 2002, pp. 657–86.

Schneider, Irving. "The Psychiatrist in the Movies: The First Fifty Years." *The Psychoanalytic Study of Literature*, edited by Joseph Reppen and Maurice Charney, Analytic Press, 1985, pp. 53–67.

Schönau, Walter. "Methoden der psychoanalytischen Interpretation aus literaturwissenschaftlicher Perspektive." *Methoden in der Diskussion: Freiburger literaturpsychologische Gespräche 15*, edited by Johannes Cremerius, Königshausen & Neumann, 1996, pp. 33–43.

Schönau, Walter, and Joachim Pfeiffer. *Einführung in die psychoanalytische Literaturwissenschaft*. Metzler, 2003.

Schwartz, Murray M. "The Literary Use of Transference." *Psychoanalysis and Contemporary Thought*, vol. 5, no. 1, 1982, pp. 35–43.

Schwartz, Murray M. "Where Is Literature?" *Transitional Objects and Potential Spaces: Literary Uses of D. W. Winnicott*, edited by Peter L. Rudnytsky, Columbia UP, 1993, pp. 50–62.

Sclater, Shelley Day. "What Is the Subject?" *Narrative Inquiry*, vol. 13, no. 2, 2003, pp. 317–30.

Searles, George J. *The Fiction of Philip Roth and John Updike*. Southern Illinois UP, 1985.

Sedgwick, Eve K. "Paranoid Reading and Reparative Reading, or, You're So Paranoid, You Probably Think This Essay Is About You." *Touching Feeling: Affect, Pedagogy, Performativity*, Duke UP, 2003, pp. 123–52.

Seel, Martin. "Ein Schritt in die Ästhetik." *Die Macht des Erscheinens: Texte zur Asthetik*, Suhrkamp, 2007, pp. 11–26.

Seidl, Otmar, and Michael Ermann. "Die Klinik als psychoanalytischer Raum: Spezifika der stationären analytischen Psychotherapie." *Psychoanalyse mit und ohne Couch: Haltung und Methode*, edited by Axel Gerlach, Anne-Marie Schlösser, and Anne Springer, Psychosozial-Verlag, 2003, pp. 180–93.

Shaffer, Peter. *Amadeus*. 1979. Penguin, 2007.

Shaffer, Peter. "Author's Note on the Book." *Equus*, Longman, 1993, pp. xix–xx.

Shaffer, Peter. "Author's Notes on the Play." *Equus*, Longman, 1993, pp. xxi–xxiii.

Shaffer, Peter. *The Royal Hunt of the Sun*. 1964. Unisa P, 1999.

Shem, Samuel. "Psychiatry and Literature: A Relational Perspective." *Literature and Medicine*, vol. 10, no. 1, 1991, pp. 42–65.

Shklovsky, Viktor. "Art as Technique." *Twentieth-Century Literary Theory*, edited by K. M. Newton, Palgrave, 1997, pp. 3–5.

Shostak, Debra B. *Philip Roth: Countertexts, Counterlives*. U of South Carolina P, 2004.

Siddall, Gillian. "'That Is What I Told Dr. Jordan...': Public Constructions and Private Disruptions in Margaret Atwood's *Alias Grace*." *Essays on Canadian Writing*, vol. 81, Winter 2004, pp. 84–102.

Simon, John. "Hippodrama at the Psychodrama." *The Hudson Review*, vol. 28, no. 1, 1975, pp. 97–106.

Skura, Meredith A. *The Literary Use of the Psychoanalytic Process*. Yale UP, 1981.

Smith, Paul J. "The Approach to Spanish Television Drama of the New Golden Age: Remembering, Repeating, Working Through." *Bulletin of Hispanic Studies*, vol. 83, no. 1, 2006, pp. 61–73.

Sontag, Susan. "Against Interpretation." *Against Interpretation and Other Essays*. Farrar, Straus & Giroux, 1986, pp. 3–14.

Sontag, Susan. *Illness as Metaphor*. Allen Lane, 1979.

Sophocles. *Oedipus Rex*. Translated by David Mulroy, U of Wisconsin P, 2011.

Spacks, Patricia M. "About Portnoy." *The Yale Review*, vol. 58, Summer 1969, pp. 623–35.

Spence, Donald P. *Narrative Truth and Historical Truth: Meaning and Interpretation in Psychoanalysis*. Norton, 1984.

Sprengnether, Madelon. "Ghost Writing: A Meditation on Literary Criticism as Narrative." *Transitional Objects and Potential Spaces: Literary Uses of D. W. Winnicott*, edited by Peter L. Rudnytsky, Columbia UP, 1993, pp. 87–98.

Stacy, James R. "The Sun and the Horse: Peter Shaffer's Search for Worship." *Educational Theatre Journal*, vol. 28, no. 3, 1976, pp. 325–37.

Staels, Hilde. "Intertexts of Margaret Atwood's *Alias Grace*." *Modern Fiction Studies*, vol. 46, no. 2, Summer 2000, pp. 427–50.

Stanley, Alessandra. "Four Days, a Therapist; Fifth Day, a Patient." *The New York Times*, January 28, 2008, http://www.nytimes.com/2008/01/28/arts/television/28stan.html?_r=0.

Stein, Karen F. "Talking Back to Bluebeard: Atwood's Fictional Storytellers." *Margaret Atwood's Textual Assassinations: Recent Poetry and Fiction*, edited by Sharon R. Wilson, Ohio State UP, 2003, pp. 154–72.

Steiner, Riccardo. "'Es ist eine neue Art von Diaspora…': Bemerkungen zur Emigrationspolitik gegenüber deutschen und österreichischen Psychoanalytikern während der Verfolgung durch die Nationalsozialisten auf der Grundlage des Briefwechsels zwischen Anna Freud und Ernest Jones sowie anderer Dokumente." *Psyche*, vol. 48, no. 7, July 1994, pp. 583–652.

Stern, Donnel B. "Field Theory in Psychoanalysis, Part I: Harry Stack Sullivan and Madeleine and Willy Baranger." *Psychoanalytic Dialogues*, vol. 23, no. 5, 2013, pp. 487–501.

Stern, Donnel B. "Field Theory in Psychoanalysis, Part II: Bionian Field Theory and Contemporary Interpersonal/Relational Psychoanalysis." *Psychoanalytic Dialogues*, vol. 23, no. 6, 2013, pp. 630–45.

Stern, Donnel B. "Partners in Thought: A Clinical Process Theory of Narrative." *The Psychoanalytic Quarterly*, vol. 78, no. 3, July 2009, pp. 701–31.

Sterngast, Tal. "Das Coming Out der Therapie." *Tageszeitung*, February 25, 2010, http://www.taz.de/!48875/.

Sträßner, Matthias. *Analytisches Drama*. Fink, 1980.

Strauß, Bernhard. "*In Treatment*: Öffentliche Psychotherapie in Film und Fernsehen." *Psychotherapeut*, vol. 56, no. 2, 2011, pp. 153–61.
Strawson, Galen. "Against Narrativity." *Ratio*, vol. 17, no. 4, December 2004, pp. 428–52.
Szondi, Peter. *Theorie des modernen Dramas 1880–1950*. Suhrkamp, 1965.
Tanner, Tony. "*Portnoy's Complaint*: 'The Settling of Scores! The Pursuit of Dreams!'" Modern Critical Views: Philip Roth, edited by Harold Bloom, Chelsea House, 1986, pp. 63–69.
Taylor, Barbara. *The Last Asylum: A Memoir of Madness in Our Times*. Hamish Hamilton, 2014.
Taylor, John R. *Peter Shaffer*. Longman, 1974.
Thomä, Helmut, and Horst Kächele. *Psychoanalytische Therapie: Grundlagen*. Springer, 2006.
Timm, Neil. "*Equus* as a Modern Tragedy." *West Virginia University Philological Papers*, vol. 25, 1979, pp. 128–34.
Tolan, Fiona. *Margaret Atwood: Feminism and Fiction*. Rodopi, 2007.
Tolan, Fiona. "The Psychoanalytic Theme in Margaret Atwood's Fiction: A Response to Burkhard Niederhoff." *Connotations: A Journal for Critical Debate*, vol. 19, no. 1–3, 2009/10, pp. 92–106.
Tomashoff, Craig. "'Veep,' 'Girls,' 'Atlanta' Scribes Reveal Secrets of Their Writers Rooms: 'Required' Arguments, 'Group Therapy.'" The *Hollywood Reporter*, June 16, 2017, https://www.hollywoodreporter.com/lists/veep-girls-atlanta-scribes-reveal-secrets-writers-rooms-required-arguments-group-therapy-1013526/item/americans-emmy-writers-room-1013512.
Tsiavou, Evangelia. "Das Modell der Gegenübertragungsanalyse als Brücke zwischen Text und Forscher." *Das Argument in der Literaturwissenschaft*, edited by Willi Benning, Athena, 2006, pp. 116–34.
Umstead, R. T. "Unusual 'Treatment' for HBO Series." *Multichannel News*, vol. 28, no. 44, 2007, p. 24.
Vermeulen, Timotheus, and Gry C. Rustad. "Watching Television with Jacques Ranciere: US 'Quality Television,' *Mad Men* and the 'Late Cut.'" *Screen*, vol. 54, no. 3, Fall 2013, pp. 341–54.
Vernadakis, George. "*In Treatment* (Season 2)." *Multichannel News*, vol. 30, no. 13, 2009, p. 54.
Vevaina, Coomi S. "Margaret Atwood and History." *The Cambridge Companion to Margaret Atwood*, edited by Coral A. Howells, Cambridge UP, 2006, pp. 86–99.
Walls, Doyle W. "*Equus*: Shaffer, Nietzsche, and the Neuroses of Health." *Modern Drama*, vol. 27, no. 3, September 1984, pp. 314–23.
Walsh, Fintan. *Theatre & Therapy*. Palgrave Macmillan, 2013.
Warstat, Matthias. "Spielen und Heilen: Zur Theatralisierung des Therapeutischen." *Theatralisierung der Gesellschaft: Soziologische Theorie und Zeitdiagnose*, edited by Herbert Willems, VS, 2009, pp. 533–47.

Weber, Dietrich. *Theorie der analytischen Erzählung*. C. H. Beck, 1975.
Weber, Tanja, and Christian Junklewitz. "Das Gesetz der Serien: Ansätze zur Definition und Analyse." *Medienwissenschaft*, vol. 1, 2008, pp. 13–31.
Wellershoff, Dieter. "Fiktion und Praxis." *Literatur und Veränderung*. Kiepenheuer & Witsch, 1969, pp. 9–32.
Wepfer, Res. "Die Alltagserzählung als Drehbuch." *Erzählen als Konfliktdarstellung: Im psychotherapeutischen Alltag und im literarischen Kontext*, edited by Brigitte Boothe and Agnes von Wyl, Lang, 1999, pp. 103–17.
White, Michael, and David Epston. *Narrative Means to Therapeutic Ends*. Norton, 1990.
Wilcox, James R., and H. L. Ewbank. "Analogy for Rhetors." *Philosophy & Rhetoric*, vol. 12, no. 1, Winter 1979, pp. 1–20.
Willi, Jürg. "Die therapeutische Beziehung aus systemischer und beziehungsökologischer Sicht." *Die therapeutische Beziehung*, edited by Wulf Rössler, Springer, 2005, pp. 59–80.
Williams, Meg H. "Conversations with Internal Objects: Family and Narrative Structure in Homer's 'Odyssey.'" *British Journal of Psychotherapy*, vol. 20, no. 2, Winter 2003, pp. 219–35.
Wilson, Sharon R. "Blindness and Survival in Margaret Atwood's Major Novels." *The Cambridge Companion to Margaret Atwood*, edited by Coral A. Howells, Cambridge UP, 2006, pp. 176–90.
Wilson, Sharon R. "Quilting as Narrative Art: Metafictional Construction in *Alias Grace*." *Margaret Atwood's Textual Assassinations: Recent Poetry and Fiction*, edited by Sharon R. Wilson, Ohio State UP, 2003, pp. 121–34.
Winnicott, Donald W. "The Capacity to Be Alone." *The International Journal of Psychoanalysis*, vol. 39, 1958, pp. 416–20.
Winnicott, Donald W. "Cure." *Home Is Where We Start From: Essays by a Psychoanalyst*, Penguin, 1990, pp. 112–20.
Winnicott, Donald W. *Playing and Reality*. London: Routledge, 2005.
Winnicott, Donald W. "The Theory of the Parent-Infant-Relationship." *The International Journal of Psychoanalysis*, vol. 41, 1960, pp. 585–95.
Winnicott, Donald W. *Therapeutic Consultations in Child Psychiatry*. Hogarth, 1971.
Wisker, Gina. *Margaret Atwood's* Alias Grace: *A Reader's Guide*. Continuum, 2002.
Wittenberg, Hermann. "Michael K and the Spatiality of Resistance." *AUETSA 96, I-II: Southern African Studies*, edited by Hermann Wittenberg and Loes Nas, U of Western Cape P, 1996, pp. 304–09.
Wright, Derek. "Chthonic Man: Landscape, History and Myth in Coetzee's *Life & Times of Michael K*." *New Literatures Review*, vol. 21, Summer 1991, pp. 1–15.
Wright, Elizabeth. "Psychoanalysis and the Theatrical: Analysing Performance." *Analysing Performance: A Critical Reader*, edited by Patrick Campbell, Manchester UP, 1996, pp. 175–90.

Wright, Laura. *Writing "Out of All the Camps": J. M. Coetzee's Narratives of Displacement*. Routledge, 2006.

Wyatt, Frederick. "The Narrative in Psychoanalysis: Psychoanalytic Notes on Storytelling, Listening and Interpreting." *Narrative Psychology: The Storied Nature of Human Conduct*, edited by Theodore R. Sarbin, Praeger, 1986, pp. 193–210.

Yalom, Irvin D. *Love's Executioner and Other Tales of Psychotherapy*. Penguin, 1991.

Yalom, Irvin D. *The Theory and Practice of Group Psychotherapy*. Basic Books, 1995.

Yeoh, Gilbert. "J. M. Coetzee and Samuel Beckett: Nothingness, Minimalism and Indeterminacy." *ARIEL*, vol. 31, no. 4, October 2000, pp. 117–37.

Young, Skip D. *Psychology at the Movies*. Wiley-Blackwell, 2012.

Zapf, Hubert. *Das Drama in der abstrakten Gesellschaft: Zur Theorie und Struktur des modernen englischen Dramas*. Niemeyer, 1988.

Zimmermann, Hannelore. *Erscheinungsformen der Macht in den Romanen Margaret Atwoods*. Lang, 1998.

Zwiebel, Ralf. "Ist psychoanalytisches Denken interkontextuell? Film-psychoanalytische Überlegungen zu Hitchcocks *Spellbound*." *Projektion und Wirklichkeit: Die unbewusste Botschaft des Films*, edited by Annegret Mahler-Bungers and Ralf Zwiebel, Vandenhoeck & Ruprecht, 2007, pp. 149–78.

Zwiebel, Ralf. "Die Position des Analytikers." *Psychoanalyse mit und ohne Couch: Haltung und Methode*, edited by Axel Gerlach, Anne-Marie Schlösser, and Anne Springer, Psychosozial-Verlag, 2003, pp. 36–59.

Zyl, Susan van. "The Creature on the Couch versus the Citizen on the Street." *JPCS: Journal for the Psychoanalysis of Culture & Society*, vol. 8, no. 1, Spring 2003, pp. 88–98.

Index

acting out 30, 66, 111, 148, 225–35, 247
Adler, Alfred 98
Agnes of God (Pielmeier) 239
Alias Grace (Atwood) 19, 192–216, 271, 273–77, 279, 281
Allen, Woody 18, 287 n.13
Amadeus (Shaffer) 232
American Ego Psychology 5
American Pastoral (Roth) 142
analogy 9–10
    dream 96
    relational 18, 96–97, 116, 120, 122, 136, 160, 277, 278, 280
    transmedial 130–34
analysis 82–88
"Analysis Terminable and Interminable" (Freud) 92
analyst–analysand relationship 110
analytic persona 58
analytic third 39, 42–45, 49, 110, 288 n.2
Anatomy Lesson, The (Roth) 142
Andrew's Brain (Doctorow) 269
Annie Hall (Allen) 287 n.13
Another Woman (Allen) 287 n.13
anti-narrative 122–26
anti-psychiatric movement 19, 271
anti-psychiatry 217–40
Appignanesi, Richard 269
archaeology 64, 65, 85, 202, 257
Are You My Mother? (Bechdel) 287 n.15
Aristotle 127
artistic creativity, theory of 99
art(s)
    and psychoanalysis 20
    as relational experience 95–137
    therapeutic promise of 126–30
    of therapeutic relationship 4–13, 53–94
    therapeutic relationship in the 13–20
Atwood, Margaret 19, 192–216, 238, 275, 282, 286 n.7, 291 n.1, 291 n.2
Atypical (Rashid) 269
authenticity 79
authorship 180–90, 278
    split 207–15
"Autobiographical Study" (Freud) 28

Bad Sex (de Kock) 166
Bakhtin, Mikhail 79–82, 156
Balint, Michael 38, 145
Baranger, Madeleine and Willy 45–46, 58, 60, 61, 70, 255
Barthes, Roland 57, 104, 106
Bechdel, Alison 287 n.15
Benjamin, Walter 102, 104, 136
Be'Tipul (Levi) 241, 242
Bettelheim, Bruno 90, 162, 289 n.4
bibliotherapy 126
Bion, Wilfred 5, 36, 115, 189
bi-personal field 39, 44–47, 49, 58, 60, 61, 255, 270
Blanchot, Maurice 290 n.1
Bloch (Fröhlich and Märtesheimer) 241
body rhetoric 36
Bonaparte, Marie 99
Boothe, Brigitte 67, 69, 82, 83, 87, 91
Breast, The (Roth) 142
Brecht, Bertolt 132, 226
Breuer, Josef 97–98, 127, 196

Brooks, Peter   7, 10, 18, 56, 59, 76, 86, 91, 92, 95, 104, 110–11, 120–21, 122, 135, 203
Buber, Martin   78

"Can the Subaltern Speak?" (Spivak)   290 n.1
catharsis   69, 127, 132
characters   57–59
Charon, Rita   6
Civilization and Its Discontents (Freud)   148
Cixous, Hélène   239, 287 n.14
co-construction   47, 75, 137, 241–68
Coetzee, J. M.   11, 19, 100, 125, 136, 166–91, 194, 215, 238, 263, 274, 278, 282, 286 n.7
Coleridge, Samuel T.   290–91 n.2
communication   23–25, 29, 32, 36, 48, 66, 67, 69, 72, 73, 75, 78, 80, 82, 87, 93, 124, 152, 181, 196, 216, 235, 258, 268
  asymmetrical   116
  oral   57, 153
  unconscious   5, 35, 42, 56, 104
  verbal, paraverbal, and nonverbal   17
  written   57
co-narrative transformation   74
constructions   63–66
"Constructions in Analysis" (Freud)   64
Contributions to a Psychology of Love (Freud)   148
Cooper, David   217, 235
co-treatment   259–67
countertransference   5, 12, 22, 23, 41, 42, 45, 48, 56, 74, 75, 103, 106–11, 118, 121, 127, 134, 180, 185, 198, 199, 221, 245, 247, 267, 269–71, 278, 282
  analysis   114–16
  analytic stance of   36–39
  working with   33–36
creation, as relational act   101–103

creativity   20, 60, 71, 97–99, 101, 119, 120, 124, 135, 218, 219, 221, 222, 232, 234, 238–40, 277
Crime and Punishment (Dostoevsky)   153
critical consciousness   133

Dalí, Salvador   286 n.8
da Vinci, Leonardo   149
"Death of the Author, The" (Barthes)   104
Deception (Roth)   141, 290 n.12
Deconstructing Harry (Allen)   287 n.13
de Kock, Leon   166
Derrida, Jacques   85
Desplechin, Arnaud   287 n.15
Dexter, John   231, 292 n.3
dialogicity   79, 82
dialogue   77–82, 285–86 n.5
  psychoanalytic   10, 118–22
Diderot, Denis   131
"Dimensions" (Munro)   19
Disgrace (Coetzee)   167
Divide the Night (Ebersohn)   205
Doctorow, E. L.   269
Don Juan de la Mancha (Menasse)   166, 287 n.14
Dostoevsky, Fyodor   153
drama therapy   68
dream analogy   96
Duet for One (Kempinski)   239

Ebersohn, Wessel   205
Eco, Umberto   90
elasticity   36–39
"Eli, the Fanatic" (Roth)   289 n.1
El Saadawi, Nawal   184
empathy   6, 38, 82, 91, 238, 248, 262
enactment   18, 19, 30, 41, 57, 71–72, 103, 131, 186, 229–33, 235, 236, 239, 240, 270, 274, 275, 281
entrapment   254

ephemerality   131
epic theater   132
Equus (Shaffer)   19–20, 217–40, 270, 271, 274, 275, 277, 280, 289 n.3

Facts, The (Roth)   141
faith   218–25
fascism   286 n.9
Felman, Shoshana   10–12, 18, 87, 94, 97, 99, 101, 111, 117–18, 121, 135, 284
Ferenczi, Sándor   27, 35, 37–39
Ferro, Antonino   39, 45–47, 49, 58–59, 63, 72, 74, 88, 110, 119, 184, 190
fictionality   62, 64, 70, 80, 82, 274, 288 n.1
fictional narratives   128
Fish, Stanley   117
Foe (Coetzee)   167
Foucault, Michel   104, 106
Fragment of an Analysis (Freud)   75–76, 85
Freud, Sigmund   3, 5, 11–13, 21–24, 41, 53–55, 66, 115, 127, 148, 149, 156, 195, 221–24, 272, 285 n.3, 286 n.7
   on analysis   84
   on art–neurosis relationship   97–100
   as conquistador   184
   on constructions   63–64, 66
   on countertransference   33–39
   on creative act   101
   on dialogue   77, 79
   as explorer   184
   on narrative work   7
   on psychoanalytic dialogue   118, 119
   on storytelling   73–75
   textile metaphor   291 n.4
   on theatricality of transference   70, 71
   on transference   4, 26–33, 56, 62–63
Freud's Last Session (St. Germain)   239, 269

Gadamer, Hans-Georg   78, 121–22
García, Rodrigo   241
Geheimnisse einer Seele (Pabst)   13
gestalt therapy   68
Girls   130–31
Goethe, Johann Wolfgang   84, 104
Graphic Freud (Appignanesi)   269
Green, André   80, 81, 103, 156
Gur, Batya   205
Gypsy (Rubin)   269

Hamlet   99, 100, 130
HBO   20, 130–31, 241, 242, 252, 253, 292 n.6
Heimann, Paula   5, 35
hermeneutics   118–21, 135, 184, 279
Huff (Lowry)   18, 241
Hug, Annette   287 n.14
Human Stain, The (Roth)   142
Hustvedt, Siri   16, 18, 59, 62, 101, 156
hysterics   97

Illouz, Eva   14
interpersonal encounter   28, 79, 131
interpretation, theory of   237–38
Interpretation of Dreams (Freud)   130, 209
Interpretation of Murder, The (Rubenfeld)   205
interpretive skills   212
In Treatment (Levi and García)   20, 69, 137, 241–75, 280–82, 287 n.14, 292 n.4
In Zeleny's Zimmer (Hug)   287 n.14
Iser, Wolfgang   108–109

Jakobson, Roman   68
James, Henry   18, 141

Jimmy P. (Desplechin) 287 n.15
Jones, Ernest 90, 130
Jung, C. G. 37, 39, 124, 195, 218, 221, 224, 292 n.2

Keats, John 115
Kempinski, Tom 239
Kleinian psychoanalysis 59
Klein, Melanie 5, 27, 35–36
Kureishi, Hanif 3, 4, 7, 11, 18, 286 n.6
Kurtz, Arabella 100, 136

Lacan, Jacques 185, 285 n.2, 288 n.2
La coscienza di Zeno (Svevo) 13
Laing, R. D. 217, 235
language 6, 9–11, 14, 22, 24, 54, 56, 63, 66–68, 72, 77, 80, 93, 94, 100, 105, 106, 108, 134, 136, 137, 141, 142, 145, 148, 150, 152–55, 165, 168, 169, 171, 172, 174, 176, 188, 191, 199, 204, 208, 210, 215, 218, 220, 235, 254, 256, 258, 265, 271, 272, 274
Laplanche, Jean 92
Last Asylum, The (Taylor) 58
Leonardo da Vinci and a Memory of His Childhood (Freud) 148
Letting Go (Roth) 141
Levi, Hagai 241, 286 n.7, 292 n.2
Levinas, Emmanuel 290 n.1
Life & Times of Michael K (Coetzee) 19, 167–91, 270, 271, 273–75, 277, 280, 281
literary scholarship 8, 16, 17, 129, 130, 282
literary theory 16, 36, 59, 104, 105, 112, 135
Loewald, Hans 53, 71–72
Lorenzer, Alfred 86
Love's Executioner (Yalom) 292 n.5

McPherson, Conor 239
Mad Men (Weiner) 241
Mann, Thomas 13
Marx, Karl 145
Mating Birds (Nkosi) 19, 184
Medical Humanities 6, 7, 124
Menasse, Robert 166, 287 n.14
metaphors 3, 8–12, 14, 33, 35, 37, 38, 41, 43–45, 54–57, 59, 60, 62, 76, 77, 80–82, 86, 87, 91, 94–96, 121, 122, 128, 135, 137, 175, 178, 179, 181, 193, 202, 203, 231, 239, 265
  of literary transference 106–13
  poetry as 63–64, 66–68
  spatial 59, 197
  theatrical 30, 58–72, 131, 230, 274
mirroring, theory of 40
Mitchell, Stephen 38–42, 47, 48, 56, 87–88, 288 n.4
MPD *see* multiple personality disorder
Mrs Klein (Wright) 239
multiple personality disorder (MPD) 193, 205, 215
Munro, Alice 19
mutuality 78, 79, 82, 106
My Life as a Man (Roth) 141
"My Lover Has Dirty Fingernails" (Updike) 287 n.15

narrative 5–6, 72–75, 77
  anti-narrative 122–26
  complexity 91
  definition of 5
  empowerment 277
  fictional 128
  therapy 100, 126, 192
  truth 288 n.2
  see also storytelling; *see also* individual entries
"Narrative Medicine" movement 6
narratology 7, 39, 46, 72, 77, 104

Necessary Roughness (Kruger and Shapiro) 241
Negative Capability 115
Negotiating with the Dead (Atwood) 209–10
Netflix 206, 269, 292 n.6
neutrality 31–34, 37, 48, 150, 189, 205, 227, 244, 247, 270, 278, 279
Nkosi, Lewis 19, 184

object relations theory 5, 27, 286 n.9
observational skills 212
Oedipus complex 4, 99, 147, 163
Oedipus 55, 82–84, 87, 89, 93, 154, 155, 206, 228, 229, 272, 276, 279
Oedipus Rex 83, 87, 228
Ogden, Thomas 23, 36, 39, 42–44, 46, 54, 55, 60, 65, 67–68, 74, 81, 82, 104, 110, 111, 136, 287–88 n.2, 288 n.4
One Thousand and One Nights 88
Operation Shylock (Roth) 142
Ordinary People (Redford) 287 n.15
Othering 170
Out of This World (Swift) 166

Pabst, Georg Wilhelm 13, 286 n.8
Parry, Benita 290 n.1
Patrimony (Roth) 142
performativity 66, 69, 131
Phillips, Adam 4, 9, 93, 95, 100, 126, 168
Pielmeier, John 239
playback theater 68
poetry 63–64, 66–68
Polley, Sarah 206
polyphony 81, 82, 209
Portnoy's Complaint (Roth) 17–19, 141–66, 271–73, 275, 276, 281, 287 n.14, 290 n.10, 290 n.13
Portrait de Dora (Cixous) 239, 287 n.14

potential space 42, 60, 61, 70, 128, 132
projective identification 35–36, 45
psychoanalysis 285 n.1
  as aesthetic experience (*see* psychoanalytic aesthetics)
  arts and 20
  definition of 4
  fundamental rule of 23–24
  see also individual entries
psychoanalytic aesthetics 53–94
  analysis 82–88
  characters 57–59
  constructions 63–66
  dialogue 77–82
  poetry 66–68
  Portnoy's Complaint 150–57
  seriality 88–93
  space and time 59–63
  storytelling 72–77
  theater 68–72
  transference texts 56–57
psychoanalytic criticism 10, 11, 102, 130, 135, 236
psychoanalytic dialogue 118–22
psychoanalytic situation 53, 71, 79, 81, 150, 152, 156, 227
"Psychoanalytic Special, The" (Roth) 141
psychodrama 68, 132

reader-response theory 108, 135, 277
Redford, Robert 287 n.15
reductionism 55, 163, 265
reenactment 22, 30, 53, 72, 93, 231, 235, 236, 274
relational analogy 18, 96–97, 100–103, 105, 106, 110, 113, 114, 116–18, 120, 122, 126, 127, 130, 131, 135–37, 160, 165, 277–80
relational matrix 39–42, 45, 47, 48, 101, 165, 270

Relational School   40, 41, 79, 288 n.4
relationships in reading   103–106
resistance   6, 15, 18, 25, 26, 28–31, 33, 35, 48, 56, 62, 66, 75, 92, 120, 122, 148, 152, 155, 157, 162, 163, 167, 171–75, 181–83, 189, 199, 200, 206, 210, 213, 217, 219, 223, 227, 239, 245, 246, 248, 260, 270, 281, 286 n.7, 290 n.7, 292 n.4
Ricoeur, Paul   118
Rilke, Rainer Maria   99
Robber Bride, The (Atwood)   192
Roth, Philip   17, 19, 137, 141–66, 215, 274, 277, 282, 286 n.7, 289 n.1, 290 n.8, 290 n.12, 290 n.13
Royal Hunt of the Sun, The (Shaffer)   232
Rubenfeld, Jed   205

Sabbath's Theater (Roth)   142
St. Germain, Mark   239, 269
Saturday Morning Murder, The (Gur)   205
Schafer, Roy   5, 7, 74, 117, 123, 285 n.1, 288 n.4
Scheherazade   55, 83, 88–91, 93, 192–216, 276
Schiller, Friedrich   84
Schmitt, Gladys   287 n.15
self-exploration   87, 239
self-reflection   136, 212, 268, 269, 277, 280
self-understanding   8, 14, 33, 73, 82, 123, 125, 188, 193
seriality   19, 88–93, 193, 206, 253, 276
serial settings   251–59
Shaffer, Peter   19, 217–40, 274, 275, 282, 286 n.7, 289 n.3, 291 n.1
Shakespeare, William   130
Sherlock (Gatiss and Moffat)   241

Shining City (McPherson)   239
Shklovsky, Viktor   73
Sinclair, Jo   13
"Sin Eater, The" (Atwood)   291 n.1
Six Feet Under (Ball)   241
Something to Tell You (Kureishi)   3, 11, 18
Sonnets for an Analyst (Schmitt)   287 n.15
Sontag, Susan   68, 121
Sophocles   84, 87
Sopranos, The (Chase)   241, 253, 255, 271, 284
Sorrows of an American, The (Hustvedt)   18, 101
spectatorship   234–39
Spellbound (Hitchcock)   13
Spence, Donald   65, 288 n.2
Spivak, Gayatri   290 n.1
storytelling   5–7, 12, 15, 19, 20, 25, 46, 47, 49, 55, 57, 59, 71–77, 79, 83, 88, 89, 91–93, 102, 107, 111, 122–26, 154, 159, 160, 172, 181, 182, 191, 193, 202, 203, 206, 207–16, 226, 232, 255, 263, 272, 274, 276, 279, 280, 283
  cyclical   93
  linear   93
  therapeutic significance of   7, 122–26
  see also narrative
Strachey, James   59
Studies on Hysteria (Freud)   26, 85
sublimation, theory of   98
suspicious interpretation   118–22
Svevo, Italo   13
Swift, Graham   166
Szasz, Thomas   217
Szondi, Peter   84

talking cure   7, 69, 107, 122, 126, 195, 257, 271
Taylor, Barbara   58, 90

television   10, 12, 13, 15, 18–20, 49, 89, 97, 119, 130–34, 139, 241, 251–59
Tell Me You Love Me (Mort)   241, 255
temporal ambiguity   61
terra incognita   195
textile metaphor   291 n.4
theater   68–72
    epic   132
    modern   133
theatrical space   70
therapeutic aesthetic   7
therapeutic discourse   14
therapeutic epistemology   167–91
therapeutic intimacy   23
therapeutic relationship   21–49, 62, 271–72
    as aesthetic experience   8, 53–55
    analytic stance of countertransference   36–39
    analytic stance of transference   31–33
    analytic third   42–44
    art of   4–13, 53–137
    in the arts   13–20
    bi-personal field   44–47
    countertransference, working with   33–36
    definition of   4, 5
    narration and   5–7
    relational matrix   39–42
    setting   23–26
    transference, working with   26–31
    see also individual entries
therapy play   227, 239, 276
transference   4, 59, 62
    analytic stance of   31–33
    dialogue and   79–81
    feelings   62
    texts   56–57
    theatricality of   69–70
    working with   26–31
    see also individual entries
transitional object   60
transitional space   46, 68, 70, 230–31
transmedial analogy   130–34
Tummelplatz   59
Turn of the Screw, The (James)   18

unconscious communication, theory of   5
Updike, John   287 n.15

virtuality   26–31, 63, 132

Waiting for the Barbarians (Coetzee)   167
Wanderlust (Payne)   269
Wasteland (Sinclair)   13
Waste Land, The (Eliot)   8
Web Therapy (Kudrow)   241
Werther (Goethe)   104
Winnicott, Donald   3, 5, 38, 60, 70, 71, 106, 119–20, 136, 290 n.12
Woman at Point Zero (El Saadawi)   184
working alliance   29
working through   92

Yalom, Irvin   130, 292 n.5

Zauberberg, Der (Mann)   13
Zuckerman Unbound (Roth)   290 n.13

www.ingramcontent.com/pod-product-compliance
Lightning Source LLC
Chambersburg PA
CBHW070013010526
44117CB00011B/1556